FAMILY CHILD CARE

2021 Tax
Workbook
& Organizer

Being a Family Child Care Professional

Family child care is a special profession for those who love young children. As a professional family child care provider, you must balance the skills required to care for children with those required to operate your business. Here are some tips that will keep your family child care business as healthy and successful as possible:

- Learn the child care regulations for your area, and follow them.
- Join your local family child care association.
- Sign up with your local child care resource and referral agency.
- Join the Child and Adult Care Food Program (CACFP).
- Find good professional advisers (such as a tax professional, insurance agent, and lawyer).
- Participate in training to acquire and improve your professional skills.

Additional Resources

Redleaf Press (www.redleafpress.org; 800-423-8309) publishes resources for family child care professionals. Redleaf Press offers the following publications to support your business:

- Starting a family child care business:
    Family Child Care Business Planning Guide

- Promoting your business:
    Family Child Care Marketing Guide, 2nd edition

- Creating contracts and policies:
    Family Child Care Contracts and Policies, 4th edition
    Sharing in the Caring: Agreement Packet for Parents and Providers
    The Redleaf Complete Forms Kit for Both Family Child Care and Center-Based Programs, Revised edition

- Keeping accurate records and filing your taxes:
    Family Child Care Record-Keeping Guide, 9th edition
    The Redleaf Calendar-Keeper: A Record-Keeping System for Family Child Care Professionals
    Family Child Care Tax Workbook and Organizer
    Family Child Care Tax Companion
    The Business of Family Child Care: Record-Keeping DVD

- Reducing business risks:
    Family Child Care Legal and Insurance Guide

- Managing your money and planning for retirement:
    Family Child Care Money Management and Retirement Guide

FAMILY CHILD CARE

2021 Tax Workbook & Organizer

TOM COPELAND, JD

UPDATED AND REVISED FOR 2021 BY BILL PORTER

Redleaf Press®
www.redleafpress.org
800-423-8309

Tom Copeland is a licensed attorney and has conducted tax workshops for family child care providers since 1982. In 2017 his website (www.tomcopelandblog.com) was chosen as one of the Top 75 Childcare Blogs and Websites for Childcare Providers and Parents by Feedspot (ranked second in the United States). In 2014 his blog was chosen as one of the top 50 money management blogs in the country by Direct Capital, a national financing company. In 1998 he won the Child Care Advocate of the Year award from the Minnesota Licensed Family Child Care Association. In 2003 he received the Friend of the National Association for Family Child Care (NAFCC) award from NAFCC. In 2004 Tom received the Advocate of the Year award from NAFCC. Tom is the author of *Family Child Care Business Planning Guide, Family Child Care Contracts and Policies, Family Child Care Legal and Insurance Guide* (with Mari Millard), *Family Child Care Marketing Guide, Family Child Care Money Management and Retirement Guide, Family Child Care Record-Keeping Guide*, and *Family Child Care Tax Companion.* Tom Copeland can be reached by email at tomcopeland@live.com, by phone at 651-280-5991, or through his website at www.tomcopelandblog.com.

Published by Redleaf Press
10 Yorkton Court
St. Paul, MN 55117
www.redleafpress.org

Cover design by Renee Hammes
Cover photograph © iStockphoto.com/DNY59
Typeset in Times
Printed in the United States of America
ISBN 978-1-60554-757-2

DISCLAIMER
This publication is designed to provide accurate information about filing federal tax returns for family child care providers. Tax laws, however, are in a constant state of change, and errors and omissions may occur in this text. We are selling this publication with the understanding that neither Redleaf Press nor the author is engaged in rendering legal, accounting, or other professional services. If you require expert legal or tax assistance, obtain the services of a qualified professional. Because each tax return has unique circumstances, neither the author nor Redleaf Press guarantees that following the instructions in this publication will ensure that your tax return is accurate or will enable you to find all the errors on your tax return. In addition, this book addresses only tax issues related to family child care. This publication is to be used for filling out 2021 tax forms only. For information on how to fill out tax forms after 2021, please consult later editions of this publication.

Contents

Acknowledgments

It is a great privilege to take part in the updating and revising of this book. Tom Copeland deserves the bulk of the credit and a gigantic thank-you as he wrote the original book. Also, a big thank-you to the many tax preparers and child care providers that gave Tom feedback for prior editions of this book as well as an extra special thank-you to the Hansell family for their support.

And of course this book would not be possible without Melissa York, Douglas Schmitz, and everybody at Redleaf Press working on its production.

If you have comments regarding how to improve future editions of this book, please email me at Bill.Porter@PrideTaxPreparation.com.

Highlights of the New Tax Laws

- The standard meal allowance rates for 2021 are $1.39 for breakfast, $2.61 for lunch and supper, and $0.78 for snacks. The rates are higher for Alaska and Hawaii. See page 94.

- The standard mileage rate for 2021 is $0.56 per business mile. See page 113.

- The income eligibility limits for the Earned Income Credit have increased to $48,108 (for married couples filing jointly with one child) and $42,158 (if single with one child). See page 122.

- The income limits to qualify for the IRS Saver's Credit has increased to $66,000 (adjusted gross income for couples filing jointly) and $33,000 for individuals or married people filing separately. See page 124.

- Money you received from the federal Stimulus Checks is not taxable income and should not be reported on your 2021 tax return.

- Money you received from the Paycheck Protection Program (PPP) is not taxable income and should not be reported on your 2021 tax return.

- Money you received from the Economic Injury Disaster Loan Program (EIDL) is not taxable income and should not be reported on your 2021 tax return.

- Money received from any state or local child care grants, including the Child Care Stabilization Grant, is taxable income. See page 102.

- For 2021, the Child Care Credit now allows for up to $8,000 of expenses ($16,000 if you have two or more children). The credit is also fully refundable. For 2021, the Child Tax Credit increases from $2,000 to $3,000 ($3,600 if the child is under age 6) per child. You may have already received a partial "advance" of this credit through monthly payments from July 2021 to December 2021.

Tax Changes and Other Things to Consider for 2021

Stimulus Checks

The third stimulus check (also known as "Economic Impact Payment" (EIP) or "Recovery Rebate" on the tax return) was $1,400 per person, including any dependents you have. That is not taxable on your tax return, so if you received the full amount you are eligible for, you do not need to mention it on the tax return. If you did not receive the full amount you are eligible for, you can claim the missing amount on **Form 1040**, line 30.

You probably received the second stimulus check ($600 per person) in January 2021. Since that was reconciled on last year's tax return, you don't need to consider it for the 2021 tax return.

Paycheck Protection Program (PPP) and Economic Injury Disaster Loans (EIDL)

If you were one of the many people to take advantage of these great provisions, there is even more good news. Neither of these are taxable on the federal tax return, even when those amounts are forgiven (you don't need to pay it back). However, it could be taxable on some state tax returns. See your state tax forms to determine if it is taxable in your state.

State and Local Grants for Your Business

These are added to your business income. Any business expenses you bought with that money are still a tax deduction.

Unemployment Compensation

Due to various pandemic conditions, you may have collected unemployment compensation in 2021. Unemployment compensation is taxed as general income on **Schedule 1**, line 7 (don't include unemployment compensation as part of your business income on **Schedule C**).

Pandemic Supplies

Due to the pandemic, you may have purchased such things as sanitizer, face masks, or gloves to use in your child care business. Like other cleaning supplies, those expenses should be included as a business supply expense.

Business Meals

If you travel out of town overnight for business, take parents out to eat, or pay for a "business meal" with other providers, the usual rule allows you to deduct only 50% of that cost on your tax return. But for 2021 and 2022, that is increased to 100% if the meal was provided by a restaurant.

Sick Pay or Family Leave

If you temporarily could not work due to certain conditions, such as having COVID-19, taking care of someone who has COVID-19, or certain other conditions, you may be eligible for a tax credit for some or all of the time you could not work. See **Form 7202** and its instructions for details.

Child Tax Credit

The Child Tax Credit has been $2,000 per child in recent years. For 2021, if your income is under $75,000 ($150,000 if married filing jointly) a special law gives you an additional $1,000 ($1,600 if the child is under age six) for each child, for a total of $3,000 per child ($3,600 if the child is under age six). If your income is over those amounts, the extra $1,000 (or $1,600) is gradually reduced or eliminated. For 2021, this credit applies for children under age 18.

You may have already received some prepayments for this credit. From July 2021 through December 2021, the IRS sent many people prepayments of up to half of this credit. When you file your tax return, you will need to reconcile these payments with the actual credit. That means you will get the remaining portion of the credit on your tax return, or if you received too much in prepayments, you might need to repay some or all of the prepayments that you received.

For example, let's say you are filing as married filing jointly, your income on your tax return is $140,000, and you have three children, ages 8, 10 and 12. That qualifies for a $9,000 credit on your tax return. But you may have already received $750 a month from July through December 2021 (a total of $4,500). In that example, your tax return will show a $4,500 credit ($9,000 total credit, minus the $4,500 prepayment that you already received).

Now let's take that example further: you realize that your ex-spouse is allowed to claim two of the children this year, so now you have only one child on your tax return. In this example, your total credit is only $3,000. Because you already received $4,500, you would need to repay $1,500 ($3,000 total credit, minus the $4,500 prepayment that you already received).

However, if your prepayments are larger than the credit you qualify for, you might qualify for "repayment protection." That means the amount you would need to repay could be reduced or eliminated. If you are married and your income is under $60,000 ($40,000 if filing as single or $50,000 if filing as head of household), you will not need to repay any of the Child Tax Credit, even if you received more prepayments than what you qualify for. If your income is over those amounts, the repayment protection is gradually phased out. If you are married and your income is over $120,000 ($80,000 if filing as single or $100,000 if filing as head of household), the repayment protection no longer applies.

Child Care Credit

This credit has been greatly expanded for 2021. If you pay anyone to watch your child so that you can work (including such things as preschool, after-school programs, and day camp), you may be eligible for this credit. In previous years, this credit was limited to $3,000 of expenses ($6,000 for two or more children), but those limits have increased to $8,000 ($16,000 for two or more children) for 2021. The percentage of the credit is also greatly increased for most people.

Earned Income Credit

It is possible that your business income is lower than it was in previous years. If you qualify for the Earned Income Credit, you have the option to use your "earned income" from 2019 ("earned income" is usually your business profit plus any wages from a W-2). You can choose to use either your 2019 earned income or your 2021 earned income and use the one that gives you the biggest credit.

There are also other new rules that make it easier for some people to qualify for the Earned Income Credit, especially if you don't have any children. The IRS forms and worksheets have been updated to reflect these other changes.

Introduction

The purpose of the *Family Child Care Tax Workbook and Organizer* is to guide you as you prepare your federal tax forms for your family child care business. Since this book covers only the federal income tax rules and forms, you may also need to complete additional forms for your state and local tax returns. Because the tax laws can change every year, the *Tax Workbook and Organizer* is updated each year to reflect the latest changes in the tax rules and forms. For this reason, it's important to use only the current year's edition of this book.

Note: Family child care providers who operate as a partnership or corporation should not use this book to file their taxes, because they must use different tax forms. Providers who are set up as a single-person limited liability company (LLC) will use all the forms as described in this book.

Getting Help

The *Family Child Care Tax Workbook and Organizer* is designed to enable you to fill out important tax forms for your business. The following resources are available if you need further help:

Getting Help from the IRS

- Call the IRS Business and Specialty Tax Line at 800-829-4933 with your questions. This number is for business-related questions. Tax help is also available at IRS offices nationwide.

- Visit the IRS website (www.irs.gov) to download tax forms, publications, and instructions or to search for answers to your questions.

- You can call 800-829-3676 to order a free copy of any IRS publication or form. Many post offices and libraries also carry the more common IRS forms and instructions.

- If you are running out of time, you can get a six-month extension (to October 15) to file your taxes. You must still pay the taxes you owe by April 15 or pay interest and a penalty on the amount you owe.

- For a list of IRS resources, revenue rulings, court cases, and publications relevant to family child care providers, see appendix C.

Getting Help from a Tax Professional

- If you need help finding a tax professional, visit my website (www.tomcopelandblog .com) for a tax preparer directory.

Finding IRS Publications and Other Resources

- For copies of all the relevant IRS publications, tax forms, revenue rulings, court cases, and other materials, visit my website at www.tomcopelandblog.com.

Notes on This Edition

New Record-Keeping and Tax Tips is a regular feature that includes IRS updates and new information to help you keep your records, file your tax return, and deal with the IRS. This year's tips cover the following topics:

- Should You Take a Distribution from Your IRA?
- Should You Claim Social Security Benefits Early?
- Time to Invest in Your 2022 IRA!
- Retirement Plan Limits for 2021

IRS Child Care Provider Audit Technique Guide

The IRS **Child Care Provider Audit Technique Guide** is one of a series of audit guides that the IRS produced to help auditors better understand specific businesses. I refer to this guide several times in this book. I have posted a copy of the guide on my website, www.tomcopelandblog.com, along with a more detailed commentary about the guide.

How to Find a Tax Professional

Many family child care providers use tax professionals to help prepare their tax returns; however, many tax preparers aren't familiar with how the IRS Tax Code affects family child care businesses. You need to find out if the tax preparer you are considering is aware of the unique tax rules for your business. (The *Record-Keeping Guide* contains more information about hiring and working with a tax preparer.) Here are some ways that you can find a qualified tax preparer:

- Ask other family child care providers or the members of your family child care association for the names of their tax preparers.
- Find out if there are any community resources you can use. For example, some communities have taxpayer assistance services for low-income people. Contact your local United Way for more information about these programs.

- Three national tax preparer organizations offer state listings of their members: the National Association of Enrolled Agents (www.naea.org or 202-822-6232), the National Association of Tax Professionals (www.natptax.com or 800-558-3402), and the National Society of Accountants (www.nsacct.org or 800-966-6679). You can also look online to find the local chapter of any of these organizations.

Using Tax Preparation Software

An increasing number of family child care providers are using tax preparation software to do their own taxes. The three leading tax preparation software programs are TurboTax, H&R Block at Home, and TaxAct. The IRS has a program by which you can use these tax preparation software programs for free if you are income eligible: https://apps.irs.gov /app/freeFile. These programs can be helpful in doing math calculations (such as depreciation) and completing your tax forms; they may also help catch some of your mistakes. They do, however, have drawbacks—specifically, tax software *will not* do the following:

- Identify the items you can deduct for your business. The software will merely list the category (for example, Supplies); it will be up to you to figure out what you can claim on that line.

- Explain how to deduct items that are used both for business and personal purposes. You will need to figure out how to claim not only the supplies you use exclusively for your business but also the supplies you use for both business and personal purposes. Here's an example: Let's say that you spent $120 on arts and crafts supplies that were used only by the children in your care and $600 on household cleaning supplies that were used by both your business and your family. In this case, you can deduct the full amount of the arts and crafts supplies but not of the cleaning supplies. You must multiply that $600 by your Time-Space percentage and add that amount to the $120 for arts and crafts supplies. The total is the number that you enter on **Schedule C**, line 22. If you don't know that you can't claim either $720 or the Time-Space percentage of $720 for your supplies, then you shouldn't be using a tax software program.

- Alert you to all the special rules that apply to your business. For example, it won't remind you that the reimbursements you received from the Food Program for your own children are not taxable income.

- Ask you detailed questions to make sure you are reporting the highest Time-Space percentage and business deductions you are allowed to claim.

Using Tax Software

- Enter your business expenses (advertising, supplies) *after* applying your Time-Space percentage or actual business-use percentage.

- Be sure to keep records of how you calculated your business-use percentage (if you will not be using your Time-Space percentage).

- Read chapter 3 for a clear explanation of depreciation rules and how to use them. Unless you know a lot about depreciation, it is easy to make a mistake claiming depreciation expenses.

- Before filing your return, compare **Form 8829**, **Form 4562**, and **Schedule C** with the numbers you entered into the Tax Workbook and the Tax Organizer to see if all your deductions are properly reported. Sometimes it's easy to lose track of a deduction you enter into a software program.

How to Use This Book

Although filling out tax forms isn't a pleasant task, it's an essential part of operating a family child care business. Many family child care providers don't claim all the business deductions they're entitled to because they're unaware of the tax rules and don't think the deductions are worth the time it takes to learn the tax rules. As a result, providers end up paying more taxes than they need to. Taking advantage of all the legal business deductions that you're entitled to, however, ends up lowering your tax bill.

Because a family child care business requires you to use your home for business purposes, the tax rules for your business are unlike those that apply to most other small businesses. A professional tax adviser might not be familiar with all the details of the tax laws as they apply to your business, which is why you need to take an active role in learning the tax rules and what they mean for your business.

This book is designed to guide you through all aspects of preparing your taxes and filling out your federal tax forms for the current year. (In most states, you will also have to pay state income taxes, but there are no special state tax forms to file if you are a family child care provider.) The *Family Child Care Record-Keeping Guide* provides additional tax preparation information about how to keep good records and how to determine which expenses are deductible.

Careful, accurate business records are an essential part of preparing your taxes; when family child care providers get into trouble with the IRS, it's usually because they can't separate their deductible business expenses from their nondeductible personal expenses. These personal and business expenses are usually closely intertwined, and the IRS requires you to have written evidence for all your business deductions.

This book provides you with two different approaches to preparing your taxes—the Tax Organizer and the Tax Workbook—as well as copies of the common tax forms that most providers need to file for their business.

The Tax Organizer

The Tax Organizer is a set of worksheets on which you can gather, calculate, and organize all the information you need to fill out your tax forms. The Tax Organizer doesn't include a lot of explanation of the tax laws, but if you don't have any unusual tax issues, it can be a great way to gather all your data, thus making it much easier to complete your tax forms. There are many ways you might use this section of the book. You might complete the Tax Organizer (referring to the Tax Workbook if you need more information about a particular topic) and then transfer the information directly to your tax forms. You might complete the Tax Organizer and then give the information to a professional tax preparer. Or if you just need information on a particular tax form or topic (such as depreciation or the Food Program), you might skip the Tax Organizer completely and just use the Tax Workbook.

The Tax Organizer worksheets help you record and organize all your business income and expenses. Once you fill in the information, the Tax Organizer provides specific directions about where to enter each line on your tax forms. After you complete the Tax Organizer, tear it out of this book and save it with your other tax records. Since the tax laws and forms are always changing, this Tax Organizer applies only to the year 2021; don't use it for any other year.

The Tax Workbook

The second section of this book is the Tax Workbook, which is designed to guide you line by line through the key tax forms you need to file for your business. For each form, it's important to read the instructions carefully and take the time to understand the rules. Most of the tax issues covered in this book are discussed in more detail in the *Family Child Care Record-Keeping Guide.* If any of your tax-preparation questions aren't addressed in this book, you can refer to the *Record-Keeping Guide* or my website (www.tomcopelandblog.com), or you can contact the IRS (www.irs.gov) for more information (also see appendix C).

Tax Forms

The final section of this book (Part V) includes copies of forms **W-10**, **1040**, **1040 Schedule C**, **1040 Schedule SE**, **4562**, and **8829**. It's best to tear out these forms, copy them, and then do your rough work on the copies so you can make adjustments as you go along. Once you have your final numbers, write them on a clean copy before submitting your forms to the IRS.

You may also need forms for special situations. For example, if you're making estimated tax payments, you'll need to file **Form 1040-ES Estimated Tax for Individuals**. If you want to change your tax return for an earlier year, you'll need to file **Form 1040X Amended U.S. Individual Income Tax Return**. In addition, if you hire employees, you must file a series of tax forms throughout the year. Copies of those tax forms are available at www.irs.gov.

Complete Your Tax Forms in the Correct Order

Since some tax forms must be filled out before others can be completed, it's important to fill out your tax forms in the proper order. For example, **Form 8829**, **Form 4562**, and **Schedule C** are closely linked; you can't complete **Schedule C** before you've completed **Form 4562**. You need to fill out Part I of **Form 8829** before you can complete most of **Form 4562** and **Schedule C**. And you need to complete most of **Schedule C** before you can finish **Form 8829**. Here's the best way to proceed:

1. Start by filling out Part I of **Form 8829** (lines 1–7) and determining your Time-Space percentage (see chapters 2 and 1, respectively).

2. Complete **Form 4562** (see chapter 3); enter the amount on line 22 of **Form 4562** on line 13 of **Schedule C**.

3. Complete lines 1–29 of **Schedule C** (see chapter 5), and enter the amount on line 29 of **Schedule C** on line 8 of **Form 8829**.

4. Finish filling out **Form 8829**; enter the amount on line 36 of **Form 8829** on line 30 of **Schedule C**.

5. Finish filling out **Schedule C** and any other tax forms you need to complete, such as your **Form 1040** and your state tax forms.

Here's a flowchart that shows the proper order for filling out your tax forms:

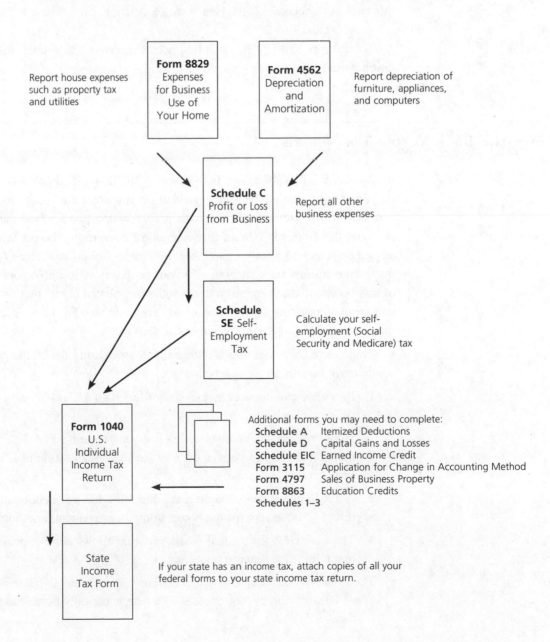

About the Math in This Book

The calculations in this book use exact amounts so you can track how to do the calculations; however, the IRS allows you to round numbers to the nearest dollar, and we recommend that you do so on your tax forms. Here's a reminder of how to round numbers correctly: If the cents portion of an amount is $0.49 or less, round down to the nearest dollar (for example, round $3.39 down to $3.00). If the cents portion of an amount is $0.50 or more, round up to the nearest dollar (for example, round $3.68 up to $4.00).

In this book we also do a lot of multiplying by percentages. Here's a reminder of how to do this: Let's say that you want to multiply $500 by 30%. To multiply by a percentage, you need to move the decimal point two places to the left before you multiply—in this case 30% becomes 0.30. Here's the calculation:

$500 × 0.30 = $150

To multiply $500 by 3%, you first need to convert 3% to 0.03. In this case, the calculation would be

$500 × 0.03 = $15

Give This Book to Your Tax Preparer

If you decide to complete the Tax Organizer and then hire a professional tax preparer to do your return, remind the preparer about tax rules that are unique to the family child care business. Unfortunately, some tax preparers don't understand the nature of this business and therefore can't do an adequate job of interpreting the tax law in your favor. (For advice on selecting a tax preparer, see the *Family Child Care Record-Keeping Guide*.) It may make an important difference in your tax return if you give your tax preparer a copy of this book and draw attention to the following eleven points that are the foundation of preparing a tax return for a family child care business. (For more information on any of these points, see the *Record-Keeping Guide*.)

- There have been four major changes in depreciation rules in the past several years that will benefit all providers:

  1. Providers can deduct any expense of less than $2,500 in one year, rather than depreciating it.

  2. House repairs can be deducted in one year, regardless of the cost. Home improvements must be depreciated over 39 years. The definition of what is a repair has been greatly expanded.

  3. A 100% bonus depreciation rule allows providers to deduct all items costing more than $2,500 except for the home, home improvement, and home addition.

  4. The Safe Harbor for Small Taxpayers rule allows eligible providers to deduct home improvements in one year.

- The standard "ordinary and necessary" test for business expenses casts a wide net in the family child care business. Child care is the only home-based business that is allowed to use hundreds of common household items for both personal and business purposes. Such items include toothpaste, lightbulbs, toilet paper, garbage bags, a lawn mower, sheets, and towels. (See the *Record-Keeping Guide* for a list of more than 1,000 allowable deductions.)

- The standard for claiming a room in the home as business use is regular use, not exclusive use. The children in a provider's care need not be present in a room for it to be used regularly for the business (storage, laundry, and so on). (See chapter 1.)

- A garage (either attached to the home or detached) and basement should be included in the total square footage of the home when calculating the business use of the home. Most family child care providers use their garage and basement on a regular basis for their business because they have a laundry room, storage room, or furnace area there. They may store a car, bicycles, tools, lawn maintenance items, firewood, or other items used for business in these spaces. (See chapter 1.)

- Providers can claim a higher business-use percentage of their home if they have one or more rooms that are used exclusively in their business. The tax preparer should add the Space percentage of this exclusive-use area to the Time-Space percentage of the rest of the home to determine the total business-use percentage of the home. (See chapter 1.)

- When counting the number of hours the home is used for business, include the number of hours the children in the provider's care are present as well as the number of hours the provider spends on business activities when the children are not present. These hours include the time the provider spends cleaning, preparing activities, interviewing parents, keeping records, and preparing meals. (See chapter 1.)

- Reimbursements from the Child and Adult Care Food Program (CACFP) are taxable income to the provider. Reimbursements for the provider's own child (if the provider is income eligible) are not taxable income. Providers are entitled to deduct all the food they serve to the children in their care, even if their food expenses are greater than their Food Program reimbursements. (See chapter 4.)

- Providers who are not licensed or registered under their state law are still entitled to claim their home expenses as business use if they have applied for a license or are exempt from local regulations. (See page 6.)

- All providers are better off financially if they claim depreciation on their home as a business expense. When a provider sells her home, she will have to pay a tax on any depreciation she claims (or was entitled to claim) after May 6, 1997. She will owe this tax even if she hasn't claimed any home depreciation as a business deduction. (See chapter 12.)

- Providers who use their home for business can avoid paying taxes on the profit on the sale of the home if they have owned the home and lived in it for at least two of the last five years before the sale. (See chapter 12 and the *Record-Keeping Guide*.)

- Providers are entitled to use the Start-Up Rule and deduct any items they owned before their business began and are used in their business, including a computer, TV, VCR, DVD player, washer, dryer, refrigerator, sofa or bed, and many other types of property. In addition, providers who have not deducted these items or not depreciated items they were entitled to in previous years can use IRS **Form 3115** to recapture all previously unclaimed depreciation on the current year tax return. This can mean hundreds of dollars in deductions for providers who have been in business for a number of years. (See chapter 10.)

If You File Electronically

If you will be filing your tax return electronically (or if your tax preparer will be doing so), be sure to keep paper copies of all your backup documentation, such as your depreciation schedules, the calculations for your Time-Space percentage, and your mileage records. The electronic documents can get lost, and you will need paper copies to provide evidence that your numbers are accurate if you are ever audited.

A Few Other Issues before We Get Started

What If You Aren't Licensed or Certified?

For tax purposes, you don't need to have a business name, be registered with your state or Chamber of Commerce, or even meet the requirements of your local regulations in order to be considered a business. Your child care business begins when you are ready to care for children and are advertising that you are ready to accept children. At this point, you can begin claiming all "ordinary and necessary" expenses for your business. You don't have to be licensed or actually caring for children to be considered a business and start claiming your expenses.

Suppose you're paid to care for children but don't meet the requirements of your local regulations. You may still deduct many expenses as business deductions, as long as you report your income. You can deduct all direct expenses, such as car expenses, depreciation on personal property (such as furniture and appliances), office expenses, equipment rental, repairs, supplies, education, food, and other miscellaneous home expenses. You may deduct these expenses even if you are caring for more children than your local regulations allow. Although we don't recommend operating outside of your local regulations, you should be aware of the tax advantages of deducting these expenses from your business income on **Schedule C**.

The only expenses you aren't entitled to deduct if you don't meet your local requirements are your home utilities, mortgage interest, home repairs, homeowners insurance, home depreciation, and real estate taxes. (These expenses appear on **Form 8829**. If you aren't entitled to claim expenses on **Form 8829**, you can still deduct all your mortgage interest and real estate taxes by itemizing on **Schedule A**.)

If your local regulations are voluntary, or if you are exempt from them, you may claim all the same business deductions as a licensed or certified provider. For example, your state rules may require that child care providers be licensed only if they care for more than four children. If you care for three children, you are exempt from the licensing rules and thus are able to deduct the same business expenses as a licensed provider.

Do You Need an Employer Identification Number?

If parents want to claim the child care tax credit, they will ask you for your Social Security or employer identification number (EIN). Because of privacy concerns, I strongly recommend that you get an EIN for your business. Using an EIN can reduce the chances that your Social Security number will get into the wrong hands and cause you problems with identity theft. If you hire an employee, you are required to have an EIN. You can get an EIN by filing **Form SS-4** (go to www.tomcopelandblog.com and click on "IRS Tax Forms" to download the form) or by calling the IRS Business and Specialty Tax Line at 800-829-4933.

Another easy way to get your EIN is by going online. The application process is quicker, with fewer questions, and a simpler format to follow. Go to www.irs.gov and enter "EIN" in the search box. Once you fill out the application online, you will instantly get your EIN. You'll be asked, "Why is the sole proprietor requesting an EIN?" This question includes the following choices for answers: started a new business, hired employee(s), banking purposes, changed type of organization, or purchased active business. Always answer "started a new business" to this question, unless you are hiring employees. This may seem like a strange answer if you've been in business for a long time, but the instructions say to choose an answer that is closest to your situation.

If you have an EIN, you should use it instead of your Social Security number on forms **Schedule C** and **Schedule SE**. On all other forms, including **Form 1040** and **Form 1040-ES**, you should use your Social Security number.

About Parent Payments and Form W-10

If the parents of children in your care want to claim the child care tax credit, they will ask you to fill out **Form W-10**. **Form W-10** is easy to complete: simply enter your name, address, and Social Security or employer identification number, and sign the form. If you have an employer identification number, you must use it, rather than your Social Security number, on this form.

If you don't fill out **Form W-10** when a parent asks you to do so, you face a penalty of $50, even if you don't file tax returns or meet state regulations. Since the parents are responsible for giving you this form, you don't have to track them down and give it to them if they don't ask for it. Don't, however, refuse to sign **Form W-10** in the hope of hiding some of your income from the IRS. Not signing this form is one of the things that can trigger an IRS audit of your tax return.

Parents don't file **Form W-10** with their tax return. Instead, they keep it for their records. When they file **Form 2441**, they take the information from **Form W-10** and record each provider's name, address, and employer identification number, and the amount paid to each provider. The IRS uses this information to check whether the providers listed filed tax returns and reported all their income.

In the past, some parents overstated the number of their dependent children, and some providers understated the amount of their income. The IRS is trying to reduce such false reporting by requiring parents to list the Social Security or employer identification number of each provider. Still, some parents may report child care expenses on their **Form 2441** that are higher than what they paid you. This can happen, for example, when parents use two providers but report all of their child care expenses under one provider because they don't have the other provider's Social Security or employer identification number.

To protect yourself, you need to keep careful records of how much each parent paid you during the year. You should also get a signed receipt from each parent that indicates how much they paid you that year and keep the receipt with your tax records.

Providing Receipts for Parent Payments

There are three types of receipts that you can use, as shown in the examples below.

1. One type of receipt is **Form W-10**, which shows the amount paid and the parent's signature. Keep a copy of all the **Form W-10**s that you fill out. You can also fill out copies of **Form W-10** and give them to parents in January each year. (See the example below.) Parents find this helpful, and it's a professional touch that many will appreciate. There's a blank copy of **Form W-10** in the back of this book that you can use.

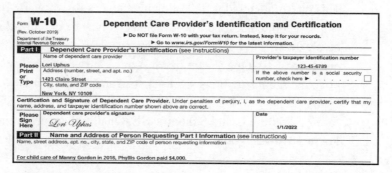

2. Another option is to use a standard book of sales receipts that you can buy in a stationery or office supply store. (See the example below.)

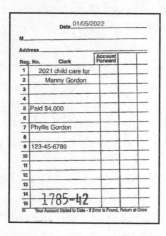

3. You can also use the receipts in the *Family Child Care Business Receipt Book,* which are designed especially for family child care providers. (See the example below.)

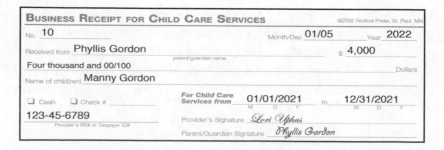

Record-Keeping and Tax Tips

New Tom Copeland Record-Keeping DVD

Redleaf Press has released my first DVD, *The Business of Family Child Care: Record-Keeping* featuring Tom Copeland. In this DVD, I share everything that new and experienced family child care providers need to know about record keeping.

The DVD is designed to be used by both trainers and family child care providers. The three-hour DVD covers the following topics:

- the three-step process for claiming business expenses

- which business deductions you can claim

- how to calculate your Time-Space percentage

- deducting your house and home improvements

- why the Food Program is so important and how to claim food expenses

- and much more!

Organizations that support providers can choose some or all of the sections of the DVD to cover in live workshops. Individual providers can watch all or parts of the DVD at their convenience.

Should You Take a Distribution from Your IRA?

These are very difficult times financially for family child care providers. Many are looking for ways to pay their bills and stay in business. One option some may want to consider is to take an early distribution from their Individual Retirement Account (IRA) or other retirement plan. Is this a good idea?

Normally, it is not advisable to take money out of your retirement plan early. The rules are that if you do so before you are age 59½ you will owe a 10% penalty on the amount you take out. In addition, you will have to pay income taxes on the amount distributed. This represents a big tax bill.

IRS rules allow you to borrow money from some retirement plans, such as a 401(k), but not your IRA. However, if your retirement plan allows you to take a loan, there could be high monthly loan payments, and you must pay back the loan within five years. Your

IRA administrator sets the interest rate on the loan. If you default on the loan, the 10% penalty withdrawal comes back.

A general warning about taking an IRA distribution or IRA loan: The decision to take a distribution or loan can have significant financial implications. In some cases a loan can be useful (if your retirement plan allows that), but a distribution should only be taken as a last resort if you cannot avoid a major financial catastrophe otherwise.

Should You Claim Social Security Benefits Early?

A financial crisis sometimes causes providers to consider taking their Social Security benefits earlier than they had originally planned. Is this a good idea?

You are eligible to start claiming your Social Security benefits as early as age 62. The amount you will receive goes up each year that you wait to claim your benefits. The last year you must start claiming benefits is age 70. Your full retirement age is either age 66 (if you were born before 1960) or 67 (if you were born in 1960 or later).

To find out how much you can expect to get in Social Security benefits, go to www.socialsecurity.gov and create your own account. You will see your annual Social Security statement, which will tell you how much you can expect to get if you start claiming benefits at age 62, your full retirement age, and age 70. These numbers are based on the assumption that you will be earning the same amount of money as you earned in 2020 until you reach these ages. If you earn more in the coming years, your benefit will rise and if you earn less, your benefit will decline.

If you start claiming Social Security benefits before your full retirement age and earn more than $19,560 in 2022, your benefit will be reduced. Once you reach your full retirement age, you can earn as much money as you want, and it will have no impact on your Social Security benefits.

From a financial viewpoint, you should wait for as long as you can before claiming Social Security benefits. For every year you wait after your full retirement age, your benefit will rise by about 8% a year, which is significant. I strongly recommend that you look at your Social Security account at www.ssa.gov/myaccount to see how your retirement age affects your monthly benefits. Before making the decision about what age to start claiming Social Security benefits, consider the reduction in benefits over your lifetime. Claiming benefits at a younger age could mean a loss of tens of thousands to hundreds of thousands of dollars over your lifetime.

Another important factor also needs to be considered: quitting work to enjoy retirement. If collecting benefits early would allow you to quit work, you may have gained something valuable: extra time to enjoy retirement, such as travel, spending time with your family, and more. So while the long-term financial benefits could be reduced by collecting benefits early, you may want to consider all factors when making your decision.

Social Security is complicated, so I would not make any decision until you talk with a financial planner.

How Much Money Do You Want to Make?

You may want to know the answer to this question because you are considering raising your rates and need help justifying higher rates. Or, you are just curious. Whatever the reason, here's the simplest way to figure this out:

First, take the number from IRS **Schedule C**, line 31. This represents your profit from last year. It takes into account all your business income minus all your business expenses. It's your profit.

Second, take the number from last year's IRS **Form 8829 Expenses for Business Use of Your Home**, line 4. This represents how many hours you worked last year.

Third, divide your profit (line 31 of **Schedule C**) by the number of hours you worked (line 4 of **Form 8829**). The result is the amount you earned per hour for your work last year.

For example, if your profit was $25,000 and you worked 3,000 hours, you earned $8.33 per hour ($25,000 ÷ 3,000).

Many providers underestimate how many hours they work by not carefully counting all the hours they spent on business activities in their home when children were not present. If this is the case for you, your hourly wage will be lower if you include all of these hours.

Some providers underreport their business expenses by not claiming all the expenses they are entitled to. My book *Family Child Care Record-Keeping Guide* lists over 1,000 allowable deductions.

How can you use this information?

If you want to raise your hourly wage, multiply the hourly wage you want by line 4 on **Form 8829** to see what your profit must be. So, in the above example, if you want to earn $10 an hour, multiply $10 by 3,000 hours = $30,000 profit.

To reach this goal, you would need to earn an additional $5,000 per year. If you care for four children, you could raise your rates by $1,250 per year or $24 per week. Or, you could cut your business expenses by $5,000 per year.

Sometimes parents look at how much they pay you, see how many other children are in your care, and assume you are earning a lot more money than you really are. The next time parents question your rates, tell them how much you make per hour.

Who Needs an Emergency Fund?

The obvious answer is that we all do.

Life is full of unexpected events. Are you ready for them?

- Your car breaks down and requires a major repair.

- You fall and break your arm and are unable to provide child care for four to six weeks.

- Your roof springs a leak and your homeowners insurance has a $1,000 deductible.

- Your mother becomes ill, and you leave town to stay with her until she recovers.

- The largest employer in your town shuts down, and three families tell you they are leaving.

If you think about it, unexpected events are such a fact of life that we really should call them expected events.

Since you are almost guaranteed to encounter a major financial disruption at some time in the next few years, you should plan ahead by setting aside at least three months of living expenses in an emergency fund.

Deposit this money in a money market fund or bank account where it can be easily accessed and has little or no risk of losing its value.

Here's what three family child care providers said about emergency funds:

> "After five years of struggling, the best thing I did was to put six months' worth of living expenses into a savings account. This completely changed the way I did business, because I didn't have to worry about the money factor when making business decisions about terminating or enrolling new children."

> "I think it's important for child care providers to have a plan B—a backup plan. Plan for bad weather, power outages, becoming ill and not being able to work, and car breakdowns and repairs. Think of everything you can that could affect your income, and develop a backup plan that will help offset the loss of income in those situations."

> "Make sure you have a three-month emergency fund before you spend any money on more supplies—and I actually feel you need more than three months. My goal is to have a six-to-eight-month backup fund. Because we have those reserves, if a family doesn't work out, I can feel okay letting them go."

Saving money for an emergency fund may not sound like an exciting project, but it's an important financial goal you should take seriously.

Don't let the prospect of setting aside three months of living expenses intimidate you. The first step is to set a specific goal ($5,000, $10,000, whatever three months of living expenses are for your family). Don't worry if this number seems impossibly high.

Second, establish a place where you are going to put the money and commit yourself to not spending this on anything except an emergency. It can be a separate savings account or a money market fund. Don't put it into a Certificate of Deposit (CD), because there is usually a penalty for taking it out early.

Third, make regular (monthly) contributions to your emergency fund. Start small: $25 a month is fine. Maintain the discipline of a monthly contribution. To start with, establishing the habit of a consistent contribution is more important than the amount of the contribution. Review your progress at the end of each year and make plans for how much you will save each month next year.

Don't be discouraged if your progress is slow. Slow but steady wins the race. As your emergency fund grows, so will your financial confidence. You will start to feel a sense of freedom and relief that will make all your hard work worthwhile!

Time to Invest in Your 2022 IRA!

Many family child care providers wait until they file their 2022 tax return before making a contribution to their 2022 IRA. Here's a simple way to boost your retirement savings. Contribute to your IRA at the beginning of the year. This will generate substantially higher returns than if you wait until after the year is over.

The reason is that money invested in January will take full advantage of the power of compound interest. Money you invest at the beginning of 2022 will earn interest throughout the year. Over the long run, money invested early in the year will make a big difference in your retirement. Let's look at some examples.

Providers Kim and Teresa are the same age. They invest $5,000 each year in their IRA and earn the same rate of interest (5%) each year. Kim invests her $5,000 each January, while Teresa waits until April of the following year to invest her $5,000. This means that Kim's contribution is earning interest for 15 extra months (January 2022–April 2023) each year.

After 30 years Kim will have $16,000 more in her IRA, and after 40 years she will have $34,000 more.

If they both earned 9% (the historic long-term return of the stock market), Kim would have $75,000 more than Teresa after 30 years and $193,000 more over 40 years.

What if Kim invested her money on January 1, 2022, for her 2021 IRA and Teresa invested on April 15? Even the 3.5 month difference would add up to $30,000 more in Kim's pocket after 30 years and $45,000 over 40 years (at 9% a year).

In all these scenarios, that's a lot of money!

It's Not Too Late

If you are in your 50s, it's not too late to boost your retirement savings. If you are age 55 and you contribute $2,400 on January 1 each year for 10 years (earning 7% a year), you will have $273,000 at age 65. Not bad.

So when is the best time to start saving money for your retirement? Answer: Today! When is the next best time? Answer: Tomorrow! Now is the time to contribute toward your 2022 IRA.

Retirement Plan Limits for 2021

Here are the contribution limits for various individual retirement account (IRA) plans for 2021:

- Traditional IRA and Roth IRA: $6,000, plus an additional $1,000 if you are age 50 or over

- SIMPLE IRA: $13,500 of your net profit, plus an additional $3,000 if you are age 50 or over (**Note**: you must have established a SIMPLE IRA by October 1, 2021, to make a 2021 contribution.)

- SEP IRA: 18.58% of your net profit

The deadline for your contribution to your 2021 IRA is April 15, 2022.

PART I

The Tax Organizer

The Tax Organizer

The Tax Organizer is a series of worksheets that help you organize all the income and expenses for your family child care business and show you where to enter the information on your tax forms. After you complete the Tax Organizer, cut it out and save it with your other tax records for the current tax season. Because the tax laws change constantly, do not use this Tax Organizer for any year other than 2021.

If you plan to give this Tax Organizer to your tax preparer, show it to the preparer before you start recording information. Some tax preparers have their own tax organizer that they will ask you to use, but ask your tax preparer if you can use this one instead. This Tax Organizer can help your tax preparer better understand the deductions that you're entitled to claim for your child care business and can save her a lot of time as she completes your tax return. Before you give your completed Tax Organizer to your tax preparer, be sure to make a copy for your records.

Once your tax return is complete, review the deductions in your Tax Organizer and make sure they've all been entered on your tax forms. If it appears that any of the deductions you listed aren't included, ask the tax preparer why.

There are several record-keeping books that can help you record and organize your tax records, including the following:

> *Redleaf Calendar-Keeper*
> *Inventory-Keeper*
> *Mileage-Keeper*

If you use these products to track your income and expenses throughout the year, you will be able to complete this Tax Organizer much more quickly (and your tax return will be more accurate). Each part of the Tax Organizer explains how to get the information from these other tools and enter it in the Tax Organizer.

Let's start with some identifying information:

Name _____

Address _____

_____

Social Security or employer ID number_____

17

Your Income

In the chart below, list all the child care income you received from both parent fees and county or state subsidy programs for parents. If necessary, continue on another sheet of paper.

Name of Parent	Income from Parents Jan 1–Dec 31	Income from Subsidy Programs Jan 1–Dec 31
_____	_____	_____
_____	_____	_____
_____	_____	_____
_____	_____	_____
_____	_____	_____
_____	_____	_____
_____	_____	_____
_____	_____	_____
_____	_____	_____
_____	_____	_____

Totals   **(A)** _____   **(B)** _____

Total parent fees **(A + B)**   _____

Plus government grants   + _____

Enter on **Schedule C**, line 1   = _____

Food Program reimbursements
received Jan 1–Dec 31   _____

Less Food Program reimbursements
for your own children (total **[C]**
from page 31 of this Tax Organizer)   – _____

Other income   = _____

Enter the total "other income" on **Schedule C**, line 6.

Your Time Percentage

Your Time percentage is the ratio of hours spent on business activities in your home during this tax year to the total hours in a year. There are two ways to calculate this ratio, depending on whether the care you provide for children is on a regular or irregular schedule throughout the year. In either case, you need to have written records of the hours you worked.

A. If You Cared for Children on a Regular Schedule throughout the Year

Complete this section if the hours you cared for children were fairly consistent from week to week during this tax year. If the hours weren't consistent, go to section B on page 21.

HOURS CARING FOR CHILDREN ON A REGULAR BASIS

	_____	Time the first child regularly arrived at your home
	_____	Time the last child regularly left your home
	_____	(A) Number of hours in a day the children were present, from the time the first child regularly arrived until the last child regularly left
x	_____	Number of days you worked per week
=	_____	Hours you worked in a week
x	_____	52 weeks
=	_____	(B) Tentative hours caring for children

You cannot count time spent on vacations, holidays, illnesses, or other days your business was closed. Below, record these days for the entire year and subtract this total from the tentative hours caring for children:

	_____	Vacations
+	_____	Holidays
+	_____	Illnesses
+	_____	Other
		(describe: _____)
=	_____	Total days closed
x	_____	(A) Hours worked in a typical day
=	_____	(C) Total hours closed
	_____	(B) Tentative hours caring for children
–	_____	(C) Total hours closed
=	_____	(D) Total hours caring for children on a regular basis

ADDITIONAL HOURS CARING FOR CHILDREN

	Average # Hours		# Times per Year		
Children arriving early or staying late	_____	x	_____	=	_____
Children staying overnight	_____	x	_____	= +	_____
Occasional care on weekends	_____	x	_____	= +	_____
Other (describe: _____)	_____	x	_____	= +	_____
Total additional hours caring for children				(E) =	_____

BUSINESS HOURS IN THE HOME WHEN CHILDREN WERE NOT PRESENT

Activity Worked	Average # Hours		# Weeks in Business		Hours
Business phone calls	_____	x	_____	=	_____
Cleaning	_____	x	_____	=	+ _____
Email/internet activity	_____	x	_____	=	+ _____
Family child care association activities	_____	x	_____	=	+ _____
Food Program paperwork	_____	x	_____	=	+ _____
Meal preparation	_____	x	_____	=	+ _____
Parent interviews	_____	x	_____	=	+ _____
Planning/preparing activities	_____	x	_____	=	+ _____
Record keeping	_____	x	_____	=	+ _____
Other (identify: _____)	_____	x	_____	=	+ _____
Other (identify: _____)	_____	x	_____	=	+ _____
Total business hours when children were not present				**(F) =**	_____

SUMMARY OF BUSINESS HOURS

Total hours caring for children on a regular basis	**(D) =**	_____
Total additional hours caring for children	**(E) +**	_____
Total business hours when children were not present	**(F) +**	_____
Total business hours	**(G) =**	_____

Enter the Total business hours **(G)** amount on **Form 8829**, line 4.

If you were not in business as of January 1 of last year, calculate and enter the number of hours in the year from the day you started your business until December 31 of last year. If you were in business the full year, enter 8,760 hours.

IF YOU USE THE *REDLEAF CALENDAR-KEEPER*
The total number of hours you worked should be recorded on the year-to-date total line in the box in the upper-right corner of the December calendar page. Enter this amount in **(G)** above or directly on **Form 8829**, line 4.

B. If You Cared for Children on an Irregular Schedule

If your hours of business were not on a regular schedule throughout the year, you will have to carefully track your hours worked for each month. Calculate the number of hours you cared for children each day, from the moment the first child arrived until the last child left. Don't count any days that your business was closed because of vacations, holidays, or illnesses. Next, calculate your business hours when children were not present by filling out the table Business Hours in the Home When Children Were Not Present on page 20.

	# Hours Caring for Children
January	_____
February	+ _____
March	+ _____
April	+ _____
May	+ _____
June	+ _____
July	+ _____
August	+ _____
September	+ _____
October	+ _____
November	+ _____
December	+ _____
Total hours caring for children:	(H) = _____

SUMMARY OF BUSINESS HOURS

Total hours caring for children	(H)	_____
Total business hours when children were not present	(F) +	_____
Total business hours	(I) =	_____

Enter the Total business hours (I) amount on **Form 8829**, line 4.

IF YOU USE THE *REDLEAF CALENDAR-KEEPER*
Follow the same directions as listed above to report your total number of business hours.

Your Space Percentage

List all the rooms in your home (including the basement and garage). Enter the square footage of each room in the column that best applies to how that space is used.

Room	Used 100% for Business	Used Regularly for Business	Not Used Regularly for Business
_____	_____	_____	_____
_____	_____	_____	_____
_____	_____	_____	_____
_____	_____	_____	_____
_____	_____	_____	_____
_____	_____	_____	_____
_____	_____	_____	_____
_____	_____	_____	_____
_____	_____	_____	_____
_____	_____	_____	_____
_____	_____	_____	_____
_____	_____	_____	_____
_____	_____	_____	_____
Total square feet	_____	_____	_____
	(J)	**(K)**	**(L)**

Total square footage of your home: (J + K + L = M)   **(M)** = _____

Your Time-Space Percentage

1) If you have no entries in column (**J**):
Enter the amount from line (**K**) on **Form 8829**, line 1.
Enter the amount from line (**M**) on **Form 8829**, line 2.

2) If you have any entries in column (**J**), you have one or more rooms that are used *exclusively* for your business. Calculate your Time-Space percentage for these rooms as follows:

Enter the amount on line (**J**) _____
Enter the amount on line (**M**) _____
Divide (**J**) by (**M**) = _____% (**N**) Space percentage for exclusive-use rooms

Enter the amount on line (**K**) _____
Enter the amount on line (**M**) _____
Divide (**K**) by (**M**) = _____% (**O**) Space percentage for regularly used rooms

Enter the amount from line (**G**) or (**I**) = _____ (**P**)
Enter the total number of hours in the year from **Form 8829**, line 5* _____ (**Q**)
Divide (**P**) by (**Q**) = _____ (**R**) Time percentage for regularly used rooms

Multiply:

    (**O**) _____
x (**R**) _____
=   _____ (**S**) Time-Space percentage for regularly used rooms

Add:

    (**N**) _____
+ (**S**) _____
=   _____ (**T**) Final Time-Space percentage

Enter the Final Time-Space percentage (**T**) amount on **Form 8829**, line 7.
Do not fill in lines 1–6. Attach a copy of these calculations to **Form 8829**.

---

*If you weren't in business as of January 1 of last year, enter the number of hours in the year from the day you started your business until December 31 of last year.

Your Business Expenses

Start by entering your business expenses in the categories below, then transfer the amounts to the indicated lines on **Schedule C**. (See the *Record-Keeping Guide* for a list of more than 1,000 deductions.)

Advertising   _____ Enter on **Schedule C**, line 8

Liability insurance   _____ Enter on **Schedule C**, line 15

Legal and professional services
(for your business)   _____ Enter on **Schedule C**, line 17

Business taxes and licenses
(payroll taxes and child care licenses) _____ Enter on **Schedule C**, line 23

Business travel expenses
(vehicle expenses go on line 9)   _____ Enter on **Schedule C**, line 24a

Deductible business meals (see page 109) _____ Enter on **Schedule C**, line 24b

Wages (paid to both family and
nonfamily employees)   _____ Enter on **Schedule C**, line 26

Your expenses may be 100% deductible or partly deductible, based on either the Time-Space percentage or the actual business-use percentage:

- **100% business use**: Items that are never used for personal purposes after business hours. Do not claim something as 100% business use unless it meets this qualification.

- **Time-Space percentage**: Items that are used for both business and personal purposes. To calculate your Time-Space percentage, see pages 39–44.

- **Actual business-use percentage**: Items that are used extensively but not exclusively for business purposes. Calculate the percentage of time the item is actually used in your business (each item will usually have a different business-use percentage). You must have written records to show how you arrived at each business-use percentage. Most providers reserve this method for more expensive items they use considerably more than items in their Time-Space percentage.

For each business category that follows, enter your expenses:

Credit Card Interest

100% business use $ _____

Time-Space percentage $_____ x _____% =   + $ _____

Actual business-use percentage $_____ x _____% =   + $ _____

Enter the total on **Schedule C**, line 16b   = $ _____

Office Expenses

100% business use $ _____

Time-Space percentage $_____ x _____% = + $ _____

Actual business-use percentage $_____ x _____% = + $ _____

Enter the total on **Schedule C**, line 18 = $ _____

Rent of Items

100% business use $ _____

Time-Space percentage $_____ x _____% = + $ _____

Actual business-use percentage $_____ x _____% = + $ _____

Enter the total on **Schedule C**, line 20b = $ _____

Repairs and Maintenance on Business Property

(doesn't include home repairs)

100% business use $ _____

Time-Space percentage $_____ x _____% = + $ _____

Actual business-use percentage $_____ x _____% = + $ _____

Enter the total on **Schedule C**, line 21 = $ _____

Supplies

(includes children's supplies and kitchen supplies)

100% business use $ _____

Time-Space percentage $_____ x _____% = + $ _____

Actual business-use percentage $_____ x _____% = + $ _____

Enter the total on **Schedule C**, line 22 = $ _____

Toys

100% business use $ _____

Time-Space percentage $_____ x _____% = + $ _____

Actual business-use percentage $_____ x _____% = + $ _____

Enter the total on one of the blank lines on **Schedule C**, Part V = $ _____

Household Items

(includes yard expenses, safety items, tools)

100% business use $ _____

Time-Space percentage $_____ x _____% = + $ _____

Actual business-use percentage $_____ x _____% = + $ _____

Enter the total on one of the blank lines on **Schedule C**, Part V = $ _____

Cleaning Supplies

100% business use $ _____

Time-Space percentage $_____ x _____% = + $ _____

Actual business-use percentage $_____ x _____% = + $ _____

Enter the total on one of the blank lines on **Schedule C**, Part V = $ _____

Activity Expenses

(includes field trips, birthday parties, special activities)

100% business use			$ _____
Time-Space percentage	$_____ x _____% =		+ $ _____
Actual business-use percentage	$_____ x _____% =		+ $ _____
Enter the total on one of the blank lines on **Schedule C**, Part V			= $ _____

Other Expenses

(items not included in any of the above expense categories)

100% business use			$ _____
Time-Space percentage	$_____ x _____% =		+ $ _____
Actual business-use percentage	$_____ x _____% =		+ $ _____
Enter the total on one of the blank lines on **Schedule C**, Part V			= $ _____

IF YOU USE THE *REDLEAF CALENDAR-KEEPER*

There are two places where you can find the totals of your **Schedule C** deductions. One is the year-to-date total at the bottom of the monthly expense report for December. The second is the list of direct business expenses on the income tax worksheet. Take the totals that best represent your deductions, and enter them in the appropriate expense category in the Tax Organizer.

Your Vehicle Expenses

To calculate the miles that you drove on trips for which the primary purpose was business, enter information from your written records, such as the *Redleaf Calendar-Keeper,* the *Mileage-Keeper,* receipts, and canceled checks on the lines below. If you used more than one vehicle for your business last year, photocopy this part of the Tax Organizer and fill out one worksheet for each vehicle you used.

Odometer Readings

Make and model of vehicle		_____
Year first used in your business		_____
Purchase price of vehicle		_____
Odometer reading December 31 of last year		_____
Odometer reading January 1 of last year	–	_____
Total miles vehicle was driven last year	**(A)**	_____

Business Mileage

Add up your business mileage and then multiply it by the standard mileage rate.

Business miles January 1–December 31	= _____	**(B)**
Standard mileage rate	x 0.56	
Total mileage deduction	= _____	**(C)**

Business-Use Percentage of Vehicle

Total business miles last year	_____	**(B)**
Divided by total miles vehicle was driven last year	÷ _____	**(A)**
Business-use percentage of vehicle	= _____	**(D)**

Other Vehicle Expenses

Vehicle loan interest	_____	
Vehicle property tax (if applicable)	+ _____	
Total other vehicle expenses	= _____	
Multiplied by business-use percentage of vehicle	x _____	**(D)**
Business-use percentage of other vehicle expenses	= _____	
Parking/tolls/ferry during business trips	+ _____	
Total business-use percentage of other vehicle expenses	= _____	**(E)**

Standard Mileage Rate Method

Mileage deduction	_____	**(C)**
Total business-use percentage of other vehicle expenses	+ _____	**(E)**
Total business deduction (standard mileage rate method)	= _____	

Enter the Total business deduction on **Schedule C**, line 9

Actual Vehicle Expenses Method

To use this method, you must have recorded all your vehicle expenses so that you can add them up at the end of the year.

Gas	_____	
Oil/lube/filter	+ _____	
Tune-up/repairs/tires	+ _____	
Lease payment (see page 117)	+ _____	
Wash/wax	+ _____	
Supplies	+ _____	
Vehicle insurance (not including extra business endorsement)	+ _____	
Other	+ _____	
Total actual vehicle expenses	= _____	
Multiplied by business-use percentage of vehicle	x _____	**(D)**
Business deduction for actual vehicle expenses	= _____	**(F)**

Vehicle Depreciation

Fair market value of vehicle when first used for business   _____

Business-use percentage of vehicle   x _____ **(D)**

     = _____

Depreciation percentage (from tables on page 92)   x _____ %*

Depreciation deduction   _____ **(G)**

Actual Business-Use Deduction

Business deduction for actual vehicle expenses   _____ **(F)**

Extra business endorsement on vehicle insurance (if any)   + _____

Depreciation deduction   + _____ **(G)**

Total business-use percentage of other vehicle expenses   + _____ **(E)**

Total business deduction (actual vehicle expenses method)   = _____

     Enter the Total business deduction on **Schedule C**, line 9

Compare your total business deduction under the standard mileage rate method and the actual vehicle expenses method. If you began your business last year or used the standard mileage rate method for this vehicle in earlier years, you may choose to use the total from either method. If you used the actual vehicle expenses method for this vehicle in earlier years, you must continue using this method. (For more information, see chapter 5.)

IF YOU USE THE *REDLEAF CALENDAR-KEEPER*

Refer to the year-to-date total mileage at the bottom of the December expense report. If you tracked your actual vehicle expense in one of the monthly expense columns, enter the year total from December on the appropriate lines above.

IF YOU USE THE *MILEAGE-KEEPER*

Enter the amounts recorded for mileage and actual vehicle expenses from pages 34–35 (if you use the standard mileage rate method) or pages 44–45 (if you use the actual vehicle expenses method) on the appropriate lines above.

---

*See chapter 3 for limitations on the depreciation deduction each year. Also, if you purchased a vehicle last year, see the Section 179 rules in chapter 3.

Your Food Expenses

You have two choices when calculating your food expenses. You can use the standard meal allowance rate or the actual cost of food. The standard meal allowance rate was established by the IRS so that providers could claim their food expenses without having to keep food receipts. (For a complete discussion of how to report Food Program reimbursements and food expenses on **Schedule C**, see chapter 4. For a detailed discussion of how to track food costs, see the *Record-Keeping Guide*.) Here's a summary of these two methods:

USING THE STANDARD MEAL ALLOWANCE RATE

You must keep the following records throughout the year: each child's name, dates and hours of attendance, and number of meals served. If you were on the Food Program during the year, save your monthly claim forms, which contain this information. Track nonreimbursed meals on your copy of the claim form or someplace else. Use the meal form to track nonreimbursed meals for last year (or all meals if you weren't on the Food Program). Use the year-end meal tally to total your reimbursed and nonreimbursed meals for last year.

USING THE ACTUAL COST OF FOOD

There are many ways to calculate your actual food costs. One way to do this is to buy and store your business food separately from buying and storing food for your personal use. Probably the simplest and most accurate method is to estimate the average cost per child per meal and multiply that number by the number of meals and snacks served. To calculate the average cost, track the ingredients you served for four typical menus for breakfast, lunch, supper, and snacks. Estimate the cost of the food for each menu, and divide that number by the number of children served. (For more information about how to calculate the actual cost of food, see the *Record-Keeping Guide*.)

IF YOU USE THE *REDLEAF CALENDAR-KEEPER*

If you tracked your food expenses each month, your yearly total will be on page 83 of your December expense report. You may also have entered your food expenses on the income tax worksheet as direct business expenses on page 85. If you haven't estimated your business food expenses, you may want to fill out the meal form and year-end meal tally in this book to get a more accurate deduction rather than using the totals on your *Redleaf Calendar-Keeper*.

Calculating Food Program Reimbursements for Your Own Children

If you received Food Program reimbursements for your own children this year, subtract this amount before reporting your reimbursements as taxable income on **Schedule C**. Your year-end statement from your Food Program might have already done this for you. To calculate the reimbursements for your own children, you'll need to calculate the first and the second half of the year separately, because the reimbursement rates go up on July 1 every year.

Begin by filling out the two worksheets below, taking the information requested from the meal counts on your monthly claim forms.

Worksheet 1:
Food Program Reimbursements
for Your Own Children, January–June 2021

Number of Meals	Breakfasts	Lunches	Snacks	Dinners
January	_____	_____	_____	_____
February	_____	_____	_____	_____
March	_____	_____	_____	_____
April	_____	_____	_____	_____
May	_____	_____	_____	_____
June	_____	_____	_____	_____
Total meals	_____	_____	_____	_____

Total meals
times CACFP Tier 1
reimbursement rate

x $ 1.39	x $2.61	x $0.78	x $2.61
(Alaska: $2.22)	(Alaska: $4.24)	(Alaska: $1.26)	(Alaska: $4.24)
(Hawaii: $1.62)	(Hawaii: $3.06)	(Hawaii: $0.91)	(Hawaii: $3.06)

CACFP
reimbursements for
your own children =

_____	_____	_____	_____
(1)	(2)	(3)	(4)

Add reimbursement totals 1–4 to get the total
reimbursements for your own children, Jan–June   = _____   **(A)**

Worksheet 2:
Food Program Reimbursements
for Your Own Children, July–December 2021

Number of Meals	Breakfasts	Lunches	Snacks	Dinners
July	_____	_____	_____	_____
August	_____	_____	_____	_____
September	_____	_____	_____	_____
October	_____	_____	_____	_____
November	_____	_____	_____	_____
December	_____	_____	_____	_____
Total meals	_____	_____	_____	_____

Total meals
times CACFP Tier 1
reimbursement rate

x $1.40	x $2.63	x $0.78	x $2.63
(Alaska: $2.23)	(Alaska: $4.26)	(Alaska: $1.27)	(Alaska: $4.26)
(Hawaii: $1.63)	(Hawaii: $3.08)	(Hawaii: $0.91)	(Hawaii: $3.08)

CACFP
reimbursements for
your own children =

_____	_____	_____	_____
(1)	(2)	(3)	(4)

Add reimbursement totals 1–4 to get the total
reimbursements for your own children, July–Dec   = _____ **(B)**

Once you have calculated amounts (**A**) and (**B**), add them together to get the total (**C**):

Reimbursements for your own children, Jan–June   _____ **(A)**
Reimbursements for your own children, Jul–Dec   + _____ **(B)**
Total reimbursements for your own children   = _____ **(C)**

Enter the total reimbursements for your own children (**C**) amount on page 18
of this Tax Organizer.

MEAL FORM Week of _____ 2021

Child	Mon	Tue	Wed	Thu	Fri	Sat	Sun	Totals
	Bkst __ Lun __ Din __ Sn1 __ Sn2 __ Sn3 __	Bkst __ Lun __ Din __ Sn1 __ Sn2 __ Sn3 __	Bkst __ Lun __ Din __ Sn1 __ Sn2 __ Sn3 __	Bkst __ Lun __ Din __ Sn1 __ Sn2 __ Sn3 __	Bkst __ Lun __ Din __ Sn1 __ Sn2 __ Sn3 __	Bkst __ Lun __ Din __ Sn1 __ Sn2 __ Sn3 __	Bkst __ Lun __ Din __ Sn1 __ Sn2 __ Sn3 __	B __ L __ D __ S __
	Bkst __ Lun __ Din __ Sn1 __ Sn2 __ Sn3 __	Bkst __ Lun __ Din __ Sn1 __ Sn2 __ Sn3 __	Bkst __ Lun __ Din __ Sn1 __ Sn2 __ Sn3 __	Bkst __ Lun __ Din __ Sn1 __ Sn2 __ Sn3 __	Bkst __ Lun __ Din __ Sn1 __ Sn2 __ Sn3 __	Bkst __ Lun __ Din __ Sn1 __ Sn2 __ Sn3 __	Bkst __ Lun __ Din __ Sn1 __ Sn2 __ Sn3 __	B __ L __ D __ S __
	Bkst __ Lun __ Din __ Sn1 __ Sn2 __ Sn3 __	Bkst __ Lun __ Din __ Sn1 __ Sn2 __ Sn3 __	Bkst __ Lun __ Din __ Sn1 __ Sn2 __ Sn3 __	Bkst __ Lun __ Din __ Sn1 __ Sn2 __ Sn3 __	Bkst __ Lun __ Din __ Sn1 __ Sn2 __ Sn3 __	Bkst __ Lun __ Din __ Sn1 __ Sn2 __ Sn3 __	Bkst __ Lun __ Din __ Sn1 __ Sn2 __ Sn3 __	B __ L __ D __ S __
	Bkst __ Lun __ Din __ Sn1 __ Sn2 __ Sn3 __	Bkst __ Lun __ Din __ Sn1 __ Sn2 __ Sn3 __	Bkst __ Lun __ Din __ Sn1 __ Sn2 __ Sn3 __	Bkst __ Lun __ Din __ Sn1 __ Sn2 __ Sn3 __	Bkst __ Lun __ Din __ Sn1 __ Sn2 __ Sn3 __	Bkst __ Lun __ Din __ Sn1 __ Sn2 __ Sn3 __	Bkst __ Lun __ Din __ Sn1 __ Sn2 __ Sn3 __	B __ L __ D __ S __
	Bkst __ Lun __ Din __ Sn1 __ Sn2 __ Sn3 __	Bkst __ Lun __ Din __ Sn1 __ Sn2 __ Sn3 __	Bkst __ Lun __ Din __ Sn1 __ Sn2 __ Sn3 __	Bkst __ Lun __ Din __ Sn1 __ Sn2 __ Sn3 __	Bkst __ Lun __ Din __ Sn1 __ Sn2 __ Sn3 __	Bkst __ Lun __ Din __ Sn1 __ Sn2 __ Sn3 __	Bkst __ Lun __ Din __ Sn1 __ Sn2 __ Sn3 __	B __ L __ D __ S __
	Bkst __ Lun __ Din __ Sn1 __ Sn2 __ Sn3 __	Bkst __ Lun __ Din __ Sn1 __ Sn2 __ Sn3 __	Bkst __ Lun __ Din __ Sn1 __ Sn2 __ Sn3 __	Bkst __ Lun __ Din __ Sn1 __ Sn2 __ Sn3 __	Bkst __ Lun __ Din __ Sn1 __ Sn2 __ Sn3 __	Bkst __ Lun __ Din __ Sn1 __ Sn2 __ Sn3 __	Bkst __ Lun __ Din __ Sn1 __ Sn2 __ Sn3 __	B __ L __ D __ S __

Child	Mon	Tue	Wed	Thu	Fri	Sat	Sun	Totals
	Bkst __ Lun __ Din __ Sn1 __ Sn2 __ Sn3 __	Bkst __ Lun __ Din __ Sn1 __ Sn2 __ Sn3 __	Bkst __ Lun __ Din __ Sn1 __ Sn2 __ Sn3 __	Bkst __ Lun __ Din __ Sn1 __ Sn2 __ Sn3 __	Bkst __ Lun __ Din __ Sn1 __ Sn2 __ Sn3 __	Bkst __ Lun __ Din __ Sn1 __ Sn2 __ Sn3 __	Bkst __ Lun __ Din __ Sn1 __ Sn2 __ Sn3 __	B __ L __ D __ S __
	Bkst __ Lun __ Din __ Sn1 __ Sn2 __ Sn3 __	Bkst __ Lun __ Din __ Sn1 __ Sn2 __ Sn3 __	Bkst __ Lun __ Din __ Sn1 __ Sn2 __ Sn3 __	Bkst __ Lun __ Din __ Sn1 __ Sn2 __ Sn3 __	Bkst __ Lun __ Din __ Sn1 __ Sn2 __ Sn3 __	Bkst __ Lun __ Din __ Sn1 __ Sn2 __ Sn3 __	Bkst __ Lun __ Din __ Sn1 __ Sn2 __ Sn3 __	B __ L __ D __ S __
	Bkst __ Lun __ Din __ Sn1 __ Sn2 __ Sn3 __	Bkst __ Lun __ Din __ Sn1 __ Sn2 __ Sn3 __	Bkst __ Lun __ Din __ Sn1 __ Sn2 __ Sn3 __	Bkst __ Lun __ Din __ Sn1 __ Sn2 __ Sn3 __	Bkst __ Lun __ Din __ Sn1 __ Sn2 __ Sn3 __	Bkst __ Lun __ Din __ Sn1 __ Sn2 __ Sn3 __	Bkst __ Lun __ Din __ Sn1 __ Sn2 __ Sn3 __	B __ L __ D __ S __
	Bkst __ Lun __ Din __ Sn1 __ Sn2 __ Sn3 __	Bkst __ Lun __ Din __ Sn1 __ Sn2 __ Sn3 __	Bkst __ Lun __ Din __ Sn1 __ Sn2 __ Sn3 __	Bkst __ Lun __ Din __ Sn1 __ Sn2 __ Sn3 __	Bkst __ Lun __ Din __ Sn1 __ Sn2 __ Sn3 __	Bkst __ Lun __ Din __ Sn1 __ Sn2 __ Sn3 __	Bkst __ Lun __ Din __ Sn1 __ Sn2 __ Sn3 __	B __ L __ D __ S __
	Bkst __ Lun __ Din __ Sn1 __ Sn2 __ Sn3 __	Bkst __ Lun __ Din __ Sn1 __ Sn2 __ Sn3 __	Bkst __ Lun __ Din __ Sn1 __ Sn2 __ Sn3 __	Bkst __ Lun __ Din __ Sn1 __ Sn2 __ Sn3 __	Bkst __ Lun __ Din __ Sn1 __ Sn2 __ Sn3 __	Bkst __ Lun __ Din __ Sn1 __ Sn2 __ Sn3 __	Bkst __ Lun __ Din __ Sn1 __ Sn2 __ Sn3 __	B __ L __ D __ S __
	Bkst __ Lun __ Din __ Sn1 __ Sn2 __ Sn3 __	Bkst __ Lun __ Din __ Sn1 __ Sn2 __ Sn3 __	Bkst __ Lun __ Din __ Sn1 __ Sn2 __ Sn3 __	Bkst __ Lun __ Din __ Sn1 __ Sn2 __ Sn3 __	Bkst __ Lun __ Din __ Sn1 __ Sn2 __ Sn3 __	Bkst __ Lun __ Din __ Sn1 __ Sn2 __ Sn3 __	Bkst __ Lun __ Din __ Sn1 __ Sn2 __ Sn3 __	B __ L __ D __ S __

Weekly Totals

Breakfasts _____   Dinners _____

Lunches _____   Snacks _____

Place a check mark (✓) next to each meal or snack you serve. Do not count meals served to your own children. If you are on the Food Program, use this form to track your nonreimbursed meals only. Add the reimbursed meals from your monthly claim forms and the nonreimbursed meals from this form together, and put the totals on the year-end meal tally on page 95. If you are not on the Food Program, use this form to track all your meals, and put the totals on the year-end meal tally on page 95.

Make copies of this form for each week of the year. If you have six or fewer children in your program, you can use one form for two weeks. You can download this form at the Redleaf Press website. Go to www.redleafpress.org, and find the page for the *Redleaf Calendar-Keeper 2021*. There will be a link to this form.

YEAR-END MEAL TALLY

If you are not on the Food Program, enter all meals and snacks in the column labeled "Number Not Reimbursed by Food Program."

	Breakfasts		Lunches		Dinners		Snacks	
	Number Reimbursed by Food Program	Number Not Reimbursed by Food Program	Number Reimbursed by Food Program	Number Not Reimbursed by Food Program	Number Reimbursed by Food Program	Number Not Reimbursed by Food Program	Number Reimbursed by Food Program	Number Not Reimbursed by Food Program
January								
February								
March								
April								
May								
June								
July								
August								
September								
October								
November								
December								
TOTAL								

2021 Standard Meal Allowance Rate*

Number of Breakfasts ____ X $1.39 = $ ____
Number of Lunches ____ X $2.61 = $ ____
Number of Dinners ____ X $2.61 = $ ____
Number of Snacks ____ X $0.78 = $ ____
Total Food Deductions $ ____ †

Do not report any meals served to your own children (even if they are reimbursed by the Food Program).

* The IRS standard meal allowance rate for 2021 used in these calculations is based on the Tier I rate as of January 1, 2021. This rate is used for all meals and snacks served throughout 2021, even though the Tier I rate goes up every July. All providers, whether on Tier I or Tier II (and all providers not on the Food Program), will use the rates listed.

† Enter this amount on Form 1040 Schedule C, Part V. Be sure to enter any reimbursements from the Food Program (with the exception of reimbursements for your own children) as income on Form 1040 Schedule C, line 6.

Your Home Expenses

Casualty losses	_____	Enter on **Form 8829**, line 9, col. b
Mortgage interest paid last year	_____	Enter on **Form 8829**, line 10*, col. b
Real estate taxes paid last year	_____	Enter on **Form 8829**, line 11*, col. b
Homeowners/renters insurance	_____	Enter on **Form 8829**, line 18, col. b
Home repairs and maintenance	_____	Enter on **Form 8829**, line 20, col. b
Other assessments	_____	Enter on **Form 8829**, line 22, col. b

*See pages 49–50.

Utilities

Gas _____
Oil _____
Electricity _____
Water _____
Sewer _____
Garbage _____
Cable TV _____

Total utilities _____ Enter on **Form 8829**, line 21, col. b

Apartment or home rent _____ Enter on **Form 8829**, line 19, col. b

You can never claim monthly costs associated with the first phone line in your home. If you have a second phone line in your home, you may claim part of its monthly costs based on your business-use percentage. Calculate your business-use percentage by tracking your business and personal use for at least two months. Divide your business hours by the total (business and personal) hours of use.

Cost of second phone line _____
Actual business-use percentage   x _____ %
= _____ Enter on **Form 8829**, line 21, col. a

IF YOU USE THE *REDLEAF CALENDAR-KEEPER*
Enter the amounts in the Total column (not the FCC Business Expense column) from the house expenses worksheet.

Your Depreciation

Enter all the depreciable items you bought last year on the worksheet on the next page. (Use the depreciation tables in chapter 3 to fill in the Table % column in the depreciation worksheet.) Enter your depreciation deductions on **Form 4562**. For depreciable items you bought before last year and after you went into business, fill out copies of this page. Enter depreciation for each year on **Form 4562**. Enter the first year of depreciation as described in chapter 3. After the first year, enter depreciation (except home and home/land improvements) on **Form 4562**, line 17.

Your Home Depreciation
(including home and land improvements)

Purchase price of your home   _____

Cost of any improvements to your
home or land that you completed
before your business began (see below)   + _____ **(A)**

Your home's adjusted value   = _____ **(B)**

Fair market value of your home when you first used it for business   _____ **(C)**

Enter the smaller of **(B)** or **(C)** on **Form 8829**, line 37

Improvements Completed before Your Business Began

Description of Project	Month/Year Completed	Cost of Project
_____	_____	_____
_____	_____	+ _____
_____	_____	+ _____
_____	_____	+ _____
_____	_____	+ _____
_____	_____	+ _____
Total cost of all projects		= _____ **(A)**

IF YOU USE THE *INVENTORY-KEEPER*
Use the numbers from page 53.

Depreciation Worksheet

Depreciation Category[1]	Date Put into Service	Cost or Other Basis[2]	Method/ Convention	Business-Use %[3]	Business Basis[4]	Table %	Depreciation Deduction	Section 179 Deduction
Computers/printers								
Furniture/appliances								
Home improvements								
Land improvements								

[1] See chapter 3 for a definition of what items belong in each depreciation category.

[2] Enter the original cost or the fair market value of the item when it was first used for business last year, whichever is lower.

[3] Enter one of the following percentages: 100% business use, Time-Space percentage, or actual business-use percentage. See chapter 5 for a definition of each option.

[4] Multiply the amount in the Cost or Other Basis column by the percentage in the Business-Use % column.

PART II

The Tax Workbook

CHAPTER 1

Calculating Your Time-Space Percentage

Before you start filling out your tax forms, calculate your Time-Space percentage for this tax year. This percentage is one of the most important numbers you will use for your taxes because it determines how much of your key expenses you will be able to deduct as business expenses. For example, the Time-Space percentage is used in calculating home expenses on **Form 8829**, personal property depreciation expenses on **Form 4562**, and shared household supplies and other expenses on **Schedule C**. The specific deductions that are based on the Time-Space percentage include these:

- casualty losses
- mortgage interest
- real estate taxes
- homeowners insurance
- home repairs and maintenance
- utilities

- rent of a house or apartment
- home depreciation
- personal property depreciation
- home improvements
- land improvements
- household supplies and toys

Since the total of these costs is usually a significant amount, it's important to calculate your Time-Space percentage correctly. The Tax Organizer includes worksheets you can use to calculate your Time-Space percentage quickly; this chapter provides a more detailed description of that process.

Computing your Time-Space percentage is a three-step process. First you calculate your Time percentage, then you calculate your Space percentage, and then you multiply the two together. The formula you will use looks like this:

$$\frac{\text{\# hours your home is used for business}}{\text{Total \# hours in a year}} \quad x \quad \frac{\text{\# square feet of your home used regularly for business}}{\text{Total \# square feet in your home}} \quad = \quad \text{Time-Space percentage}$$

Step One: Calculate Your Time Percentage

The Time percentage is how much time your home is used for your business. You calculate it by using the following formula:

$$\frac{\text{\# hours your home is used for business}}{\text{Total \# hours in a year}} = \text{Time percentage}$$

You can include the following activities in calculating how many hours your home is used for your business:

- caring for children

- cleaning the home for your business

- cooking for the children in your care

- planning and preparing activities for your business

- keeping business records, including paperwork for the Child and Adult Care Food Program (CACFP)

- conducting interviews with parents

- talking to parents on the telephone about your business

- locating resources and information on the internet

- any other business-related activities you do in your home

In calculating your Time percentage, you may not count time you spend outside your home on activities such as shopping or transporting children to school. For those activities, you are not using your home for business purposes.

Maximize Your Claim

Many family child care providers don't include all their working hours in calculating their Time percentage and therefore do not take full advantage of the law. Although there is no maximum Time percentage, it is important to track your working hours so that you have evidence to back up your claim. Also, you must recalculate your Time percentage each year because the number of hours you work usually isn't exactly the same from year to year. Here are some tips for recording your business hours:

HOURS SPENT CARING FOR CHILDREN

Throughout the year, keep records that show how much time you spend caring for the children in your business. Keep attendance records, or save a copy of a document that describes your normal working day, such as a parent contract or a flyer advertising your business.

EXAMPLE

This year you cared for children from 7:00 a.m. to 5:00 p.m. five days a week and took one week of vacation. In this case, you spent 2,550 hours caring for children (10 hours a day x 5 days a week x 51 weeks = 2,550 hours).

To come up with this number, count all the hours when children are in your care from the time the first child arrives to the time the last child leaves. If you usually work from 7:00 a.m. to 5:00 p.m. but a child regularly arrives early or stays late, note this on a calendar or in your record book and count the additional time. If a child stays overnight occasionally, count all the hours the child is in your house. If you regularly care for children overnight, your Time percentage could be very high. In this case, it is extremely important to keep exact records of when children are present.

If you take a vacation, don't count this time as business hours. You probably should not count the hours for paid holidays, either, although there are no IRS guidelines on this point.

Hours Working When Children Are Not Present

In addition to counting all the hours you spend caring for children, you should also include all the hours your home is used for business purposes when the children in your care are not present. This includes time spent cleaning, cooking, planning activities, keeping records, interviewing, making phone calls, and doing other activities related to your business. Don't count hours spent on general home repairs or maintenance activities, such as cutting the lawn, repairing fixtures, or putting up storm windows.

You may not count the same hours twice. For example, if you clean the house during the day while the children sleep, you cannot count the cleaning hours because you are already counting this time as caring for children. You may only count these hours if the children you care for are not present. For example, if between 7:00 a.m. and 8:00 a.m. you are preparing breakfast for the children in your care and your spouse is cleaning your home, you can only count one hour toward your Time percentage. If your spouse did the cleaning the night before while you were not conducting business activities, then you can count the time spent doing both tasks.

Keep records showing that you spent these hours on business activities and not on personal activities. If you spend one hour cleaning after the children leave, count this hour as business time. If you are cleaning your house in general, count only the time that is associated with the mess created by your business. Mark on a calendar when you do these business activities, or make up a weekly schedule that you regularly follow.

Example

In addition to the 2,550 hours you spent actually caring for children, you spent 60 hours a month (720 hours a year) on business activities such as cleaning, preparing meals, planning activities, record keeping, meeting parents, and making business phone calls. You add this to your total business hours for the year and get 3,270 hours, which gives you a Time percentage of 37% (3,270 ÷ 8,760 hours [24 hours a day x 365 days = 8,760 hours]).

Step Two: Calculate Your Space Percentage

The Space percentage is how much space you use in your home on a regular basis for your business. You calculate it by using the following formula:

$$\frac{\text{\# square feet of your home used regularly for business}}{\text{Total \# square feet in your home}} = \text{Space percentage}$$

For a room to be counted as child care space, it must be used on a *regular* basis for your business. Regular means consistent, customary use. Using a room only occasionally for business is not regular use. A room doesn't have to be used every day to be considered regularly used, but using it once every two weeks probably isn't regular use. If the children in your care sleep in your bedroom for an hour a day, count the bedroom as being regularly used for the business. However, using the bedroom for sick children once a month would not be regular use.

If there are any rooms in your home that you use exclusively for your business, refer to the section titled Exclusive-Use Rooms (in this chapter) before you calculate your Space percentage.

In the total square footage of your home, include every area of your home, including your basement, porch, deck, carport, detached garage, basement, and other structures on your land, such as a barn. Do not include the following spaces: lawn, garden area, driveway, sidewalk, sandbox, or outdoor play space.

IRS Child Care Provider Audit Technique Guide on the Space Percentage

The guide explicitly states that providers should count both their basements and garages as part of the total square footage of their home. A Tax Court case (see the *Uphus and Walker v. Commissioner* case in appendix C) has also ruled that providers can claim their laundry room, storage room, and garage as regularly used in the business, even if the children in care never use the rooms.

This means that when you count your basement in the total square footage of your home, you may be able to count areas such as the following as regularly used by your business: the furnace and water heater area (if used regularly to heat the home and water used by the business), the laundry room (if used regularly to wash children's clothes, bedding, and blankets), and the storage areas (if used regularly to store toys, holiday decorations, or home maintenance equipment used in the business).

The inclusion of basements and garages into the Space percentage calculation can have different consequences for providers. For providers who use these areas on a regular basis for their business and have other rooms that are not regularly used in their business, this is good news because it will increase their Space percentage. For providers who have exclusive-use rooms and did not previously count these areas, this is bad news because it will decrease their Space percentage. For providers who use all their rooms on a regular basis for their business as well as their basement and garage, this will not make any difference. In my experience working with thousands of child care providers, I have found that it is very common for providers to use all the rooms of their home on a regular basis for their business. If this applies to you, don't hesitate to claim 100% Space percentage.

Let's look at an example of a Space percentage calculation:

	Used regularly for business?	Count as business space	Don't count as business space
Living room	Yes	300 sq ft	
Dining room	Yes	200 sq ft	
Kitchen	Yes	150 sq ft	
Entryway or stairs	Yes	150 sq ft	
Second-floor hallway	Yes	75 sq ft	
Master bedroom	Yes	200 sq ft	
Child's bedroom	Yes	150 sq ft	
Child's bedroom	No		250 sq ft
Bathroom	Yes	100 sq ft	
Basement playroom	Yes	275 sq ft	
Basement furnace/ laundry area	Yes	50 sq ft	
Basement storage area	Yes/No	150 sq ft	250 sq ft
Garage/carport	Yes	200 sq ft	
Total		2,000 sq ft	500 sq ft

$$\frac{\text{\# square feet of your home used regularly for business}}{\text{Total \# square feet in your home}} = \frac{2,000}{2,500} = 80\% \text{ Space percentage}$$

Step Three: Calculate Your Time-Space Percentage

To find your Time-Space percentage, multiply your Time percentage by your Space percentage. In our example:

37% Time x 80% Space = 30% Time-Space percentage

Here's the Time-Space percentage formula again:

$$\frac{\text{\# hours your home is used for business}}{\text{Total \# hours in a year}} \quad x \quad \frac{\text{\# square feet of your home used regularly for business}}{\text{Total \# square feet in your home}} = \frac{\text{Time-Space}}{\text{percentage}}$$

Use your 2021 Time-Space percentage only for the expenses you are claiming in 2021. *Remember that you will have to recalculate your Time-Space percentage each year and apply the new percentage to your expenses.*

If you discover that in previous years you have not been counting all the business space in your home or all your business hours, you may want to file **Form 1040X** (see chapter 9) to amend your previous tax returns and collect refunds from the IRS.

Exclusive-Use Rooms

If you use one or more of the rooms in your home exclusively for your business, you will need to calculate your Space percentage a bit differently. For example, an exclusive-use room might be a separate playroom that is used only by the children in your care. Exclusive use means 100% business use—it means that you don't use the room for any personal purposes at all, at any time. You can walk through the area during your personal time to get to another room or to go outside, but if you use the room for personal use at all, it is no longer used exclusively for business.

Let's say that in the example on the previous page the basement playroom is an exclusive-use room that is used 100% for the child care business. This room will serve as an example of how to calculate the Space percentage if you have an exclusive-use room:

1. Divide the square feet of the exclusive-use room by the total square feet of the home: 275 ÷ 2,500 = 11%

2. Divide the square feet of the rooms used regularly for business by the total square feet of the home: 1,725 ÷ 2,500 = 69%

3. Multiply the Space percentage of the shared rooms by the Time percentage: 69% x 37% = 26%

4. Add the percentages that resulted from Step 1 and Step 3: 11% + 26% = 37% Time-Space percentage

Notice that this Time-Space percentage is significantly greater than the 30% that we calculated previously for this example. If you use any rooms exclusively for your business, you should use this formula and claim the higher Time-Space percentage.

If you use some rooms exclusively for business, try not to set aside any other rooms exclusively for personal use, if you can avoid it. If you use one room exclusively for business and all your other rooms regularly for business, you will have a higher Time-Space percentage than if you use one room exclusively for business and all your other rooms exclusively for personal use.

You don't need to have a physical barrier around an area that is used exclusively for business. If a room has an area used exclusively for business but is otherwise a personal area, measure the two parts of the room and claim the exclusive-use rule for the exclusive area.

Because of the significant impact that an exclusive-use room can have on your Time-Space percentage, an IRS auditor is likely to look closely at the measurements of these rooms. If you claim any exclusive-use rooms, draw a simple diagram of your home showing which areas you used exclusively for your business, and keep this diagram with your records. This is important because your use of the rooms or the square footage of the rooms may change (if you remodel, for example). Save any copies of your house plans, blueprints, or other documents that can verify the square footage of your home.

Actual Business-Use Percentage

An actual business-use percentage is an alternative to the Time-Space percentage for items that you regularly use for business. It results in a much higher rate than your Time-Space percentage. You determine an item's actual business-use percentage by dividing the number of hours you use it for business by the total number of hours you use it for all purposes. If you use this method, you must document your business use in writing and be prepared to back up your number if the IRS challenges it.

Here's an example: You bought a swing set this year for $1,000; your Time-Space percentage is 25%. Using your Time-Space percentage, you could only depreciate $250 ($1,000 x 25%) of this expense this year. (See chapter 3 for an explanation of depreciation.) You determine that the children in your care use the swing set 10 hours a week (2 hours/day x 5 days), while your own children only use it 7 hours a week (1 hour/day x 7 days). In this case, your business-use percentage would be 59% (10 hours of business use ÷ 17 hours of total use), and you would be able to depreciate $590 ($1,000 x 59%). Since this item represents a large expense, and 59% is significantly greater than 25%, you should definitely use your business-use percentage in this case.

If you use a business-use percentage, you must keep records to support your calculation. If the IRS challenges it, it will be up to you to prove that your figure is accurate. This doesn't mean that you have to keep a log every day to show the business use, but you may need several weeks or months of logs to show a pattern. The higher your business-use percentage, the more evidence the IRS may request to justify your number.

You may use a business-use percentage for a few items and your Time-Space percentage for everything else. You can use either method for any items you are depreciating.

For more information about the tax issues discussed in this chapter, refer to the related topics in the other chapters of this book and the Redleaf Press *Family Child Care Record-Keeping Guide*.

CHAPTER 2

Claiming Your Home Expenses: Form 8829

This chapter explains how to fill out **Form 8829 Expenses for Business Use of Your Home**. The following expenses are listed on this form:

- casualty losses
- mortgage interest
- real estate taxes
- homeowners insurance
- home repairs and maintenance
- utilities
- rent
- home depreciation

The goal of **Form 8829** is to determine how much of your home expenses you can claim as a business deduction. There are limits on this amount; for example, you cannot claim a loss from your business because of home expenses (other than real estate taxes and mortgage interest). You can carry forward any home expenses that aren't allowable this year and claim them in a later year. (If you live on a military base and pay no home-related expenses, you don't need to fill out **Form 8829**.)

To finish **Form 8829**, you will have to complete **Schedule C** through line 29 (see chapter 5). It's a good idea to read this chapter first so you'll know what to do when you reach that point on **Form 8829**. You may want to begin **Form 8829** while the Time-Space percentage calculation is fresh in your mind, then switch to other forms needed to complete **Schedule C** and return to **Form 8829** when you're done with **Schedule C**.

New Simplified Method

You may use a new IRS Simplified Method to claim up to $1,500 of your house expenses without receipts on **Schedule C**, line 30. If you choose to use this new rule, you will not fill out IRS **Form 8829** and you will not be able to deduct house depreciation, utilities, property tax, mortgage interest, homeowners insurance, or house repairs. You will be able to claim 100% of your property tax and mortgage interest on **Schedule A Itemized Deductions**. The vast majority of providers should not use this Simplified Method. See chapter 5 for an explanation.

How to Fill Out Form 8829

This section explains how to fill out **Form 8829** for your business by taking you through the form line by line and referring to the filled-out example at the end of this chapter. Before you start filling out **Form 8829**, you should also skim the section titled Special Cases for **Form 8829** on page 55 to see if any of the situations described there apply to your business in this tax year.

Part I: Part of Your Home Used for Business

Line 1: Enter the number of square feet of your home that you use regularly for your business. Ignore the phrase "area used exclusively for business" on this line. Every other kind of business is only allowed to count the space that is used exclusively for business, but family child care providers are exempt from this regulation (see IRS **Publication 587 Business Use of Your Home**).

Line 2: Enter the total square footage of your home. Some providers use the number of rooms in their home on lines 1 and 2 instead of the square footage of those rooms. This might lower your business use of your home by a greater margin than if you were counting square feet.

Line 3: Divide line 1 by line 2 to get your Space percentage. If you used 2,200 square feet of your 2,200-square-foot home regularly for your business, you would enter 100% on this line (2,200 ÷ 2,200 = 100%).

Line 4: Enter the number of hours you used your home for business purposes in this tax year. Be sure to include both the hours that children were present and the hours you spent on business activities when they weren't present.

Line 5: If you operated your business every day of the year, enter 8,760 (365 days x 24 hours = 8,760 hours). If you didn't operate your business every day of the year, enter the total number of hours your home was available for business use. To find this number, multiply the number of days you were in business by 24 hours. Include Saturdays, Sundays, and holidays between working days. Here's an example: You began your business on April 1 of last year and were still in business at the end of the year. Since there are 275 days between April 1 and December 31, on line 5 you would enter 6,600 hours (275 days x 24 hours).

Line 6: Divide line 4 by line 5. If you worked 3,514 hours last year and you were in business the entire year, your Time percentage would be 40% (3,514 ÷ 8,760).

Line 7: Multiply line 6 by line 3. If your Space percentage was 100% and your Time percentage was 40%, your Time-Space percentage would be 40% (100% x 40%). This percentage will affect your other tax forms, so be sure to double-check your math. An error will mean mistakes on all your tax forms. Be sure to save the records that show how you calculated your numbers for Part I. The Time-Space percentage is a favorite area for IRS audits, so it's important to have good, clear documentation.

If You Weren't in Business the Entire Year
Recall that the total number of hours your home was available for business use was calculated on line 5 of Part I. When you enter your home expenses in Part II, you may list only the expenses that you incurred when your home was

available for business use; the dates of your expenses must match the dates you used for that calculation.

If you based that calculation on the 275 days between April 1 and December 31 of last year, you may enter only expenses you incurred between April and December. You may not include the March utility bill that you paid in April, but you may include the January bill for December's utilities.

You will also need to enter a prorated amount of your home expenses for the year, such as property tax and homeowners insurance. In our example, you would enter 75% of these yearly expenses (275 days ÷ 365 days = 75%).

Let's look at an example to see how being in business for less than the full year will affect **Form 8829** and **Schedule A**. Last year you began your business on April 1, and your Time-Space percentage between April 1 and December 31 was 40%. Your mortgage interest for the year was $5,000, and your property tax was $2,000. Since you were in business for only 75% of the year, multiply these expenses by this percentage:

Mortgage interest	$5,000 x 75% = $3,750
Property tax	$2,000 x 75% = $1,500

Next, multiply the results by your Time-Space percentage (40%):

Mortgage interest	$3,750 x 40% = $1,500
Property tax	$1,500 x 40% = $600

These numbers represent the amount you can deduct on **Form 8829**. If you itemize your tax return, enter the remaining amounts on **Schedule A**:

Mortgage interest	$5,000 – $1,500 = $3,500
Property tax	$2,000 – $600 = $1,400

Remember, the amount you claim for mortgage interest and property tax on **Form 8829** (after multiplying by the Time-Space percentage) and **Schedule A** should equal (and never exceed) 100%.

Part II: Figure Your Allowable Deduction

Before you fill out this part of **Form 8829**, go to **Schedule C** and complete lines 1–29 (see chapter 5). Then return to this point and continue.

Line 8:   Enter the amount from **Schedule C**, line 29. If you sold any items you used in your business during the last year (see chapter 11), add the net gain or loss from these items on this line. If you sold your home last year, don't include the net gain or loss from the sale on this line.

If there is a negative number on line 8, your mortgage interest and real estate taxes (lines 10 and 11) will be the only home expenses you can claim this year. Complete the rest of this form anyway, because you may be able to carry over any excess expenses to next year.

The next several lines of **Form 8829** include two columns. The following numbers are an example of how you might fill out lines 9–36. For this example, assume that the provider was in business for the entire year.

Time-Space percentage	40%
Net income from line 29 of **Schedule C**	$3,500
Casualty losses	$0
Mortgage interest	$2,000

Real estate taxes	$1,500
Home insurance	$900
Child care homeowners insurance endorsement	$400
Repairs and maintenance	$800
Utilities	$1,000

Col. (a): Under column (a) you will enter only your *direct* expenses—expenses that were incurred 100% for your business or for which you are using an actual business-use percentage instead of a Time-Space percentage. Continue reading for a description of each line in this column.

Col. (b): Under column (b) you will enter your *indirect* expenses—expenses that were incurred partly for your business and partly for your personal use. Continue reading for a description of each line in this column.

Line 9: Hurricanes and fires have certainly made people aware of the terrible damage that can be caused by a natural disaster. A casualty loss is defined as the damage, destruction, or loss of property resulting from an identifiable event that is sudden, unexpected, or unusual, such as an earthquake, tornado, flood, storm, fire, vandalism, theft, or car accident.

You must file an insurance claim in a timely manner in order to deduct a sudden or unexpected loss. If your insurance fully covers your losses, then you can't claim them as losses for tax purposes. If your insurance doesn't fully cover them (for example, if you have to pay a deductible or are underinsured), then you may be able to claim some business deductions that will reduce your taxes at the end of the year.

You are entitled to deduct any casualty losses of items used in your business (not covered by insurance), including your home, furniture, appliances, and business equipment. Expenses that result from a casualty loss or theft may also be deductible. These expenses include medical treatment, cleanup, minor repairs, temporary housing, a rental car, replacing spoiled food, and boarding up your home or sandbagging your property in anticipation of a flood.

If a natural disaster forces you to shut down your business temporarily, you cannot deduct your loss of income as a business expense. You will simply report less income on your tax return and therefore pay less in taxes.

If an item is completely destroyed, the business loss is the purchase price of the item minus the depreciation you have claimed on it or were entitled to claim on it. For example, let's say that you have a Time-Space percentage of 40% and are uninsured. You buy a swing set for $1,000 and depreciate it for two years, and then it is destroyed in a fire. In this case, your business loss would be $245 ($1,000 x 40% = $400 – $155 [two years of depreciation deductions] = $245).

If you received an insurance payment of $200 for this loss, the business portion of that payment would be $80 ($200 x 40% Time-Space), and your business loss would be $165 ($245 – $80). If you received a payment of $1,000 for this loss, you would have a business gain of $155 ($245 – $400 [$1,000 x 40% Time-Space = $400] = – $155), which you would report on **Form 4797**.

If an item you use in your business is damaged but not destroyed, use the lower of the adjusted value of the property (the original cost minus the depreciation claimed) or the difference between the fair market value of the item immediately before and immediately after the casualty. In other words, in the above example the adjusted value of the swing set was $245. If the business portion of the swing set's value before damage was $300 and its value after the damage was $100, the difference would be $200 ($300 – $100 = $200). You would compare the $200 to the adjusted value ($245) and use the lower number ($200) as your business loss.

Calculate your business loss (or gain) on a separate piece of paper and enter the total on line 9, column (a). Notice that the expenses entered on this line are taken out on line 34 and transferred to **Form 4684**. From that form, the business losses (or gains) are transferred to **Form 4797** and then to **Form 1040**, where they are deducted. This means that you will not actually claim your business losses as an expense on **Form 8829**. (Personal losses are calculated on **Form 4684** and then transferred from there to **Schedule A**.)

Although casualty losses can't create a loss on **Form 8829** (see the IRS instructions for **Form 8829**), you can carry the excess amount forward to next year. If you suffer a loss in an event that leads to your community being declared a federal disaster area, see the instructions to **Form 4684**. If you buy new property to replace the damaged or destroyed property, begin depreciating the new property under the rules described in chapter 3.

An Insurance Note

Many homeowners insurance policies only cover up to $2,000 worth of property used in a family child care business. Examine your policy to find out if your business property is properly covered. If it's not, you should purchase additional business property insurance. Business liability insurance usually will not cover the loss of business property. See the *Family Child Care Legal and Insurance Guide* for detailed information about how to protect your home and business through insurance.

To help prepare for a natural disaster, you should conduct an inventory of all the property in your home. Use the *Family Child Care Inventory-Keeper* to help you identify and track all your property and estimate its fair market value. Take photographs of all the rooms in your home, and store the photographs and your inventory records in a safe-deposit box.

Line 10: If you itemized your deductible mortgage interest using **Schedule A**, enter your total deductible mortgage interest in column (b), including any interest paid on a contract-for-deed mortgage and mortgage insurance. If you used the standard deduction on **Form 1040**, enter your total deductible mortgage interest on line 16, column (b). Don't include interest on a mortgage loan that didn't benefit your home (such as a second mortgage used to pay off your credit cards or buy a car). If you are including mortgage insurance premiums and your adjusted gross income on **Form 1040**, line 11 is more than $100,000 (married filing jointly), see the instructions to **Form 8829**.

Refinancing Points

The points, or mortgage closing fees, paid on a home loan are treated as prepaid interest. You can deduct on line 10, column (b), the business portion of points paid on a loan to buy, build, remodel, or improve a home in the same year. (Deduct the personal portion of the points on **Schedule A** as personal interest.) You must deduct any points paid to refinance a loan over the term of the loan.

If you refinance with the same lender, add the remaining points of the old loan to the points of the new loan and spread the total over the life of the new loan. For example, let's say that you're paying $200 a year in points for a twenty-year loan. Six years into the loan, you refinance with the same lender and get a new twenty-year loan, and the points for the new loan amount to

$3,000. Add the remaining points of the old loan ($4,000 – $1,200 = $2,800) to the new points ($3,000) and spread the total ($5,800) over twenty years, at $290 a year. Put $290 on line 10, column (b) each year for the next twenty years (where it will be multiplied by your Time-Space percentage to calculate business use).

If you refinance with another lender, you can deduct all the remaining points from the old loan on line 10, column (b) in the year you refinance.

Line 11: If you itemized your real estate taxes using **Schedule A**, enter this total amount in column (b). If your total taxes on **Schedule A**, line 5d is over $10,000, see the instructions for **Form 8829**. You will be able to deduct only part of this amount on **Form 8829**, but you will be able to claim the remaining amount of your real estate taxes on **Schedule A**, line 6. If you used the standard deduction on **Form 1040**, enter your total real estate taxes on line 17, column (b).

You are always entitled to claim the business portion of property tax and mortgage interest on **Form 8829** whether or not you itemize your personal taxes using **Schedule A**.

Line 12: Enter the total of lines 9, 10, and 11. (In the example at the end of this chapter, $0 + $2,000 + $1,500 = $3,500.)

Line 13: Enter the total of line 12, column (b), multiplied by line 7. (In the example, $3,500 x 40% = $1,400.)

Line 14: Enter the total of line 12, column (a), and line 13. (In the example, $0 + $1,400 = $1,400.)

Line 15: Enter the total of line 8 minus line 14. (In the example, $3,500 – $1,400 = $2,100.)

The amount on line 15 ($2,100) is the most that you can claim on **Form 8829** for the remaining home expenses. You *must* claim the business amount of your mortgage interest and real estate taxes on this form; you can claim the rest of these expenses as itemized deductions on **Schedule A**. Use your Time-Space percentage to determine your business deduction. Here's the calculation, building on the previous example, using a 40% Time-Space percentage:

	Total Expense	Form 8829 Expense 40%	Schedule A Expense 60%
Mortgage interest	$2,000	$800	$1,200
Property tax	$1,500	$600	$900

You may wish to claim all of your mortgage interest and real estate taxes on **Schedule A** rather than dividing them between **Schedule A** and **Form 8829**; however, this is both against the law and not in your best interests. Unlike your personal income, your business income is subject to Social Security and Medicare taxes as well as income tax. For this reason, a business deduction will reduce your taxes more than a personal deduction will.

Don't make the error of claiming your Time-Space percentage of these expenses on **Form 8829** and then claiming 100% of the same expenses on **Schedule A**. You are never allowed to claim more than 100% of any deduction. In addition, if your state offers a property tax rebate, you must calculate the amount of your rebate based on your personal-use percentage of the property tax, not the business- and personal-use percentage of the property tax. For example, if a family child care provider has a Time-Space percentage of 40%, then her personal use of the home is 60%, and she is entitled to use only 60% of her property tax to calculate her rebate.

Remember that only mortgage interest and real estate taxes can create a loss on **Form 8829**. What happens if they do? Building on the previous example, if the business share of the mortgage interest and real estate taxes was greater than $3,500, that amount could be claimed as a loss for the business. If the mortgage interest was $6,000 and real estate taxes were $4,000, the amount on line 12 would be $10,000. Multiply this by 40% (line 7), and line 13 would be $4,000 ($10,000 x 40%). Line 14 would also be $4,000. Since $4,000 is more than $3,500 (line 8), 0 would be entered on line 15.

No other expenses could be claimed on **Form 8829**. Line 34 would be $4,000, and this amount would transfer to **Schedule C**, line 30, where it would create a $500 loss on that form. The other expenses on this form would be put on Part IV and carried over to **Form 8829** in the next year.

Line 16: If you used the standard deduction to claim your personal deductions, enter your mortgage interest here on column (b). **Note**: As of 2018 you may deduct mortgage interest only if the loan is used to improve your home. So, a home equity loan that you use to buy a car or boat or anything else besides improving your home is no longer deductible.

Line 17: If you used the standard deduction to claim your personal deductions, enter your real estate taxes here on column (b).

Line 18: Enter your homeowners insurance in column (b). If you purchased a special policy just for your business or bought a business endorsement for your homeowners insurance policy, enter this amount in column (a). You cannot deduct home mortgage insurance premiums paid on cash-out refinances or home equity loans.

Line 19: If you rent your home, enter your total rent payments in column (b). As a renter, you may claim the Time-Space percentage of your monthly rent and any utilities you pay, plus a portion of any home improvements you make and any losses due to the theft of personal property used in your business.

Line 20: Enter your home repair and maintenance expenses in column (b). (See chapter 3 for a discussion of the difference between a repair and a home improvement.) Repairs (painting, wallpapering, fixing a broken window, or mending a leak) keep your home in good working order. Repairs to an exclusive-use room are 100% deductible; enter these expenses in column (a).

Line 21: Enter your total utility expenses (gas, electricity, water, sewage, garbage, and cable TV) in column (b), even if you rent your home. Monthly fees for telephone service are not deductible. If your phone service includes charges on a cost-per-minute basis, however, you can deduct the cost of your local business calls. Enter the cost of local business calls on line 20, column (a).

Actual Business-Use Percentage of Utilities Costs

Because of the significant cost of heating oil, gas, and electricity, you may benefit from using your actual business-use percentage of utility expenses. The actual business-use percentage of utilities costs for heating a home during the day for ten or more hours, Monday through Friday, is probably significantly more than the cost calculated by using a typical 30%–40% Time-Space percentage, especially since you can turn down the heat in the evening.

How can you determine the actual business-use percentage of your utility expenses? If you have been in business only for a short time, look at your energy usage before and after your business began. You might also call your local utility company to see if it can determine your energy usage during daytime hours.

If you decide to use a method other than your Time-Space percentage to calculate your utility expenses, be sure to keep careful records of your calculations and save them. Enter the actual business-use amount of your utilities on line 20, column (a).

Line 22: If you have other house expenses not claimed elsewhere, claim them here.

Line 23: Enter the total of lines 16–22. (In the example, $0 + $900 + $0 + $800 + $1,000 + $0 = $2,700.)

Line 24: Enter the total of line 23, column (b), multiplied by line 7. (In the example, $2,700 x 40% = $1,080.)

Line 25: If you had any home operating expenses in 2020 that you were unable to deduct that year because of the home expense limitation, enter that amount here.

Line 26: Enter the total of line 23, column (a), and lines 24–25. (In the example, $400 + $1,080 + $0 = $1,480.)

Line 27: Compare the amounts on line 15 and line 26, and enter whichever is the least. (In the example, $2,100 is the larger of the two, so $1,480 is entered.)

Line 28: Enter the amount of line 15 minus line 27. (In the example, $2,100 – $1,480 = $620.) In the example, this is the upper limit of the home depreciation expenses that can be claimed.

Line 29: Enter any excess casualty losses.

Line 30: Enter your home depreciation total from line 42. (The same example will be used in the next section to illustrate how to depreciate a home.) In the example, $963 is entered ($11 will be added later for a home improvement; see the instructions for line 42 on page 54).

Line 31: Enter any excess casualty losses and depreciation you carried over from 2020.

Line 32: Enter the total of your home depreciation, excess casualty losses, and carryover of excess casualty losses and home depreciation from 2020. In the example, $963 is entered.

Line 33: Compare the amounts on line 28 and line 32, and enter whichever is the least. (In the example, $620 is entered because it is less than $963.)

Line 34: Enter the total of lines 14, 27, and 33. (In the example, $1,400 + $1,480 + $620 = $3,500.)

Line 35: If you had any casualty loss from line 14 or 33, enter that amount here. The example does not have anything to record.

Line 36: Subtract line 35 from line 34. (In our example, $3,500 – $0 = $3,500.)

Line 36 has the allowable expenses for the business use of your home that you can claim on **Schedule C**. Enter this amount on **Schedule C**, line 30.

Using an Actual Business-Use Percentage

Although in most cases you will apply the Time-Space percentage from line 7 to all your indirect home expenses on **Form 8829**, in some cases you can use an actual business-use percentage instead. (See the section titled Actual Business-Use Percentage at the end of chapter 1 for a discussion.)

If a home expense is partly for your business and partly for personal use, you would normally enter it in column (b) and use the Time-Space percentage from line 7 to calculate the allowable business portion of the expense.

You aren't required to use the Time-Space percentage if you can show that one or more of your home expenses should be allocated in a different way. This is most common in the case of repairs to a room that is used heavily, but not exclusively, for your business. (If the room was used exclusively for business, you would enter 100% of the cost of the repair in column [a].)

Let's say that your Time-Space percentage is 37%, and you incurred a $200 repair to fix the radiator in a room that you use 80% of the time for your business. In this case you can claim 80% of the cost of this repair, or $160. To do this, simply enter the amount you calculate according to the business-use percentage in column (a), and enter nothing in column (b). In this example, you would list $160 in column (a). All the amounts you list in column (a) are deducted 100% as business expenses.

Part III: Depreciation of Your Home

If you first began using your home for your business last year, you must fill out **Form 4562**, line 19i (see chapter 3). Next, fill out lines 36–41 of **Form 8829**. If you used your home for your business before last year, don't enter any information about home depreciation on **Form 4562**; just fill out lines 36–41 of **Form 8829**, as described below.

Line 37: Enter your home's adjusted basis or its fair market value, whichever is the least. In the example, this amount is $103,800. Your home's adjusted basis is the sum of the purchase price of your home plus the value of any home improvements before you began using your home for your business (for more information, see chapter 3).

Line 38: Enter the value of the land at the time you purchased your home ($10,000 in the example). This amount should be included in the purchase price of your home on line 36; however, land can't be claimed as a business expense.

Line 39: Subtract line 38 from line 37. This is the basis of your home ($93,800 in the example). This number doesn't change from year to year. You'll enter the same numbers on lines 37–38 of **Form 8829** each year that you own this home.

Line 40: Enter the amount of line 39 multiplied by line 7 ($37,520 in the example). This is the business basis of your home.

Line 41: If you first began using your home for business before 1987, consult IRS **Publication 534 Depreciating Property Placed in Service Before 1987** to determine what rules were in effect when you began using your home for business. If you first used your home for business after 1986 but before May 13, 1993, enter 3.175% on this line. If you first used your home for business after May 12, 1993, but before last year, enter 2.564% on this line.

If you first began using your home for business last year, enter the percentage from the chart below, based on the first month you used your home for business:

January	2.461%	July	1.177%
February	2.247%	August	0.963%
March	2.033%	September	0.749%
April	1.819%	October	0.535%
May	1.605%	November	0.321%
June	1.391%	December	0.107%

In the example, the business began in January, so 2.461% is entered on this line. For years 2 through 39, 2.564% will be used for our depreciation calculations (for information about home depreciation, see chapter 3).

Line 42: Enter the amount of line 40 multiplied by line 41. This is the amount of home depreciation you can claim. In the example, this amount is $922. After $41 is added for a home improvement, the total ($963) is entered on line 30. (See the example form at the end of this chapter.)

Part IV: Carryover of Unallowed Expenses

Line 43: Subtract line 27 from line 26. A positive number here represents excess operating expenses that can't be deducted this tax season but can be carried forward and deducted next tax season. If you have a carryover here, put a copy of your **Form 8829** in your files for next tax season so you won't forget to claim it.

Line 44: Subtract line 33 from line 32 ($963 – $620 = $343). A positive number here represents excess casualty losses and home depreciation that can't be deducted this tax season but can be carried forward and deducted next tax season. If you have a carryover here, put a copy of your **Form 8829** in your files for next tax season so you won't forget to claim it.

If you go out of business in a tax year and don't operate your business the following year, you won't be able to claim any carryover expenses. If you go back into business in a later year, however, you will be able to claim your carryover expenses at that time.

What You Can't Claim on Form 8829

You can't claim the following kinds of expenses on **Form 8829**:

- **Property assessments**
  Property assessments (sidewalks, sewer, other improvements to your land made by your local government) are usually included with your property tax bill. Subtract them from your property tax before you enter your property tax on line 11. The cost of a property assessment can be deducted as a land improvement. For an explanation of how to deduct these expenses, see pages 83–84.

- **Monthly mortgage payments**
  Don't put your monthly mortgage payments on **Form 8829**. These payments consist of interest and payments toward the principal of your loan. Your monthly principal payments have nothing to do with how much you can deduct as a business expense. Your mortgage interest is claimed on line 10 or 16, column (b), of **Form 8829**. The principal is accounted for when you depreciate your home. Your home depreciation is based on the purchase price of your home, which you claim on line 30 of **Form 8829**.

- **Home expenses if you aren't a sole proprietor**
  If you have formed a partnership or a corporation and are working out of your home, you can't claim your home expenses on **Form 8829** because a partnership or a

corporation can't file **Form 8829**; it is for individuals only. If you have established a single-person limited liability company (LLC), however, you are entitled to claim all home expenses on **Form 8829**.

Special Cases for Form 8829

If You Have Any Exclusive-Use Rooms

You can claim a higher Time-Space percentage on **Form 8829** if you use one or more rooms in your home exclusively for business. The following example shows you how to calculate the Time-Space percentage in this situation:

- Polly Jones's home totals 2,000 square feet.

- She has one 300-square-foot room that she uses exclusively for her business.

- She uses the other 1,700 square feet regularly for her business.

- Polly works 2,628 hours during the year in the 1,700-square-foot area.

Because Polly has a room she uses exclusively for her business, she can't complete Part I of **Form 8829**. Instead, she will have to write "see attached" across Part I of the form and attach a separate sheet of paper that shows her Time-Space calculation.

Here's what her attachment would say:

Supporting Statement for Form 8829, Part I

Name: Polly Jones
Social Security #146-28-3333
Total square footage of home: 2,000
Square footage of room used exclusively for business: 300
Remaining 1,700 square feet are used regularly for child care
Hours 1,700-square-foot area is used for child care: 2,628
$300 \div 2,000$ = 15% actual business-use percentage of exclusive-use area
$1,700 \div 2,000$ = 85% Space percentage for business use of remainder of home
$2,628 \div 8,760$ = 30% Time percentage for business use of remainder of home
$85\% \times 30\%$ = 25.5% Time-Space percentage for business use of
                remainder of home
$15\% + 25.5\%$ = 40.5% Time-Space percentage for business use of entire home

---

If You Provide Child Care Outside Your Home

Child care providers operating at locations other than their own homes is a growing trend. If you only provide child care in a building that's separate from your home, you can claim 100% of the expenses associated with that space, such as rent, utilities, furniture, and supplies. But if you operate out of another building, or two separate locations, you won't be eligible to file **Form 8829**. Instead, you will show your expenses for the other building on **Form 4562** and **Schedule C**, as follows:

ENTER ON **FORM 4562**

- depreciation (line 19i)

ENTER ON **SCHEDULE C**

- insurance (line 15)
- mortgage interest (line 16a)
- rent (line 20b)
- repairs and maintenance (line 21)
- property taxes (line 23)
- utilities (line 25)

Since you can only claim one location for your business, you won't be able to claim a Time-Space percentage for your home expenses if you're using both your home and a building separate from your home for your business. This is true even if you're still using your home for business activities such as keeping records and planning lessons. You can claim part of the cost of the business equipment that you use in your home, such as your computer, printer, file cabinet, and desk. Follow the depreciation rules described in chapter 3, and use your actual business-use percentage.

You won't be eligible to claim travel to and from your home and your place of business as business trips; this travel will be considered commuting to work. You can still count a trip for business purposes as business mileage if you are departing from and returning to your place of business.

If you provide child care at a location other than your home, you won't be eligible to use the IRS standard meal allowance rate in calculating your food expenses (see chapter 4). In addition, you may not be eligible to participate in the Food Program (check with your sponsor). Also, check your state regulations, which may prohibit you from providing child care in a home that you do not live in.

If You Receive a Military Housing Allowance

The IRS **Child Care Provider Audit Technique Guide** clarifies how to treat housing allowances if you are a family child care provider living in military housing.

If you live in on-base housing, you can't claim any home expenses except for those you pay out of your own pocket. Since you have no property tax or mortgage interest expenses, you can't deduct these expenses. If you spend your own money on a home repair, fence, or improvement, you can deduct the business portion of this expense on **Form 8829** or **Form 4562**.

If you live in off-base housing, you're entitled to claim the Time-Space percentage of your property tax and mortgage interest on **Form 8829** and the personal portion of these expenses on **Schedule A**. (You can do this even if your housing allowance covers these expenses.)

The **Child Care Provider Audit Technique Guide** offers a detailed formula to determine how much of your other home expenses not covered by your housing allowance (such as utilities, home depreciation, homeowners insurance, and home repairs) you can deduct as a business expense. Enter the allowable portion of these expenses on **Form 8829**, line 21, column (a). (For more information about how to claim these expenses, see the *Record-Keeping Guide*.)

If You Went Out of Business

If you went out of business last year, you can't claim a full year's worth of home depreciation. Instead, you can claim a prorated percentage of the full year's depreciation based on how many months you used your home for your business. Count the month that you stop using your home for business as a half month (this is according to the Mid-Month Convention rule; see chapter 3).

For example, let's say that you went out of business in November of last year. The business basis of your home is $17,550 and you have been in business for three years. Normally, your depreciation deduction would be $449.98 ($17,550 x 2.564% [the percentage of depreciation for a 39-year-old property]); however, in this case your deduction would be $449.98 x (10.5 months ÷ 12 months), or $393.73.

If Your Spouse Also Claims a Home Office Deduction

If your spouse is self-employed and also claims a deduction for home office expenses, you must file **Form 8829** and **Schedule C** for your business, and your spouse must file his own **Form 8829** and **Schedule C** for his business. Since the space that he claims for his business cannot also be claimed as space for your child care business, your Space percentage will be less than 100%.

If your spouse uses 10% of the home exclusively for his business, then he can claim 10% of the home expenses (such as utilities, real estate taxes, and mortgage interest). If you regularly use the rest of the home for your child care business, your Space percentage will be 90%. If your Time percentage is 35%, your Time-Space percentage will be 31.5% (90% x 35%), and you will claim 31.5% of the home expenses on your **Form 8829**.

If your spouse doesn't use any rooms exclusively for his business, then he won't file **Form 8829** because he won't be entitled to claim any home expenses (although he can still claim other business expenses on his **Schedule C**).

If you both use the same office for your business, he is using it nonexclusively, and you are using it regularly, you can claim the office space in your Time-Space calculation. Under these circumstances, you might have a Space percentage of 100% even if your husband runs his business in the home.

If You Made Home Improvements

If you made a home improvement before your business began, include the cost of the improvement in the cost of your home when you depreciate it in Part III of **Form 8829**.

If you made a home improvement after your business began but before 2020, calculate the depreciation deduction (see chapter 3), and include that amount on **Form 8829**, line 40. Write "see attached" next to this line, and attach a supporting statement showing how you calculated your home improvement deduction.

Here's an example:

Supporting Statement for Form 8829, Part III

Name: Polly Jones
Social Security #146-28-3333
Total square footage of home: 2,000
$4,000 new deck installed in 2015
x 40% Time-Space percentage
$1,600
x 2.564% depreciation amount for 39-year-old property
$41.02 enter on line 42

If you made a home improvement in 2020, first fill out **Form 4562**, line 19i (see chapter 3). Transfer the depreciation deduction from **Form 4562**, column (g), line 19i, to **Form 8829**, line 42. Don't include this amount in the depreciation deduction carried forward from **Form 4562**, line 22, to **Schedule C**, line 13. You can't claim an expense twice.

If You Moved

If you moved during the last year and continued to provide child care in your new home, you must file two copies of **Form 8829**, one for each home. You will need to calculate a separate Time-Space percentage for each home. On both forms, cross out the number printed on line 5 (8,760), and enter the number of hours you occupied the home during the last year. For example, if you moved on May 1, enter 2,880 hours (January–April = 120 days x 24 hours) on line 5 for the first house and 5,880 hours (May–December = 245 days x 24 hours) on line 5 for the second house. List your expenses for each home on the appropriate form. Add together lines 36 on both forms, and enter the total on **Schedule C**, line 30.

To determine what Time-Space percentage to use on shared items you are claiming on **Schedule C** (toys, household items, activity expenses, cleaning supplies, and so on), use the average of the two Time-Space percentages for each home. To account for the different number of months that each house was used for your business, use the following formula: multiply your Time-Space percentage for each house by the number of months the business was in each home. Add the two totals together and divide by 12. This is the Time-Space percentage to use for all shared expenses on **Schedule C**. For example, your Time-Space percentage was 35% for your first home (used January–April), and it was 25% for the second home (May–December): 35% x 4 months = 140%; 25% x 8 months = 200%; 140% + 200% = 340%, divided by 12 months = 28%.

For more information about the tax issues discussed in this chapter, refer to the related topics in the other chapters of this book and the Redleaf Press *Family Child Care Record-Keeping Guide*.

Form **8829**	**Expenses for Business Use of Your Home**	OMB No. 1545-0074
Department of the Treasury Internal Revenue Service (99)	▶ File only with Schedule C (Form 1040). Use a separate Form 8829 for each home you used for business during the year. ▶ Go to *www.irs.gov/Form8829* for instructions and the latest information.	20**21** Attachment Sequence No. **176**

Name(s) of proprietor(s)	Your social security number
POLLY JONES	123-45-6789

Part I — Part of Your Home Used for Business

1	Area used regularly and exclusively for business, regularly for daycare, or for storage of inventory or product samples (see instructions)	**1**	2,200
2	Total area of home	**2**	2,200
3	Divide line 1 by line 2. Enter the result as a percentage	**3**	100 %

For daycare facilities not used exclusively for business, go to line 4. All others, go to line 7.

4	Multiply days used for daycare during year by hours used per day . .	**4**	3,514 hr.		
5	If you started or stopped using your home for daycare during the year, see instructions; otherwise, enter 8,760	**5**	8,760 hr.		
6	Divide line 4 by line 5. Enter the result as a decimal amount	**6**	. 40		
7	Business percentage. For daycare facilities not used exclusively for business, multiply line 6 by line 3 (enter the result as a percentage). All others, enter the amount from line 3 . . . . . ▶	**7**			40 %

Part II — Figure Your Allowable Deduction

8	Enter the amount from Schedule C, line 29, **plus** any gain derived from the business use of your home, **minus** any loss from the trade or business not derived from the business use of your home. See instructions.		**8**	$3,500

	See instructions for columns (a) and (b) before completing lines 9–22.		**(a)** Direct expenses	**(b)** Indirect expenses		
9	Casualty losses (see instructions)	**9**				
10	Deductible mortgage interest (see instructions) .	**10**				
11	Real estate taxes (see instructions)	**11**				
12	Add lines 9, 10, and 11	**12**				
13	Multiply line 12, column (b), by line 7	**13**			
14	Add line 12, column (a), and line 13			**14**	0
15	Subtract line 14 from line 8. If zero or less, enter -0-			**15**	$3,500
16	Excess mortgage interest (see instructions) . .	**16**		$2,000		
17	Excess real estate taxes (see instructions) . . .	**17**	$400	$1,500		
18	Insurance	**18**		$900		
19	Rent	**19**				
20	Repairs and maintenance	**20**		$800		
21	Utilities	**21**		$1,000		
22	Other expenses (see instructions)	**22**				
23	Add lines 16 through 22	**23**	$400	$6,200		
24	Multiply line 23, column (b), by line 7	**24**	$2,480		
25	Carryover of prior year operating expenses (see instructions)	**25**			
26	Add line 23, column (a), line 24, and line 25			**26**	$2,880
27	Allowable operating expenses. Enter the **smaller** of line 15 or line 26			**27**	$2,880
28	Limit on excess casualty losses and depreciation. Subtract line 27 from line 15			**28**	$620
29	Excess casualty losses (see instructions)	**29**			
30	Depreciation of your home from line 42 below	**30**	$963		
31	Carryover of prior year excess casualty losses and depreciation (see instructions)	**31**			
32	Add lines 29 through 31			**32**	$963
33	Allowable excess casualty losses and depreciation. Enter the **smaller** of line 28 or line 32 . . .			**33**	$620
34	Add lines 14, 27, and 33			**34**	$3,500
35	Casualty loss portion, if any, from lines 14 and 33. Carry amount to **Form 4684.** See instructions .			**35**	
36	**Allowable expenses for business use of your home.** Subtract line 35 from line 34. Enter here and on Schedule C, line 30. If your home was used for more than one business, see instructions. ▶			**36**	$3,500

Part III — Depreciation of Your Home

37	Enter the **smaller** of your home's adjusted basis or its fair market value. See instructions . . .	**37**	$103,800
38	Value of land included on line 37	**38**	$10,000
39	Basis of building. Subtract line 38 from line 37	**39**	$93,800
40	Business basis of building. Multiply line 39 by line 7	**40**	$37,520
41	Depreciation percentage (see instructions)	**41**	2.431 %
42	Depreciation allowable (see instructions). Multiply line 40 by line 41. Enter here and on line 30 above	**42**	$963

Part IV — Carryover of Unallowed Expenses to 2022

43	Operating expenses. Subtract line 27 from line 26. If less than zero, enter -0-	**43**	
44	Excess casualty losses and depreciation. Subtract line 33 from line 32. If less than zero, enter -0-.	**44**	$343

For Paperwork Reduction Act Notice, see your tax return instructions.	Cat. No. 13232M	Form **8829** (2021)

CHAPTER 3

Calculating Your Depreciation: Form 4562

Major Change in Depreciation Rules

As a result of a significant change in depreciation rules, as of 2018 providers can depreciate 100% of the business portion of new expenses in one year, except for their home, a home improvement, and a home addition! This means most providers will not have to depreciate items. This is great news because it allows providers to deduct in one year expenses that would normally have to be deducted over a number of years.

In some situations, you may want to spread your deductions over the years rather than claiming them all in 2020. This may happen if you want to show more profit in 2020 because you are applying for a loan, or your tax bracket is going up in later years, or other personal circumstances. If any of these apply to you, then this chapter can explain how to depreciate larger expenses.

But in general, you probably want to take advantage of the new tax laws and not depreciate expenses for your business, except for a home, a home improvement, and a home addition. A deck, new garage, or large shed would be considered a home addition. Here is a summary of these changes:

- Any item you purchase that costs $200 or less may be deducted in one year.

- Any item you purchase that costs between $201 and $2,500 may be deducted in one year, as long as you attach a special statement to your tax return.

- House-related repairs can be deducted in one year as always. However, there is a new, expanded definition of what can be treated as a repair, rather than a home improvement, that could include roof shingles, windows, wood and tile floors, and more.

- **Any item you purchase that costs more than $2,500 may also be deducted in one year, with the exception of a home, a home improvement, or home addition. This is called the 100% bonus depreciation rule and is the major change that will be in effect through 2022!**

$2,500 Rule

For decades, the IRS rules said that you must depreciate items costing more than $100 (with certain exceptions). As of 2015, according to Treasury Regulation Section 1.263(a), providers may deduct in one year any item costing $200 or less. You may also deduct items costing between $201 and $2,500 in one year as long as you attach a special statement to your tax return.

This rule applies to any individual purchase, and there is no limit as to how many items you can deduct. Therefore, you could buy twelve items costing less than $2,500 each and apply this rule to all of them. If you use an item 100% for your business, you can deduct 100% of its cost in 2021. If you also use this item for personal purposes, multiply the cost by your Time-Space percentage (scc chapter 1) and deduct the business portion in 2021.

To use this $2,500 rule, you must elect it by filing the following statement with your tax return:

"Section 1.263(a)-1(f) De Minimis Safe Harbor Election

[Your name, address, and EIN or Social Security number]

For the year ending December 31, 2021, I am electing the de minimis safe harbor under Treas. Reg. Section 1.263(a)-1(f) for my business expenses of less than $2,500."

You must file such a statement for each year you wish to use this $2,500 rule. Put this deduction on **Schedule C**, Part V, line 27a, and call it "De minimis Equipment." Doing so will make it clear that you elected this rule. See page 247 for a copy of this statement.

When you choose to use thc $2,500 rule, you must apply it to all items purchased that year costing between $201 and $2,500. Using this $2,500 rule is a choice, so you can decide whether to depreciate items under the rules described in this chapter or deduct them in onc year.

What About 2018, 2019, or 2020? What can you do if you were eligible to use this rule in 2018, 2019, or 2020 but you instead depreciated an item instead of deducting it in one year? You cannot amend your return back to these years, elect to use this new Treasury Regulation, and deduct the cost in one year. This is because you did not attach the statement of election to your tax return. Once you elect to use this rule, you cannot later amend your tax return to undo it.

The Old 50% Bonus Depreciation Rule

In 2017 a 50% bonus depreciation rule allowed providers to deduct 50% of the normal depreciation of most items in one year. Exceptions to this rule were home improvements, the home itself, and home additions. For example, if you bought a $4,000 swing set in 2017 and used it 100% for your business, you could have deducted $2,000 (50% of the cost) in one year and depreciated the other $2,000 over seven years.

With the new 100% bonus depreciation rule (see below), it no longer makes sense to use the 50% bonus depreciation rule for items purchased in 2021 because it fell to zero in 2020 and after.

New 100% Bonus Depreciation Rule

The Tax Cuts and Jobs Act (www.congress.gov/115/plaws/publ97/PLAW-115publ97.pdf) passed in December 2017. As of 2018, the act allows providers to deduct in one year the business portion of all expenses except for a home, a home improvement, and home addition. Computers and other office equipment must be used more than 50% of the time to qualify for this rule. Effectively, this amends the old 50% bonus depreciation rule to a 100% bonus depreciation rule.

In other words, if you purchased a $10,000 fence and your Time-Space percentage is 40%, you can deduct $4,000 on your 2020 tax return. Enter $4,000 on **Form 4562**, line 14.

The 100% bonus rule applies to the purchase of both new and used items. It is available for the tax years 2018–2022. In 2023 it will be reduced to 80%, then 60% in 2024, 40% in 2025, and 20% in 2026.

This is one of the most important tax changes for family child care providers in decades! No longer will you have to spread out the deduction for your furniture, appliances, fences, playground equipment, patio, or driveway. If you go out of business in the next few years, there is no recapture of these deductions. In other words, you won't ever have to pay back these deductions. You do not have to attach a statement to your tax return electing this rule as you must do for items that cost less than $2,500. You are considered to have automatically elected this rule unless you specifically elect out by doing so on your tax return. Claiming expenses under the 100% bonus depreciation rule can create a loss for your business on **Schedule C**. If you realized you should have used the 100% bonus depreciation rule in 2018, you can amend your tax return and claim this deduction and get a refund.

Note: The 100% bonus depreciation rule applies to your federal taxes, not your state taxes. Your state may not adopt this rule when calculating your state income taxes. If it does, your business profit will be higher for state tax purposes. Contact your state department of revenue to see if they have adopted this rule or not.

Home Improvements

Home improvements are a complicated topic, one that has seen many changes recently. In general, home improvements made in 2021 must be depreciated over 39 years. There are three possible situations where you may be able to deduct them in one year:

1. A home improvement may meet the definition of a repair.
2. You use the home improvement for more than 50% of the time in your business.
3. You qualify for the Safe Harbor for Small Taxpayers rule.

Home Improvements vs. Repairs

Treasury Regulation Section 1.263(a) expands what can be treated as a repair and offers the clearest explanation yet of the difference between a repair and a home improvement. A repair may be deducted in one year, regardless of the cost, while a home improvement must be depreciated over 39 years. This is a big difference!

Repairs deal with normal wear and tear and routine maintenance. They are expenses that do not materially add to the value of a home or prolong its life: they simply keep it in good operating condition. Examples of repairs include painting, wallpapering, fixing a broken window, and mending leaks. Repairs can sometimes include replacing the shingles on a home or garage. If you replaced the shingles and the roofing boards underneath the shingles, the work should be treated as a home improvement.

A home improvement is something that results in the betterment of the property, restores the property, or adapts the property to a new or different use. If you replace a significant or substantial portion of a major component of your home (walls, windows, floors, plumbing, electrical, or heating), you must depreciate these items over 39 years. Examples of home improvements include building a new addition, installing a furnace, remodeling your kitchen or bathroom, and adding a deck or garage.

It's not exactly clear what replacing a "substantial portion" of a major component of your home means. I talked to the author of the Treasury Regulation, who said that replacing 20% of the windows or floors would not be a "substantial portion" and could be treated as a repair. When asked if replacing fewer than 50% of windows or floors would be considered a repair, she said, "Maybe" and wouldn't be more precise.

This creates a problem for providers trying to determine when they can treat an expense as a repair or home improvement. In the examples provided with the new regulations described in Section 1.263(a), the replacement of 8 of 20 sinks (40%) was treated as a repair, as was the replacement of 100 of 300 windows (33%). Replacing 200 of 300 windows (67%) was treated as an improvement. In my opinion, you can argue that the replacement of less than half of a major component of the home could be treated as a repair. I think this is a reasonable interpretation of the rule, but I can't guarantee that's what an IRS auditor would conclude.

Under my interpretation, if you replace 8 out of 20 windows, treat the cost as a repair and deduct the Time-Space percentage of the cost in one year (regardless of the cost). If you replace 12 of 20 windows, depreciate the cost as a home improvement over 39 years. If you add a new wood or tile floor that represents less than half the square footage of your home, treat it as a repair. **Note**: carpeting should always be considered eligible for the 100% bonus depreciation rule and thus can be deducted in one year, regardless of the cost. If you have two bathrooms and remodel one of them, treat it as a home improvement. If you have three bathrooms and remodel one of them, I believe you could treat it as a repair. If you remodel your kitchen, it's a home improvement.

Remember, if something is a home improvement but costs less than $2,500, you can still deduct the business portion of the cost in one year.

Because this rule is relatively new, we can expect future clarifications about what is a repair versus a home improvement. Talk to your tax professional for further guidance.

The Section 179 Rule Exception

If you used your home improvement (but not a home addition) more than 50% of the time for your business, you can now use the Section 179 rule and deduct the business portion in one year for 2021. To take advantage of this rule, your Time-Space percentage should be more than 50%. If it's not, you should keep records to show that you did use the home improvement more than 50% of the time for your business. The best way to show that is to track the hours of business and personal use on a calendar for several months.

For example, if you spent $6,000 to build a deck that is filled with child care toys and equipment and you have no children of your own, you could probably claim that you use the deck more than 50% for your business. After tracking your actual use of the deck for two months, you determine that it's used 60% for your business. You can then deduct $3,600 ($6,000 x 60%) on **Form 4562**, Part I. See pages 72–73 for an expanded discussion of the Section 179 rule.

Should you use the Section 179 exception? The drawback to using this exception is that if you go out of business or use the item 50% or less in later years, you will have to pay back some of the deduction you claimed. For example, if you go out of business five years after deducting the $3,600 for the deck, you will have to report the $3,600 as income, minus the amount of depreciation you would have taken over five years instead. Five years of depreciation on a deck amounts to $461 ($3,600 ÷ 39 years x 5 years = $461). Assuming you are in the same tax bracket (30%) in five years, you will owe

$942 in taxes when you go out of business ($3,600 – $461 x 30% = $942). However, by deducting $3,600 in the first year, you saved $1,080 in taxes ($3,600 x 30% = $1,080). The longer you use the deck before you go out of business, the greater the tax advantage of using this exception. So financially you are always better off using the Section 179 exception. However, you must fill out **Form 4797 Sale of Business Property** when you do go out of business. See chapter 11 for more details on how to recapture depreciation when using the Section 179 rule.

Note: In some cases, using the Section 179 rule can't create a business loss on your tax return. See page 72.

Safe Harbor for Small Taxpayers Rule Exception

This rule also allows some providers to deduct in one year the cost of home improvements but not home additions.

Here's how this works. If the amount of home improvements you make in one year plus the amount of any home repairs made in that year is the lesser amount of $10,000 or 2% of the unadjusted basis of your home, you may deduct the business portion of the home/land improvements in one year.

Let's sort this out.

The unadjusted basis of your home is the purchase price of your home minus the value of the land at the time you bought it, plus the value of any home improvements you made before the year you are using this rule. For example, if you purchased your home for $300,000, and the value of land when you bought it was $30,000, and you made $50,000 in home improvements before 2021, the unadjusted basis of your home would be $320,000 ($300,000 – $30,000 + $50,000 = $320,000). Therefore, the lesser of $10,000 or 2% of the unadjusted basis of your home is $6,400 ($320,000 x 2% = $6,400, which is less than $10,000).

Let's look at two examples.

EXAMPLE #1

Bernice installed a new deck for $4,500 and made no home repairs in 2021. Her Time-Space percentage is 40%. Her home's unadjusted basis is $250,000. Because $4,500 is less than $5,000 ($250,000 x 2% = $5,000), she can use this rule. She could deduct $1,800 for the deck in one year ($4,500 x 40% = $1,800). Enter on **Form 4562**, line 14. To use this rule you must elect it by filing a statement with your tax return.

EXAMPLE #2

Bernice installed the same deck but also spent $2,000 on house repairs. She can't use this rule because the $6,500 of repairs and improvements ($4,500 + $2,000) is higher than $5,000. She can deduct $800 of the repairs ($2,000 x 40% = $800) in one year, but she must depreciate the deck over 39 years.

Note: Repairs to your personal property (items not attached to your home or land) are not counted as a home repair. For example, Keri had the following expenses in 2021: $4,000 kitchen remodel, $500 to recover a sofa, $600 for deck stain, $250 furnace and duct cleaning, and $250 computer repair. Her Time-Space percentage is 35%. The unadjusted basis of her home is $260,000. Her deduction limitation is $5,200 ($260,000 x 2% = $5,200). She can deduct separately the business portion of her sofa and computer expenses because these are considered repairs to her personal property, not to her home.

Therefore, she can deduct $500 + $250 = $750 x 35% = $262.50 in 2020. The remaining expenses total $4,850 ($4,000 + $600 + $250). Since this is less than $5,200, she can deduct $1,698 ($4,850 x 35% = $1,698) in 2020.

To use this rule you must elect it by filing a statement with your tax return. Here's the statement you should use:

"Section 1.263(a)-3(h) Safe Harbor Election for Small Taxpayers

[Your name, address, and EIN or Social Security number]

For the year ending December 31, 2021, I am electing the safe harbor election for small taxpayers under Treas. Reg. Section 1.263(a)-3(g) for the following: [list your improvements]."

You must file such a statement each year you use this small taxpayer safe harbor rule. See page 247 for a copy of this statement.

Notes on the safe harbor election for small taxpayers: What can you do if you were eligible to use this rule before 2021 but you instead depreciated a home improvement? You cannot amend your return and elect to use this new Treasury Regulation and deduct the cost in one year. This is because you must have attached the statement of election to your tax return in the year you purchased it. Once you elect to use this rule, you cannot later amend your tax return to change it. You can use the safe harbor election if you rent your home and spend money on a home improvement.

Summary

These new tax rules are fantastic news for many family child care providers! They allow providers to deduct in one year many items that in previous years had to be depreciated. In fact, any purchase other than a home, a home improvement, and home addition can be deducted in one year, regardless of the cost. This eliminates practically all of the calculations for depreciation, and thus providers can skip over much of the rest of this chapter!

Here's a summary of depreciation rules. If an item costs $200 or less, you can deduct it in one year. Later in this chapter I explain how to depreciate each type of expense in detail.

OFFICE EQUIPMENT

Costing less than $2,500: deduct in one year and attach statement to your tax return

Costing more than $2,500:

If you use less than 50% for your business, depreciate over five years

If you use 50% or more for your business:

- Use the Section 179 rule, or
- Use the 100% bonus depreciation rule and deduct in one year, or
- Depreciate over five years

PERSONAL PROPERTY

Costing less than $2,500: deduct in one year and attach statement to your tax return

Costing more than $2,500:

Use the 100% bonus depreciation rule and deduct in one year, or

Depreciate over seven years

If you use 50% or more for your business:

- Can use the Section 179 rule

LAND IMPROVEMENT

Costing less than $2,500: deduct in one year and attach statement to your tax return

Costing more than $2,500:

Use the 100% bonus depreciation rule and deduct in one year

- Can depreciate over 15 years

HOME IMPROVEMENT

Costing less than $2,500: deduct in one year and attach statement to your tax return

Costing more than $2,500:

Depreciate over 39 years

If used more than 50% for business, can use the Section 179 rule

Does the Safe Harbor for Small Taxpayers rule apply (effective for 2014 and after)?

- If yes, deduct in one year

HOME

Depreciate over 39 years

See appendix B for a chart summarizing these rules.

General Rules about Depreciation

The following is a discussion about how to apply the rules for items you are depreciating. Since the vast majority of providers will take advantage of either the $2,500 rule or the 100% bonus depreciation rule, much of what follows in this chapter is irrelevant. If you are using the 100% bonus depreciation rule, enter your deductions on **Form 4562**, line 14. The exceptions to this are depreciations of the home, home improvement, home additions, and vehicles. See pages 84–89 for details on these items.

This chapter explains how to fill out **Form 4562 Depreciation and Amortization**. Many child care providers feel that depreciation is the most complex tax concept that they have to deal with, so I will try to keep it as simple as possible. Basically, depreciation is a way to spread the deductible cost of an item over several years by deducting a certain percentage of the total amount each year. (When dealing with depreciation, remember that the deductible portion of any expense depends on how the item is used; for more information, see chapter 5.)

If you buy an item before your business begins and later start using it in your business, the following rules apply (see the section titled Start-Up Costs on page 89).

If you began depreciating an item last year, you must continue depreciating this item according to the depreciation rules for that year, even if the rules change in later years.

The IRS divides depreciable items into categories and sets a depreciation period for the items in each category—in other words, it tells you over how many years you must spread the cost for items in each category. The depreciation method and the length of the depreciation period determine the percentage of the total amount you can deduct each year. The depreciation tables at the end of this chapter show the percentages that will be used this year.

Here are the categories of items and the number of years the IRS says you must depreciate them. Every item you depreciate must fall into one of these categories:

Category	Number of Years of Depreciation
Personal computers/office equipment	5
Other personal property	7
Home improvements	39
Land improvements	15
Home	39
Vehicle	5

The years of depreciation rules for 2021 (as shown above) are the same as those for 2020. This chapter describes how to apply those depreciation rules and fill out **Form 4562**. In many cases, home depreciation will be shown on **Form 8829**. Bear in mind that before you fill out **Form 4562**, you should complete Part I of **Form 8829**, since you will need your Time-Space percentage calculation from **Form 8829** to determine your depreciation deductions on **Form 4562**.

IRS Child Care Provider Audit Technique Guide on Depreciation
The guide lists a number of items that are commonly depreciated in the family child care business, including computers, office equipment, kitchen equipment, playground equipment, furniture, appliances, DVD players, televisions, and pianos. The guide clearly states that providers may depreciate items that were purchased before their business began that were originally exclusively personal use and then later put into business use. The guide states, "The fact that the asset was only used for personal purposes prior to being placed in service does not disqualify it from being converted to use in the business."

The Benefits of Depreciation

If you began your business before 2021 and haven't been depreciating your home, home or land improvements, and household items, you may be entitled to claim this previously unclaimed depreciation on **Form 3115**, which could result in hundreds or even thousands of dollars of deductions this year (see chapter 10 for more information).

Taking a Household Inventory

Are you claiming *all* of your allowable depreciation deductions? To find out, conduct an inventory of the items in your home that are used regularly in your business. All new providers should take an inventory their first year in business, and experienced providers should review their inventory each year.

To conduct an inventory, record all the items you are using in your business, room by room. Include any home improvements that were made before and after your business began. Estimate the fair market value of each item at the time you began using it in your business. Next, determine the depreciation of each item as a business expense.

Gather and keep records that support your business deductions for these items. You can do this with receipts or photographs of the property. To claim depreciation, you must have written evidence. When filling out **Form 4562**, always answer yes to the questions on lines 24a and 24b that ask whether you have evidence to support your claim and whether the evidence is written. *Failure to answer these questions could trigger an audit.* See page 89 for a discussion of how to deduct items you owned before you went into business.

Need Inventory Help?

The *Family Child Care Inventory-Keeper* includes a series of forms that make it easy to inventory your property and claim depreciation. The *Inventory-Keeper* includes detailed room-by-room listings of household items and charts for your home and for home and land improvements, as well as instructions on how to estimate the fair market value of depreciable items.

Determining Your Depreciation

The following section of this chapter goes into detail about how to depreciate an item rather than using the 100% bonus depreciation rule for everything except a home, a home improvement, and a home addition. The depreciation rules can be difficult to understand because there are so many of them. To simplify things, the depreciation process is broken down here into four steps. You must go through these four steps for each item you are depreciating.

Step One: What Is the Business Amount of the Item?

The first step is to determine the business amount of the property you are depreciating. Start with the lower of (a) the cost of the property or (b) its fair market value at the time you first used it for business. If you bought the item (new or used) last year, use its actual cost. Multiply the value of the item by your Time-Space percentage or an actual business-use percentage (as described in chapter 1). The result is the business amount (or business basis) of the item you are depreciating.

EXAMPLE

You bought playground equipment in 2021 for $3,000. If your 2021 Time-Space percentage is 35%, the business amount of this item would be $3,000 x 35% = $1,050.

You could then deduct $1,050 in 2021. If you decided to depreciate the playground equipment over seven years, your Time-Space percentage could change over that time. If so, it will affect the amount of business deduction that you can claim. In the following example, $3,000 worth of playground equipment is depreciated using seven-year straight-line depreciation. Watch what happens as the Time-Space percentage (T/S%) changes:

2020	$3,000 x	35%	(T/S%)	= 1,050	x 7.14%	= $74.97
2021	$3,000 x	30%	(T/S%)	= 900	x 14.29%	= $128.61
2022	$3,000 x	31%	(T/S%)	= 930	x 14.29%	= $132.90
2023	$3,000 x	32%	(T/S%)	= 960	x 14.28%	= $137.09

Step Two: How Long Must You Depreciate the Item?

The next step is to determine the number of years over which the property must be depreciated. You must put all your depreciable items into one of the categories listed on page 67. The category that an item falls into determines the number of years over which it must be depreciated. Once you begin depreciating an item, you must stick to the number of years on this chart, even if the rules change in later years.

Step Three: What Depreciation Method Can You Use?

The third step is to determine which depreciation method to use. In some cases, you will have a choice between the straight-line method and the accelerated method, which is also called the 150% or 200% declining balance method. (For a summary of these methods, see the depreciation tables at the end of this chapter.)

- Under the straight-line method, you claim an equal amount of depreciation each year. Generally, you can't use this method unless you choose it the first year you use the property for business.

- Under the accelerated depreciation method, you claim more depreciation in the first few years and less in later years. Although the accelerated method is usually more beneficial, you may not want to use it if doing so would cause a loss for your business this year or large fluctuations in your deductions from year to year.

EXAMPLE

You decide to use the 200% declining balance depreciation method for your playground equipment, which entitles you to deduct 28.58% of the $1,050 business amount in the first year. Using this method, the amount of depreciation you could claim in the first year would be $1,050 x 28.58% = $300. (See below to determine if you must use the Half-Year Convention rule.)

Once you choose a depreciation method for an item, you generally must continue using that method for the life of that item; you can't change methods. Also, you must use the same method for all the items in each category that you start depreciating in the same year. For example, if you use straight-line depreciation for a freezer you bought last year, you must use that method for all other personal property you bought or first used for business last year. You can use another method for a land improvement (such as a fence) that you purchased in that year. (This rule doesn't apply to the Section 179 rule; you can use Section 179 for one furniture item and still use accelerated or straight-line depreciation for other furniture items you bought that year.)

Each year you can choose again for the items you buy and start depreciating that year. So for last year's purchases, you could use accelerated depreciation for other personal property and straight-line depreciation for land improvements, but this year you can make a different choice for your new purchases in those categories.

Step Four: Do Any Special Rules Apply?

The final step is to determine if there are any special depreciation rules that apply to the item. There are five special depreciation rules—three conventions, the 100% bonus depreciation rule, and Section 179. Section 179 allows you to deduct the entire cost of some depreciable items in the first year, and the three convention rules are applied to items in the first year they are used for business. These rules—the Half-Year Convention, the Mid-Month Convention, and the Mid-Quarter Convention—may affect the first-year depreciation you can take in certain circumstances.

THE 100% BONUS DEPRECIATION RULE

As described on pages 60–61, this new rule as of 2018 allows you to deduct the business portion of all expenses in one year without having to depreciate them. The exceptions to this rule are the home, a home improvement, and a home addition.

THE HALF-YEAR CONVENTION

Since the items you're depreciating were bought at various times during the year, the IRS won't allow you to claim a full year's worth of depreciation the first year you use an item in your business. Instead, for all items except home improvements and home depreciation, you must apply the Half-Year Convention rule in the first year of depreciation.

This rule says that no matter when you purchased the item or put it into business use, it will be treated as if it were put into business use in the middle of the year. This means that you only get one-half of the normal depreciation deduction in the first year. The other half of that year's deduction is picked up at the end of the depreciation period. In other words, if you are using seven-year straight-line depreciation rules, you will claim half of the normal depreciation in the first year, then six years of full depreciation, and then another half year. This means that you must actually depreciate the item over eight calendar years. In the depreciation tables at the end of this chapter, the Half-Year Convention rules are already built into the percentages listed.

THE MID-MONTH CONVENTION

To depreciate your home and home improvements, you must apply the Mid-Month Convention rule instead of the Half-Year Convention rule. Under this rule, the deduction for the first year is based on the month that you first used the home or home improvement in the business, and it doesn't matter when during the month. The rule treats every item as if it was first put into business use in the middle of the first month that it was used for business. The percentages for each month are listed in the depreciation table for home and home improvements.

THE MID-QUARTER CONVENTION

This rule applies if you purchased over 40% of items you are depreciating during the last quarter of last year, which might happen, for example, if you started your business during that quarter. If you didn't purchase over 40% of such items during the last quarter of the year, this rule doesn't apply to you. There are some expenses that you don't have to include in your capital expenditures in determining if you must apply the Mid-Quarter Convention rule:

- property that you purchase and sell in the same tax year

- the purchase of a home

- home improvements (you still have to include land improvements)

- deductions for personal property that you claim under Section 179 rules

When you apply the Mid-Quarter Convention in computing your depreciation, it imposes limits on the amount of depreciation you can claim this year for the items you purchased in each quarter of the year. The depreciation limits for the items you purchased in each quarter are as follows:

First quarter	(January, February, March)	87.5%
Second quarter	(April, May, June)	62.5%
Third quarter	(July, August, September)	37.5%
Fourth quarter	(October, November, December)	12.5%

If this convention applies to you, you will only be able to deduct 87.5% of what you would otherwise be entitled to for the items you purchased in the first quarter of the year. And you will only be able to deduct 12.5% of the depreciation you would otherwise be entitled to for the items you purchased in the last quarter of the year.

EXAMPLE

You purchased a $2,800 swing set in November last year and a $3,000 jungle gym in February last year, and these are your only capital expenditures in this tax year. Your Time-Space percentage is 25%. If you choose to apply seven-year straight-line depreciation to these items, you would get the following results:

| $2,800 swing set | x 25% | = | $700 | x 7.14% | = $49.98 |
| $3,000 jungle gym | x 25% | = | $750 | x 7.14% | = $53.55 |

Since you purchased more than 40% of your capital expenditures during the last quarter of last year, however, you must apply the Mid-Quarter Convention. Under the straight-line depreciation rules, 7.14% represents only one-half of the first year of depreciation. This means that you must multiply by two before applying the limitations:

$2,800 swing set purchased in fourth quarter:	$49.95 x 2 x 12.5% = $12.50
$3,000 jungle gym purchased in first quarter:	$53.55 x 2 x 87.5% = $93.71
Total	$106.21

In the second year of depreciation for these items (and beyond), you will be able to claim the full amount of your normal depreciation:

$2,800 swing set	x 25%	=	$700	x 14.29%	= $100.03
$3,000 sofa	x 25%	=	$750	x 14.29%	= $121.47
Total					$221.50

Is all this work worth it? In our example, the first year doesn't look like much. However, in subsequent years, the numbers will add up.

These calculations get far more complicated if you use accelerated depreciation instead of straight-line depreciation, because in every subsequent depreciation year you must use a different depreciation percentage. Because of this, you may consider choosing straight-line depreciation whenever you use the Mid-Quarter Convention rule, unless you are using computer software to calculate your depreciation.

Section 179

Section 179 is a special rule that allows you to claim up to $1,040,000 of your new or used items purchased in the year they are incurred. This rule does not apply to land improvements or home depreciation. **Note: As discussed earlier, home improvements may be eligible for the Section 179 rule as of 2018.**

To be eligible to apply it to an item, you must meet all four of these conditions:

1. You must use the rule that applies to the year you first used the item in your business. This means you can't use Section 179 on your tax return for any item you used in your business before last year. But you can claim Section 179 if you amend your taxes for earlier years (see Changing Your Election of Section 179 on page 73).

2. The expenses you claim under Section 179 can't result in a loss on your tax return for this year. (But you can carry forward any unused Section 179 deductions to the next tax year.) If you file jointly, Section 179 expenses can't create a loss on the combined earned income of both spouses. In other words, any wage income your spouse reports on your joint **Form 1040** can offset Section 179 losses from your business. If your **Schedule C** shows $5,000 in losses and your spouse reports more than $5,000 in wages on **Form 1040**, you can claim those losses. If you file separately, your spouse's tax return doesn't play any role in these limits.

3. You must be using the item more than 50% of the time for your business. Most child care providers use their Time-Space percentage to calculate their personal property depreciation. It's unusual to have a Time-Space percentage greater than 50%, so few providers can use Section 179 for these items.

4. You may not use Section 179 for an item you purchased from a related party, such as a spouse, child, parent, grandparent, or grandchild (siblings—that is, brothers and sisters—are not covered by this restriction). You can't use Section 179 if you acquired the property as a gift or inheritance.

Note: Your state may or may not recognize the Section 179 rule. If not, you may be required to add back to your income (for state income tax purposes) the amount of extra depreciation you claimed because of this rule.

Put Your Section 179 Expenses on the Right Form

To take advantage of the Section 179 rule, you must claim the expense on **Form 4562**, Part I. So if you purchased an item that cost over $2,500 this year, used it mostly for business, and want to claim the entire deduction this year, be sure to put it on **Form 4562**.

The Consequences of Using Section 179

There are some potentially negative consequences of using Section 179 that you should take into consideration before you decide to use this method:

1. If you go out of business before the end of the normal depreciation period for the item, you will have to pay back (recapture) some of the depreciation you claimed and file **Form 4797** (see chapter 11) to report it as income. The sooner you go out of business, the more income you will have to report. Before using Section 179, consider whether you plan to be in business at the end of the normal depreciation period

for that item (five years for a personal computer or a car; seven years for other personal property). If you shut down your business for several months and then start up again, your Section 179 deductions will not be affected.

2. Recapturing some of the depreciation you claimed also comes into play if you sell an item before the end of its normal depreciation period. If this is the case, you must also fill out **Form 4797** (see chapter 11). If you sell the item for a gain, you have to report the gain as income. If you sell it for a loss while you are still in business, you can deduct that loss on your **Form 1040**.

3. You will also have to recapture some of the depreciation you claimed if your business-use percentage of a Section 179 item falls to 50% or less in a later year. To avoid this, only apply Section 179 to items you will be using more than 50% of the time for business over their entire lives.

When Should You Use the Section 179 Rule?

Now that I've explained all the restrictions and potential negative consequences of using the Section 179 rule, you might wonder: are there any circumstances when you should consider using it? In most situations, the items you purchased are eligible for either the $2,500 rule or the 100% bonus depreciation rule, allowing you to deduct the business portion in one year without regard to having to be used more than 50% in your business.

As we discussed on pages 63–64, using the Section 179 rule on a home improvement does make sense rather than depreciating it over 39 years.

Section 179 after the First Year

Once you use Section 179 to claim the business deduction for an item, you can't claim any further deductions for that item in future years. In other words, you won't record anything on **Form 4562** for this item in any future years. However, if your business use falls below 50%, you will need to recapture some of the depreciation you claimed. See chapter 11 for details.

Changing Your Election of Section 179

The IRS allows you to choose or revoke your choice of the Section 179 rule by amending your tax return for the tax years 2018 through 2020. Once you amend your return to elect or revoke the Section 179 rule, this change cannot be reversed without the consent of the IRS. If you did not take advantage of the Section 179 rule between 2018 and 2020, you may want to consider amending your tax return to get a refund. Here's an example of how this rule might benefit you. Let's say that you bought a computer in 2018 for $2,600 and used it 80% of the time in your business. You depreciated the computer over five years and claimed $320 in depreciation deductions ($2,600 x 80% business use x 20% first-year accelerated depreciation = $416).

If you amend your tax return and elect to use the Section 179 rule, you can claim $1,664 as a deduction on your 2018 amended tax return ($2,600 x 80% = $1,600 – $416 = $1,664). This will mean a tax refund of about $499 (30% tax bracket) or $655 (40% tax bracket). If you use this rule, it will eliminate any depreciation deduction for this item on all subsequent tax returns.

Depreciation Tip

Don't subtract the first year's depreciation deduction from the cost of the property before calculating the depreciation for the second year. Use the original cost to calculate your depreciation each year.

Calculating Depreciation by Category

The rest of this chapter will review each of the categories of depreciable items in more detail, explaining the specific rules and options that apply to each one. The examples will show the straight-line method, an accelerated method, and Section 179 (where applicable) but will always show the straight-line method first. Straight-line depreciation is the easiest to use, and there are many pitfalls and restrictions involved in using Section 179.

You may prefer to use accelerated rules rather than the straight-line rules. If you depreciate an item under the accelerated rules and go out of business before the end of the recovery period, you won't have to recapture (pay back) any of the depreciation you've claimed. If you sell an item you've used for your business, however, there may be some tax consequences, and if you were using accelerated rules, you'd be more likely to owe tax at this point than if you'd been using straight-line rules (see chapter 11).

Check the Tables for More Information

As you read the following examples, refer to the tables at the end of this chapter. These tables list the percentages that you can deduct each year under each of the depreciation methods described on the following pages.

Keep Written Records of All Your Business Deductions

Remember that you need to keep written records to support all the business deductions you claim, in the form of receipts, canceled checks, or other records.

Personal Computer/Office Equipment

Under an IRS regulation, you can make an election to deduct in one year office equipment that individually costs less than $2,500! If it cost more than $2,500, it may be eligible for the Section 179 rule or 100% bonus depreciation rule. This category of depreciation includes personal computers and office equipment, including printers, fax machines, copiers, scanners, and electric typewriters. If you do use the 100% bonus depreciation rule, enter the deduction on **Form 4562**, line 14. We'll use a computer as an example. You can use your Time-Space percentage or an actual business-use percentage to depreciate the items in this category. If you use an actual business-use percentage, track how much time you use each item for your business (children's games, business record keeping, and so on) and how much time you use it for personal purposes. Divide the number of hours of business use by the total number of hours you use the item. For example, if you use your computer three hours a week for business and nine hours a week for personal purposes, your business-use percentage would be 25% (3 ÷ [3 + 9]).

In this category, your options for depreciation methods are based on your business-use percentage. If it is 50% or less, you must depreciate the item over five years. If it is higher, you can choose from three depreciation periods as described below, after an explanation about a change in recommendations for depreciating listed property.

100% Bonus Depreciation Rule

In the first example below, we will not use the 100% bonus depreciation rule because the computer was not used more than 50% for business. In the second example, we will use the new rule because the computer was used 70% for business.

What Is Listed Property?

Clearly, a vehicle weighing less than 6,000 pounds would be listed property and should be depreciated on **Form 4562**, Part V. See pages 76–77 for an example of how to fill out Part V. The IRS Regulation Section 1.280F-6 says, "Exception for computers. The term 'listed property' shall not include any computer (including peripheral equipment) used exclusively at a regular business establishment. For purposes of the preceding sentence, a portion of a dwelling unit shall be treated as a regular business establishment if (and only if) the requirements of Section 280A(c)(1) are met with respect to that portion."

Family child care providers don't meet the requirements under Tax Code Section 280A(c)(1) because it allows taxpayers to claim expenses for their home only if they use part of the home exclusively in their business. Family child care providers have their own rule under Section 280A(c)(4), which allows them to claim expenses for their home if they're using rooms on a regular basis. But technically that doesn't meet the requirements under Section 280A(c)(1), so a provider's computer should be listed property.

The one exception is that a provider who has an exclusive-use room and uses a computer in that room would be able to claim that the computer was not listed property because it meets the above exception. However, providers who use their computer in a regularly used room in their home do not meet this exception and must claim their computer as listed property.

Claiming a computer as listed property means providers must keep track of business use based on the hours the computer is used for business purposes. The IRS **Child Care Provider Audit Technique Guide** indicates that auditors may be stricter about demanding logs showing the business use of computers. Most providers, as a practical matter, do not keep such logs and instead use their Time percentage. This could be challenged in an audit. You must keep careful records to show this computer use. Such a record might be a log that tracks business and personal use for several months.

Business Use Equal to or Less Than 50%

If your business-use percentage is 50% or less, use the five-year straight-line depreciation rule. See the tables at the end of this chapter for the percentages that you can deduct each year. If you bought a $3,000 computer last year and your business-use percentage was 25%, the amount you can claim as a business expense would be $75:

Five-Year Straight-Line

$3,000 computer x 25% business use	=	$750 business basis
$750 x 10% (1st-year depreciation)	=	$75

Enter this amount on **Form 4562**, Part V, line 27. column (h).

Business Use Greater Than 50%

If your business-use percentage is more than 50%, you have four choices—you can use the five-year straight-line method, the five-year 200% declining balance method, the 100% bonus depreciation rule, or Section 179. (To use the Section 179 rule, you must have bought the computer in 2021.) If your business-use percentage is 70%, this is what these three calculations would look like (refer to the tables at the end of this chapter for more information).

Five-Year Straight-Line

$3,000 computer x 70% business use	=	$2,100
$2,100 x 10%	=	$210

Enter this amount on **Form 4562**, Part V, line 26, column (h).

Five-Year 200% Declining Balance

$3,000 computer x 70% business use	=	$2,100
$2,100 x 20%	=	$420

Enter this amount on **Form 4562**, Part V, line 26, column (h).

100% Bonus Depreciation

$3,000 computer x 70% business use	=	$2,100
$2,100 x 100%	=	$2,100

Enter this amount on **Form 4562**, Part V, line 14

Form 4562 (2021)									Page **2**
Part V	**Listed Property** (Include automobiles, certain other vehicles, certain aircraft, and property used for entertainment, recreation, or amusement.)								
	Note: For any vehicle for which you are using the standard mileage rate or deducting lease expense, complete **only** 24a, 24b, columns (a) through (c) of Section A, all of Section B, and Section C if applicable.								
	Section A—Depreciation and Other Information (Caution: See the instructions for limits for passenger automobiles.)								

24a Do you have evidence to support the business/investment use claimed? ☐ Yes ☐ No			24b If "Yes," is the evidence written? ☐ Yes ☐ No					
(a) Type of property (list vehicles first)	**(b)** Date placed in service	**(c)** Business/ investment use percentage	**(d)** Cost or other basis	**(e)** Basis for depreciation (business/investment use only)	**(f)** Recovery period	**(g)** Method/ Convention	**(h)** Depreciation deduction	**(i)** Elected section 179 cost

25	Special depreciation allowance for qualified listed property placed in service during the tax year and used more than 50% in a qualified business use. See instructions				**25**	$2,100
26	Property used more than 50% in a qualified business use:					
COMPUTER	1/1/2021	70 %	$2,100	$1,550	5 YEAR	DB	$210	
		%						
		%						
27	Property used 50% or less in a qualified business use:					
		%				S/L –		
		%				S/L –		
		%				S/L –		
28	Add amounts in column (h), lines 25 through 27. Enter here and on line 21, page 1				**28**		
29	Add amounts in column (i), line 26. Enter here and on line 7, page 1					**29**	

SECTION 179

$3,000 computer x 70% business use = $2,100

Using this method, you can claim the entire business-use percentage of the expense. If you go out of business within five years, however, you will have to pay back some of it. Enter $2,100 on **Form 4562**, Part I, line 2.

After filling out Part I, line 2, notice that there is a limitation amount for line 1 ($1,040,000) and a business income limitation on line 11 (see the IRS instructions for **Form 4562**). Your business income is your earned income—your net profit from line 31 of **Schedule C**, plus the wages you (or your spouse) report on line 7 of **Form 1040**. Because of these limitations, you can't take more than the lesser of $1,040,000 or your earned income as a Section 179 deduction.

If your business income is $25,000, you will enter $25,000 on line 11, since this is the lesser of the two amounts (see example). If this is the case, you will have no problem claiming the full $2,100 for your computer this year, since it is far less than the lower of the two limitations.

Form **4562**	**Depreciation and Amortization** (Including Information on Listed Property) ▶ Attach to your tax return. ▶ Go to *www.irs.gov/Form4562* for instructions and the latest information.	OMB No. 1545-0172 **2021** Attachment Sequence No. **179**
Department of the Treasury Internal Revenue Service (99)		
Name(s) shown on return	Business or activity to which this form relates	Identifying number

Part I	**Election To Expense Certain Property Under Section 179**		
	Note: If you have any listed property, complete Part V before you complete Part I.		
1	Maximum amount (see instructions)	**1**	
2	Total cost of section 179 property placed in service (see instructions)	**2**	$2,100
3	Threshold cost of section 179 property before reduction in limitation (see instructions)	**3**	
4	Reduction in limitation. Subtract line 3 from line 2. If zero or less, enter -0-	**4**	
5	Dollar limitation for tax year. Subtract line 4 from line 1. If zero or less, enter -0-. If married filing separately, see instructions	**5**	

6	**(a)** Description of property	**(b)** Cost (business use only)	**(c)** Elected cost	
	COMPUTER	$2,100	$2,100	

7	Listed property. Enter the amount from line 29	**7**	
8	Total elected cost of section 179 property. Add amounts in column (c), lines 6 and 7	**8**	$2,100
9	Tentative deduction. Enter the **smaller** of line 5 or line 8	**9**	$2,100
10	Carryover of disallowed deduction from line 13 of your 2020 Form 4562	**10**	
11	Business income limitation. Enter the smaller of business income (not less than zero) or line 5. See instructions	**11**	$25,000
12	Section 179 expense deduction. Add lines 9 and 10, but don't enter more than line 11	**12**	$2,100
13	Carryover of disallowed deduction to 2022. Add lines 9 and 10, less line 12 ▶	**13**	

Computer Software

Because any computer software you purchase will cost less than $2,500, you can deduct the cost in one year if you make that election. Apply your Time-Space percentage if you use it for business and personal use.

Other Personal Property

Under an IRS regulation, you can make an election to deduct in one year personal property that individually costs less than $2,500! If it cost more than $2,500, you can use the 100% bonus depreciation rule and deduct it in one year. If you do use the 100% bonus depreciation rule, enter the deduction on **Form 4562**, line 14. Therefore, it's unlikely you will choose to depreciate this category of expenses unless you want to show a higher profit this year. For example, if you bought a $4,000 swing set used 40% in your business, you can enter $1,600 ($4,000 x 40%) on **Form 4562**, line 14.

If you do wish to depreciate these expenses, you should depreciate them over seven years using either the seven-year straight-line method or the 200% declining balance method. To demonstrate, we'll use the example of a purchase of a $4,000 swing set used 40% in your business.

This category of depreciation includes all personal property other than computers and computer software. It includes large play equipment, furniture, appliances, TVs, VCRs, DVD players, lawn and garden equipment, household tools, and other household expenditures.

SEVEN-YEAR STRAIGHT-LINE

To use this method, you would prepare a supporting schedule such as the following.

2021 Tax Return
Supporting Schedule for Form 4562, Part III, line 19c
Polly Jones
Social Security #474-66-1234

Item	Date Put in Service	Method	Cost	Business-Use %	Business Basis	Table % Year 1	Deduction 2021
Swing set	1/21	7 YR/SL	$4,000	40%	$1,600.00	7.14%	$114.24
Total			$4,000		$1,600.00		$114.24

Using this method, the amount you can claim as a depreciation expense this year is $114.24. Enter this amount on **Form 4562**, Part III, line 19c, column (g). In column (e), enter "HY" for the Half-Year Convention (see pages 70–71). If you're depreciating more than three items, include your supporting schedule with your tax return.

Part III MACRS Depreciation (Don't include listed property. See instructions.)						
Section A						
17 MACRS deductions for assets placed in service in tax years beginning before 2021					**17**	
18 If you are electing to group any assets placed in service during the tax year into one or more general asset accounts, check here . . . . ▶ ☐						
Section B—Assets Placed in Service During 2021 Tax Year Using the General Depreciation System						
(a) Classification of property	(b) Month and year placed in service	(c) Basis for depreciation (business/investment use only—see instructions)	(d) Recovery period	(e) Convention	(f) Method	(g) Depreciation deduction
19a 3-year property						
b 5-year property						
c 7-year property		$1,600	7 YEAR	HY	S/L	$114
d 10-year property						
e 15-year property						
f 20-year property						
g 25-year property			25 yrs.		S/L	
h Residential rental			27.5 yrs.	MM	S/L	
property			27.5 yrs.	MM	S/L	
i Nonresidential real			39 yrs.	MM	S/L	
property				MM	S/L	

SEVEN-YEAR 200% DECLINING BALANCE

To use this method, you would prepare a supporting schedule, such as the following.

2021 Tax Return
Supporting Schedule for Form 4562, Part III, line 19c
Polly Jones
Social Security #474-66-1234

Item	Date Put in Service	Method	Cost	Business-Use %	Business Basis	Table % Year 1	Deduction 2021
Swing set	1/21	7YR/200% DB	$4,000	40%	$1,600.00	14.29%	$228.64
Total			$4,000		$1,600.00		$228.64

Using this method, the amount you can claim as a depreciation expense this year is $228.64. Enter this amount on **Form 4562**, Part III, line 19c, column (g). Enter "HY" in column (e). If you're depreciating more than three items, include a supporting schedule.

Part III MACRS Depreciation (Don't include listed property. See instructions.)						
Section A						
17 MACRS deductions for assets placed in service in tax years beginning before 2021					**17**	
18 If you are electing to group any assets placed in service during the tax year into one or more general asset accounts, check here . . . . ▶ ☐						
Section B—Assets Placed in Service During 2021 Tax Year Using the General Depreciation System						
(a) Classification of property	(b) Month and year placed in service	(c) Basis for depreciation (business/investment use only—see instructions)	(d) Recovery period	(e) Convention	(f) Method	(g) Depreciation deduction
19a 3-year property						
b 5-year property						
c 7-year property		$1,600	7 YEAR	HY	200%	$229
d 10-year property						
e 15-year property						
f 20-year property						
g 25-year property			25 yrs.		S/L	
h Residential rental			27.5 yrs.	MM	S/L	
property			27.5 yrs.	MM	S/L	
i Nonresidential real			39 yrs.	MM	S/L	
property				MM	S/L	

If you used the swing set more than 50% of the time for your business, you can use the Section 179 rule:

SECTION 179

Item	Method	Cost	Business Use %		Business Basis	Deduction 2021
2021 Tax Return						
Supporting Schedule for Form 4562, Part I						
Polly Jones						
Social Security #474-66-1234						
Swing set	Section 179	$4,000	x 75%	=	$3,000	$3,000
Total		$4,000			$3,000	$3,000

Using this method, the amount you can claim as a depreciation expense this year is $3,000. Enter this amount on **Form 4562**, Part I.

Personal Property Expenses before Last Year

If you were in business before last year, enter your depreciation deductions for the items first used in your business before last year on **Form 4562** as follows:

- Enter computer depreciation on **Form 4562**, line 17.
- Enter other personal property depreciation on **Form 4562**, line 17.

You do not have to attach a supporting schedule to your tax return after the first year you begin depreciating an item. Just enter the proper amount of depreciation for the items from earlier years onto the lines noted above.

Warning: Choose Wisely!
Remember that once you begin depreciating an item using one of the methods described in this chapter, you must continue using that method for the entire life of the item, even if the depreciation rules change in later years.

Home Improvements

A home improvement is something that is attached to your home and adds to its value or substantially prolongs its useful life. Home improvements include room additions, a new garage, or an outdoor deck. If you made home improvements since you began using your home for business, you must depreciate these improvements separately from your home depreciation. Remember, you may be able to deduct a home improvement in one year if it meets the definition of a repair, you use it more than 50% of the time in your business, or you meet the requirements for the safe harbor election for small taxpayers. See pages 60–63.

You may depreciate a home improvement expense even if you are renting your home or apartment. The only requirement is that you must be the person who paid for the improvement. If you have paid for the home improvement in lieu of rent payments, you should claim the cost of the home improvement as rent and deduct it all in the current year. Enter this amount on **Form 8829**, line 18. Remember, you can elect out of using the 100% bonus depreciation rule if you want to show lower expenses this year.

Home improvements are depreciated with the same method used for the home itself, the 39-year straight-line method. To calculate the depreciation deduction for a home improvement, first multiply the cost of the improvement by your Time-Space percentage to get the business basis of the improvement. (When your Time-Space percentage changes, the total you can depreciate will also change.) Multiply the business basis by the percentage for the month you completed the improvement (as listed in the depreciation tables at the end of this chapter).

If you completed a $3,000 garage remodeling project in April of last year, your depreciation calculation might look something like this:

$3,000	Total cost of garage remodeling
x 25%	Time-Space percentage
$ 750	
x 1.819%	Depreciation percentage for April
$13.64	Amount you can deduct

The amount you can claim as a depreciation expense this year for your garage remodeling project is $13.64. Enter this amount on **Form 4562**, Part III, line 19i, column (g). After the first year of depreciation, you will use 2.564% each year to calculate your deduction.

Section A						
17 MACRS deductions for assets placed in service in tax years beginning before 2021						**17**
18 If you are electing to group any assets placed in service during the tax year into one or more general asset accounts, check here . . . . ▶ ☐						
Section B—Assets Placed in Service During 2021 Tax Year Using the General Depreciation System						
(a) Classification of property	(b) Month and year placed in service	(c) Basis for depreciation (business/investment use only—see Instructions)	(d) Recovery period	(e) Convention	(f) Method	(g) Depreciation deduction
19a 3-year property						
b 5-year property						
c 7-year property						
d 10-year property						
e 15-year property						
f 20-year property						
g 25-year property			25 yrs.		S/L	
h Residential rental property			27.5 yrs.	MM	S/L	
			27.5 yrs.	MM	S/L	
i Nonresidential real property	4/21	$750	39 yrs.	MM	S/L	$13.64
				MM	S/L	

You can use your actual business-use percentage instead of your Time-Space percentage in calculating your home improvement depreciation. It may make sense to do this if your business-use percentage is much higher than your Time-Space percentage. If you do use your business-use percentage, you'll need written evidence to support it. It probably isn't possible to claim a higher business-use percentage for home improvements that are an integral part of the structure of your home, such as a new roof or new windows.

Depreciating Unfinished Home Improvement Projects

If you started a home improvement project last year but won't finish it until this year, you can depreciate part of the project this tax season if you were able to start using the improvement by the end of last year. Here are your options:

- Wait to take any depreciation on the project until it is finished. If you started a project in 2021 and didn't use the improvement at all that year, start depreciating the project in 2022 in the month the project is finished.

- Treat the unfinished home improvement as two projects. If you began using part of the improvement in December of last year, you can depreciate your expenses for the project starting that month. Depreciate your expenses for this year starting the month the project is finished.

Home Improvement Savings Are Small

Since home improvements must be depreciated over 39 years, the amount you will be able to claim in any one year will be relatively small. Some providers spend thousands of dollars fixing up their homes for their businesses under the mistaken belief that they will be able to write off much of the cost in the first year. As they soon discover, spending money on home improvements is not a good way to create deductions for your business.

In the previous example, a $3,000 remodeling expense resulted in a $13.64 deduction in the first year. If you are in the 12% income tax bracket, this would be a federal tax savings of only $3.55 (12% income tax plus 14% net self-employment tax rate). Your state income taxes will also produce a small tax savings. If you make a home improvement, it's always good to take the depreciation deduction, no matter how small, because it will run for many years. But remember that large home improvement expenses for your business will not translate into significant tax savings.

The Mid-Quarter Convention rule (see pages 70–71) doesn't apply to home improvements. You can now take Section 179 for home improvements. If you make home improvements that are necessary to become licensed or regulated or to maintain your license, you may be able to depreciate 100% of the cost.

Home Improvements before Last Year

Use Part III of **Form 4562** only for improvements that you paid for last year. If you made a home improvement before last year and before you began using your home for business, determine whether the cost of the improvement or its fair market value at the time your home was first used for your business is the lesser amount. (Since most home improvements increase in value along with the home, the lower number will usually be the original cost.) Add this amount to the cost of your home, and depreciate it as part of your home depreciation.

If you made a home improvement before last year but after you began using your home for your business, enter the depreciation for that improvement on **Form 8829**, following the instructions given in chapter 2. Calculate the depreciation deduction separately from your home and add that amount to **Form 8829**, line 42. The home improvements you make after you begin using your home for business aren't depreciated with your home because the depreciation periods end on different dates.

Land Improvements

Land improvements are eligible for either the $2,500 rule or the 100% bonus depreciation rule and therefore do not have to be depreciated. If you do use the 100% bonus depreciation rule, enter the deduction on **Form 4562**, line 14. Land improvements are not eligible for the Section 179 rule. Land improvements include installing a fence around your property or a patio, paving your driveway, adding a cement walkway, or installing a well.

To calculate the depreciation deduction for a land improvement, first multiply its cost by your Time-Space percentage to get the business basis of the improvement. (When your Time-Space percentage changes, the total you can depreciate will also change.) If you purchased a fence in 2021 for $11,000, your depreciation calculation might look something like this:

> Cost of fence $11,000 x 30% Time-Space percentage = $3,300
> $3,300 x 5% (first year using 15-year 150% declining balance method) = $165.00
> Enter this on **Form 4562**, Part III, line 19c, column (e).

Part II	Special Depreciation Allowance and Other Depreciation (Don't include listed property. See instructions.)						
14	Special depreciation allowance for qualified property (other than listed property) placed in service during the tax year. See instructions.					14	$1,650
15	Property subject to section 168(f)(1) election					15	
16	Other depreciation (including ACRS)					16	
Part III	MACRS Depreciation (Don't include listed property. See instructions.)						
	Section A						
17	MACRS deductions for assets placed in service in tax years beginning before 2021					17	
18	If you are electing to group any assets placed in service during the tax year into one or more general asset accounts, check here ▶ ☐						
Section B—Assets Placed in Service During 2021 Tax Year Using the General Depreciation System							
(a) Classification of property	(b) Month and year placed in service	(c) Basis for depreciation (business/investment use only—see instructions)	(d) Recovery period	(e) Convention	(f) Method	(g) Depreciation deduction	
19a 3-year property							
b 5-year property							
c 7-year property							
d 10-year property							
e 15-year property		$3,300	15 YEARS	HY	150% DB	$165	
f 20-year property							
g 25-year property			25 yrs.		S/L		
h Residential rental property			27.5 yrs.	MM	S/L		
			27.5 yrs.	MM	S/L		
i Nonresidential real property			39 yrs.	MM	S/L		
				MM	S/L		

Again, you may want to use your actual business-use percentage instead of your Time-Space percentage in calculating the depreciation for land improvements. This may make sense for a fence that you install for your business if you have no young children of your own or if you can show that it is mostly for your business. As noted above, you must be able to support this business-use claim.

Landscaping Is Not a Land Improvement

Landscaping includes trees, shrubbery, sod, plantings, grading, and landscape architect's fees. Deduct it in one year as a repair on **Form 4562**, line 19 (see page 79). If your landscaping is located immediately adjacent to your home and would be destroyed if your home was moved or replaced, then it should be treated as a home improvement and depreciated over 39 years. Landscaping that costs more than $2,500, is installed away from your home and would not be harmed if your home was moved or replaced is considered part of the land and cannot be depreciated at all.

Land Improvements before Last Year

Use Part II of **Form 4562** only for the land improvements you paid for last year. If you made a land improvement before you began your business, determine whether the cost of the improvement or its fair market value at the time it was first used in your business is the lesser amount. (Since many land improvements increase in value along with the home, the original cost will often be the lower number.) Add this amount to the cost of your home when determining the depreciation deduction for your home.

If you made a land improvement before last year but after you began using your home for your business, enter the depreciation for that land improvement on **Form 8829**. (Follow the instructions under Home Improvements.) Calculate your depreciation deduction and add that amount to **Form 8829**, line 42.

Home Depreciation

The purchase of a home is not eligible for the 100% bonus depreciation rule or the Safe Harbor for Small Taxpayers rule (see pages 60–65). It's always financially beneficial to depreciate your home. There are two important reasons to depreciate your home. First, it will reduce your taxable income while you're in business. Second, any higher taxes that you may have to pay later because you used your home in your business will be the same whether or not you claimed the depreciation you were entitled to. (The rules about the tax consequences when you sell your home don't change the fact that you are still better off claiming all the home depreciation you're entitled to; see chapter 12.)

If you own a mobile home that is fastened to the land and connected to local utilities, use the home depreciation rules described in this section. If your mobile home wears out within 39 years, you can deduct all the unused depreciation in the final year.

Most taxpayers must show that they use part of their home regularly and exclusively for business purposes to qualify to deduct depreciation for their home. Family child care providers are exempt from this requirement. You only need to show that you use part of your home regularly for your business. If that is the case, you can claim part of the value of your home as a depreciation expense each year you are in business.

If you're married and your name isn't on the deed of the home, you can still claim home depreciation for your business. If you aren't married and your companion owns the home, you can't claim home depreciation (see the *Record-Keeping Guide*). You can't take a business deduction for your mortgage payments; instead, depreciate your home using the rules described below.

If You Rent Your Home

If you rent your home instead of own it, deduct your Time-Space percentage of your rent instead of depreciation. To do this, enter your total rent payments on **Form 8829**, line 18, column (b) (see chapter 2).

If You Started Claiming Home Depreciation before Last Year

If you claimed depreciation on your home before last year, enter your depreciation by filling out **Form 8829**, lines 37–42. Don't claim this deduction on **Form 4562**.

If you or your spouse claimed home depreciation in earlier years for another business, continue depreciating your home under the rules for that business. Once your child care business begins, start a separate depreciation calculation for your home for this business. In other words, use two different depreciation schedules to depreciate your home for the two different businesses.

If You Started Claiming Home Depreciation Last Year

If you first began using your home for your business last year, you must enter information on **Form 4562**, Part III, line 19i. Enter the month you started using your home for business in column (b). Enter the business basis of your home in column (c). To calculate the business basis of your home, follow these steps:

STEP ONE

Record the purchase price of your home. If you hired a contractor or built part of the home yourself, record only the amount of money you actually spent to build your home; don't include the value of your labor.

The basis for depreciating your home is either its purchase price or its fair market value at the time you first started to use it for your business, whichever is lower. Therefore, if you bought your home in 2011 for $150,000 and its fair market value when you started using it for your business in 2020 was $180,000, use $150,000 as the basis of your home.

Note: If the fair market value of your home declines after you begin using it for business, don't reduce its value in calculating your home depreciation in later years.

STEP TWO

Add to the above amount the value of any home improvements you made before you first used your home for business. These improvements might include remodeling expenses, a new roof, room additions, siding, or a new deck. Don't include repairs or maintenance expenses, such as painting, wallpapering, or fixing a broken window.

STEP THREE

Subtract from the above the value of the land (land is not depreciable) to get the adjusted basis of your home. If you don't know the value of the land when you bought the house, use the relationship between the value of your land and home today to calculate the value of your land when you bought your house. Check your property tax statement, or call your county assessor's office for an estimate of the value of your land today.

EXAMPLE

You bought your home in 2014 for $100,000. According to your property tax statement, it's worth $120,000 now. Your county assessor says the land is worth $12,000 today, and $12,000 ÷ $120,000 = 10%. Therefore the value of your land in 2014 was roughly 10% of the purchase price of your home, or $10,000 ($100,000 x 10% = $10,000). Keep a copy of your tax assessment report for your records.

If you buy more land or are given land and pay for surveying, you can't claim these expenses as business deductions. (For more information, see the *Record-Keeping Guide*.)

STEP FOUR

Multiply the adjusted basis of your home by your Time-Space percentage to get the business basis of your home—the amount you can depreciate. Enter this number in column (c) of **Form 4562**, Part III, line 19i. Here are the calculations:

Step One:	$100,000	purchase price of home in 2014
Step Two:	+ $3,800	new roof in 2015
	$103,800	
Step Three:	–$10,000	value of land in 2014
	$93,800	adjusted basis of home
Step Four:	x 30%	Time-Space percentage
	$28,140	business basis of home

The next step is to determine the percentage of the business basis of your home that you can deduct in the first year of business. This depends on the month you began your business last year; see the depreciation tables at the end of this chapter.

Let's use our example to calculate your first year's home depreciation deduction. If you went into business in January 2021, you would use 2.461%:

$28,140	business basis of home
x 2.461%	began business in January
$692.53	home depreciation deduction

Enter the amount you calculate here in line 19i, column (g). After the first year of depreciation, you will use 2.564% each year to calculate your deduction.

Part III	**MACRS Depreciation (Don't** include listed property. See instructions.)						
Section A							
17	MACRS deductions for assets placed in service in tax years beginning before 2021					**17**	
18	If you are electing to group any assets placed in service during the tax year into one or more general asset accounts, check here . . . . ▶ ☐						
Section B—Assets Placed in Service During 2021 Tax Year Using the General Depreciation System							
(a) Classification of property	**(b)** Month and year placed in service	**(c)** Basis for depreciation (business/investment use only—see instructions)	**(d)** Recovery period	**(e)** Convention	**(f)** Method	**(g)** Depreciation deduction	
19a 3-year property							
b 5-year property							
c 7-year property							
d 10-year property							
e 15-year property							
f 20-year property							
g 25-year property			25 yrs.		S/L		
h Residential rental property			27.5 yrs.	MM	S/L		
			27.5 yrs.	MM	S/L		
i Nonresidential real property	1/2021	$28,140	39 yrs.	MM	S/L	$693	
				MM	S/L		

If you first began using your home for your business last year, fill out Part III of **Form 4562**, as described above. Enter the depreciation deduction ($692.53 in our example) on **Form 4562**, line 22. Don't carry this deduction forward to **Schedule C**, line 13. You will claim your home depreciation on **Form 8829**.

Vehicle Depreciation

You can use either the standard mileage rate method or the actual vehicle expenses method to deduct the vehicle expenses for your business (see chapter 5 and the *Record-Keeping Guide* for information on claiming other expenses for your vehicle). If you choose the actual vehicle expenses method, you may take a depreciation deduction on your vehicle. Vehicles are subject to the Half-Year or Mid-Quarter Convention rule (see pages 70–71).

To report the depreciation on your vehicle, fill out **Form 4562**, Part V, Section A. If you began depreciating your vehicle in an earlier year, you must continue depreciating it under the rules that were in effect when you began to depreciate it.

Caution

If you decide to use the actual vehicle expenses method in the first year you use a vehicle in your business, you'll be locked into this method for the life of that vehicle; you can't switch back to the standard mileage rate method in later years. This means that you'll have to keep detailed records of all your vehicle expenses for every year you use the vehicle in your business.

To depreciate your vehicle, you must first figure out if the vehicle was used more or less than 50% for your business. Next, determine if the vehicle weighs more or less than 6,000 pounds gross vehicle weight. Look for this information on the inside front door panel of your vehicle. Once you have these two facts, follow the instructions below that apply to your situation.

Rules for 50% or less versus more than 50% for your business

If your vehicle is used 50% or less for business, you must use straight-line depreciation and you do not qualify to use the 100% bonus depreciation rule.

If your vehicle is used more than 50% for business, you can use accelerated depreciation (200% declining balance). If you purchased the vehicle after September 28, 2017, and first started using it for your business in 2021, you can also use the 100% bonus depreciation rule. However, if your business percentage drops to 50% or less in a later year, you will need to recapture some depreciation. It is done just like recapturing Section 179 (see pages 204–205), except you use column (b) for **Form 4797**, lines 33–35 instead of column (a).

If the Vehicle Weighs Less Than 6,000 Pounds

Vehicles are normally depreciated over five years. If your vehicle is expensive (over $50,000), your depreciation deduction is subject to limitations each year, based on the first year the vehicle is used for your business.

If you first started using your vehicle in your business in 2021, the first-year depreciation limit is $10,200 for 2021, $16,400 for 2022, $9,800 for 2023, and $5,860 each year thereafter until the vehicle is fully depreciated. If you use the 100% bonus depreciation rule (as mentioned above, the vehicle must be used more than 50% for business) the limit is $18,200 for 2021, and the same limits as described above for the subsequent years.

You must reduce these limitations by your business-use percentage of the vehicle. In other words, if you use a car 35% of the time for your business, your depreciation limit in 2021 would be $3,570 ($10,200 x 35%).

For example, if you bought a $60,000 vehicle (new or used) and your business use was 60%, your business basis would be $36,000 ($60,000 x 60%). The first year of accelerated depreciation (200% declining balance) would be $7,200. If you choose to not use the 100% bonus depreciation rule, the limitation would be $6,120 ($10,200 x 60%). Your deduction would be subject to the limitation, so you would enter $6,120 on **Form 4562**, Part V, line 27.

Part V	Listed Property (Include automobiles, certain other vehicles, certain aircraft, and property used for entertainment, recreation, or amusement.)								
	Note: For any vehicle for which you are using the standard mileage rate or deducting lease expense, complete **only** 24a, 24b, columns (a) through (c) of Section A, all of Section B, and Section C if applicable.								
	Section A—Depreciation and Other Information (Caution: See the instructions for limits for passenger automobiles.)								
24a Do you have evidence to support the business/investment use claimed? ☐ Yes ☐ No			24b If "Yes," is the evidence written? ☐ Yes ☐ No						
(a) Type of property (list vehicles first)	(b) Date placed in service	(c) Business/ investment use percentage	(d) Cost or other basis	(e) Basis for depreciation (business/investment use only)	(f) Recovery period	(g) Method/ Convention	(h) Depreciation deduction	(i) Elected section 179 cost	
25 Special depreciation allowance for qualified listed property placed in service during the tax year and used more than 50% in a qualified business use. See instructions .						25			
26 Property used more than 50% in a qualified business use:									
VAN	1/1/2021	60 %	$60,000	$36,000	5 YEAR	200%DB-HY	$6,120		
		%							
		%							
27 Property used 50% or less in a qualified business use:									
		%				S/L –			
		%				S/L –			
		%				S/L –			
28 Add amounts in column (h), lines 25 through 27. Enter here and on line 21, page 1 .						28			
29 Add amounts in column (i), line 26. Enter here and on line 7, page 1							29		

If the Vehicle Weighs 6,000 Pounds or More

Only very large vehicles weigh over 6,000 pounds. If this applies to your vehicle, the limits no longer apply. In the example above, you could use the full $7,200 of first year depreciation rather than being limited to $6,120. Then you would continue to depreciate it over five years without any limits.

If the business use was 50% or more, there is no limitation for the 100% bonus depreciation rule either, so you can deduct the entire business portion in the first year. In the example above, you could deduct the entire business basis of $36,000 in the first year.

Note: If you are able to claim all the vehicle depreciation in the first year, you are not entitled to any further depreciation in later years. If you weren't able to claim all the depreciation in the first year due to the limitations, the calculation to determine how much you can depreciate in later years is very complicated. Use tax preparation software or a tax preparer to help you calculate depreciation in later years.

Depreciation and Vehicle Expenses

In addition to depreciation, you can claim actual vehicle expenses on **Schedule C**, line 9 (see Vehicle Expenses in chapter 5). If you depreciate a vehicle you first started using in business last year, you can't use the standard mileage rate to claim expenses for it in later years. If you use Section 179 and go out of business, or use the vehicle 50% or less within five years, you'll have to file **Form 4797** to recapture some of the depreciation you claimed (see chapter 11).

If You Sold Your Vehicle Last Year

If you've been depreciating your vehicle before last year and you sold it last year, use the following to determine how much depreciation to claim.

If you placed your vehicle in business use between January 1 and September 30 of the first year you used it in your business, you can deduct one half of the regular depreciation amount. If you placed your vehicle in business use between October 1 and December 31 of the first year you used it in your business, multiply the full-year depreciation amount by the following percentages, based on the month you sold the vehicle:

January–March	12.5%
April–June	37.5%
July–September	62.5%
October–December	87.5%

(For a description of the tax consequences of selling a vehicle, see chapter 11.)

Congratulations!

You have entered your depreciation expenses on either **Form 4562** or **Form 8829**. Now enter the total of all your depreciation deductions on **Schedule C**, line 13.

Next, take a deep breath. The most difficult part of doing your taxes is done! Nothing else you'll do on your tax forms will be as complicated as what you have just completed. Your next step will be completing **Schedule C**.

Start-Up Costs: A Special Rule

To the IRS, your business begins when you're ready to enroll children and are advertising that fact to the public. Whether you are licensed or have any children in your care at that point is not important. Here's an example: In February you are ready to care for your first child and put up a sign at your church announcing your business. In March you apply for your license, in April you get your license, and in May you enroll your first child. In this case, the IRS would say that your business began in February. On the other hand, if you get your license in June and aren't ready to care for your first child until August, then the IRS would say that your business began in August.

You are entitled to deduct items you owned before your business began. Conduct an inventory of all these items and estimate their value at the time your business began. See my *Family Child Care Record-Keeping Guide* for an explanation of how to do this.

If you went into business in 2021, you can use the Start-Up Rule to deduct in one year up to $5,000 worth of items that cost $200 or less. Amounts over $5,000 can be amortized over 180 months using **Form 4562**, Part VI. Items that cost more than $200 can be deducted in one year using the 100% bonus depreciation rule. Remember, there is an exception to this rule for the home, home improvements, and home additions. If you didn't claim these expenses in 2020, you can amend your tax return.

For example, let's say you owned 150 items before you went into business in 2021 (washer, dryer, refrigerator, tables, couch, bed, pots and pans, lawn mower, patio furniture, rugs, and so on). The total amount of items valued at $200 or less was $6,000 and the total value of items costing more than $200 was $4,000. Let's assume these values are determined after applying your Time-Space percentage. You can deduct $5,000 of the $6,000 as start-up expenses and amortize the other $1,000 over 180 months. You can also deduct the $4,000 in 2021 under the 100% bonus depreciation rule.

If you went into business before 2020 and didn't claim the items you owned before you went into business, you can use IRS **Form 3115** to recapture previously unclaimed depreciation. See chapter 10 for how to do this.

Special Cases for Depreciation

If You've Gone In and Out of Business

What if you started depreciating an item, went out of business, and then started up your business again? When you start up again, determine whether the fair market value of the item at that time or the adjusted basis of the item is the lesser amount. The adjusted basis is the cost of the item minus the amount of depreciation you claimed (or were entitled to claim) while you were in business. Then begin depreciating the item as Year 1 for this new amount.

EXAMPLE
In Year 1 you bought a $4,000 fence. You started using the fence in your business in Year 2; its fair market value at that time was $3,000. From Year 2 through Year 4, you claimed $369 in depreciation (fifteen-year straight-line depreciation with a 40% Time-Space percentatge). You stopped doing child care in Year 5 and Year 6.

In Year 7 you started up your business again. At that time, the fair market value of the fence was $1,000. The adjusted basis is the original cost ($4,000) less the depreciation you have claimed ($369), or $3,631. Since the fair market value is lower than the adjusted basis of the item, use $1,000 to begin depreciating all over again using the fifteen-year depreciation rules. The depreciation you can now claim in the new Year 1 is $20 ($1,000 x 5% first year depreciation = $20).

If You Haven't Been Taking All Your Depreciation

What if you discover that you didn't take all the depreciation you were entitled to in a previous year? What if you haven't been taking any depreciation at all on your home or some other item? In these cases, you have three options:

1. You can file an amended tax return for 2020 and claim the depreciation you were entitled to for that year. You will get a refund plus interest. (For missed depreciation, you can only amend your return from last year.)

2. If you didn't deduct the full amount of depreciation you were entitled to and the error goes back before 2020, you should file **Form 3115** to recapture all the unclaimed depreciation you are entitled to. (For instructions on filing **Form 3115**, see chapter 10.) To use **Form 3115**, you must have failed to claim the full amount of your depreciation for at least two consecutive years.

3. You can decide not to take advantage of **Form 3115** and just claim the depreciation you would be entitled to this year if you had depreciated the previous years correctly. To do this, calculate the amount of depreciation you are entitled to under the rules that were in effect when the depreciation period began. If you bought the item for

your business in 2015, for example, you would claim depreciation based on the fourth year of the seven-year depreciation tables. If you choose this option, you would permanently forget about your unclaimed depreciation from earlier years.

If You Incurred Expenses to Meet Local Regulations

In some parts of the country, the local regulations require you to purchase safety equipment (such as smoke detectors or fire extinguishers) or make home improvements (such as enlarging a basement window or installing a fence) in order to operate a family child care business. These expenses aren't automatically 100% deductible. What matters is how you use the item, not why you bought it.

- In the case of smoke detectors and fire extinguishers, you can deduct only your Time-Space or business-use percentage of the cost. If these items are in an exclusive-use room, however, you can deduct 100% of the cost.

- If you enlarge a basement window in order to become licensed and you use that area of the basement 100% for your business, you can deduct the total cost as a repair. If you use that area of the basement for both business and personal purposes, you must apply your Time-Space or business-use percentage to the cost before deducting it.

If an Item Wears Out during the Depreciation Period

If an item wears out before its depreciation period ends, you're normally entitled to claim all the remaining depreciation as a business deduction in the year it wears out (start-up costs are an exception to this rule). For instructions on how to claim this amount, see chapter 11. If you buy a new item to replace the old one, you will start a new depreciation period for the new item.

Obtain a Copy of Your Depreciation Schedule

When your tax preparer depreciates items for your business, he or she will prepare a depreciation schedule showing each item, cost, depreciation method, and convention. It's important to ask your tax preparer for a copy of this schedule each year. This can be extremely useful for you in preparing future tax returns whether you do them yourself or use a new tax preparer.

For more information about the tax issues discussed in this chapter, refer to the related topics in the other chapters of this book and the Redleaf Press *Family Child Care Record-Keeping Guide*.

2021 Depreciation Tables

If you are required to use the Mid-Quarter Convention (see pages 70 and 71), see appendix A of IRS **Publication 946** for the proper percentage to use.

	3-Year Straight-Line (computer software)	5-Year Straight-Line (computers, office equipment, and vehicles)	5-Year 200% Declining Balance (computers, office equipment, and vehicles)
Year 1	16.67%	10%	20%
Year 2	33.33%	20%	32%
Year 3	33.33%	20%	19.20%
Year 4	16.67%	20%	11.52%
Year 5		20%	11.52%
Year 6		10%	5.76%
Section 179?	Maybe	No	Yes

	7-Year Straight-Line (furniture and appliances)	7-Year 200% Declining Balance (furniture and appliances)
Year 1	7.14%	14.29%
Year 2	14.29%	24.49%
Year 3	14.29%	17.49%
Year 4	14.28%	12.49%
Year 5	14.29%	8.93%
Year 6	14.28%	8.92%
Year 7	14.29%	8.93%
Year 8	7.14%	4.46%
Section 179?	Maybe	Yes

	15-Year Straight-Line (land improvements)	15-Year 150% Declining Balance (land improvements)
Year 1	3.33%	5.00%
Year 2	6.67%	9.50%
Year 3	6.67%	8.55%
Year 4	6.67%	7.70%
Year 5	6.67%	6.93%
Year 6	6.67%	6.23%
Year 7	6.67%	5.90%
Year 8	6.66%	5.90%
Year 9	6.67%	5.91%
Year 10	6.66%	5.90%
Year 11	6.67%	5.91%
Year 12	6.66%	5.90%
Year 13	6.67%	5.91%
Year 14	6.66%	5.90%
Year 15	6.67%	5.91%
Year 16	3.33%	2.95%
Section 179?	Maybe	Maybe

39-Year Straight-Line (home and home improvements)

For the first year of depreciation, use this table:		*After the first year of depreciation, use:*
January	2.461%	2.564%
February	2.247%	
March	2.033%	
April	1.819%	
May	1.605%	
June	1.391%	
July	1.177%	
August	0.963%	
September	0.749%	
October	0.535%	
November	0.321%	
December	0.107%	
Section 179?	No	No

CHAPTER 4

Reporting Your Food Program Income and Food Expenses

The first part of this chapter explains how to report your income from the Child and Adult Care Food Program (CACFP). The Food Program is a federal program that reimburses family child care providers for serving nutritious food. The second part of this chapter explains how to claim your food expenses. It's important to claim these expenses properly because food is the single biggest business deduction most family child care providers have. The standard meal allowance rates for 2021 are $1.39 for breakfast, $2.61 for lunch or supper, and $0.78 for snack. The rates are higher for Alaska and Hawaii. See page 94.

Reporting Your Income from the Food Program

All family child care providers who meet their state regulation standards are eligible to participate in the CACFP. All family child care providers should participate in the Food Program because it offers a major source of income. (For a full discussion of the benefits of the Food Program, see the *Record-Keeping Guide*.)

Reimbursement Rates

There is a great new rule for reimbursements from July 1, 2021 to June 30, 2022! All family child care providers that participate in the Food Program will receive the higher Tier 1 rate. Below is a discussion of the usual rules of the Tier I rates versus the Tier II rates, but that will only apply for reimbursements after June 30, 2022.

The Food Program's reimbursement rates are raised on July 1 every year. If you have a low income, live in a low-income area, or serve low-income children, you will be eligible for the Tier I reimbursement rates. If you don't have at least one of these qualifications, you will get the Tier II reimbursement rates.

For your family to be considered low income in 2021, you must meet the following income eligibility guidelines (July 1, 2021–June 30, 2022):

Annual Income	Family of one	Family of two	Each additional person
All states except Alaska and Hawaii	$23,828	$32,227	$8,399
Alaska	$29,767	$40,275	$10,508
Hawaii	$27,417	$37,074	$9,657

FOOD PROGRAM REIMBURSEMENT RATES (PER SERVING)

	Tier I Regular Rate		Tier II Reduced Rate	
	Jan–June	July–Dec	Jan–June	July–Dec
Breakfast	$1.39	$1.40	$0.50	$0.51
Lunch/Supper	$2.61	$2.63	$1.58	$1.59
Snack	$0.78	$0.78	$0.21	$0.21
Total	$4.78	$4.81	$2.29	$2.31

If you live in Alaska and Hawaii, the reimbursement rates are higher:

Alaska

Breakfast	$2.22	$2.23	$0.78	$0.79
Lunch/Supper	$4.24	$4.26	$2.55	$2.57
Snack	$1.26	$1.27	$0.35	$0.35
Total	$7.72	$7.76	$3.68	$3.71

Hawaii

Breakfast	$1.62	$1.63	$0.58	$0.58
Lunch/Supper	$3.06	$3.08	$1.84	$1.86
Snack	$0.91	$0.91	$0.25	$0.25
Total	$5.59	$5.62	$2.67	$2.69

As of July 1, 2021, the Tier I reimbursement per child equaled $1,250 per year for serving a daily breakfast, lunch, and snack. The Tier II reimbursement equaled $600 per year.

These rates are based on a consumer price index that tracks the cost of food served in a home on a national basis. Despite the fact that the Food Program reimbursement rate has not increased as fast as providers would like, you are still always better off financially by joining and remaining on the Food Program.

Reporting CACFP Reimbursements

I recommend that you enter your Food Program reimbursements on **Schedule C**, line 6, and write "CACFP Income" next to this number. This will clearly show the IRS that you are reporting this income. Some providers prefer to include these reimbursements in the parent fees they report on line 1; however, the IRS is always on the alert for unreported income in the child care field. If you combine your Food Program reimbursements with your parent fees, they won't be as identifiable. The IRS may wonder if you have reported all this income properly and might audit your return to find out.

F	Accounting method: (1) ☑ Cash (2) ☐ Accrual (3) ☐ Other (specify) ▶		
G	Did you "materially participate" in the operation of this business during 2021? If "No," see instructions for limit on losses	☑ Yes	☐ No
H	If you started or acquired this business during 2021, check here ▶ ☐		
I	Did you make any payments in 2021 that would require you to file Form(s) 1099? See instructions	☐ Yes	☐ No
J	If "Yes," did you or will you file required Form(s) 1099?	☐ Yes	☐ No

Part I   Income

1	Gross receipts or sales. See instructions for line 1 and check the box if this income was reported to you on Form W-2 and the "Statutory employee" box on that form was checked ▶ ☐	1	
2	Returns and allowances	2	
3	Subtract line 2 from line 1	3	
4	Cost of goods sold (from line 42)	4	
5	**Gross profit.** Subtract line 4 from line 3	5	
6	Other income, including federal and state gasoline or fuel tax credit or refund (see instructions)	6	CACFP $4,250
7	**Gross income.** Add lines 5 and 6 ▶	7	

Form 1099

If you have received **Form 1099 Miscellaneous Income** from your Food Program sponsor, be sure to put the amount listed on it on line 6 and identify it as "1099 Income" instead of "CACFP Income." The IRS computers can check whether all **Form 1099** income was properly reported by those who received this form. You want to make sure that anyone who looks at your **Schedule C** can see that you have reported all of your **Form 1099** income.

Reimbursements for Your Own Children

If you received reimbursements from the Food Program for your own children last year, this income is not taxable; however, some Food Program sponsors don't tell you how much of your monthly reimbursement is for your own children. To calculate how much you were reimbursed for your own children, you can use the worksheets in the Tax Organizer (see pages 30–31). Once you've calculated the total reimbursement for your own children, subtract it from your total reimbursements for the year and enter the result on line 6 of **Schedule C**. Show how you got this total in the space next to line 6 ("$5,000 CACFP, $750 own child").

The IRS can find out the total amount you received from the Food Program and is likely to look for this number on your **Schedule C**. By showing how you got the amount entered there, you'll explain why line 6 doesn't match your total reimbursement amount.

If in a previous year you reported the reimbursements for your own child as income and claimed the same amount as a food expense, then the two amounts almost canceled each other out, and no damage was done. If you reported the reimbursements for your own child as income but didn't claim your food expenses for that child, you should file an amended tax return to get a refund, plus interest (see chapter 9).

Reimbursements for a Foster Child

If you have a foster child and you receive Food Program reimbursements for that child, treat these reimbursements the same way you would for your own children. You're receiving them because your family is income eligible. Therefore, these reimbursements are not taxable income, and the food you serve to a foster child is not a deductible business expense.

Food Stamps

If you receive food stamps, don't report them as income on **Schedule C**, because they are not taxable income. This means that the food you purchase with food stamps can't be deducted as a business expense either. If you receive food stamps, be sure to save records that show how much you received in food stamps.

If One of Your Employees Receives a Check from the Food Program

Some family child care providers operate their business from more than one location and hire employees to care for the children in one or both locations. In this situation, the Food Program will probably issue some of the reimbursement checks to your employee, and your employee should turn over the checks to you. Here's how to handle this transaction on your tax forms:

If your Food Program sponsor sends a **Form 1099** to the employee, the employee should send a **Form 1099** back to you. If the sponsor doesn't use this form, the employee shouldn't do so either. In either case, the employee should show the reimbursement as income on her own **Schedule C** and report the same amount as an expense under line 27 (other expenses). If she does this, she won't owe any tax on this income. You should show the reimbursements as income on your **Schedule C**, line 6 (other income).

Don't Assume That Food Expenses Equal Food Program Reimbursements
Instead of keeping careful food records, some providers just assume that their food expenses equal their Food Program reimbursements, so they report neither of these amounts on their tax return on the assumption that they will "wash out." For example, a provider who received $3,000 from the Food Program would assume that she spent $3,000 on food and not report either number on her **Schedule C**. This is a bad practice.

If you are a Tier I provider, you can justify your deduction by using the standard meal allowance rule and show the IRS your monthly Food Program claim forms to defend your position. If you served extra meals and snacks that weren't reimbursed by the Food Program, then your food deduction will be too low. You can easily claim a higher food deduction by tracking the nonreimbursed meals you serve.

If you are a Tier II provider who evens out your food income and expenses, you are probably cheating yourself out of hundreds of dollars. If you use the standard meal allowance rule, you will always be able to claim food deductions that are at least twice as much as your Food Program income, because you will be claiming food expenses based on the Tier I rate, while reporting income based on the lower Tier II rate. It makes no sense not to claim this extra deduction.

Why Should You Report Your Food Reimbursements This Way?
The instructions in **Publication 587** tell you to report only your net income or expense for food reimbursements. This means that if you received $3,000 in reimbursements and spent $3,500 on business food, you would report no income and a $500 food expense. I recommend that you always show your taxable reimbursement on line 6 and all deductible food expenses on line 27 of **Schedule C**. The tax result is the same with both methods, but showing only the net income or expense is likely to increase your chance of being audited. Many providers spend far more on food than they receive from the Food Program, and showing a large food expense on **Schedule C** without any reimbursement income will draw attention from the IRS, especially for a Tier II provider.

For example, let's say that you are a Tier II provider who has received $2,000 in reimbursements and spent $5,000 on food. If you follow the IRS instructions, you would report $0 income and $3,000 in food expenses. In this case the IRS may assume that you didn't report your Food Program reimbursements and will audit you to find out if you did. All the IRS agents I have consulted recommend that you show your taxable Food Program reimbursements and all your business food deductions on **Schedule C**.

IRS Child Care Provider Audit Technique Guide on Food Expenses
The guide clearly rejects the netting method described in **Publication 587** saying, "The netting method is not a preferred method since an Examiner will always be looking for the food reimbursement amounts." The guide says that the recommended method is to report Food Program reimbursements as income and report all food expenses as expenses on **Schedule C**.

Determining the Cost of Your Food

You now have two choices for how to claim your food expenses: use the IRS standard meal allowance rule or estimate your actual cost of business food. See the *Record-Keeping Guide* for a complete discussion of these two choices.

Using the Standard Meal Allowance Rule

The IRS meal allowance rule allows you to calculate your food expenses by multiplying the meals and snacks you serve to the children in your care by the Tier I Food Program reimbursement rates in effect at the beginning of the calendar year. The rates for calendar year 2021 are $1.39 for breakfast, $2.61 for lunch or supper, and $0.78 for snacks. (The rates are higher in Alaska and Hawaii; see page 94.) **If you use these rates, you won't have to save any of your business or personal food receipts.**

You can use the meal allowance for up to one breakfast, one lunch, one supper, and three snacks per child per day. (The Food Program rules haven't changed; they still only reimburse up to three servings a day.) You must actually serve a meal in order to count it.

All family child care providers are eligible to use this rule, including those who aren't licensed or registered, those who receive the lower Tier II reimbursement rate, those who aren't on the Food Program, and those who are operating illegally. You can use the meal allowance one year and estimate your actual cost of food the next year. If you spend less on food than the standard meal allowance, you can still use it.

You can't use the meal allowance rate if you provide care in a building that isn't your home, and you may not count a meal if the child's parent has supplied the food. You also can't count any meals you serve to your own child. (Food Program reimbursements for your own children aren't taxable income.)

You can count meals you serve to employees as an actual food cost separate from the meal allowance rate (you must save the receipts). Or you could use the standard meal allowance. You may deduct only 50% of the cost of food served to employees while they are working. So either deduct 50% of the actual food cost or 50% of the standard meal allowance rate. A special rule for 2021 and 2022 allows you to deduct 100% of the food cost of your employee if the food is provided by a restaurant. If you hire your child to work for you, you can deduct the actual cost of the food served to your child if that child is eating in the middle of his workday. You may deduct any food you serve as part of an activity (rather than a meal or snack) as a separate activity expense rather than a food expense. For example, you can deduct the cost of a cake that you serve at a birthday party or the ingredients for a gingerbread house. Nonfood meal preparation supplies, such as containers, paper products, and utensils, continue to be deductible.

To use the standard meal allowance rule, you must maintain the following records: the name of each child, the dates and hours each child was in your care, and the number of breakfasts, lunches, suppers, and snacks served. The IRS provides a meal and snack log you can use to track this information. In addition, the *Redleaf Calendar-Keeper* has two pages of charts that meet IRS requirements, and those are included in Part I of this book.

Estimating Your Actual Cost of Food

If you are trying to decide whether to use the standard meal allowance rule or your actual cost of food, you may want to estimate the actual cost of the food you serve based on several weeks of menus and compare it with the standard meal allowance rate. It's important to keep in mind that if you choose to estimate your actual cost of food rather than using the standard meal allowance, you will have to keep receipts for all the business and personal food you purchase.

There are many ways to estimate your actual food expenses (the *Record-Keeping Guide* describes several). Usually the simplest and most accurate method is to estimate your average cost per meal per child, and then multiply this by the total number of meals you served.

Reporting Your Food Expenses

It's best to claim your deduction for food expenses on one of the blank lines in **Schedule C**, Part V, Other Expenses, although you can also put it elsewhere on this form. Wherever you choose to put it, be sure to identify it clearly as "Food" rather than including it under a general heading, such as "Other," because the IRS will be looking for it. If you're a Tier II provider who spends thousands of dollars more for food than you're reimbursed by the Food Program, you should identify yourself as such by writing "Food (Tier II Provider)" next to your food deduction, rather than simply "Food."

Since large individual expense amounts on **Schedule C** can trigger an audit, don't include any nonfood items in your food expenses. Remove items such as paper products and kitchen supplies from your food receipts and claim them on a different line, such as line 22 (supplies). The food expenses you list on Part V are carried over to line 27 (other expenses) on the front page of **Schedule C**.

If you serve meals to your employees, you can deduct 50% of the cost of the food (for 2021 and 2022, 100% if the food was provided by a restaurant), and your employees don't have to report these meals as income. You can either include this cost with your other food expenses or list it separately as "Employee meals" on one of the blank lines in Part V. You could enter employee meals on line 24b. (If you are reporting "Employee meals," make sure you have filed all the proper payroll forms for these employees [see chapter 8].)

Part V	Other Expenses. List below business expenses not included on lines 8–26 or line 30.	
FOOD		$5,540
or NOT ON FOOD PROGRAM		$5,540
or FOOD (TIER II PROVIDER)		$5,540
EMPLOYEE MEALS		$600

Summary of Food Income and Expenses

Here's a summary of the rules about which food expenses you can deduct as a business expense and how to treat your income from the Food Program and food stamps:

	Report as Taxable Income?	Deduct as a Food Expense?
FOOD INCOME		
Food Program reimbursements for children in your care	Yes	
Food Program reimbursements for your own child	No	
Food Program reimbursements for your foster child	No	
Food stamps for your own family	No	
FOOD EXPENSES		
Food eaten by the children in your care		Yes
Food eaten by you during business hours at home		No
Food eaten by your own child during business hours		No
Lunch leftovers eaten by your family		No
Nonreimbursed meals eaten by the children in your care		Yes
Noncreditable food (ice cream, potato chips, and so on) eaten by the children in your care		Yes
Food eaten by a paid employee during business hours		Yes (but only 50% of the cost)
Food eaten by foster children		No

> **For more information about the tax issues discussed in this chapter, refer to the related topics in the other chapters of this book and the Redleaf Press** *Family Child Care Record-Keeping Guide*.

CHAPTER 5

Reporting Your Business Income
and Expenses: Schedule C

This chapter explains how to fill out **Schedule C** Profit or Loss from Business. On this form you'll report both your business income and your business expenses. You'll find more information about how to calculate and report specific kinds of business income and expenses, such as depreciation, in other chapters of this book. This chapter will take you step-by-step through **Schedule C**. (A copy of **Schedule C** is included in the tax forms at the back of this book.)

If you and your husband work side by side caring for children, you may want to consider filing two **Schedule C**s (see pages 117–118). You can then split the income and expenses between the two of you. This may be an option if you want your husband to show more income to increase his Social Security benefits. Before taking this step, consult with a Social Security expert to see the long-term impact on Social Security benefits for both of you. Before reading about how to fill out each line of **Schedule C**, some general issues about how to enter your income and expenses on this form will be addressed.

Reporting Income (Part I of Schedule C)

Part I of **Schedule C** is where you will enter all your income. In addition to parent fees, you must report as income any payments you received from county social service agencies for care you provide to low-income parents. Report all of this income on **Schedule C**, line 1. If you received reimbursements from the Food Program, see chapter 4 for instructions on how to report this income.

IRS Child Care Provider Audit Technique Guide on Reporting Income
The guide makes it clear that the IRS will look very closely to make sure a provider is reporting all her income. They may examine a provider's contract and policies to see if she got paid additional amounts for late pickup, overnight care, transportation, diaper fees, holding fees, and so on. Providers should keep careful records showing the source of all deposits into checking and savings accounts (both business and personal). If you did not receive the full amount from a parent, as stated in your contract, make a note of the reason. For example, if your contract says that your fee is $150 a week, the IRS would assume you received $7,800 a year from the parent ($150 x 52 weeks). Reasons why you may not have received this full amount could include unpaid vacation or

sick time, part-time care, forgiving payments for a laid-off parent, or debt from a parent who left child care. Without records showing deposits of parent payments, you may have trouble showing why you earned less than the full amount.

Cash Payments

If you receive any cash payments, you should record them in a cash journal. Enter the dates you provided child care, the child's and parent's names, the amount, and the date of payment. The IRS is always looking for signs of unreported income, and a cash journal will help your case if you need to show that you didn't earn any more money than you reported. Here's a sample entry from a cash journal:

CASH JOURNAL

Dates of Care	Child/Parent	Amount Pd.	Date Pd.
Jan 3–Jan 7	Jenny/Carol Martinez	$100	Jan 3
Jan 10–Jan 14	Jenny/Carol Martinez	$100	Jan 10

Here's how to report some of the other kinds of business income you may have received last year.

Grants

If you received grants from a government agency (usually for start-up expenses or home renovations), this money is most likely taxable income. If the granting agency has sent you **Form 1099G** Certain Government Payments, the IRS will be sure to check to see that you have reported this income. Even if you didn't receive **Form 1099G**, you should report the grant as income. Enter your income from grants on **Schedule C**, not on **Form 1040**.

Since you are reporting the grant as income, you will deduct the items you buy with the grant money according to the usual rules for claiming deductions. For example, if you use the grant money to buy a home improvement (such as a deck), you will have to depreciate that expense over several years (see chapter 3). This will reduce your deductions and increase your taxes in the current year.

The only situation in which you don't have to report a grant as income is if you qualify for it because your family has a low income. If a grant is offered only to low-income families, it may be considered a welfare payment (like food stamps) rather than taxable income. (If you don't know if your grant qualifies, contact the granting agency.) You can't deduct the items you buy with nontaxable grant money as a business deduction.

Loans

Some loans given to family child care providers for purchasing business equipment are structured so that the loan is forgiven (you don't have to pay it back) if you stay in business for two years. Normally you don't have to report a loan as income; however, when a business loan is forgiven, you need to report the amount of the loan as income on **Schedule C**, line 6. In the year you receive the loan, don't report any of the money as income; simply deduct the items that you purchased with the loan money as business expenses.

Gifts from Parents

In general you must report as business income any cash, gift certificates, or items you receive from the parents of the children in your care. Report these gifts on **Schedule C**, line 1. However, if a parent gives you a gift that is not directly related to your business, you do not have to report these gifts as income. Examples would include birthday gifts or holiday gifts. If you use any of these gifts in your business, don't treat them as an expense.

If a parent gives you a noncash gift as a partial or total payment for child care services, then the item isn't really a gift, and you do have to report it as income. For example, if the parent gives you a $20 scarf as partial payment for child care, you have to report it as income.

Refunds to Parents

Some providers offer a discount to parents who pay for blocks of time in advance. If one of your parents moves away before the end of the paid-up period and you refund some of her money, then subtract the refund from the original payment and report only the net income. If you reported the original payment as income in one year and gave the refund in the next year, the refund becomes a business expense, and you will report it on **Schedule C**, Part V.

Military Housing Allowances

Some family child care providers receive military housing allowances that are called BAQ (Basic Allowance for Quarters) or VHA (Variable Housing Allowance). These housing allowances are not taxable income, so don't report them on **Schedule C**. If you receive a housing allowance but live off-base, see page 56. See the *Record-Keeping Guide* for a full discussion of military housing allowances.

Foster Care Allowances

Some family child care providers receive payments for child or foster care under an arrangement with a charitable organization or governmental agency. These payments don't have to be reported on **Schedule C** if they are received from a foster care placement agency that is licensed or certified by a state or local government or from an agency that is designated by a state or local government to make such payments, because those payments are exempt from federal taxes. Since the payments aren't taxable, you can't deduct any expenses you incur for these children. See the *Record-Keeping Guide* for a full discussion of foster care allowances.

Respite Care Payments

If you receive payments from a government agency for offering respite care for a family, this money is taxable income. (Respite care is usually provided for families that need to be separated from their children on a short-term basis.) Report these payments as income on **Schedule C**, line 1. You can deduct the expenses you incur in caring for a child in respite care in the same way you do your expenses for regular child care children.

Interest

If you have earned any interest on a business checking or savings account, don't enter it on **Schedule C**. You must report that type of interest income on **Schedule B**.

Claiming Expenses (Part II of Schedule C)

Part II of **Schedule C** is where you will show all the deductions for your business expenses (sometimes after transferring the information from another tax form). The major expense lines that are listed on **Schedule C** are as follows:

- Line 8: Advertising
- Line 9: Car and truck expenses
- Line 13: Depreciation
- Line 14: Employee benefit programs
- Line 15: Insurance (other than health)
- Line 16: Interest
- Line 17: Legal and professional services
- Line 18: Office expenses
- Line 20: Rent or lease
- Line 21: Repairs and maintenance (of personal property used in the business)
- Line 22: Supplies
- Line 23: Taxes and licenses
- Line 24: Travel, meals, and entertainment
- Line 26: Wages
- Line 27: Other expenses (the total of all the items you've listed on the blank lines in Part V, such as food, toys, household items, cleaning supplies, and activity expenses)

Some of these major line items are covered in more detail in other parts of this book. For example, there's a section on vehicle expenses at the end of this chapter. The topic of depreciation is covered in chapter 3, and issues related to paying wages and hiring employees are covered in chapter 8. If you have any questions about how to calculate the deductions for any of these items, see the relevant part of this book.

If some of your business expenses don't seem to fit on any of the lines on **Schedule C**, bear in mind that it doesn't matter on which line you enter your expenses. The IRS won't penalize you for listing a business expense on one line rather than another. This means that you can make your own decision about what to categorize as supplies or office expenses or any other line on **Schedule C**; however, use the words *de minimis equipment* to describe toys, cribs, or other items that cost less than $2,500. (For suggestions on how to categorize your expenses, see the *Record-Keeping Guide*.)

To reduce your chance of an audit, don't lump large expense items together on one line. Instead, use the blank spaces under line 27, other expenses, to list items such as food, cleaning supplies, and activity expenses. If any line on your **Schedule C** is unusually high in comparison with your income, it may trigger an audit. For example, if your income on **Schedule C** is $15,000 and you list $8,000 for cleaning supplies, this will draw attention to your return. If your total expenses are reasonable, and you have just put all your food expenses, kitchen supplies, and children's supplies on line 22, then you don't need to worry. If you're audited, you will need to show the IRS all your records to demonstrate that your expenses are valid.

Calculating the Deductions for Your Business Expenses

You can deduct only the portion of an expense that relates to your business. To calculate how much you can deduct for each business expense, you need to follow the instructions given in chapters 1 through 3 for completing **Form 4562** and Part I of **Form 8829**. If you haven't completed those sections yet, you should do it now. (Calculating the deductions for your business expenses can be a complicated process. If you have any questions about this topic, refer to the *Record-Keeping Guide*, which lists over 1,000 potential business expenses and explains how to deduct them.)

As I described in the previous chapters of this book, you will need to divide all your expenses into three categories:

1. 100% personal use (such as jewelry and cigarettes)

2. 100% business use (such as child care food and the toys used only in your business)

3. Shared business and personal use (such as cleaning supplies and lightbulbs)

If an expense is 100% personal use, you can't deduct any of it as a business expense. If it is 100% business use, you can deduct all of it as a business expense. If it has both business and personal uses, you can deduct only part of it as a business expense.

There are two ways to determine the business portion of a shared expense; you can multiply the cost of the item either by your Time-Space percentage (covered in chapter 1) or by the item's actual business-use percentage. For most items, you will use your Time-Space percentage; for some items you may prefer to use an actual business-use percentage, especially if the expense was large and the business-use percentage is significantly higher than your Time-Space percentage.

Determining the Actual Business-Use Percentage

To determine the actual business-use percentage of an item, you need to track how much time you use the item for your business and how much time you use it for personal purposes. Divide the number of hours of business use by the total number of hours you used the item. For example, if you used an item three hours a week for business and nine hours a week for personal purposes, your business-use percentage would be 25% ($3 \div [3 + 9]$).

You must keep careful notes about how you calculated your business deductions and be able to support them if you are audited. Do your calculations on another sheet of paper, and enter only the business portion of your expenses on **Schedule C**. For example, let's say that you spent a total (business and personal) of $100 for paper towels last year. If your Time-Space percentage is 30%, you can enter $30 on **Schedule C** (probably on line 22). If you determine that 55% of the towels were used for your business, your business-use percentage is 55%, and you can enter $55 instead.

In addition, on line 18 for office expenses, you're claiming the following: books $50 (100% business); business birthday cards $20 (100% business); computer paper $15 (60% actual business use); internet access fees $250 (50% actual business use); office supplies $100 (40% Time-Space percentage); and magazines $50 (40% Time-Space percentage).

The best way to organize these expenses is to list them by category:

100% Business		Time-Space Percentage		Actual Business-Use Percentage	
books	$50	office supplies	$100	computer paper $15 x 60% =	$9
birthday cards	<u>$20</u>	magazines	<u>$50</u>	internet fee $250 x 50% =	<u>$125</u>
Subtotal:	$70	Subtotal:	$150	Subtotal:	$134
			x 40% = $60		

Total Office Expense: $264 ($70 + $60 + $134)

In this example, you would keep this calculation for your files and enter $264 on line 18.

If You Operate Two Home-Based Businesses

If you operate two businesses out of your home, you must file a separate **Schedule C** for each business and report your income and expenses for each business separately. If you earn money on child care–related activities (such as child care training or consulting), enter all your income and expenses for these activities on the same **Schedule C** as your child care business.

Allocate your expenses on a reasonable basis between the two **Schedule C**s. Transfer the net income from both of them to one **Form 1040 Schedule SE**. If you're entitled to claim the home office deduction for your other business, you must also file a separate **Form 8829** for each business. If your other business claims part of your home on **Form 8829**, you won't be able to claim a 100% Space percentage for your child care business.

How to Fill Out Schedule C

On the first few lines of **Schedule C**, enter your name and Social Security number at the top of the page, and then proceed as follows:

Line A: Enter "Family Child Care."

Line B: Enter your principal business code: 624410 Child Day Care Services.

Line C: If your business has an official name, enter it here. If not, leave the line blank. See your state rules regarding any requirements for having a business name.

Line D: Enter your employer identification number, if you have one.

Line E: Enter your business address.

Line F: Select method (1) Cash. This doesn't mean that you're paid in cash; it means that you report your income when you receive it and your expenses when you incur them. For example, if a parent pays you in January of this year for services provided in December of last year, you will report the payment as income next tax season. If you received a check in December of last year that you don't deposit until January of this year, you count it as income for this tax season. If you buy something for your business with a credit card, you count it as an expense the month you sign the credit card receipt, not the month you pay your credit card bill. (Once you charge something on your credit card, you are legally obligated to pay the bill.)

Line G: Enter "yes." You are considered to have materially participated in your business if you meet any one of the following tests: (1) you worked more than 500 hours in the year, (2) you were the sole participant in your business (no employees), or (3) you worked more than 100 hours, and no other person worked more time than you.

Line H: If this is the first year you have filed **Schedule C**, check the box.

Line I: If you hired an independent contractor and paid any person $600 or more, you are required to file **Form 1099**. If this is true for you, check "yes." If not, check "no." See the form's instructions for details. If you paid a house cleaner, gardener, or someone to mow your lawn or plow your driveway, and you wrote a check to a corporation, you do not need to submit **Form 1099**. If you paid the individual directly, you do. **Note**: If you hire an assistant to help you care for children, this person is an employee, not an independent contractor; this is true no matter how little you pay the person. See chapter 8 for details.

Line J: If you are required to file **Form 1099**, check "yes." If you check "yes" on line I and fail to check it on line J, your chance of being audited will increase.

Part I: Income

Line 1:   Enter all your income from parent fees here, including cash payments. Also enter any payments from social service agencies for care you provided to low-income parents.

Lines 2, 3, and 4.   Leave these lines blank.

Line 5:   Enter the amount from line 1.

Line 6:   Enter any other business income you received, such as CACFP reimbursements, grants, gifts, and loans that have been forgiven.

Line 7:   Add lines 5 and 6. This is your gross income.

Part II: Expenses

Line 8:   **Advertising**. Enter any advertising expenses, which may include business cards, welcome mats, newspaper ads, keepsakes, and children's T-shirts (for more information, refer to the *Family Child Care Marketing Guide,* which lists over 100 advertising deductions).

Line 9:   **Car and truck expenses**. Enter the vehicle expenses you have incurred for business purposes here. For information on how to calculate this amount, see the section on vehicle expenses at the end of this chapter.

Line 10:   **Commissions and fees**. Leave blank.

Line 11:   **Contract labor**. Enter the amount you paid to independent contractors (see pages 147–148).

Line 12:   **Depletion**. Leave blank.

Line 13:   **Depreciation**. Enter the amount from **Form 4562**, line 22 (see chapter 3). Make sure you have not included in this amount any depreciation expenses for your house or home improvements. Instead, claim these expenses on **Form 8829** (see chapter 2).

Line 14:   **Employee benefit programs**. Enter the cost of any benefits you provide your employees such as health, life, or disability insurance.

Line 15: **Insurance**. Enter the total of any liability insurance you carry for your business and any workers' compensation insurance you purchase for yourself or your employees. Workers' compensation insurance protects a provider or employee who is injured while working. Insurance coverage can include medical benefits, disability income, rehabilitation expenses, and other costs. Liability and workers' compensation insurance is 100% deductible. Life insurance and disability income insurance for yourself are not deductible. Health insurance premiums for yourself aren't deductible on **Schedule C**, but they may be deductible on **Form 1040** (see chapter 6). Don't deduct your homeowners or renters insurance here; put these on **Form 8829** instead (see chapter 2). For a complete discussion of insurance, see the *Family Child Care Legal and Insurance Guide*.

Line 16: **Interest**. Enter the business portion of any interest you paid on items purchased for your business. For example, in January of last year, you bought some large play equipment on credit for $750. Your Time-Space percentage is 25%. By the end of last year, you paid $75 in interest on this purchase. In this case, you can deduct $18.75 ($75 x 25% = $18.75) as a business interest deduction on line 16.

You can put the business-use percentage of your vehicle loan interest on this line or include it in your vehicle expenses on line 9. Don't enter mortgage interest here; instead, enter it on **Form 8829** (see chapter 2). Report any interest you've earned on your business checking or saving accounts on **Schedule B**.

Loan Payments

You can't deduct the loan payments you make on an item purchased for your business. You can depreciate the item or take a Section 179 deduction, even if you're still making payments on it. You can also deduct the business portion of the interest you're paying on the loan.

Line 17: **Legal and professional services**. Enter the total of any legal and professional services you incurred for your business. This includes any costs you incur if you go to small-claims court over a business matter as well as the tax preparation fees to do your business tax forms (**Form 4562**, **Schedule C**, **Form 8829**, **Schedule SE**, **Form 1040-ES**, **Form 8826**, **Form 3115**, payroll tax forms, and others). Ask your tax preparer how much of the fee is for your business tax forms. (You can no longer deduct the tax preparation fees for your personal tax forms).

Line 18: **Office expenses**. Enter the total of any office expenses you incurred (such as bank charges, books, magazines, desk supplies, receipt books), as well as any education or training expenses for yourself.

Line 19: **Pension and profit-sharing plans**. Enter the cost of any pension or profit-sharing plans you have set up for your employees.

Line 20: **Rent or lease**. Enter your total expenses for renting videotapes, carpet cleaning machines, and other business property. If you rent your home, don't enter that expense here; list it on line 19 of **Form 8829** (see chapter 2).

Line 21: **Repairs and maintenance**. Enter your total expenses for repair or maintenance of your personal property, such as appliance service contracts or repair of broken toys. Enter the costs of repair and maintenance of your home on **Form 8829**, line 20 (see chapter 2).

Line 22: **Supplies**. Enter your total expenses for supplies, such as children's supplies (craft items and games) and kitchen supplies (plastic wrap, garbage bags, and food containers).

Line 23: **Taxes and licenses**. Enter the total you've paid for taxes and licenses. Include any payroll taxes you've paid for the employer portion of Social Security, Medicare, and federal unemployment taxes. Also include any license fees you've paid. The sales taxes you've paid on items bought for your business can either be entered here or be included in the cost of each item. Enter your property taxes on **Form 8829**, line 11 (see chapter 2).

Line 24: **Travel, meals, and entertainment**. On line 24a, enter the total lodging and travel costs (such as airfare, bus fare, train fare, vehicle rental, or mileage) you incurred when traveling away from home overnight for a child care conference or other business activity.

On line 24b, enter your deductible meal costs. You can keep receipts for all your meal expenses, or you can claim a per diem meal rate. For trips to many areas of the United States, that rate is $55 a day for 2021. (See the U.S. General Services Administration website for a list of the per diem rates across the country: www.gsa.gov/perdiem.) You don't need any receipts to claim the standard rate, but you must use only one of these methods for all your trips in the year.

You can usually only deduct 50% of your business meal expenses, including the meal per diem rates. But for 2021 and 2022, you can deduct 100% of your business meal expenses if the meals were provided by a restaurant. If you use the per diem meal rate for out-of-town travel overnight, you can also use the special rule to deduct 100% of that meal rate. Add up your total deductible meal expenses and enter that amount on line 24b.

Note: If you use the per diem meal rate, you may be only to deduct 50% of that rate, even if the meals were from a restaurant. However, the IRS has not clarified that situation yet. If you are limited to 50%, it may be better to use the actual expense so you can claim 100% of the meals provided by restaurants. Don't enter your food expenses for the children in your care on line 24b; enter them in Part V (see chapter 4).

If you go out and eat a meal with another child care provider, you can deduct 100% (50% if meal is not provided by a restaurant) of the cost of your meal if the discussion during the meal is primarily business related. You should be fairly conservative in claiming such meals as business deductions. If you deduct a meal with another provider, keep a record of who attended the discussion and what topics were discussed. If you take the parent of a child in your care out for a meal, you can deduct 100% (50% if meal is not provided by a restaurant) of the amount that you paid for your meal and the parent's meal on line 24b.

Line 25: **Utilities**. Don't enter your home utilities (gas, electricity, water, sewer, garbage, and cable television) here; put them on line 21 of **Form 8829**, where they'll be added to the home expenses you carry over to line 30 of **Schedule C** (see chapter 2).

The utilities expense that remains to be put on line 25 is usually telephone service. You can't claim a business deduction for basic monthly service for the first phone line into your home, even if you only installed the phone as a requirement to be licensed. If your phone bill is charged on a cost-per-minute basis, see line 21 on page 51.

If you install a second phone line and use it exclusively for your business, you can deduct 100% of this expense. If you use a second phone line partly for your business, you can deduct the Time-Space percentage of its cost.

Note: A cell phone is not deductible if it is the first line into your home. If you don't have a landline phone and have only one cell phone line, you cannot deduct any portion of your cell phone use.

You can deduct all other phone-related business expenses, such as long-distance calls, call waiting, an answering machine, and Yellow Pages advertising. If you wish, you can depreciate the cost of buying a phone (as other personal property; see chapter 3).

Schedule C versus Form 8829

Both **Schedule C** and **Form 8829** have lines for utilities, mortgage interest, repairs and maintenance, and insurance, which can give rise to some confusion about where to record certain expenses. The answer is that you should enter all the expenses related to your home on **Form 8829** and only the expenses related to your personal property on **Schedule C**. Here's a guide to which expenses to enter on each form:

Form 8829	**Schedule C**
Home utilities	Business repairs: toys, lawn mower,
Real estate taxes	furniture, freestanding appliances, etc.
Mortgage interest	Payroll taxes
Renters insurance	Liability insurance
Home repairs: furnace, plumbing,	Insurance on personal property
electrical, built-in appliances, etc.	Interest from home equity loan used
Home maintenance	to purchase nonhome items
Homeowners insurance	
Home depreciation	

If you run your business out of a building other than your home, don't follow this guide; instead, enter all your expenses for the building in which your business is located on **Schedule C**; you won't fill out **Form 8829** at all, since you don't have a home-based business.

Line 26: **Wages**. Enter any gross wages you paid to employees, including each employee's share of Social Security, Medicare, and any state taxes you have withheld. (For more information about paying employees, see chapter 8.)

Line 27: **Other expenses**. This is the total of the expenses listed on the blank lines in Part V of **Schedule C**. To get this total, go to Part V and list there all your remaining business expense categories, including food, toys, household items, cleaning supplies, and activity expenses (which are all major expenses for most family child care providers). Refer to the *Record-Keeping Guide* for many other kinds of expenses that you might include here. Because of the $2,500 rule (see pages 60–61), many more items may appear here rather than on **Form 4562**. These items could include furniture, appliances, playground equipment, fences, patios, and driveways. You can put them here on Line 27 and call them whatever you want: "$2,500 Property" or "Equipment" or "Household Items" or "Fence." It doesn't matter what you call these expenses. The following are special considerations for toys and gifts:

Toys. The IRS **Child Care Provider Audit Technique Guide** places special emphasis on toy expenses. If a provider is deducting a significant amount for toys, the guide suggests that the auditor investigate whether some of those expenses were really toys for her own children. You should keep receipts for the toys that you purchase for your own children to help prove that your business deduction is reasonable.

Gifts. You can deduct up to $25 (plus any cost of shipping and wrapping) per person each year for gifts to the parents of a child in your care. (You must spend the money on gifts to be able to take the deduction.) Any gifts you give to the children themselves may be a gift or it may be an activity expense. If it's an activity expense, there is no $25 per person limitation. A gift is an item that is used by only one child in your care, such as a gift card or clothing. A gift is also a wrapped present that the child opens at her own home and doesn't bring back to your home for the other children to play with it. An activity expense is a present you give to the child in your home who then allows the other children to play with it. It's still an activity even if the child then takes the present home and never returns with it. Don't list activity expenses as "gifts," or the IRS will assume that the $25 rule applies to them; instead, list them as activity expenses.

Line 28: Enter the subtotal of your direct business expenses by adding lines 8 through 27.

Line 29: Enter the total of line 28 minus line 7. This represents your tentative profit before subtracting the expenses for the business use of your home that you entered on **Form 8829**. You must complete **Form 8829** before you can continue with **Schedule C** (see chapter 2).

Line 30: A 2013 rule allows providers to choose between two methods when claiming house expenses. The first method is to claim these expenses from **Form 8829** (enter the amount from line 35). The second method (the Simplified Method) requires no receipts and involves using the following formula: $5 x your Time percentage x the number of square feet you use your home for your business (not to exceed 300 square feet). Almost all providers use at least 300 square feet of their home. Here's an example, if your Time percentage was 40%: $5 x 40% x 300 = $600. Thus, this provider would claim $600 on line 30 of **Schedule C**. She would also be entitled to claim 100% of her property tax and mortgage interest on **Schedule A**, if she itemized. Follow the instructions to **Schedule C** to use this method.

   Warning: The vast majority of providers will be better off using their house expenses as shown on **Form 8829**, rather than using the Simplified Method. If you use the Simplified Method and later discover that you would have been better off using your **Form 8829** expenses, you cannot amend your tax return to fix this. Therefore, do not use the Simplified Method unless you have compared it to what you could have claimed using **Form 8829**.

Line 31: Subtract line 30 from line 29. This is your net profit or loss from your business. Enter this amount on **Form 1040 Schedule 1**, line 12, and **Schedule SE**, line 2.

Line 32: If you have a loss on line 31, check box 32a, "All investment is at risk."

Showing a Loss on Schedule C
If you don't show a profit at least three years out of every five, the IRS may look more closely at your tax returns to determine if you're really trying to make a profit. You must be able to show that you're acting in a businesslike manner in a serious effort to make a profit. Most providers won't need to worry about this, but if you only care for children infrequently, you should not try to claim a loss.

   The IRS **Child Care Provider Audit Technique Guide** states that it is unusual for a family child care business to show a loss. Although this is an overstatement, if you have a legitimate loss, you should be prepared to defend it with good records.

If you claim regular losses, the IRS may take the position that you could have taken in more children or worked longer hours to make a profit. If it rules that you aren't in business to make a profit, it may reduce your business expenses.

Part III: Cost of Goods Sold

Lines 33–40: Skip this section; it doesn't apply to family child care businesses.

Part IV: Information on Your Vehicle

See the example under the section titled Standard Mileage Rate Method on the following pages for instructions on filling out this section.

Congratulations!

You have completed the second-most time-consuming tax form (according to the IRS). For most of you, the hard work is done. After calculating your self-employment tax on **Schedule SE**, you'll be ready to fill out **Form 1040** and file your return. If you need to fill out any other tax forms that address issues such as the Earned Income Credit, the sale of your home, or education credits, see the relevant chapters of this book. If you deliver child care out of a building that is not your home, enter all of your home expenses on **Schedule C** (mortgage interest, house depreciation, homeowners insurance, property tax, rent, house repairs, and utilities), not on **Form 8829**.

Vehicle Expenses (Line 9)

There are two ways to calculate the vehicle expenses that you deduct on line 9—the standard mileage rate method and the actual vehicle expenses method. Which method is better for you?

- The standard mileage rate method allows you simply to multiply your business miles by a set rate and claim the result as your deduction. In addition, you can claim the business portion of your vehicle loan interest and personal property tax, as well as your expenses for parking and tolls.

- The actual vehicle expenses method allows you to claim the business portion of all the expenses associated with your vehicle (gas, repairs, insurance, and so on). If you use this method, you must keep all your receipts for those expenses.

Traditionally, most providers have chosen the standard mileage rate over the actual vehicle expenses method, since the record keeping is simpler. You can calculate your business deduction using both methods and use the one that offers the higher deduction.

If you are now considering using the actual vehicle expenses method, you should try hard to save all your receipts for vehicle expenses. You may be able to reconstruct some of these records; for example, if you bought gas with a credit card, save the copies of your credit card statements that show this. If you bought gas with cash, divide the miles you have driven by your car's average miles per gallon to calculate how many gallons of gas you have used. Then reconstruct what you spent by multiplying the number of gallons by the average price of gas over that period.

If you used the actual vehicle expenses method in the first year you used your vehicle for your business, you can't switch to the standard mileage rate method in later years. If you used the standard mileage rate in the first year you used your vehicle for your business, you can switch to the actual vehicle expenses method in later years. (After you change to the actual vehicle expenses method, you must use straight-line depreciation on your vehicle; see chapter 3. If you lease a vehicle, you cannot switch methods after the first year, no matter which method you use.)

Whichever method you use, you will need to track all your business miles, even if you use the vehicle 100% for business purposes. To track your business trips, refer to records such as receipts, canceled checks, credit card statements, field trip permission forms, training certificates, and calendar notations, or keep a mileage log. (The *Family Child Care Mileage-Keeper* makes it easy to record your mileage.)

If the Vehicle Isn't Registered in Your Name

If you are married, you can claim business expenses for both your vehicle and your spouse's vehicle, even if your name isn't on the vehicle registration.

If you aren't married and use a vehicle that isn't registered to you, you can't claim vehicle expenses for that vehicle. For example, if you use your boyfriend's vehicle, you can't claim any expenses for it, even if he drives it for your business trips.

If you pay your boyfriend for the use of his vehicle or to make a business trip for you, you can deduct these expenses as rent on **Schedule C**, line 20a, and your boyfriend will have to report this payment as income on line 21 of his **Form 1040**. The same is true if you pay anyone else for the use of a vehicle.

Is the Trip Business or Personal?

To determine the vehicle expenses you have incurred for your business, you need to decide which trips are deductible and which aren't. If you take a trip that involves both business and personal activities, you may still deduct the entire mileage as a business expense if the trip is primarily for business purposes.

What if you take a trip to the grocery store and buy both business and personal groceries? That can be the hardest kind of trip to judge, and there's no firm rule about whether you can deduct the mileage. The only rule is that if the trip was primarily to buy business groceries, you can deduct it as a business trip. Some factors that might make the trip a business expense include the following:

- You purchased more business than personal groceries.

- You spent more time shopping for business items than for personal items.

- You made other separate personal trips to the grocery store; this trip was for regular business shopping.

IRS Child Care Provider Audit Technique Guide on Car Expenses
The guide says that if there is a business destination and a personal destination in one trip that only the round trip miles to and from the business destination are deductible. For example, if a provider drove 5 miles to point A (business purpose) and then 3 miles to point B (personal purpose) and then 4 miles home, she could count 10 miles as business miles (the round-trip miles to and from point A).

The Standard Mileage Rate Method

The standard mileage rate is $0.56 per business mile for 2021. In addition to your mileage, you may also deduct the following:

- parking fees and tolls

- bus, subway, and train fares for business trips

- any casualty or theft losses on your vehicle

- the business percentage of the interest payments on your vehicle loan

- the business percentage of the local personal property tax on your vehicle

Some tax preparers and IRS auditors are unaware that you are entitled to claim these last two deductions even when you're using the standard mileage rate. (See IRS **Publication 463** for a clear statement of this rule.)

When you use the standard mileage rate method, you need to keep adequate records of how many miles you have driven your vehicle for business. Here's how to calculate your deduction using the standard mileage rate method:

STEP ONE

Go through your business records for last year and write down the destination of every trip you took for your business. Look through your checkbook receipts and calendar for evidence of business trips. If you took more than one trip to the same destination (grocery store, bank, and so on), count the number of trips to each destination.

STEP TWO

Determine the number of miles to each destination. Try to make a habit of recording your trip mileage as you make trips throughout the year. If you haven't done this, use an internet mapping service (such as Waze or Google Maps) to find the length of the trip (or drive to the destination again and record the mileage).

STEP THREE

Multiply the mileage to and from each destination by the number of trips you took to each destination last year. Add the miles together for all the destinations, and multiply the total by the standard mileage rate, which will give you your business-mileage deduction. Here's an example:

Al's Grocery Store	3 miles	x	48 trips	=	144 miles
First Bank	2 miles	x	60 trips	=	120 miles
Como Park	5 miles	x	12 trips	=	60 miles
Tots Toy Store	4 miles	x	10 trips	=	40 miles
Safeway Grocery Store	5 miles	x	40 trips	=	200 miles
Other trips (list)					266 miles
Total miles					830 miles

830 miles (Jan 1–Dec 31) x $0.575 = $477.25

STEP FOUR

Add to the Step Three total any parking fees, tolls, or bus, subway, or train fares you paid while conducting business activities, and enter the total on **Schedule C**, line 9. Keep records showing how you calculated these amounts. If you drive more than one vehicle, you can claim the business mileage rate for both vehicles. Enter any expenses for renting or leasing a vehicle on **Schedule C**, line 20a.

The advantage of the standard mileage rate method is that you don't have to remember to record your mileage every time you take a business trip. Your check stubs, receipts, or notes on your calendar constitute evidence that a trip was taken. To make your record keeping easier, remember to record the odometer reading on your vehicle on January 1 of each year. Once you have measured the mileage to and from each destination, you can use that mileage number forever.

If you use the standard mileage rate method, you can't deduct the cost of vehicle insurance (even for a separate business policy) or vehicle repairs (even if the damage results from using the vehicle for business). To deduct these expenses, you must use the actual vehicle expenses method. When you use the standard mileage rate method, fill out **Schedule C**, Part IV, only if you don't have any depreciation expenses to show on **Form 4562**. Otherwise, fill out **Form 4562**, Part V, Section B, instead of **Schedule C**, Part IV.

Enter the date you first began using your vehicle for your business on line 43 of **Schedule C**. Enter the total business miles you drove last year on line 44a. (This may include mileage from more than one vehicle.) Don't enter anything under Commuting on line 44b. Put your personal vehicle miles on line 44c. Answer yes on line 45 if you use your car for personal purposes. Line 46 asks if your family had another vehicle available

---

Part IV **Information on Your Vehicle.** Complete this part **only** if you are claiming car or truck expenses on line 9 and are not required to file Form 4562 for this business. See the instructions for line 13 to find out if you must file Form 4562.

43   When did you place your vehicle in service for business purposes? (month/day/year)   ▶   1 / 1 / 2021

44   Of the total number of miles you drove your vehicle during 2021, enter the number of miles you used your vehicle for:

a   Business _____ 830 _____   b Commuting (see instructions) _____   c Other _____ 11,000 _____

45   Was your vehicle available for personal use during off-duty hours? . . . . ☑ Yes   ☐ No

46   Do you (or your spouse) have another vehicle available for personal use?. . . . . ☑ Yes   ☐ No

47a   Do you have evidence to support your deduction? . . . . ☑ Yes   ☐ No

b   If "Yes," is the evidence written? . . . . ☑ Yes   ☐ No

---

for personal use. Answer yes to this question unless you don't have a second car. If you have kept records of the business use of your vehicle, answer yes to lines 47a and 47b.

You can use the standard mileage rate method even if you are operating more than one vehicle in your business. This is true whether or not you and your spouse are using each of your vehicles at the same time for business purposes.

Selling a Vehicle Used in Your Business
To report the sale of a vehicle used in your business, fill out **Form 4797 Sales of Business Property** (see chapter 11). If you sell a vehicle after using the standard mileage rate method for business expenses, you must reduce the business basis of the vehicle by a certain amount for every mile you drove for business purposes. This amount varies according to the year the vehicle was used. For 2021 it's $0.26 per mile. This means that if you drove your vehicle 10,000 business miles last year, your gain from selling it will be raised by $2,600 (10,000 miles x $0.26).

The Actual Vehicle Expenses Method

Under this method you can deduct the business portion of the following:

- gasoline, oil, antifreeze, and windshield wiper fluid

- tires, repairs, tune-ups, car washes, and waxes

- vehicle insurance, vehicle loan interest payments, and lease payments

- vehicle depreciation

- garage rent

- personal property tax on the vehicle and vehicle license fees

- membership in automobile clubs

- casualty or theft losses on the vehicle

- other actual vehicle expenses

In addition, you can still deduct your parking fees, tolls, and bus, subway, and train fares, as you can under the standard mileage rate method. Here's how to calculate your deduction using the actual vehicle expenses method:

STEP ONE

First, calculate the actual business-use percentage for each vehicle by dividing the number of business miles you drove the vehicle that year by the total miles you drove it that year. For example, if you drove your vehicle 12,875 miles, and 1,875 of those miles were for your business, your business use would be 15% (1,875 ÷ 12,875 = 15%).

STEP TWO

List all your actual expenses for all the vehicle expenses listed above (gasoline, oil, antifreeze, and so on). Make sure you have records for all the expenses you claim. Add up your vehicle expenses, and multiply the total by your business-use percentage. In the example below, the vehicle expenses total $1,550, and the vehicle deduction is $432.50.

Gasoline	$175.00
Oil	$20.00
Repairs	$205.00
Insurance	$700.00
Taxes and license	$100.00
Vehicle loan interest	$350.00
$1,550.00 x 15% =	$232.50
Additional business vehicle insurance ($200 x 100%)	$200.00
Vehicle deduction	$432.50

STEP THREE

Add to the total from step two any parking fees, tolls, or bus, subway, or train fares you paid while conducting business activities, and enter the total on **Schedule C**, line 9. Keep the records showing how you calculated these amounts. Enter any expenses for renting or leasing a vehicle on **Schedule C**, line 20a (rent or lease of vehicle).

STEP FOUR

In addition to claiming your actual expenses, this method allows you to take a depreciation deduction for your vehicle. Claim this depreciation on **Form 4562**, Part V, Section B, not on **Schedule C**, Part IV. You will transfer the depreciation expense on **Form 4562** to **Schedule C**, line 13 (see chapter 3 for instructions on how to depreciate your vehicle).

Leasing versus Owning

For a leased vehicle, you can choose between the standard mileage rate method and the actual vehicle expenses method. If your vehicle lease is actually a purchase contract and you want to claim the cost of the purchase contract by depreciating your vehicle, you must use the actual vehicle expenses method.

To use the standard mileage rate method for a leased vehicle, follow the rules described in this chapter. This method doesn't allow you to claim any portion of the cost of the lease. If you use the standard mileage rate method for a leased vehicle, you must continue to use it for the entire lease term.

To use the actual vehicle expenses method for a leased vehicle, follow the rules described in this chapter. Calculate your business-use percentage, and apply it against your actual expenses (lease payments, gasoline, insurance, and any other expenses).

Most vehicle leases involve a large payment at the beginning of your lease. If you are claiming actual vehicle expenses, that amount is to be spread out over the life of the lease. Do not deduct it all in the first year you paid it. For example, if you paid $2,700 at the start of your lease and your lease term is 3 years (36 months), that means you would not count the $2,700 in the first year, but you can count an additional $75 per month in addition to your regular monthly lease payment ($2,700 divided by 36 months equals $75 per month).

If the fair market value of a vehicle you leased in 2021 is more than $50,000, you must reduce your deduction by a small amount for each year that you lease the vehicle (see IRS **Publication 463 Travel, Entertainment, Gift, and Car Expenses** for tables).

In general, you're better off purchasing a vehicle than leasing it. The benefits of leasing are that you get to drive a newer (and usually more expensive) vehicle than if you own one; however, leasing is usually more expensive than buying, and at the end of the lease period you must return the vehicle.

Should You and Your Spouse File Two Schedule Cs?

If you and your spouse work side by side caring for children, each of you can be filing your own **Schedule C** and splitting the income and expenses.

Why would you do this? Because by doing so, your spouse could show a profit that could help him or her earn higher Social Security benefits. IRS rules allow a married couple in this situation to split the profit, pay self-employment taxes under both their names, and thus spread the future Social Security benefits between the two of them. This can be done without the couple filing as a partnership.

To do this, the two spouses should each file a separate **Schedule C**. They should split the income and expenses on these two forms and each pay self-employment tax under their own names. This will not increase the total self-employment tax they will pay. The two should split the income and expenses according to the amount of work they perform for the business. A spouse who works two hours a week doing the record keeping should not claim 50% of the income and expenses.

Warning

The reason to file two **Schedule C**s for one business is to allow the spouse to contribute more to his or her Social Security account and, later, earn higher benefits. However, before you take this action, I strongly recommend that you find out the long-term impact on the Social Security benefits for both you and your spouse.

Social Security rules are complex. You qualify to receive Social Security benefits by working for at least 10 years and earning enough income each of those years. If your spouse also works, you both can receive Social Security benefits. If your spouse dies, you can receive some of his or her benefits. Depending on how much you and your spouse have earned over the years, it may be more beneficial to have future earnings credited to your spouse.

To find out the impact of crediting the profit from your business to you alone or splitting it between you and your spouse, use the Social Security Retirement Estimator at www.socialsecurity.gov. Talk to someone at your local Social Security office if either of you are within five years of retiring. They can answer your questions to help you make the best decision.

Other Considerations

You can file two separate **Schedule C**s only if you are married under state law (including same-sex couples) and filing jointly. Unmarried couples cannot do this. In most cases you cannot do this if you are a Limited Liability Company (LLC) or a corporation.

If you do this, parents can still pay you, and, therefore, your husband does not need to obtain his own EIN. You don't have to put your husband's name on your child care license or contract. You don't have to change how you operate your program.

For more information about the tax issues discussed in this chapter, refer to the related topics in the other chapters of this book and the Redleaf Press *Family Child Care Record-Keeping Guide*.

CHAPTER 6

Completing Your Tax Return

In recent years there have been significant changes in IRS **Form 1040** and the numbered schedules that affect all family child care providers. The forms can be complicated to fill out, so read through things carefully. This chapter explains how to fill out the remaining tax forms that most family child care providers are likely to need to complete their tax returns. It covers the following:

- **Schedule SE**, which you use to show how much self-employment tax you owe
- **Schedule EIC**, which you use to claim the Earned Income Credit
- **Form 8863**, which you use to claim education credits
- **Form 1040**, to which you transfer the amounts from your business tax forms to finish your individual tax return
- **Form 1040-ES**, which you use to estimate your quarterly taxes for the next tax year
- **Form 8995**, Qualified Business Income Deduction Simplified Computation

You may also need to fill out other tax forms, especially if you are affected by one of the special situations described in Part III; however, the forms covered in this chapter represent the remaining forms that most family child care providers will need to file for a normal tax year.

Note: A special rule allows providers to reduce their federal taxable income by 20% of either their profit or their family's taxable income, whichever is lower. See pages 126–127.

Filing an Extension

If you need more time to file your tax return, you can file for an extension. This may be helpful if you need more time to calculate your depreciation, sort your records, or deal with a family emergency; however, filing for an extension doesn't give you more time to pay your taxes. Your taxes are due on April 15. If at that time you aren't sure how much you'll owe, pay what you estimate you'll owe. If you underestimate this amount, you will owe interest on the taxes that you didn't pay on April 15.

You may file for an automatic extension of your tax return until October 15. (There is no further extension after this.)

To get this extension, file **Form 4868 Application for Automatic Extension of Time to File U.S. Individual Income Tax Return**.

Self-Employment Tax: Schedule SE

This section explains how to fill out **Schedule SE Self-Employment Tax**. This form shows how much Social Security and Medicare tax, if any, you owe for operating your business. Before you can complete it, you will have to fill out **Form 4562**, **Schedule C**, and **Form 8829**. A blank copy of **Schedule SE** is included in the tax forms in Part V of this book.

Self-employment tax is the tax that entitles you to Social Security benefits. If you have a net profit of $400 or more on **Schedule C**, line 31, you must pay this self-employment tax. If you're self-employed and have more than one business, you must pay this tax if you have a combined net profit of $400 or more for all your businesses.

If your spouse is self-employed, you owe self-employment tax only if the $400 threshold is met by each of your businesses. For example, if your net self-employment income is $300 and your spouse's net self-employment income is $20,000, then you don't have to pay self-employment tax and fill out **Schedule SE**, but your spouse does. (It doesn't matter if you're filing jointly or separately.)

Your Social Security benefits are based partly on the Social Security taxes you pay. To receive Social Security benefits, you or your spouse must pay into the Social Security fund. If you haven't worked much outside the home, you can make sure that you'll qualify for Social Security by paying self-employment tax.

Plan for Retirement

When you claim all your allowable deductions, you reduce your taxable income and Social Security taxes, which may result in lower Social Security benefits when you retire. To offset this, save money for retirement by investing in IRAs or other investment plans.

How to Fill Out Schedule SE

In most cases, this is how a child care provider should fill out Schedule SE. If you had another business or a job from which you received a W-2, look at each line carefully to determine how to fill out Schedule SE.

Line 1: Leave blank.

Lines 2 and 3: Enter your net profit from **Schedule C**, line 31.

Lines 4b, 4c, and 6: Multiply line 3 by 92.35% (0.9235). If this amount is less than $400 or if you have a net loss from **Schedule C**, don't fill out the rest of **Schedule SE**.

Line 9: Look at the preprinted amount on line 7 and enter it again here.

Line 10: Multiply line 6 by 12.4% (0.124).

Line 11: Multiply line 6 by 2.9% (0.029).

Line 12: Add lines 10 and 11. This represents your self-employment tax. Enter this amount on **Schedule 2 Form 1040**, line 4. If line 6 is more than the preprinted amount on line 7, see the instructions.

Line 13:   Multiply line 6 by 12.4% (0.124).

You can deduct half of your self-employment tax from your income on **Schedule 1 Form 1040**, line 15, as an adjustment to your income. For example, if your self-employment tax is $1,000, put $500 on **Schedule 1 Form 1040**, line 15. This reduces your taxable income by $500. If you are in the 25% tax bracket, it would reduce your taxes by $125 ($500 x 25%).

SCHEDULE SE (Form 1040)	Self-Employment Tax	OMB No. 1545-0074
Department of the Treasury Internal Revenue Service (99)	▶ Go to *www.irs.gov/ScheduleSE* for instructions and the latest information. ▶ Attach to Form 1040, 1040-SR, or 1040-NR.	2021 Attachment Sequence No. **17**

Name of person with self-employment income (as shown on Form 1040, 1040-SR, or 1040-NR) AMANDA WILSON	Social security number of person with **self-employment** income ▶ 123-56-6789

Part I Self-Employment Tax

Note: If your only income subject to self-employment tax is **church employee income,** see instructions for how to report your income and the definition of church employee income.

A   If you are a minister, member of a religious order, or Christian Science practitioner **and** you filed Form 4361, but you had $400 or more of **other** net earnings from self-employment, check here and continue with Part I . . . . ▶ ☐

Skip lines 1a and 1b if you use the farm optional method in Part II. See instructions.

1a	Net farm profit or (loss) from Schedule F, line 34, and farm partnerships, Schedule K-1 (Form 1065), box 14, code A . . .	1a	
b	If you received social security retirement or disability benefits, enter the amount of Conservation Reserve Program payments included on Schedule F, line 4b, or listed on Schedule K-1 (Form 1065), box 20, code AH	1b	( )
	Skip line 2 if you use the nonfarm optional method in Part II. See instructions.		
2	Net profit or (loss) from Schedule C, line 31; and Schedule K-1 (Form 1065), box 14, code A (other than farming). See instructions for other income to report or if you are a minister or member of a religious order	2	$1,000
3	Combine lines 1a, 1b, and 2 . . .	3	$1,000
4a	If line 3 is more than zero, multiply line 3 by 92.35% (0.9235). Otherwise, enter amount from line 3 .	4a	
	Note: If line 4a is less than $400 due to Conservation Reserve Program payments on line 1b, see instructions.		
b	If you elect one or both of the optional methods, enter the total of lines 15 and 17 here	4b	
c	Combine lines 4a and 4b. If less than $400, **stop;** you don't owe self-employment tax. **Exception:** If less than $400 and you had **church employee income,** enter -0- and continue . . . . ▶	4c	$923.50
5a	Enter your **church employee income** from Form W-2. See instructions for definition of church employee income	5a	
b	Multiply line 5a by 92.35% (0.9235). If less than $100, enter -0-	5b	
6	Add lines 4c and 5b . . .	6	
7	Maximum amount of combined wages and self-employment earnings subject to social security tax or the 6.2% portion of the 7.65% railroad retirement (tier 1) tax for 2021	7	142,800
8a	Total social security wages and tips (total of boxes 3 and 7 on Form(s) W-2) and railroad retirement (tier 1) compensation. If $142,800 or more, skip lines 8b through 10, and go to line 11	8a	
b	Unreported tips subject to social security tax from Form 4137, line 10 . . .	8b	
c	Wages subject to social security tax from Form 8919, line 10	8c	
d	Add lines 8a, 8b, and 8c . . .	8d	
9	Subtract line 8d from line 7. If zero or less, enter -0- here and on line 10 and go to line 11 . . . ▶	9	
10	Multiply the **smaller** of line 6 or line 9 by 12.4% (0.124)	10	
11	Multiply line 6 by 2.9% (0.029) . . .	11	
12	**Self-employment tax.** Add lines 10 and 11. Enter here and on **Schedule 2 (Form 1040), line 4** . .	12	$141.30
13	**Deduction for one-half of self-employment tax.** Multiply line 12 by 50% (0.50). Enter here and on **Schedule 1 (Form 1040), line 15**	13	$70.65

Part II Optional Methods To Figure Net Earnings (see instructions)

Farm Optional Method. You may use this method **only** if **(a)** your gross farm income[1] wasn't more than $8,820, **or (b)** your net farm profits[2] were less than $6,367.

14	Maximum income for optional methods	14	5,880
15	Enter the **smaller** of: two-thirds (⅔) of gross farm income[1] (not less than zero) **or** $5,880. Also, include this amount on line 4b above	15	

Nonfarm Optional Method. You may use this method **only** if **(a)** your net nonfarm profits[3] were less than $6,367 and also less than 72.189% of your gross nonfarm income,[4] **and (b)** you had net earnings from self-employment of at least $400 in 2 of the prior 3 years. **Caution:** You may use this method no more than five times.

16	Subtract line 15 from line 14 . . .	16	
17	Enter the **smaller** of: two-thirds (⅔) of gross nonfarm income[4] (not less than zero) **or** the amount on line 16. Also, include this amount on line 4b above	17	

[1] From Sch. F, line 9; and Sch. K-1 (Form 1065), box 14, code B.
[2] From Sch. F, line 34; and Sch. K-1 (Form 1065), box 14, code A—minus the amount you would have entered on line 1b had you not used the optional method.
[3] From Sch. C, line 31; and Sch. K-1 (Form 1065), box 14, code A.
[4] From Sch. C, line 7; and Sch. K-1 (Form 1065), box 14, code C.

For Paperwork Reduction Act Notice, see your tax return instructions.   Cat. No. 11358Z   Schedule SE (Form 1040) 2021

Education Credits: Form 8863

If you or any members of your family attend a postsecondary school, even for just one class, you may be able to take advantage of the Lifetime Learning Credit or the American Opportunity Credit. Postsecondary schools include community colleges, vocational education schools, colleges, universities, and any U.S. institution eligible to participate in the Department of Education student aid program. You can't claim both of these credits for the same student in the same year.

The Lifetime Learning Credit

The Lifetime Learning Credit is for those who take a class at a postsecondary school, such as a class to obtain a Child Development Associate (CDA) credential. (The class does not have to be about family child care to be eligible for the credit.) The tax credit is 20% of up to $10,000 of tuition and related expenses incurred during the last year. Unrelated expenses include books, meals, lodging, student activities, athletics, transportation, insurance, and personal living expenses.

To be eligible for this credit, your adjusted gross income must be less than $139,000 (if you're married and filing jointly) or $69,000 (if you're single). The credit is phased out when your adjusted gross income is between $119,000 and $139,000 (married filing jointly) or between $59,000 and $69,000 (single). There is a $2,000 maximum credit per family (you, your spouse, and your child). You don't need to be enrolled for any minimum amount of time or be trying to earn a degree.

American Opportunity Credit (Formerly the Hope Credit)

This credit covers the first four years of postsecondary education and is a refundable maximum tax credit of $2,500. To be eligible, your adjusted gross income must be less than $180,000 (married filing jointly) or $90,000 (all others). Education expenses that are eligible for this credit include tuition, fees, and course materials (books, supplies, and equipment). Students must be enrolled at least half-time.

To claim these credits, fill out **Form 8863 Education Credits**. Enter the amount of your credit from this form onto **Form 1040**, line 18c.

Caution about Education Credits

You should use these tax credits for courses that aren't related to family child care or for classes that are taken by other members of your family. If you're taking workshops or classes that are related to your business at a postsecondary school, it's better to claim your education costs as a direct business expense on **Schedule C** rather than using these tax credits.

For example, if you spend $100 on a child care workshop, claim it as a business deduction on **Schedule C**; if you are in the 12% bracket, you would save about $26 (12% income tax and 14% net self-employment tax). If you are in the 24% bracket, you would save about 38% (24% income tax and 14% net self-employment tax). On the other hand, if you used the Lifetime Learning Credit, your savings would be only $20 ($100 x 20% credit = $20).

You can't use the Lifetime Learning Credit for the $20 and claim the other $80 as a business deduction.

The Earned Income Credit: Schedule EIC

This section covers how to claim the Earned Income Credit using **Schedule EIC Earned Income Credit**. The Earned Income Credit is designed to help low-income families reduce their taxes. When you claim this credit, you will subtract the credit from the taxes you owe. Read the **Form 1040** instructions to determine if you are eligible for this credit. A special new law for 2021 allows more people to qualify for this credit. Here are the income eligibility limits and maximum benefits for 2021:

Family Type	Maximum Income Single or Head of Household	Maximum Income Married Filing Jointly	Maximum Benefit
Families with 1 child	$42,158	$48,108	$3,618
Families with 2 children	$47,915	$53,865	$5,980
Families with 3 or more children	$51,464	$57,414	$6,728
Workers without children	$21,430	$27,830	$1,502

Eligibility for the Earned Income Credit is based on your family's earned income and adjusted gross income, which is the amount on your **Form 1040**, line 11. This amount includes your net income from **Schedule C**, line 31, any earned income from **Form 1040**, lines 1–7, and any money you received from a military housing allowance.

A child must meet all three of the following criteria to be eligible for this credit:

1. The child must be your son, daughter, adopted child, grandchild, stepchild, or eligible foster child. A brother, sister, stepbrother, or stepsister (or the child or grandchild of your brother, sister, stepbrother, or stepsister) may also be a qualifying child if you care for this individual as you would for your own child. A foster child is a child you care for as if she were your own child.

2. The child must be either under age 19 at the end of last year, under age 24 and a full-time student, or any age and permanently and totally disabled.

3. The child must have lived with you for more than six months last year (unless the child was born last year). If a foster child, he or she must have lived with you for more than half the year.

You can file under any filing status except married filing a separate return. You must provide a correct Social Security number for each child, as well as for yourself and your spouse. You can apply for a Social Security number by filing **Form SS-5** with your local Social Security Administration office. It takes about two weeks to receive a number. If you don't have the number by April 15, you can request an automatic extension (**Form 4868**) to October 15, but you must still pay your taxes by April 15.

How to Fill Out Schedule EIC

If you meet the above qualifications, you can either figure out the credit yourself or have the IRS do it for you. If you have a qualifying child and you want the IRS to figure out your credit, complete and attach **Schedule EIC** to your tax return. Proceed as follows:

- Instead of calculating the amount for line 27a on **Form 1040**, simply write "EIC" in that space.

- If you want to figure the credit yourself, use worksheet B in the instructions for **Form 1040** to determine your credit. Enter the credit amount on **Form 1040**, line 27a. Don't attach the worksheet to your return, but do keep it with your tax records. If you have a qualifying child, you must fill out **Schedule EIC** and file it with **Form 1040**.

Fraudulent Claims for the Earned Income Credit

Some taxpayers discover that if they lower some of their expenses on **Form 8829** or **Schedule C**, they will be eligible for a higher EIC that would offset the taxes on their higher business profit. However, the IRS does not allow this. You may not adjust your expenses to claim a higher EIC.

If you make a fraudulent or reckless claim for the Earned Income Credit, you won't be entitled to receive it for either two years (if the IRS finds that you intentionally disregarded the rules) or ten years (if the IRS finds that you made a fraudulent claim).

IRS COMPLIANCE FORM TO PREVENT FRAUD

To reduce fraud, the IRS has begun a pilot program that uses **Form 8836 Qualifying Children Residency Statement** to certify that a child lived with a parent for more than half the year. This proof involves the signature of a child care provider, clergy, employer, health-care provider, landlord, school official, social service agency official, Indian tribal official, or community-based organization official who can certify where the child lived.

Although you can sign a parent's form, if you claim the EIC for your own child, you can't ask a parent of one of the children in your care to sign your form, since they aren't authorized to do so.

Other Tax Credits

Child Care Credit

You may be eligible to claim the child care credit for expenses associated with paying someone to care for your own child while you are working. This can be the case when you attend a training workshop or conference and have someone watch your child. It can also apply if you send your child to a preschool program while you are caring for child care children. To qualify for this tax credit, you must meet these tests:

- Your child must be age 12 or younger.

- The care must be provided while you are working.

- You cannot pay your spouse, the parent of the child, someone you can claim as a dependent, or your own child who is under age 19.

- Your child must have lived with you for more than half of the year.

Due to a special rule for 2021, the maximum amount of child care expenses you can claim for one child is $8,000 ($16,000 for two or more). For 2021, the tax credit can be up to 50%, depending on your adjusted gross income.

For more information, see IRS **Publication 503 Child and Dependent Care Expenses**, and IRS **Form 2441 Child and Dependent Care Expenses**. Claim the credit on **Form 1040 Schedule 3**, line 2.

Saver's Credit

If you are a low-income taxpayer, you may be eligible to receive a tax credit for any contributions you have made to a retirement plan—a 401(k), traditional IRA, Roth IRA, Simplified Employee Pension (SEP), or SIMPLE IRA. This credit is in addition to the tax deductibility of the IRA contribution. If you are married filing jointly, your adjusted gross income must be less than $66,000 to qualify for this credit. If you are single, the income limit is $33,000. The tax credit ranges from 10% to 50% of an IRA contribution up to $2,000. To claim this credit, fill out **Form 8880 Credit for Qualified Retirement Savings Contribution**, and then put the credit amount on **Form 1040 Schedule 3**, line 4.

If you made a contribution to an IRA between 2018 and 2020 and did not claim this credit, you can still file an amended tax return (see chapter 9) this year and get a refund.

Completing Your Tax Return: Form 1040

This section explains how to enter the information from your child care tax forms onto your **Form 1040**. (There's a blank copy of **Form 1040** and the new schedules in Part V of this book.) You must complete all your business tax forms before you can fill out **Form 1040**. The earlier chapters in this book have covered the business forms that you need to file along with **Form 1040**. Work carefully and make sure you transfer the numbers accurately from one form to another, as follows:

- Enter your depreciation expenses from **Form 4562** on **Schedule C**, line 13.
- Enter your home expenses from **Form 8829** on **Schedule C**, line 30.
- Enter your net profit (if any) from **Schedule C** on **Schedule SE**, line 2.

Once you have completed these business forms and your other personal tax forms (such as **Schedule A**, if you itemize), you're ready to begin filling out **Form 1040**.

Over the last few years the IRS has repeatedly changed Form 1040. You must fill out a number of new schedules before completing the form.

Form 1040

Line 1: Enter any wages from your spouse or wages you earned outside of child care.

Line 8: Enter amounts from **Schedule 1**, line 10 (see below).

Line 10: Enter amounts from **Schedule 1**, line 26 (see below).

Line 12a: Enter your standard deduction ($12,550 single or $25,100 married filing jointly) or your itemized deductions on **Schedule A**.

Line 13: Enter your qualified business income deduction from **Form 8995** (see below).

Line 19 or 28: Enter any eligible amounts for the child tax credit (see pages 129–130).

Line 26: Enter any 2021 estimated tax payments and amount applied from your 2020 return here.

Line 27a: Enter any eligible amounts for the Earned Income Credit (see pages 122–124).

Now let's look at the three new schedules for **Form 1040**.

Schedule 1 Additional Income and Adjustments to Income

Line 3: Report your profit from **Schedule C**, line 31 here.

Line 4: Report any capital gains or losses from **Form 4797** here (see chapter 11).

Line 10: Enter this total on **Form 1040**, line 8.

Line 15: Report one-half of your Social Security/Medicare tax form from **Schedule SE**, line 6 here.

Line 16: Report any contributions to a SEP or SIMPLE IRA plan here.

Line 17:   If you aren't eligible to receive health insurance through an employer (usually your spouse's employer) and you buy health insurance for yourself, you can claim 100% of the insurance premium here. You may claim this deduction even if the health insurance isn't purchased in your name. You aren't eligible for this deduction if you qualify for insurance through your spouse's employer and choose not to purchase it. You also aren't eligible if you receive payments under COBRA. If you are eligible to claim this health insurance deduction, it can't exceed your net income on **Schedule C**, line 31.

Line 20:   Report any contributions to a deductible IRA (not a SEP, SIMPLE, or Roth IRA) here.

Line 26:   Enter this total on **Form 1040**, line 10.

Schedule 2 Additional Taxes

Line 4:   Enter your self-employment tax (Social Security/Medicare tax) from **Schedule SE**, line 12.

Line 16:   Enter this total on **Form 1040**, line 23.

Schedule 3 Additional Credits and Payments

Line 2:   Report any amounts eligible for the child and dependent credit. This is explained on page 129. Enter amounts from **Form 2441** if you are eligible.

Line 3:   Enter any amounts for education credits from **Form 8863**. This is explained on pages 124–125.

Line 4:   If you made a contribution to an IRA and were eligible for the Saver's Credit, enter your credit amount here. See page 124.

Line 5:   If you are eligible for any residential energy credits, enter the amount from **Form 5695** here.

Line 8:   Enter the totals from lines 1–7 and enter on **Form 1040**, line 20.

In summary, all providers must fill out **Schedule 1** and **Schedule 2**. Depending on your circumstances, you may have to fill out **Schedule 3**.

Standard Deduction vs. Itemized Deduction

All providers can reduce their federal taxable income by the higher of a standard deduction or itemized deductions on **Schedule A**. For 2021 the standard deduction has risen. If you are single, it rises from $12,400 (2020) to $12,550 (2021), and if you are married, from $24,800 to $25,100. This means that many providers will find it beneficial to claim the standard deduction, rather than itemizing using **Schedule A**. **Schedule A** is where providers claimed the personal portion of their property tax and mortgage interest (as well as other personal expenses). **If you itemized in previous years and now claim the standard deduction, you will not lose the ability to claim the business portion of your property tax and mortgage interest on Form 8829 Expenses for Business Use of Your Home.**

Qualified Business Income Deduction

Form 1040 now allows providers to reduce their federal taxable income by 20% of the lower of their adjusted gross income or family's taxable income. **Note**: This rule does not affect your Social Security/Medicare tax or your state income tax (if any).

You are eligible to take advantage of this rule if your family's adjusted gross income is less than $163,300 (single) or $326,600 (married, filing jointly). If you make more than this, the deduction is subject to some limitations. You are not eligible for this rule if you are incorporated as a C corporation. Your adjusted gross income is on **Form 1040**, line 11.

Your profit is found on **Schedule C**, line 31. If you have a loss on **Schedule C**, you aren't eligible for the Qualified Business Income Deduction. You would carry over any loss to your 2021 tax return to see if you would be eligible for this deduction in 2021. If your spouse is also self-employed or is incorporated (other than a C corporation) or in a partnership, you must net your business income. So if your spouse is self-employed and has a profit of $40,000 and your profit is $30,000, your joint profit is $70,000, which you would compare to your family's taxable income.

Here's how to calculate your qualified business income deduction. Note: I'm using a simple example and avoiding other tax issues, such as sale of property, retirement contributions, and health insurance deductions. Enter your profit from **Schedule C**, line 31, onto IRS **Form 1040 Schedule 1**, line 3. Then transfer this amount to IRS **Form 1040**, line 8. If you are married, enter your spouse's income on **Form 1040**, line 1. Next, enter half of your Social Security/Medicare tax from **Form 1040 Schedule 1**, line 15, to **Form 1040**, line 10. Subtract line 10 from line 9. The result on line 11 is your family's adjusted gross income.

Enter your standard deduction of either $12,550 (single) or $25,100 (married filing jointly) on **Form 1040**, line 12a.

Line 10 represents your qualified business income deduction. To calculate this number you will need to fill out the new IRS **Form 9885 Qualified Business Income Deduction Simplified Computation**. This form will tell you to compare two numbers and use the lower of the two. The first number is your business profit multiplied by 20%. The second number is your family's adjusted gross income (line 11) minus your standard deduction and then multiplied by 20%. Put the lower of these two numbers on **Form 1040**, line 13. This is your qualified business income deduction.

Let's look at an example.

You are single and your business profit is $40,000. One-half of your Social Security/ Medicare tax is $2,826. Your standard deduction is $12,550.

First number: $40,000 - $2,826 = $37,174 x 20% = $7,425.

Second number: $40,000 – $2,826 – $12,400 = $24,774 x 20% = $4,955

The lower of these two numbers is $4,955, and that's your qualified business income deduction.

Here's how **Form 1040** and **Form 8995** would be filled out using this example:

Form 1040 Schedule 1

Line 3:	$40,000 business profit
Line 10:	$40,000 transfer to **Form 1040**, line 8
Line 14:	$2,826 half of your Social Security/Medicare tax
Line 22:	$2,826 transfer to **Form 1040**, line 10

Form 1040

Line 8:	$40,000

Line 9: $40,000

Line 10: $2,826

Line 11: $40,000 – $2,826 = $37,174 adjusted gross income

Line 12a: $12,400 standard deduction

Line 13: $4,925 based on filling out **Form 8995**

Form 8995

Lines 1, 2, and 4: $40,000 business profit minus **Schedule 1**, line 15 = $37,174

Line 5: $37,174 x 20% = $7,435

Lines 6–9: Zero

Line 10: $7,435

Line 11: $37,174 adjusted gross income – $12,550 standard deduction = $24,624

Line 13: $24,624

Line 14: $24,624 x 20% = $4,925

Compare line 5 ($7,435) with line 14 ($4,925) and transfer the lower number to **Form 1040**, line 13.

Form **1040** — Department of the Treasury—Internal Revenue Service (99) — U.S. Individual Income Tax Return — 2021 — OMB No. 1545-0074 — IRS Use Only—Do not write or staple in this space.

Filing Status Check only one box. ☐ Single ☐ Married filing jointly ☐ Married filing separately (MFS) ☐ Head of household (HOH) ☐ Qualifying widow(er) (QW)
If you checked the MFS box, enter the name of your spouse. If you checked the HOH or QW box, enter the child's name if the qualifying person is a child but not your dependent ▶

Your first name and middle initial	Last name	Your social security number
If joint return, spouse's first name and middle initial	Last name	Spouse's social security number

Home address (number and street). If you have a P.O. box, see instructions. | Apt. no.

City, town, or post office. If you have a foreign address, also complete spaces below. | State | ZIP code

Foreign country name | Foreign province/state/county | Foreign postal code

Presidential Election Campaign Check here if you, or your spouse if filing jointly, want $3 to go to this fund. Checking a box below will not change your tax or refund. ☐ You ☐ Spouse

At any time during 2021, did you receive, sell, exchange, or otherwise dispose of any financial interest in any virtual currency? ☐ Yes ☐ No

Standard Deduction Someone can claim: ☐ You as a dependent ☐ Your spouse as a dependent
☐ Spouse itemizes on a separate return or you were a dual-status alien

Age/Blindness You: ☐ Were born before January 2, 1957 ☐ Are blind Spouse: ☐ Was born before January 2, 1957 ☐ Is blind

Dependents (see instructions):
If more than four dependents, see instructions and check here ▶ ☐

(1) First name Last name	(2) Social security number	(3) Relationship to you	(4) ✔ if qualifies for (see instructions): Child tax credit	Credit for other dependents
			☐	☐
			☐	☐
			☐	☐
			☐	☐

Attach Sch. B if required.

Standard Deduction for—
• Single or Married filing separately, $12,550
• Married filing jointly or Qualifying widow(er), $25,100
• Head of household, $18,800
• If you checked any box under *Standard Deduction,* see instructions.

1	Wages, salaries, tips, etc. Attach Form(s) W-2		1
2a	Tax-exempt interest . . . 2a	b Taxable interest	2b
3a	Qualified dividends . . . 3a	b Ordinary dividends	3b
4a	IRA distributions 4a	b Taxable amount	4b
5a	Pensions and annuities . . 5a	b Taxable amount	5b
6a	Social security benefits . . 6a	b Taxable amount	6b
7	Capital gain or (loss). Attach Schedule D if required. If not required, check here . . . . ▶ ☐		7
8	Other income from Schedule 1, line 10		8 $40,000
9	Add lines 1, 2b, 3b, 4b, 5b, 6b, 7, and 8. This is your **total income** . . . . . . ▶		9 $40,000
10	Adjustments to income from Schedule 1, line 26		10
11	Subtract line 10 from line 9. This is your **adjusted gross income** . . . . . . ▶		11 $37,174
12a	**Standard deduction or itemized deductions** (from Schedule A)	12a $2,826	
b	Charitable contributions if you take the standard deduction (see instructions)	12b	
c	Add lines 12a and 12b		12c $2,826
13	Qualified business income deduction from Form 8995 or Form 8995-A		13 $4,955
14	Add lines 12c and 13		14 $7,781
15	**Taxable income.** Subtract line 14 from line 11. If zero or less, enter -0-		15 $29,393

For Disclosure, Privacy Act, and Paperwork Reduction Act Notice, see separate instructions. | Cat. No. 11320B | Form **1040** (2021)

Form **8995**	**Qualified Business Income Deduction Simplified Computation**	OMB No. 1545-2294
Department of the Treasury Internal Revenue Service	► Attach to your tax return. ► Go to *www.irs.gov/Form8995* for instructions and the latest information.	**2021** Attachment Sequence No. **55**

Name(s) shown on return | Your taxpayer identification number

Note. You can claim the qualified business income deduction **only** if you have qualified business income from a qualified trade or business, real estate investment trust dividends, publicly traded partnership income, or a domestic production activities deduction passed through from an agricultural or horticultural cooperative. See instructions.
Use this form if your taxable income, before your qualified business income deduction, is at or below $164,900 ($164,925 if married filing separately; $329,800 if married filing jointly), and you aren't a patron of an agricultural or horticultural cooperative.

1	(a) Trade, business, or aggregation name	(b) Taxpayer identification number	(c) Qualified business income or (loss)
	FAMILY CHILD CARE		$40,000
i			
ii			
iii			
iv			
v			

2	Total qualified business income or (loss). Combine lines 1i through 1v, column (c)	2	$37,174		
3	Qualified business net (loss) carryforward from the prior year	3	(---)		
4	Total qualified business income. Combine lines 2 and 3. If zero or less, enter -0-	4	$37,174		
5	Qualified business income component. Multiply line 4 by 20% (0.20)			5	$7,435
6	Qualified REIT dividends and publicly traded partnership (PTP) income or (loss) (see instructions)	6	---		
7	Qualified REIT dividends and qualified PTP (loss) carryforward from the prior year	7	(---)		
8	Total qualified REIT dividends and PTP income. Combine lines 6 and 7. If zero or less, enter -0-	8	$0		
9	REIT and PTP component. Multiply line 8 by 20% (0.20)			9	$0
10	Qualified business income deduction before the income limitation. Add lines 5 and 9			10	$7,435
11	Taxable income before qualified business income deduction (see instructions)	11	$24,624		
12	Net capital gain (see instructions)	12	---		
13	Subtract line 12 from line 11. If zero or less, enter -0-	13	$24,624		
14	Income limitation. Multiply line 13 by 20% (0.20)			14	$4,925
15	Qualified business income deduction. Enter the smaller of line 10 or line 14. Also enter this amount on the applicable line of your return (see instructions) ►			15	$4,925
16	Total qualified business (loss) carryforward. Combine lines 2 and 3. If greater than zero, enter -0-			16	( )
17	Total qualified REIT dividends and PTP (loss) carryforward. Combine lines 6 and 7. If greater than zero, enter -0-			17	( )

For Privacy Act and Paperwork Reduction Act Notice, see instructions.   Cat. No. 37806C   Form **8995** (2021)

Child Tax Credits

If you have dependents (including children, grandchildren, stepchildren, or foster children) who were under age 18 at the end of last year, you're entitled to a tax credit for each child if your adjusted gross income is less than certain amounts. The usual credit is $2,000 per child, but a special new rule for 2021 increases the credit to $3,000 per child ($3,600 per child under age 6). You will qualify for the full amount if your adjusted gross income is less than

• $150,000 if married and filing a joint return,

• $112,500 if filing as head of household, or

• $75,000 if you are a single filer or are married and filing a separate return.

If your income is over those amounts, the credit may be reduced to $2,000 per child. The $2,000 is further reduced if your adjusted gross income is over

- $200,000 for single, head of household, or married filing separately, or

- $400,000 for married filing jointly.

If you earn more than this, your credit will be reduced by $50 for each $1,000, or fraction thereof, above the limit. For 2021, this credit is fully refundable (meaning it is payable to you even when you owe no taxes) as long as you lived in the United States for at least half of the year. This credit goes with the parent who claims the dependency exemption for the child. Be sure to check the box in column 4 on the Dependents section on page 1 of **Form 1040**. To get this credit, you must enter the name and Social Security number of each qualifying child on **Form 1040**. To claim the credit, fill out the Child Tax Credit worksheet in the instructions to **Form 1040** and in many cases you enter the credit amount on line 19. However, if you couldn't take full advantage of the Child Tax Credit on line 19, use **Form 8812 Additional Child Tax Credit** to calculate this credit, and enter the credit amount on line 28.

You may have received some advance payments of this credit starting in July 2021. If you received those payments, you will subtract the amount of those advance payments from your total credit, and enter the net amount on your **Form 1040**. If the amount of your advance payments was higher than the credit you qualify for, you may need to repay part or all of the advanced credit you received. However, there is an exception if your income is under certain amounts, so see the instructions if you received more advance payments than the total amount of credit that you qualify for.

Credit for Other Dependents

As of 2018 there is a tax credit called the Credit for Other Dependents. You are eligible for this credit if you have a dependent who does not qualify for the larger Child Tax Credit. This credit is worth $500. Complete the worksheet in the instructions to **Form 1040**. Include the credit on line on **Form 1040**, line 19.

Filing Quarterly Taxes: Form 1040-ES

As a family child care provider, you're self-employed and don't have any income taxes withheld from your earnings, unlike most wage-earning taxpayers. The IRS doesn't want to wait until the end of the year to get all the taxes you'll owe for 2021. If after subtracting all your withholding payments and estimated tax payments, you expect to owe $1,000 or more in federal taxes (federal income tax plus self-employment tax) this year, you may be subject to estimated quarterly tax payments. Many family child care providers aren't aware that they should be paying their taxes quarterly.

Estimated tax payments are due four times a year, on April 15, June 15, September 15, and January 15 of the next year. If you're reading this in early 2022, and you file your 2021 taxes by January 31, 2022, you won't have to file the fourth quarter estimated tax payment that is due on January 15. You may be able to avoid paying quarterly estimated taxes (see below), but if you can't avoid it, bear in mind that you can now pay these taxes with a credit card. (You may also have to pay quarterly estimated taxes to your state or locality; check your local laws.)

Avoiding the Quarterly Requirement

You don't have to pay any estimated taxes if you meet at least one of the following conditions:

- You estimate that you will receive a tax refund for the year on your individual, joint, or separate return.

- You estimate that you will owe less than $1,000 in taxes (after subtracting any withholding) by the end of the year.

- You estimate that the total tax payments that you or your spouse (if filing jointly) will make during the year will be at least 90% of your total tax bill for the year. Example: your husband has $6,400 in taxes withheld from his paycheck during 2021. You work only in your family child care business. You estimate that your total tax bill this year will be $7,000. Since $6,400 in withholding is 91% of your total tax bill, you won't have to pay estimated tax. If your husband had less than $6,300 in taxes withheld, you would have to pay some estimated tax.

- You had no income tax liability in the previous year.

- You estimate that the income tax that will be withheld from you and your spouse in 2022 will be equal to or greater than your total tax liability for 2021.

Another way to avoid worrying about estimated tax is to have your spouse file a new **Form W-4** to withhold more taxes to cover any taxes that are due because of your business earnings. For more information, see IRS **Publication 505**.

How to Fill Out Form 1040-ES

To find out if you will need to pay quarterly estimated tax this year, use the worksheet and payment vouchers on **Form 1040-ES**. The worksheet takes you through the calculations to determine how much tax you will owe by the end of 2022 after subtracting any withholding payments.

If you find that you need to make estimated tax payments, you will divide by four the total tax you will owe for the year after any withholding payments and pay this amount on April 15. For example, if you're single, have no other job besides your family child care business, and estimate that you will owe $4,000 in taxes by the end of this year, you will pay $1,000 ($4,000 ÷ 4) on April 15. In this case, you will have no withholding payments, because you do not earn a paycheck from an employer.

If your income or expenses rise or fall dramatically during the year, you can adjust your declared estimated tax and quarterly payments accordingly. There's a penalty for not paying enough estimated tax.

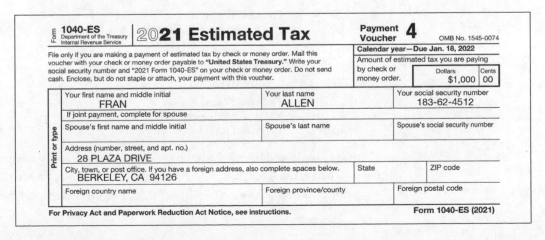

The name you enter on this form must be shown exactly as it appears on your **Form 1040**. If your spouse's name is listed first on your **Form 1040**, list your spouse first on **Form 1040-ES**. If you separated from your spouse or were divorced last year, consult a tax professional before completing this form.

Example of Estimated Tax Calculations

Let's look at an example to determine whether you must make estimated tax payments. Assume it is January 2021. You care for four children and earn $600 a week.

STEP ONE: ESTIMATE YOUR INCOME

> $600 week x 52 weeks = $31,200
> Food Program reimbursement: $4,000
> Total estimated income: $35,200

STEP TWO: ESTIMATE YOUR EXPENSES

If you provided child care in 2021, revise your 2022 number to take into account any expected changes for 2022. If you have only been providing child care for a short time, calculate your average weekly expenses. Don't forget to include depreciation for your house and personal property. A rough rule of thumb might be to estimate that your expenses will be about 40% of your parent income.

> Estimated expenses: $12,480

STEP THREE: ESTIMATE YOUR SELF-EMPLOYMENT TAX

> $22,720 net income x 92.35% x 15.3% = $3,210 (See **Form 1040-SE** for details.)

STEP FOUR: ESTIMATE YOUR INCOME TAX

Your federal income tax rate is determined by your family status and income. The tax brackets for 2021 are listed below. If your income is higher than the table below, there are higher tax brackets of 32%, 35%, and 37%.

Tax Brackets

Filing Status	10%	12%	22%	24%
Single/married filing sep.	$0–$9,950	$9,951–$40,525	$40,526–$86,375	$86,376–$164,925
Head of household	$0–$14,200	$14,201–$54,200	$54,201–$86,350	$85,351–$164,900
Married filing jointly	$0–$19,900	$19,901–$81,050	$81,051–$172,750	$172,751–$329,850

If you're single:

$22,720	Taxable income
$995	The first $9,950 is taxed at 10%
+$1,532	The remaining $12,770 is taxed at 12%
$2,527	Estimated income taxes due

STEP FIVE: TOTAL YOUR ESTIMATED TAXES

$2,527	Estimated income taxes
+$3,210	Estimated self-employment tax
$5,737	Estimated total taxes due

If you're single and have no withholding payments to apply toward your taxes, you'll have to pay estimated taxes; however, your estimated tax payment will be less than shown above because you can subtract the standard deduction from your income.

If you're married, you must make sure that your business income is offset by your spouse's withholding. If in our example none of your taxes are offset by the standard deduction, then by April 15 you should pay one-fourth of the taxes you will owe this year, which would be $5,737 x 0.25 = $1,434.25.

If your estimates change later in the year, you can adjust your estimated tax payments. If you pay too much, you'll get a refund at the end of the year. See the estimated tax worksheet in **Form 1040-ES**. If you're making estimated tax payments by filing **Form 1040-ES**, don't claim these payments as an expense on **Schedule C**. These payments represent your advanced tax deposits; you'll report them on **Form 1040**, line 26.

Filing Your Tax Return Electronically or via the Internet

An increasing number of taxpayers are filing their tax returns electronically with the IRS e-file system. You can bring your completed tax return to an authorized IRS e-file provider or have a tax preparer prepare your tax return and have it electronically filed. To find an authorized IRS e-file provider, go to www.irs.gov. You can also purchase software and e-file your own tax return with your computer and an internet connection. For more information, go to www.irs.gov.

Paying Your Taxes Online

You can now pay all your federal taxes via a secure website, www.eftps.gov or at www.irs.gov/payments/direct-pay. Now you can pay directly via the internet, including your quarterly **Form 1040-ES** estimated tax payments. You must use the EFTPS system to pay any payroll taxes you may owe when you hire employees. See chapter 8 for details. On the EFTPS website, you can also review your tax payment history and print out a confirmation of your payment. To use this site to pay online, you need to enroll first, and the enrollments take two to four weeks to process. For enrollment information, go to www.eftps.gov or call 800-945-8400.

Save Your Records

You should save all the records you used to complete your tax return for at least three years after you file your return. (Your state laws may require you to save your federal tax records for longer than three years, so check with your state department of revenue.) If you file your federal tax return on March 1, 2022, you will need to save your tax records until April 15, 2025. Many family child care providers save their records for an extra year.

You must save records associated with items that you are depreciating for as long as you are depreciating the item plus three years. So if you bought a washer and dryer last year and filed your taxes on March 1, 2022, you would save the receipt until April 15, 2033 (eight years of depreciation, plus three years). But remember that in 2021 you probably won't be depreciating anything except your house, home improvements, and home additions.

When you go out of business, you need only to keep records of the items you are depreciating for three more years. We recommend that you keep copies of your tax returns for as long as you live.

For more information about the tax issues discussed in this chapter, refer to the related topics in the other chapters of this book and the Redleaf Press *Family Child Care Record-Keeping Guide.*

This concludes the Tax Workbook section of this book. The next chapter is a Tax Return Checklist that you can use to ensure that you haven't made any common errors or forgotten anything important while doing your taxes.

CHAPTER 7

Catching Your Errors:
The Tax Return Checklist

The following checklist is designed to help you identify the most common mistakes before you send in your tax return. Review this list after you fill out all your tax forms.

Form 8829

Did you provide child care in a building that you didn't live in? You can't file **Form 8829**; instead, claim your house expenses directly on **Schedule C**.

Part I

❑ Did you enter the number of square feet of your home that you used on a regular basis for your business on line 1? *Regular use* means you used it at least two to three times per week on some business activity. You can count rooms that aren't used by the children in your care if *you* are using it for business purposes. This can include an office, laundry room, storage room, garage, and bedrooms used for storage.

❑ What should you include as the total number of square feet of your home on line 2? Make sure you also count your basement, garage (attached or unattached), and deck. Don't count a driveway, patio, or yard, since these areas aren't attached to your home. Count a shed if it is permanently attached to the ground.

❑ Does line 3 show 100%? Don't worry, it's not unusual.

❑ The instructions for this line—"Multiply days used for daycare during the year by hours used per day"—can be very misleading. So what should you enter? Put down the number of hours you worked in your home, including the number of hours children were present and the number of hours you used your home for business purposes when children were not present. Many providers fail to keep at least two months of careful records showing all the hours they spent on activities when children were not present: cleaning, record keeping, activity and meal preparation, time on the internet, and so on. If you didn't carefully track at least two months of hours for last year, plan ahead to do so for this year.

❑ Were you in business for the entire year? If so, enter 8,760 hours on line 5. If you were not in business for the full year, enter the number of hours in the year for the weeks you were in business.

❑ Line 6 represents your Time percentage. If you cared for children 11 hours a day, 5 days a week, this would represent 33% of the year. After adding the number of hours you worked on business activities when children were not present, this percentage would be 30% to 40% for most providers. If your percentage on this line is below 25%, this means that you either cared for children for fewer than 9 hours a day, 5 days a week—or you undercounted your hours.

❑ Is line 7 between 30% and 40%? This line represents your Time-Space percentage. But your Time-Space percentage can certainly be a lot higher if you work longer hours or have an exclusive-use room. If you used one or more rooms exclusively for your business, attach a statement to **Form 8829** showing how your Time-Space percentage was calculated. Lines 1–6 should be left blank. To have an exclusive-use room, you can never, ever use it for personal purposes.

Part II

❑ Line 8: Enter the amount from **Schedule C**, line 29 here. This number is called your tentative profit, since it is your profit before house expenses. Your deduction for house business expenses on **Form 8829** cannot exceed this amount. If it does, you will have to carry forward some of these expenses to the next year. See Part IV.

❑ Expenses entered under column (a): Direct expenses are those that are used 100% for your business. Expenses entered under column (b): Indirect expenses are those that are used for both business and personal purposes.

❑ Have you claimed expenses on **Schedule C**? Check to see that you are not claiming these same expenses on **Form 8829** on lines 9 through 22. This is most likely to happen with expenses for insurance, repairs, and utilities, since these categories appear on both forms. Check the following lines carefully. Utilities belong on **Form 8829**.

❑ Your full mortgage interest expense goes on line 10 or 16 (see pages 51–53) in column (b) where it will be multiplied by your Time-Space percentage.

❑ Have real estate taxes? Enter the full amount on line 11 or 17 (see pages 51–53) in column (b) where it will be multiplied by your Time-Space Percentage.

❑ Did you itemize your personal expenses on **Schedule A**? Check to see that you didn't claim 100% of your mortgage interest and real estate taxes there. These expenses should be split between **Schedule A** and **Form 8829**. If you didn't itemize using **Schedule A**, you are still entitled to your Time-Space percentage of these expenses on **Form 8829**.

❑ Enter your homeowners insurance in column (b) on line 18. Remember that your liability insurance goes on **Schedule C**, not here.

❑ Did you pay rent in 2021? Enter that amount on line 19 in column (b).

❑ List all your house repairs (for example, repairing a broken window, plumbing and electrical work, interior or exterior painting) on line 20. If you had repair expenses that were 100% business, enter them in column (a). Otherwise they should appear in column (b). Remember that repairs on your personal property used for your business (such as furniture, appliances, and equipment) go on **Schedule C**, not here.

❑ Enter your total utility expenses on line 21 in column (b). They can include gas, oil, electric, water, sewer, cable television, garbage, wood, and propane.

❑ Did you have a carryover amount from of your house expenses from line 43 on your 2020 **Form 8829**? You should enter that amount on line 25.

❑ Did you have a carryover amount from of your house depreciation from line 44 on your 2020 **Form 8829**? You should enter that amount on line 31.

❑ Line 36 represents the amount of house expenses from **Form 8829** that can be claimed on **Schedule C**, line 30.

Part III

❑ If you own your home, make sure you show an expense on line 37. You are always financially better off depreciating your home. Enter the lower of the purchase price of your home or its value at the time you first started using it for your business. For most providers, this will be the original purchase price of your home, not its current value.

❑ If you used the purchase price of your home on line 37, enter the value of the land at the time you bought it on line 38. If you used the value of your home at the time you first started using it for your business, enter the value of the land at that time.

❑ If your expenses on **Form 8829** create or increase a loss on your **Schedule C**, you won't be able to claim all of your house depreciation this year and must carry it forward to the next year. See Part IV.

❑ Not your first year using your home for your business? Enter 2.564% on line 41 as you are depreciating your home over 39 years.

❑ The amount on line 42 represents your house depreciation deduction. It should also appear on line 30.

Part IV

❑ Subtract line 27 from line 26. You will enter this amount on line 43 and carry it over onto your 2022 **Form 8829**. This will happen when your house expenses exceed your tentative profit from **Schedule C**.

❑ Subtract line 33 from line 32. You will enter this amount on line 44 and carry it over onto your 2022 **Form 8829**. This will happen when your house depreciation expense exceeds your tentative profit from **Schedule C**.

Form 4562

Are you still depreciating items? Because of tax law changes in 2018, many family child care providers may no longer need to depreciate items used in their business. All items except a home, home improvement, and home addition can be deducted in one year, and it's usually better to deduct items in one year rather than depreciating them. If you use a tax preparer, and they are showing depreciation deductions on **Form 4562**, you should ask them to explain why. If you do need to depreciate items, ask for a copy of the worksheet they used to calculate the depreciation deduction. This worksheet will be helpful in preparing your 2022 tax return, especially if you do not use the same tax professional.

Part I

❑ Have you or your tax professional listed an item on line 6? Doing so means using the Section 179 rule to deduct the item in one year. Because of the restrictions to the Section 179 rule, in most cases it doesn't make sense to use this rule, but a home improvement that is used more than 50% for your business could be an exception. Items showing on this line should probably be moved directly to **Schedule C**.

Part II

❑ Did you have any items that individually cost more than $2,500 that you purchased in 2021? Enter them on line 14. Tax changes effective in 2018 allow providers to deduct in one year all items except a home, home improvement, and home addition. Items costing $2,500 or less belong on **Schedule C** if you make that election.

❑ Enter items you purchased and began depreciating before 2021 on line 17. If you previously used a tax professional, get a copy of their worksheet showing how this number was calculated. If it's not clear to you where this number comes from, ask for clarification.

❑ Providers are entitled to claim deductions for items they owned before their business began. This includes furniture, appliances, and a host of household items. If you didn't claim these expenses under the Start-Up Rule, you may still be able to deduct them using **Form 3115 Application for Change in Accounting Method**. To claim previously unclaimed depreciation, you will need to conduct an inventory of these items and estimate their value at the time you first started using them in your business.

❑ Entering any expenses on lines 19(a–i) would be unusual. That's because most providers will no longer be depreciating items that can be deducted in one year. Again, it is almost always better to claim expenses in one year (on line 14 or on **Schedule C**) than to depreciate them here.

❑ Does a number appear on line 22? Make sure it also shows up on **Schedule C**, line 13.

❑ Are you depreciating your vehicle? Make sure "yes" is checked next to the two boxes on line 24.

❑ Items shown on lines 26 and 27 will probably be either a vehicle or a computer. If the computer costs $2,500 or less, it should be deducted in one year on **Schedule C** and not depreciated here. If the computer cost more than $2,500 and is used more than 50% of the time for your business, it should be deducted on line 14 in one year. If it is used less than 50% of the time for your business and costs more than $2,500, it should appear on line 26. The rules for depreciating a vehicle are complicated, and this deduction could appear on line 26 or 27. Recent changes in vehicle depreciation may allow you to deduct most or all the cost of the vehicle in the first year.

❑ Are you using the standard mileage rate for your vehicle expenses? You should still fill out lines 30–36 unless you don't need to otherwise file **Form 4562**.

Schedule C

Part I

❑ What goes on line 1? Enter all money received from parents, subsidy programs, and grants. This includes parent fees and copays. I recommend reporting your Food Program income on line 6, but you can put it here if you want. If you receive a **Form 1099** from your Food Program or a grant, enter these amounts on line 6.

❑ Have any amounts on lines 2–4? You shouldn't. You don't have any returns and allowances, and you aren't selling goods, so there is no need to fill out these lines or Part III.

❑ I recommend putting your Food Program income on line 6. Don't enter any reimbursements received for your own children, because they are not taxable.

Part II

❏ Did you know you are not required to list any of your deductions on any particular line on **Schedule C**? It doesn't matter if you put your calculator under Office Expenses (line 18) or under Supplies (line 22), but you need to know which deductions went on which line so you can produce receipts to support your return if you are ever audited.

❏ Do you do child care out of a home you do not live in? Do not fill out **Form 8829**—instead enter all your house-related expenses on **Schedule C**, including mortgage interest, property tax, rent, homeowners insurance, house repairs, utilities, and house depreciation. If you provide child care out of your home, do not enter these expenses on **Schedule C**.

❏ Want to reduce your chances of being audited? Make sure that the amount shown on any given line of 8–26 is not significantly larger than another. If you lump a lot of expenses under Supplies, this can attract the attention of the IRS. Instead, break out some of the expenses and put them in different categories.

❏ Did you claim the business portion of your car loan interest and any state personal property tax you pay each year on your car on line 9? You are always entitled to this deduction, even if you use the standard mileage rate method. If you used the actual vehicle expenses method for a vehicle, you can also claim depreciation for that vehicle. Check to see that your tax professional has entered that deduction on line 25 or 26 of **Form 4562**. You can't depreciate your vehicle if you use the standard mileage method.

❏ Do you have expenses from a house cleaner, gardener, music teacher, or other independent contractors? Those costs only belong on line 11. If you hire someone to help you care for children, that person is likely an employee and you should be paying payroll taxes. Report these amounts on line 26.

❏ Did you claim any depreciation on **Form 4562**? The total from line 22 on that form should appear here on line 13.

❏ Enter the amount of your business liability insurance on line 15. Homeowners insurance belongs on **Form 8829**, line 18.

❏ Don't put your mortgage interest on line 16 (a)—that belongs on **Form 8829**.

❏ Enter the cost of tax preparation fees to file only your business tax forms on line 17.

❏ Not sure where to put your food expenses? I recommend putting it on line 27(a) rather than 24(b). Be sure you are deducting 100% of your business food expenses. Line 24(b) should be used if you take parents out to eat or you pay for a "business meal" with other providers. The usual rule is you can deduct only 50% of the cost of that food but a special rule for 2021 and 2022 allow a 100% deduction if the food is provided by a restaurant.

❏ Transfer the amount from **Form 8829**, line 36 to line 30. The vast majority of providers will not use the Simplified Method as described here. That's because your house expenses from **Form 8829** are almost always going to be higher than what you could deduct using the Simplified Method.

Part III

❑ Lines 33–42: Since you do not sell any goods, you should not fill out this section.

Part IV

❑ Did you not file **Form 4562**? You should fill out this section. If you did file **Form 4562**, enter this same information on Part V of that form and leave this section blank.

Part V

❑ Not sure what to put here? You can create your own expense categories. I suggest using the following categories: Food, Household Items, Cleaning Supplies, Activity Expenses, and Toys. Do not use the category Gifts unless you are referring to items given to parents or children that are only used by them personally. You can deduct only up to $25 per year per person as a gift. If a child opens a present in your home before taking it to their home, this is an activity expense, not a gift.

❑ Compare your food expenses in Part V with the Food Program income you reported on line 6 of **Schedule C** (or line 1). If you received the higher Food Program reimbursement rate (Tier I) but served extra snacks that weren't reimbursed by the Food Program, your food deduction should be at least several hundred dollars higher than the amount on lines 1 or 6. If you received the lower Food Program reimbursement rate (Tier II), your deduction for food expenses should be at least twice as much as the amounts on line 1 or 6.

Schedule SE

❑ If you had a profit of more than $400 on **Schedule C**, line 31, you must fill out this form and pay self-employment tax. Transfer this amount to **Form 1040 Schedule 2**, line 4.

Form 4797

❑ If you sold or traded in your vehicle last year, did you check to see if you have a gain or loss as a result of the sale or trade-in? Any business gains or losses should be reported on **Form 4797**. See chapter 11.

Form 1040

❑ Did you enter your profit from **Schedule C**, line 31, onto **Form 1040 Schedule 1**, line 3? Then transfer it to **Form 1040**, line 7a.

❑ Did you claim one-half of your self-employment tax on **Form 1040 Schedule 1**, line 14? Then transfer it to **Form 1040**, line 8a. Don't forget this deduction. See chapter 6.

❑ Your health insurance deduction on **Form 1040 Schedule 1**, line 16, may not exceed your net business income (**Schedule C**, line 31). If it does, reduce your health insurance deduction until it equals the amount on **Schedule C**, line 31.

❑ If you have children of your own who were under the age of 18 at the end of last year, did you claim the Child Tax Credit on **Form 1040**, line 19 or 28? If so, did you also check the box on page 1 of **Form 1040**? See chapter 6.

❑ Did you enter the correct Social Security numbers for your spouse and your dependents on **Form 1040**?

❑ If you're married filing jointly, did both of you sign your **Form 1040**?

❑ Certain situations (such as capital gains) require you to use worksheets in addition to the tax tables. Did you double-check the taxes you owe according to the tax tables and worksheets in the IRS instruction book?

❑ Did you recheck the math on all your forms?

End-of-Year Record-Keeping Checklist

❑ Gather all your records together, and store them with your tax return.

❑ Record the odometer readings for all your vehicles on January 1 each year.

❑ Collect receipts from all the parents indicating how much they paid you for the year. Have each parent sign your copy.

❑ Save all your canceled checks, from personal as well as business checking accounts.

❑ Ask your tax preparer for copies of all the backup worksheets or forms used to prepare your tax return.

❑ Organize your expense receipts by category (utilities, food, toys) rather than by month. If you're audited, this will make it easier to present your records to the IRS.

❑ Put all your tax records in a sealed plastic storage box (to protect them from water damage), and put the box in a safe place. Save the records for at least three years after the filing date.

PART III

Tax Instructions
for Special Situations

CHAPTER 8

Hiring Employees and Paying Payroll Taxes

There were several new laws for payroll taxes that only apply to 2020 and 2021. As of now they do not affect the 2022 payroll tax forms that you will be filling out, but the laws and rules seem to be changing frequently, so you may consider consulting a tax professional about any changes for 2022.

This chapter explains how to withhold and pay taxes for your employees. Although the rules are complicated, the consequences of not following them can be serious. This chapter covers only federal tax rules about employees; if you have employees, you'll need to find out if your state has other rules regarding state and local income taxes, state unemployment taxes, and/or workers' compensation insurance.

There are two types of workers—independent contractors and employees—and there are two types of employees—those who are family members and those who are not. First we will discuss the difference between an independent contractor and an employee, and then we will explain how to withhold and pay taxes for the two types of employees.

Domestic Workers versus Employees

Don't confuse the kinds of employees discussed in this chapter with household employees—domestic workers, such as nannies or house cleaners who work in the home. The people who work for your family child care business are not household employees.

Parents who hire a nanny to care for their children don't need to pay Social Security taxes if they pay $2,300 or less per year or hire someone under the age of 18. This rule does not apply to family child care employees, because they are considered to be hired by your business rather than as household employees.

Employee or Independent Contractor?

If you pay anyone else to work with the children in your care, you need to understand that in almost every case the IRS will consider those workers to be your employees rather than independent contractors—and this fact has major tax implications.

When you hire an independent contractor, you don't withhold any taxes; you simply deduct what you pay the person as a miscellaneous expense. When you hire an employee, withhold taxes from their pay. You usually must also pay federal and state employer taxes.

It doesn't matter if the person works for only a few hours. A person who works for you 20 hours every week is your employee, and so is a person whom you hire once as a substitute while you go to the doctor. The main reason why someone you hire to care for children is considered your employee is because you have the right to direct and control the work of this person.

Independent Contractors

There are two circumstances in which the IRS might consider a family child care worker to be an independent contractor. The following situations are the exceptions to the general rule that everyone you pay to help with the children in your care is your employee:

1. A person who comes into your home on special occasions to perform specific services is not usually considered an employee. Someone who cleans your home for your business, occasionally repairs your toys, or offers swimming lessons or other activities programs for the children in your care is not an employee. Since these people aren't working under your control and direction, they can be considered independent contractors.

2. A person who is in the business of providing backup child care or who serves as an employee to several other child care providers *may* be considered an independent contractor. To have a chance of being considered an independent contractor, a worker should meet the following conditions:

   • She should advertise to the public that she's available to provide substitute or part-time child care.

   • She should have her own federal (and state, if required) employer identification number and report her income on **Schedule C**.

   • She should work under a business name ("Sally's Substitute Service") that's registered with the state. She may also need a business license (check your state law).

   • She should provide a business contract for you to sign that states her rates and the fact that she's self-employed and in the business of providing substitute child care to the public.

Even if a worker meets all the above qualifications, there's no guarantee that the IRS will consider her to be an independent contractor. However, it's far more likely to occur if she meets these qualifications than if she doesn't.

For a full discussion of the issue of employees versus independent contractors, refer to the *Record-Keeping Guide.*

A Word to the Wise

Despite the above facts, many family child care providers don't consider their workers to be employees. If the IRS rules that you have employees, you'll be responsible for back Social Security taxes, interest, and penalties. You may also owe state and local taxes, interest, and penalties.

The most likely triggers for an IRS challenge are the following situations:

• One of your workers files an unemployment claim and lists you as a previous employer.

- One of your workers is injured on the job and files a workers' compensation claim. (Your state is likely to turn your name over to the IRS and penalize you for not having workers' compensation insurance.)
- You list a deduction for an employee on **Schedule C**, line 26.
- You file **Form 1099-NEC** for a worker (this form reports payments to an independent contractor). This often triggers an IRS investigation to determine if the payee is actually an independent contractor.

Although it may be tempting to avoid treating your workers as employees to avoid filing withholding forms and paying payroll taxes, you need to take your legal responsibilities seriously. I know how frustrated many family child care providers feel about trying to comply with the legal requirements; however, there are ways to satisfy them at a relatively low cost, such as the following (for more information, see the *Record-Keeping Guide*):

- You can hire a payroll service company to set up a payroll system, withhold the proper amount of taxes, and file the required forms at a relatively low cost. Payroll service companies include, but are not limited to, QuickBooks (https://quickbooks .intuit.com/payroll), Paychex (www.paychex.com/payroll/small-business-payroll), and ADP (www.adp.com/what-we-offer/payroll). See also the article "Best Payroll Services for 2021" (www.businessnewsdaily.com/7509-best-payroll-services.html). You can also look under Bookkeeping Services in the Yellow Pages. We do not recommend any particular company
- You can use an employee leasing company instead of hiring your own employees. The advantage of this approach is that the leasing company will handle all the payroll and tax paperwork. Its disadvantage is that you won't be able to choose your own workers. Look under Employee Leasing Companies in the Yellow Pages. We do not recommend any particular company.

Note: If you have not treated your assistants as your employees in the past three years, there is some good news. The IRS will not audit you for your mistakes in past years if you apply for the Voluntary Classification Settlement Program. To be eligible, you must pay about 1% of the wages paid to your assistants for the past year; for $1,000 in wages paid, you'll owe $10.68. Apply for this program at least 60 days before the end of any tax quarter, and use IRS **Form 8952 Application for Voluntary Classification Settlement Program**. The IRS will not share this information with your state department of revenue. For more information, go to http://tinyurl.com/m9qm5rj.

Reporting Payments to Independent Contractors

If you pay any individual independent contractor $600 or more during the year, you must fill out **Form 1099-NEC**, give a copy to the independent contractor by January 31 of the following year, and file it with the IRS by January 31.

The purpose of **Form 1099-NEC** is to inform the IRS of payments that you make to independent contractors who are responsible for reporting that income to the IRS. If you don't file this form properly, you will be subject to a $50 penalty, but you won't be penalized if the independent contractor fails to report the income. If you didn't pay any independent contractors $600 or more during the year, you don't need to submit any records to the IRS.

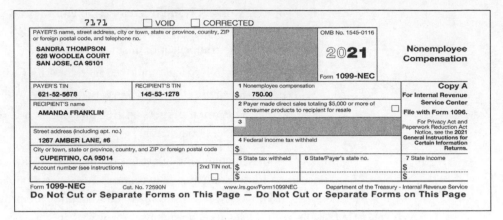

To report payments to independent contractors on your **Schedule C**, enter the total that you paid to independent contractors on line 11. *Don't enter anything on Schedule C, line 26, Wages* (unless you do have an employee). If you do, the IRS will assume that you have an employee and will check to see if you have withheld the proper amount of payroll taxes.

Employee Liability

Hiring an employee brings new risks and responsibilities. Before you start the hiring process, you need to check several things:

- Ask your licensor if there are any state regulations about the qualifications of your employees, if your state requires background checks of new employees, and if it requires you to buy workers' compensation insurance for employees.

- Find out if there are any deed restrictions, homeowners association covenants, or zoning laws that restrict your right to hire.

- Find out if your business liability insurance policy will cover you for any allegations of child abuse against your employees and for any medical expenses that are caused by the actions of your employees.

For a detailed discussion of the risks of having employees and how to reduce them, see the *Family Child Care Legal and Insurance Guide.*

Hiring Employees

When you hire someone, you must have an EIN (Form SS-4 or apply online) and fill out **Form I-9** and **Form W-4**. During the year you must file the quarterly **Form 941**, and at the end of the year you must file **Form 940**, **Form W-2**, and **Form W-3**. You can avoid filing the quarterly **Form 941** (by filing a **Form 944**) if you pay less than $4,000 in total wages for the year. See this chapter for details.

All employers are also required to file a report with their state whenever they hire or rehire an employee (including their own children), usually within 15 to 30 days of hiring the employee. This usually involves filling out a simple form and usually doesn't cost anything. Submit this form to your state, not the IRS. Check with your state for further details.

When you hire someone, you must save all your employment records for four years after filing your tax return.

Minimum Wage

Although the federal minimum wage for 2021 is $7.25 per hour, most child care providers are not subject to that requirement. Although you may not be required to pay a federal minimum wage to your employee, your state law may require you to pay a minimum wage. If the state or federal minimum wage law does apply to you and you pay someone to work more than 40 hours a week, you may be required to pay that person overtime (usually one-and-a-half times the regular rate). Even though you may not be required to pay a federal or state minimum wage, you can pay your employees these wage rates or higher. If you hire your own children, you may want to pay them the minimum wage to increase your business deductions.

Child Labor Laws

You may not hire anyone under age 14 who is not a family member. (Check with your state department of labor to see if your state laws restrict your ability to hire your own child under age 14.) If you hire someone under age 16 who is not a family member, there are restrictions on how many hours the person may work. Employees who are 14 and 15 years old may only work outside of school hours, no more than 3 hours on a school day and 8 hours on a nonschool day. They can only work 18 hours during a school week and 40 hours during a nonschool week.

Hiring Your Spouse or Children

Although the rules about hiring family members to work in your business are somewhat different from those for hiring nonfamily employees, you must still treat any family member you hire as an employee and fill out **Form SS-4**, **Form I-9**, **Form W-4**, **Form 941** (or possibly **Form 944**), and **Form 940**.

The IRS may also question the business expenses that you deduct for family employees. To protect yourself, you will need to keep good records that show specifically what work was done, how long it took, and how much you paid the employee for it.

Treat these financial transactions in a businesslike manner. For example, don't deposit the money that you pay to your spouse in a joint checking account; it will look as if you're simply paying yourself.

Your spouse or children must report the wages you pay them on their own **Form 1040**. For more information about the tax and financial benefits (and pitfalls) of hiring your spouse or children, see the *Record-Keeping Guide.*

Hiring Your Spouse

If you hire your spouse to work for your business, you must file the same tax forms as you would for any other employee, with one exception. The wages you pay to a spouse are not subject to federal unemployment taxes; however, you must still fill out **Form 940**. Your spouse's wages are subject to federal income tax withholding and Social Security and Medicare withholding. You must file **Form 941** (or possibly **Form 944**), **Form W-2**, and **Form W-3**. Your spouse must report all money earned by working in your business as wages and pay taxes on it.

Because your spouse will probably pay the same taxes that you would have paid if you had kept the money yourself, there's only a slight payroll tax advantage involved.

The advantage is that you can deduct as a business expense the 7.65% you withhold as an employer for Social Security and Medicare taxes.

HIRING YOUR OWN CHILDREN

Hiring your own children has two potential financial benefits. First, the wages you pay to your children under age 18 aren't subject to Social Security, Medicare, or federal unemployment taxes. Second, a child who earns less than $12,500 doesn't have to file a tax return.

Between ages 18 and 21, children are subject to Social Security and Medicare withholding, but their wages are not subject to federal unemployment taxes. This means that there is little financial incentive to hire them rather than nonfamily employees. Wages paid to children over 21 are subject to federal unemployment taxes.

If you hire your own child, you may need to file all the usual federal tax forms: **Form W-4**, **Form 941**, **Form W-2**, and **Form W-3**. Your child can claim an exemption from income tax withholding if he or she doesn't anticipate owing any federal taxes. In this case, the child wouldn't need to file **Form 1040**, although if he or she also worked for another employer who did withhold taxes, the child could file **Form 1040** to get a refund.

Federal law allows parents to hire their own children under or over the age of 14. In some states, you can't hire your own children who are younger than age 14. Check your state and local laws for any other restrictions on hiring your own children. As with hiring your spouse, keeping good records and treating the work in a proper, businesslike fashion is important. This means that the child must be doing work for your business, and the wages you pay must be distinguished from the child's allowance. See the *Record-Keeping Guide* for more information. Here are some tips to follow:

• Prepare a job description that details the responsibilities of the job: play with the children, clean up before and after the children, prepare meals for the children, clean toys, keep records, and so on. Do not include personal activities such as shopping, mowing the lawn, and running family errands.

• Prepare a written agreement between you and your family member that describes the employment arrangement: days and hours of work, pay, and so on. Both parties should sign this agreement.

• Keep a daily record of when the work is done. If the work is done at the same time every day, simply record the days and hours worked: Monday 9:00 a.m.–10:00 a.m., Tuesday 9:00 a.m.–10:00 a.m., Wednesday 9:00 a.m.–10:00 a.m., and so on.

• Write out a receipt for each payment, get the family member to sign it, and keep a copy: "Payment of $25 cash for 5 hours of work January 3–7." It is not necessary to pay by check; you can pay with cash. Make this payment out of a separate business account if you have one.

• Payments to family members must be reasonable. If you have a $15,000 business profit, it is unreasonable to pay your own children $6,000 in wages. Payment of $20 per hour to your 15-year-old is also unreasonable. The test of what is reasonable is probably how much you would be willing to pay someone who is not a family member.

• If you also give your child an allowance, keep a record of when you gave this allowance and how much it was.

Labor Law Posters

If you hire employees, you are required to post posters in your home explaining the rights of employees concerning minimum wage and workplace safety. You can put these posters in a back room, as long as it's accessible to employees. You can get these posters for free from the U.S. Department of Labor (www.dol.gov/general/topics/posters). This site also gives links to your state department of labor where there may be additional posters you must post. Scammers charge employers fees for these posters. Don't be fooled; you can get them for free.

Applying for an EIN

Before you can report your employment taxes, you must apply for an employer identification number (EIN). To get an EIN go to the IRS website at www.irs.gov. Enter "Online EIN" in the search box and answer the questions that appear on the screen. If you expect to pay less than $4,000 in total wages for the year, you may be eligible to file the annual **Form 944** rather than the quarterly **Form 941** (see this chapter for further information).

You can also get your EIN by filling out **Form SS-4** (available on the IRS website). Call the IRS Business and Specialty Tax Line (800-829-4933) for help in filling out this form.

If your employee doesn't have a Social Security number, she can apply for one by filling out **Form SS-5 Application for a Social Security Card**, which she can find at the nearest Social Security office.

Don't be fooled into paying anyone to receive your EIN. Some companies (EIN Filing Service, for one) charge a fee to help you get your EIN. Stay away from such "services."

Form I-9 Eligibility of the Employee

Every employer must verify that a new employee is a U.S. citizen or is eligible to work in the United States legally. To prove this, the employee must show evidence (such as a birth certificate, Social Security card, or passport) to the employer. Both parties must fill out and sign **Form I-9**.

The employer must keep **Form I-9** for three years after the date of hire or one year after the employment is terminated, whichever is later.

Form **SS-4**	**Application for Employer Identification Number**	OMB No. 1545-0003

Form SS-4 (Rev. December 2019)
Department of the Treasury
Internal Revenue Service

Application for Employer Identification Number
(For use by employers, corporations, partnerships, trusts, estates, churches, government agencies, Indian tribal entities, certain individuals, and others.)
▶ Go to www.irs.gov/FormSS4 for instructions and the latest information.
▶ See separate instructions for each line. ▶ Keep a copy for your records.

OMB No. 1545-0003

EIN

Type or print clearly.

1 Legal name of entity (or individual) for whom the EIN is being requested
SONJA OLSON

2 Trade name of business (if different from name on line 1)
FAMILY CHILD CARE

3 Executor, administrator, trustee, "care of" name

4a Mailing address (room, apt., suite no. and street, or P.O. box)
421 PORTLAND AVENUE

5a Street address (if different) (Don't enter a P.O. box.)

4b City, state, and ZIP code (if foreign, see instructions)
BOISE, ID 83701

5b City, state, and ZIP code (if foreign, see instructions)

6 County and state where principal business is located
SMITH COUNTY, ID

7a Name of responsible party

7b SSN, ITIN, or EIN

8a Is this application for a limited liability company (LLC) (or a foreign equivalent)? ☐ Yes ☑ No

8b If 8a is "Yes," enter the number of LLC members ▶

8c If 8a is "Yes," was the LLC organized in the United States? ☐ Yes ☐ No

9a Type of entity (check only one box). Caution: If 8a is "Yes," see the instructions for the correct box to check.
☑ Sole proprietor (SSN) 465-12-7748
☐ Partnership
☐ Corporation (enter form number to be filed) ▶
☐ Personal service corporation
☐ Church or church-controlled organization
☐ Other nonprofit organization (specify) ▶
☐ Other (specify) ▶
☐ Estate (SSN of decedent)
☐ Plan administrator (TIN)
☐ Trust (TIN of grantor)
☐ Military/National Guard ☐ State/local government
☐ Farmers' cooperative ☐ Federal government
☐ REMIC ☐ Indian tribal governments/enterprises
Group Exemption Number (GEN) if any ▶

9b If a corporation, name the state or foreign country (if applicable) where incorporated | State | Foreign country

10 Reason for applying (check only one box)
☐ Started new business (specify type) ▶
☑ Hired employees (Check the box and see line 13.)
☐ Compliance with IRS withholding regulations
☐ Other (specify) ▶
☐ Banking purpose (specify purpose) ▶
☐ Changed type of organization (specify new type) ▶
☐ Purchased going business
☐ Created a trust (specify type) ▶
☐ Created a pension plan (specify type) ▶

11 Date business started or acquired (month, day, year). See instructions. 1/1/2021

12 Closing month of accounting year

14 If you expect your employment tax liability to be $1,000 or less in a full calendar year and want to file Form 944 annually instead of Forms 941 quarterly, check here. (Your employment tax liability generally will be $1,000 or less if you expect to pay $5,000 or less in total wages.) If you don't check this box, you must file Form 941 for every quarter. ☐

13 Highest number of employees expected in the next 12 months (enter -0- if none). If no employees expected, skip line 14.

Agricultural	Household	Other

15 First date wages or annuities were paid (month, day, year). Note: If applicant is a withholding agent, enter date income will first be paid to nonresident alien (month, day, year) ▶ 1/1/2021

16 Check one box that best describes the principal activity of your business.
☐ Construction ☐ Rental & leasing ☐ Transportation & warehousing
☐ Real estate ☐ Manufacturing ☐ Finance & insurance
☐ Health care & social assistance ☐ Wholesale-agent/broker
☐ Accommodation & food service ☐ Wholesale-other ☐ Retail
☑ Other (specify) ▶ FAMILY CHILD CARE

17 Indicate principal line of merchandise sold, specific construction work done, products produced, or services provided.

18 Has the applicant entity shown on line 1 ever applied for and received an EIN? ☐ Yes ☑ No
If "Yes," write previous EIN here ▶

Third Party Designee
Complete this section only if you want to authorize the named individual to receive the entity's EIN and answer questions about the completion of this form.
Designee's name
Address and ZIP code
Designee's telephone number (include area code)
Designee's fax number (include area code)

Under penalties of perjury, I declare that I have examined this application, and to the best of my knowledge and belief, it is true, correct, and complete.
Name and title (type or print clearly) ▶ SONJA OLSON
Signature ▶ Sonja Olson Date ▶ 1/5/2021
Applicant's telephone number (include area code) (418) 222-7261
Applicant's fax number (include area code)

For Privacy Act and Paperwork Reduction Act Notice, see separate instructions. Cat. No. 16055N Form **SS-4** (Rev. 12-2019)

Employment Eligibility Verification
Department of Homeland Security
U.S. Citizenship and Immigration Services

USCIS
Form I-9

OMB No. 1615-0047
Expires 10/31/2022

▶**START HERE:** Read instructions carefully before completing this form. The instructions must be available, either in paper or electronically, during completion of this form. Employers are liable for errors in the completion of this form.

ANTI-DISCRIMINATION NOTICE: It is illegal to discriminate against work-authorized individuals. Employers **CANNOT** specify which document(s) an employee may present to establish employment authorization and identity. The refusal to hire or continue to employ an individual because the documentation presented has a future expiration date may also constitute illegal discrimination.

Section 1. Employee Information and Attestation *(Employees must complete and sign Section 1 of Form I-9 no later than the **first day of employment**, but not before accepting a job offer.)*

Last Name *(Family Name)*	First Name *(Given Name)*	Middle Initial	Other Last Names Used *(if any)*
OLSON	SONJA		

Address *(Street Number and Name)*	Apt. Number	City or Town	State	ZIP Code
421 PORTLAND AVENUE			MN	55118

Date of Birth *(mm/dd/yyyy)*	U.S. Social Security Number	Employee's E-mail Address	Employee's Telephone Number
01/10/1990	1 2 3 - 4 5 - 6 7 8 9		651-123-9876

I am aware that federal law provides for imprisonment and/or fines for false statements or use of false documents in connection with the completion of this form.

I attest, under penalty of perjury, that I am (check one of the following boxes):

- [✓] 1. A citizen of the United States
- [ ] 2. A noncitizen national of the United States *(See instructions)*
- [ ] 3. A lawful permanent resident   (Alien Registration Number/USCIS Number): _____
- [ ] 4. An alien authorized to work   until (expiration date, if applicable, mm/dd/yyyy): _____
     Some aliens may write "N/A" in the expiration date field. *(See instructions)*

Aliens authorized to work must provide only one of the following document numbers to complete Form I-9:
An Alien Registration Number/USCIS Number OR Form I-94 Admission Number OR Foreign Passport Number.

1. Alien Registration Number/USCIS Number: _____
   OR
2. Form I-94 Admission Number: _____
   OR
3. Foreign Passport Number: _____
   Country of Issuance: _____

QR Code - Section 1
Do Not Write In This Space

Signature of Employee	Today's Date *(mm/dd/yyyy)*
Leland Mullen	01/01/2021

Preparer and/or Translator Certification (check one):

- [ ] I did not use a preparer or translator.   [ ] A preparer(s) and/or translator(s) assisted the employee in completing Section 1.

(Fields below must be completed and signed when preparers and/or translators assist an employee in completing Section 1.)

I attest, under penalty of perjury, that I have assisted in the completion of Section 1 of this form and that to the best of my knowledge the information is true and correct.

Signature of Preparer or Translator	Today's Date *(mm/dd/yyyy)*

Last Name *(Family Name)*	First Name *(Given Name)*

Address *(Street Number and Name)*	City or Town	State	ZIP Code

STOP *Employer Completes Next Page* STOP

Employment Eligibility Verification
Department of Homeland Security
U.S. Citizenship and Immigration Services

USCIS
Form I-9
OMB No. 1615-0047
Expires 10/31/2022

Section 2. Employer or Authorized Representative Review and Verification

(Employers or their authorized representative must complete and sign Section 2 within 3 business days of the employee's first day of employment. You must physically examine one document from List A OR a combination of one document from List B and one document from List C as listed on the "Lists of Acceptable Documents.")

Employee Info from Section 1	Last Name *(Family Name)*	First Name *(Given Name)*	M.I.	Citizenship/Immigration Status
	MULLEN	LELAND	P	1

List A	OR	List B	AND	List C
Identity and Employment Authorization		Identity		Employment Authorization

List A	List B	List C
Document Title PASSPORT	Document Title	Document Title
Issuing Authority US DEPARTMENT OF STATE	Issuing Authority	Issuing Authority
Document Number 54321	Document Number	Document Number
Expiration Date *(if any) (mm/dd/yyyy)* 09/04/2021	Expiration Date *(if any) (mm/dd/yyyy)*	Expiration Date *(if any) (mm/dd/yyyy)*
Document Title		
Issuing Authority	Additional Information	QR Code - Sections 2 & 3 Do Not Write In This Space
Document Number		
Expiration Date *(if any) (mm/dd/yyyy)*		
Document Title		
Issuing Authority		
Document Number		
Expiration Date *(if any) (mm/dd/yyyy)*		

Certification: I attest, under penalty of perjury, that (1) I have examined the document(s) presented by the above-named employee, (2) the above-listed document(s) appear to be genuine and to relate to the employee named, and (3) to the best of my knowledge the employee is authorized to work in the United States.

The employee's first day of employment *(mm/dd/yyyy):*   01/01/2021   *(See instructions for exemptions)*

Signature of Employer or Authorized Representative *Sonja Olson*	Today's Date *(mm/dd/yyyy)* 01/01/2021	Title of Employer or Authorized Representative OWNER
Last Name of Employer or Authorized Representative OLSON	First Name of Employer or Authorized Representative SONJA	Employer's Business or Organization Name CHILD CARE BUSINESS

Employer's Business or Organization Address *(Street Number and Name)* 421 PORTLAND AVE.	City or Town BOISE	State ID	ZIP Code 83701

Section 3. Reverification and Rehires *(To be completed and signed by employer or authorized representative.)*

A. New Name *(if applicable)*			B. Date of Rehire *(if applicable)*
Last Name *(Family Name)*	First Name *(Given Name)*	Middle Initial	Date *(mm/dd/yyyy)*

C. If the employee's previous grant of employment authorization has expired, provide the information for the document or receipt that establishes continuing employment authorization in the space provided below.

Document Title	Document Number	Expiration Date *(if any) (mm/dd/yyyy)*

I attest, under penalty of perjury, that to the best of my knowledge, this employee is authorized to work in the United States, and if the employee presented document(s), the document(s) I have examined appear to be genuine and to relate to the individual.

Signature of Employer or Authorized Representative	Today's Date *(mm/dd/yyyy)*	Name of Employer or Authorized Representative

The Rules of Tax Withholding

There are different requirements for withholding and paying payroll taxes for different types of employees. The federal payroll taxes that are subject to withholding include the following:

- federal income tax
- Social Security/Medicare taxes
- federal unemployment taxes

You need to fill out and file different forms for each of the above kinds of taxes, and you may also need to pay or withhold state and local taxes. Here's a chart that summarizes the employer's responsibilities for federal payroll taxes:

	Must withhold federal income taxes	Must withhold and pay Social Security/ Medicare taxes	Must pay federal unemployment taxes***
Nonfamily employee*	Yes**	Yes	Yes
Spouse	Yes	Yes	No
Provider's own child 18 or over	Yes**	Yes	No
Provider's own child under 18	Yes**	No	No
Independent contractor	No	No	No

For the purposes of payroll taxes, siblings, nieces or nephews, and other relatives with whom you don't have a parent child relationship aren't considered to be family members, and you must withhold payroll taxes for them just as you would for a nonfamily employee. For example, if you hire your 16-year-old granddaughter, you must withhold Social Security and Medicare taxes from her wages.

IF YOU PAY SMALL AMOUNTS

If you pay a nonfamily member a small amount of money during the year, you still have to treat the person as an employee. If the total paid is small, you may not have to pay any unemployment taxes, but you'll still have to withhold Social Security and Medicare taxes and file the appropriate payroll forms. The minimum requirements for withholding are as follows:

- If you pay any amount, you must withhold Social Security and Medicare taxes.
- If you pay less than $1,500 in a calendar quarter, you don't have to pay any federal unemployment taxes unless you had employees for 20 or more weeks during the year.
- If the employee doesn't expect to owe any taxes, you don't have to withhold federal income taxes.

Federal Income Tax Withholding

To calculate how much federal income tax you must withhold, have the employee fill out **Form W-4**. Ask the employee to fill it out when she starts work. If your employee doesn't return a completed **Form W-4** to you, withhold taxes as if the employee were single with no adjustments. You won't generally file **Form W-4** with the IRS; instead, you'll keep it with your records to determine how much tax to withhold.

*A nonfamily employee is anyone except your spouse and your own children.
**Only if the employee requests that you do so.
***This assumes that the employer pays any employee $1,500 or more in any calendar quarter or that an employee worked for some part of a day in any 20 different weeks of the year. Unemployment tax is due for provider's own child age 21 or over.

Income tax withholding can be figured a number of ways; they're listed in **Publication 15**. You must withhold income taxes for each payroll period. The payroll period is the period of service for which you usually pay wages (for example, once a week, once every two weeks). The amount you need to withhold will depend on the amount of wages, the adjustments the employee entered on the **W-4**, and if the employee is married or single.

MAKING FEDERAL INCOME TAX DEPOSITS

The deadline for depositing the income taxes you've withheld depends on how much these taxes amount to. If you withhold $500 or more in income taxes, Social Security, and Medicare taxes in a three-month period, you should deposit the taxes monthly by the fifteenth day of the following month. If the total you withhold is less than $500 for a three-month period, you can deposit the taxes by the end of the month following that quarter. Your federal tax deposit must be made electronically using the Electronic Federal Tax Payment System (EFTPS). If you do not want to use the EFTPS, you can arrange for your tax professional, bank, or payroll service to make deposits on your behalf. The EFTPS is a free service. To enroll in the EFTPS, visit www.eftps.gov or call 800-555-4477. For more information, see IRS **Publication 966 Electronic Federal Tax Payment System: A Guide to Getting Started**.

Social Security and Medicare Withholding

You must also withhold and pay Social Security and Medicare taxes. For wages paid last year, the Social Security tax rate is 6.2% for you as an employer and 6.2% for the employee. The rate for Medicare is 1.45% for you as an employer and 1.45% for the employee. In other words, you must withhold a total of 7.65% of the gross wages you pay an employee. As the employer, you must pay 7.65% into the Social Security and Medicare fund. Refer to **Publication 15** for the tables that show how much tax to withhold.

MAKING SOCIAL SECURITY AND MEDICARE DEPOSITS

If you owe less than $2,500 in taxes for federal income tax, Social Security, and Medicare withholding (employer and employee share) in any calendar quarter, you must deposit the money by the end of the month following the calendar quarter (by April 30, July 31, October 31, and January 31). If you owe more than $2,500 in a quarter, you must file monthly. You must pay these taxes electronically using the EFTPS (www.eftps.gov).

Continue to file **Form 941** as long as you have an employee, even if you don't owe any payroll taxes, because it proves that you have an employee. Without this form, the IRS may assume that you don't have an employee and may not allow you to take employee expenses as a business deduction. If you temporarily stop hiring an employee, continue filing **Form 941** even if you have no taxes to report. When you stop paying wages, file a final return.

Form 944

You can avoid filing **Form 941** if you owe less than $1,000 in payroll taxes for the year. (The IRS created **Form 944 Employer's Annual Federal Tax Return** in response to my request to reduce the paperwork for taxpayers who pay small amounts to their employees.) Payroll taxes include Social Security and Medicare taxes (15.3%) and withheld federal income taxes (10% or 12% or 22% or 24% or more). You can use **Form 944** if you pay less than $4,000 in wages to all your employees during a year. This option is something to consider as you look forward to 2022. If you use **Form 944**, you must use the Electronic Federal Tax Payment System (EFTPS) to pay your payroll taxes.

You may have already been notified by the IRS to file **Form 944**. If not, and you wish to use **Form 944**, you must contact the IRS to request permission. Call the IRS at 800-829-4933 by April 1, 2021, or send a written request postmarked by March 15, 2021. See the instructions to **Form 944** for the mailing address.

If you are a new employer, you can indicate that you want to file **Form 944** when you apply for an employer identification number (see page 151). For more information, visit www.irs.gov/forms-pubs/about-form-944.

Federal Unemployment Tax (FUTA)

If you paid an employee $1,500 or more in any calendar quarter or had any employee who worked for some part of a day in any 20 different weeks during the year, you must pay federal unemployment tax (FUTA). The unemployment tax is based on the first $7,000 of wages paid during the year to each employee. This rate assumes that you have paid state payroll or unemployment taxes on time. If not, you will owe unemployment taxes at a rate of 6.0%. You do not have to pay a FUTA tax on wages over $7,000 for each employee. (In some states, you may be entitled to a reduction in your federal unemployment tax because of your state unemployment tax rules.) The unemployment tax rate is 0.6% for 2021.

You must pay this tax in addition to the wages you pay your employee; you may not withhold or deduct these taxes from the employee's wages.

MAKING FUTA DEPOSITS

If your total FUTA tax is less than $100 (or $12,500 in wages), pay it when you file your **Form 940**. You need to file this form by January 31 of the following year. If you owe more than $500 in FUTA taxes at the end of any quarter (you can accumulate the tax owed from one quarter to the next), you must make deposits by the end of the month following the quarter. You must pay your FUTA taxes electronically using the EFTPS. If you do not want to use the EFTPS, you can arrange for your tax professional, bank, or payroll service to make deposits on your behalf. The EFTPS is a free service. To enroll in the EFTPS, see www.eftps.gov or call 800-555-4477. For more information, see IRS **Publication 966**.

If You Haven't Filed Any Payroll Forms This Year

If you haven't yet filed the proper payroll forms and it's now early 2022, your best option is to file **Form 941** for the fourth quarter by January 31 and pay all the taxes you owe. You should file **Form 941** as soon as possible, even if you're filing late. The sooner you file, the less interest will accumulate on any taxes you owe. If you miss the January 31 deadline, you can file an amended tax return after April 15 and include the fourth-quarter filing of **Form 941** to cover the year.

Forms W-2 and W-3

In addition to the above forms, you must also file forms **W-2** and **W-3** at the end of the year for all types of employees:

- **Form W-2**
  You must file this form if you have withheld any income, Social Security, or Medicare taxes. It summarizes the wages you've paid and taxes you've withheld for each employee. You must give a copy to each employee as soon as possible after the end of the year, and no later than January 31. You must also send a copy of the **W-2** to the IRS by January 31. An employee who stops working for you during the year may ask you to provide this form within 30 days.

- **Form W-3**
  Use this form to transmit a copy of **Form W-2** to the Social Security Administration. That agency will send the income tax data on **Form W-2** on to the IRS. You must submit **Form W-3** by January 31. Mail **Form W-2** and **Form W-3** to the address indicated on the instructions for **Form W-3**.

Note

Payroll taxes that you pay (Social Security/Medicare tax, federal and state unemployment tax) are deductible in the year you pay them. Taxes withheld from your employee's paychecks are part of wages, so you claim that as part of your wage deduction for the year you paid your employee. But if you did not send the payroll payment to the IRS until January 2022, the employer portion would not be deductible until 2022. So if you withheld $200 in Social Security/Medicare taxes for the last quarter of 2021 and sent them in to the

IRS along with the employer share of these taxes ($200), you can deduct the withheld taxes in 2021 (as part of wages), but you must wait until 2022 to deduct the employer share.

How to Fill Out Payroll Tax Forms

Filling out all the payroll tax forms for an employee can be a real pain in the neck, but the first year is usually the hardest. After that, it becomes easier because the forms are more familiar. And once you've completed all the proper forms, you'll be able to claim the wages and taxes (Social Security, Medicare, and federal and state unemployment taxes) that you paid as a business deduction on **Schedule C**, line 26. Let's look at three examples of filling out employee payroll tax forms—for a nonfamily employee, your own child under age 18, and your spouse. You'll find samples of some of the forms for the first two examples at the end of this chapter. (Check for other state or local rules in your area.)

Example 1: Hiring a Nonfamily Employee

You hire your first employee, Jill, on January 1 of last year. Jill works three days a week, eight hours a day, and you pay her $7.25 per hour. You write her a check at the end of every week. What obligations do you have to withhold and pay taxes to the IRS?

STEP ONE: EMPLOYEE ELIGIBILITY
When you hire Jill, ask her to fill out **Form I-9** to affirm that she isn't an undocumented worker.

STEP TWO: EMPLOYER IDENTIFICATION NUMBER
As soon as you know that you will be hiring an employee, file **Form SS-4** to get an employer identification number. Use this number on all your employer forms.

STEP THREE: FEDERAL INCOME TAX WITHHOLDING
Jill is single, has no dependents, and declares no adjustments on her **Form W-4**, which she filled out the day she started work. Her weekly wages amount to 8 hours x 5 days x $7.25/hour = $290. According to the the wage bracket tables, you need to withhold $5.00 in income tax. You therefore reduce Jill's weekly paycheck by $5.00 for income tax withholding.

In the first quarter of the year, Jill will earn $3,770 ($290 per week x 13 weeks). The income tax on this will be $65.00 ($5.00 x 13). Since this amount, plus Jill's quarterly Social Security and Medicare taxes, will be less than $2,500 per quarter, you don't have to deposit it with the IRS every month; you can wait and pay it when you file your quarterly **Form 941**.

STEP FOUR: SOCIAL SECURITY AND MEDICARE TAX WITHHOLDING
To calculate Jill's Social Security and Medicare taxes, multiply her weekly wages by 7.65%: $290 x 7.65% = $22.19. This will further reduce her weekly paycheck by $22.19. Jill's actual take-home pay is now $290 – $5.00 – $22.19 = $262.81. Each week you must also pay $22.19 ($290 x 7.65%) of your own money into Social Security and Medicare.

Complete **Form 941** by April 30 to cover the first three months of the year. At this time you will owe the IRS $641.81 for Social Security and Medicare taxes:

$576.81	$290 x 13 x 15.3% (7.65% withheld plus 7.65% paid by you)
+$65.00	Income tax withheld ($5.00 x 13 weeks)
$641.81	Amount you owe the IRS

As long as Jill's hours and wages remain the same, you'll keep paying the IRS $641.81 every quarter. Pay this amount electronically using the EFTPS (www.eftps.gov).

Step Five: Federal Unemployment Tax

Jill earned $15,080 last year ($290 per week x 52 weeks). Since this is more than $1,500, you must pay federal unemployment tax (FUTA) on the first $7,000. At the end of the year, you will fill out **Form 940** and file it by January 31. You will owe $42 on **Form 940**:

$7,000	Jill's wages subject to FUTA tax
x 0.6%	FUTA tax
$42.00	Total FUTA tax

This amount is not withheld from Jill's paycheck; it's paid directly by you. Pay this amount electronically using the EFTPS (www.eftps.gov).

Step Six: End-of-the-Year Reporting

At the end of the year, fill out **Form W-2** and **Form W-3**. These forms will show the following:

$15,080.00	Wages paid to Jill (**W-2** and **W-3**, lines 1, 3, and 5)
$260.00	Federal income tax withheld ($22.30 x 52 weeks) (**W-2** and **W-3**, line 2)
$934.96	Social Security tax withheld ($15,080 x 6.2%) (**W-2** and **W-3**, line 4)
$218.66	Medicare tax withheld ($15,080 x 1.45%) (**W-2** and **W-3**, line 6)

Summary

$15,080.00	Jill's yearly wages
− $260.00	Federal income tax withheld
− $1,153.62	Social Security and Medicare tax withheld (7.65%)
$13,666.38	Jill's take-home pay
$1,153.62	Additional Social Security and Medicare taxes you paid (7.65%)
+ $42.00	Federal unemployment tax you paid
$1,195.62	Total taxes you paid for having Jill as an employee

Example 2: Hiring Your Own Child

You have hired your daughter Clarisse, age 16, to clean your home before children arrive in the morning. She works one hour a day, five days a week, and you pay her $5.00 per hour. You keep a record of the work she does and write her a check at the end of every week. You have an employment agreement stating her job description and pay. (See the *Record-Keeping Guide* for a sample.) Clarisse will earn $1,300 a year ($25 a week x 52 weeks). You keep records of your payments to her and make out a receipt each time you pay her. You must file the following IRS forms for this employee:

Step One: Employee Eligibility

Fill out **Form I-9**.

STEP TWO: EMPLOYER IDENTIFICATION NUMBER
File **Form SS-4**.

STEP THREE: FEDERAL INCOME TAX WITHHOLDING
Clarisse must fill out **Form W-4**. She declares no withholding allowance because she is a child and you don't have to withhold income tax on weekly wages of $25.

STEP FOUR: SOCIAL SECURITY AND MEDICARE TAX WITHHOLDING
Since Clarisse is under age 18, you don't have to withhold any Social Security or Medicare taxes for her. File **Form 941**, and check the box on line 4. Continue filing this form quarterly, even though you don't owe any taxes.

Note: Since you paid less than $4,000 in wages to Clarisse, you could use the annual **Form 944** instead of the quarterly **Form 941**. If you have not already been contacted by the IRS and told that you can use **Form 944**, fill out **Form 941**. To find out if you can use **Form 944**, call the IRS at 800-829-4933. See the end of this chapter for a sample of how to fill out **Form 944**.

Forms for Family Employees
If you have hired nonfamily employees or your own children, enter the total wages paid on line 2 of **Form 941**.

Although the instructions indicate that **Form 941** may not be required, filing **Form 941** may help support that the payments to your children were wages and not an allowance. Even if you choose not to file **Form 941**, filing a **W-2** and **W-3** is still required.

STEP FIVE: FEDERAL UNEMPLOYMENT TAX
Since Clarisse is under age 21, you don't owe any federal unemployment taxes. File **Form 940** and claim an exemption for wages on line 4.

STEP SIX: END-OF-THE-YEAR REPORTING
At the end of the year, fill out **Form W-2** and **Form W-3**.

SUMMARY

Wages paid to Clarisse	$1,300
Federal income tax withheld	$0
Social Security and Medicare taxes withheld	$0
Federal unemployment tax withheld	$0

Example 3: Hiring Your Spouse
You've hired your husband, John, to help with your business. He works five hours a week, and you pay him $10 per hour. You keep a record of the work he does and write him a check at the end of every week. John will earn $2,600 a year ($50 a week x 52 weeks).

STEP ONE: EMPLOYEE ELIGIBILITY
Fill out **Form I-9**.

STEP TWO: EMPLOYER IDENTIFICATION NUMBER
File **Form SS-4**.

STEP THREE: FEDERAL INCOME TAX WITHHOLDING
You can avoid withholding federal income tax if John is having enough withheld from the paycheck of another employer. If he does this, you don't have to fill out **Form W-4**.

STEP FOUR: SOCIAL SECURITY AND MEDICARE TAX WITHHOLDING
You must withhold Social Security and Medicare taxes on John's earnings. Multiply his weekly wages by 7.65%: $50 x 7.65% = $3.83. His weekly paycheck is now $46.17. You must pay $3.83 ($50 x 7.65%) of your own money into Social Security and Medicare. Complete **Form 941** by April to cover the first three months of the year. At the end of three months, John will have earned $650 ($50 x 13 weeks = $650). You will owe the IRS $99.45 for Social Security and Medicare taxes ($50 per week x 13 weeks x 15.3% [7.65% from John's paycheck and 7.65% from your pocket] = $99.45). Enter $99.45 on lines 5e, 6, 10, 12, and 14.

Note: Since you paid your husband less than $4,000 in wages, you can use the annual **Form 944** (see below) instead of the quarterly **Form 941** as long as you received permission to do so from the IRS. Call the IRS at 800-829-4933 to receive permission.

STEP FIVE: FEDERAL UNEMPLOYMENT TAX
You do not have to pay the federal unemployment tax.

STEP SIX: END-OF-THE-YEAR REPORTING
At the end of the year, fill out **Forms W-2** and **W-3**. You will show $322.40 in Social Security taxes withheld on line 4 ($2,600 x 12.4%) and $75.40 in Medicare taxes withheld on line 6 ($2,600 x 2.9%).

Example 4: Hiring a Part-Time Employee

You may be able to avoid filing the quarterly **Form 941** and instead use **Form 944** if you paid less than $4,000 in total wages last year. To be able to file **Form 944** for your taxes, you either must have been notified by the IRS or must call the IRS to receive permission. *Do not file **Form 944** unless you have IRS approval.*

Let's say you paid Ophelia Lopez $1,000 to provide substitute care for 50 hours last year. You should have withheld 7.65% of her pay ($76.50) when you paid her. Use **Form 944V** to make your payment. See pages 173–175 for how **Form 944** should be filled out. The deadline to file these forms is January 31. In this example, you would still file forms **I-9**, **W-2**, and **W-3**, but not **Form 941** or **Form 940** (because the amount paid was less than $1,500 in any calendar quarter).

Note: Most states still require you to file quarterly state payroll taxes (state unemployment) even when you file **Form 944**.

For more information about the tax issues discussed in this chapter, refer to the related topics in the other chapters of this book and the Redleaf Press *Family Child Care Record-Keeping Guide*.

For Employee Jill

Form **941 for 2021:** **Employer's QUARTERLY Federal Tax Return**
(Rev. June 2021)   Department of the Treasury — Internal Revenue Service

951121

OMB No. 1545-0029

Employer identification number (EIN) 9 2 – 1 2 3 4 5 6 7

Name (not your trade name) SONJA OLSON

Trade name (if any)

Address 421 PORTLAND AVENUE
Number   Street   Suite or room number

BOISE   ID   83701
City   State   ZIP code

Foreign country name   Foreign province/county   Foreign postal code

Report for this Quarter of 2021
(Check one.)

[✓] **1:** January, February, March

[ ] **2:** April, May, June

[ ] **3:** July, August, September

[ ] **4:** October, November, December

Go to *www.irs.gov/Form941* for instructions and the latest information.

Read the separate instructions before you complete Form 941. Type or print within the boxes.

Part 1:   **Answer these questions for this quarter.**

1	Number of employees who received wages, tips, or other compensation for the pay period including: *June 12* (Quarter 2), *Sept. 12* (Quarter 3), or *Dec. 12* (Quarter 4)	1	1
2	Wages, tips, and other compensation	2	$3,770 . 00
3	Federal income tax withheld from wages, tips, and other compensation	3	$65 . 00
4	If no wages, tips, and other compensation are subject to social security or Medicare tax		[ ] Check and go to line 6.

		Column 1			Column 2	
5a	Taxable social security wages*	$3,770 . 00	× 0.124 =		$467 . 48	*Include taxable qualified sick and family leave wages for leave taken after March 31, 2021, on line 5a. Use lines 5a(i) and 5a(ii) **only** for wages paid after March 31, 2020, for leave taken before April 1, 2021.
5a (i)	Qualified sick leave wages*	.	× 0.062 =		.	
5a (ii)	Qualified family leave wages*	.	× 0.062 =		.	
5b	Taxable social security tips	.	× 0.124 =		.	
5c	Taxable Medicare wages & tips	$3,770 . 00	× 0.029 =		$109 . 33	
5d	Taxable wages & tips subject to Additional Medicare Tax withholding	.	× 0.009 =		.	

5e	Total social security and Medicare taxes. Add Column 2 from lines 5a, 5a(i), 5a(ii), 5b, 5c, and 5d	5e	$576 . 81
5f	Section 3121(q) Notice and Demand—Tax due on unreported tips (see instructions)	5f	.
6	Total taxes before adjustments. Add lines 3, 5e, and 5f	6	$641 . 81
7	Current quarter's adjustment for fractions of cents	7	.
8	Current quarter's adjustment for sick pay	8	.
9	Current quarter's adjustments for tips and group-term life insurance	9	.
10	Total taxes after adjustments. Combine lines 6 through 9	10	$641 . 81
11a	Qualified small business payroll tax credit for increasing research activities. Attach Form 8974	11a	.
11b	Nonrefundable portion of credit for qualified sick and family leave wages for leave taken before April 1, 2021	11b	.
11c	Nonrefundable portion of employee retention credit	11c	.

▶ **You MUST complete all three pages of Form 941 and SIGN it.**   Next ▶

For Privacy Act and Paperwork Reduction Act Notice, see the back of the Payment Voucher.   Cat. No. 17001Z   Form **941** (Rev. 6-2021)

951221

Name *(not your trade name)*	Employer identification number (EIN)
SONJA OLSON	92-1234567

Part 1: Answer these questions for this quarter. *(continued)*

11d Nonrefundable portion of credit for qualified sick and family leave wages for leave taken after March 31, 2021 . . . . **11d** [.   ]

11e Nonrefundable portion of COBRA premium assistance credit (see instructions for applicable quarters) . . . . **11e** [.   ]

11f Number of individuals provided COBRA premium assistance [   ]

11g Total nonrefundable credits. Add lines 11a, 11b, 11c, 11d, and 11e . . . . **11g** [.   ]

12 Total taxes after adjustments and nonrefundable credits. Subtract line 11g from line 10 . **12** [$641 . 81]

13a Total deposits for this quarter, including overpayment applied from a prior quarter and overpayments applied from Form 941-X, 941-X (PR), 944-X, or 944-X (SP) filed in the current quarter **13a** [.   ]

13b Reserved for future use . . . . **13b** [.   ]

13c Refundable portion of credit for qualified sick and family leave wages for leave taken before April 1, 2021 . . . . **13c** [.   ]

13d Refundable portion of employee retention credit . . . . **13d** [.   ]

13e Refundable portion of credit for qualified sick and family leave wages for leave taken after March 31, 2021 . . . . **13e** [.   ]

13f Refundable portion of COBRA premium assistance credit (see instructions for applicable quarters) . . . . **13f** [.   ]

13g Total deposits and refundable credits. Add lines 13a, 13c, 13d, 13e, and 13f . . . . . **13g** [.   ]

13h Total advances received from filing Form(s) 7200 for the quarter . . . . **13h** [.   ]

13i Total deposits and refundable credits less advances. Subtract line 13h from line 13g . . . **13i** [.   ]

14 Balance due. If line 12 is more than line 13i, enter the difference and see instructions . . . **14** [$641 . 81]

15 Overpayment. If line 13i is more than line 12, enter the difference [.   ] Check one: ☐ Apply to next return.   ☐ Send a refund.

Part 2: Tell us about your deposit schedule and tax liability for this quarter.

If you're unsure about whether you're a monthly schedule depositor or a semiweekly schedule depositor, see section 11 of Pub. 15.

16 Check one: **[X]** **Line 12 on this return is less than $2,500 or line 12 on the return for the prior quarter was less than $2,500, and you didn't incur a $100,000 next-day deposit obligation during the current quarter.** If line 12 for the prior quarter was less than $2,500 but line 12 on this return is $100,000 or more, you must provide a record of your federal tax liability. If you're a monthly schedule depositor, complete the deposit schedule below; if you're a semiweekly schedule depositor, attach Schedule B (Form 941). Go to Part 3.

☐ **You were a monthly schedule depositor for the entire quarter.** Enter your tax liability for each month and total liability for the quarter, then go to Part 3.

Tax liability: Month 1 [.   ]

Month 2 [.   ]

Month 3 [.   ]

Total liability for quarter [.   ]   **Total must equal line 12.**

☐ **You were a semiweekly schedule depositor for any part of this quarter.** Complete Schedule B (Form 941), Report of Tax Liability for Semiweekly Schedule Depositors, and attach it to Form 941. Go to Part 3.

▶ **You MUST complete all three pages of Form 941 and SIGN it.**   Next ▶

Page **2**   Form **941** (Rev. 6-2021)

951921

Name *(not your trade name)*	Employer identification number (EIN)
SONJA OLSON	92-1234567

Part 3:   Tell us about your business. If a question does NOT apply to your business, leave it blank.

17 **If your business has closed or you stopped paying wages** . . . . □ Check here, and

enter the final date you paid wages [/ /] ; also attach a statement to your return. See instructions.

18a **If you're a seasonal employer and you don't have to file a return for every quarter of the year** . . . □ Check here.

18b **If you're eligible for the employee retention credit solely because your business is a recovery startup business** □ Check here.

19	Qualified health plan expenses allocable to qualified sick leave wages for leave taken before April 1, 2021	19	.
20	Qualified health plan expenses allocable to qualified family leave wages for leave taken before April 1, 2021	20	.
21	**Qualified wages for the employee retention credit**	21	.
22	**Qualified health plan expenses for the employee retention credit**	22	.
23	**Qualified sick leave wages for leave taken after March 31, 2021**	23	.
24	Qualified health plan expenses allocable to qualified sick leave wages reported on line 23	24	.
25	Amounts under certain collectively bargained agreements allocable to qualified sick leave wages reported on line 23	25	.
26	Qualified family leave wages for leave taken after March 31, 2021	26	.
27	Qualified health plan expenses allocable to qualified family leave wages reported on line 26	27	.
28	Amounts under certain collectively bargained agreements allocable to qualified family leave wages reported on line 26	28	.

Part 4:   May we speak with your third-party designee?

Do you want to allow an employee, a paid tax preparer, or another person to discuss this return with the IRS? See the instructions for details.

□ **Yes.** Designee's name and phone number [   ] [   ]

Select a 5-digit personal identification number (PIN) to use when talking to the IRS. □ □ □ □ □

□ **No.**

Part 5:   Sign here. You MUST complete all three pages of Form 941 and SIGN it.

Under penalties of perjury, I declare that I have examined this return, including accompanying schedules and statements, and to the best of my knowledge and belief, it is true, correct, and complete. Declaration of preparer (other than taxpayer) is based on all information of which preparer has any knowledge.

✗ **Sign your name here** *Sonja Olson*	Print your name here	SONJA OLSON
	Print your title here	OWNER
Date 4 / 11 / 2021	Best daytime phone	612-222-2222

Paid Preparer Use Only

Check if you're self-employed . . . □

Preparer's name	[ ]	PTIN	[ ]
Preparer's signature	[ ]	Date	[/ /]
Firm's name (or yours if self-employed)	[ ]	EIN	[ ]
Address	[ ]	Phone	[ ]
City	[ ] State [ ]	ZIP code	[ ]

Form **941** (Rev. 6-2021)

Form **940 for 2021:** **Employer's Annual Federal Unemployment (FUTA) Tax Return**

Department of the Treasury — Internal Revenue Service

850113

OMB No. 1545-0028

Employer identification number (EIN) 9 2 – 1 2 3 4 5 6 7

Name *(not your trade name)* SONJA OLSON

Trade name *(if any)*

Address 421 PORTLAND AVENUE

Number   Street   Suite or room number

BOISE   ID   83701

City   State   ZIP code

Foreign country name   Foreign province/county   Foreign postal code

Type of Return
(Check all that apply.)

- [ ] **a.** Amended
- [ ] **b.** Successor employer
- [ ] **c.** No payments to employees in 2021
- [ ] **d.** Final: Business closed or stopped paying wages

Go to *www.irs.gov/Form940* for instructions and the latest information.

Read the separate instructions before you complete this form. Please type or print within the boxes.

Part 1: **Tell us about your return. If any line does NOT apply, leave it blank. See instructions before completing Part 1.**

1a	If you had to pay state unemployment tax in one state only, enter the state abbreviation .	1a
1b	If you had to pay state unemployment tax in more than one state, you are a multi-state employer .	1b ☐ Check here. Complete Schedule A (Form 940).
2	If you paid wages in a state that is subject to **CREDIT REDUCTION** .	2 ☐ Check here. Complete Schedule A (Form 940).

Part 2: **Determine your FUTA tax before adjustments. If any line does NOT apply, leave it blank.**

3	Total payments to all employees .	3	$15,080 .
4	Payments exempt from FUTA tax .	4	.
	Check all that apply: **4a** ☐ Fringe benefits **4c** ☐ Retirement/Pension **4e** ☐ Other		
	4b ☐ Group-term life insurance **4d** ☐ Dependent care		
5	Total of payments made to each employee in excess of $7,000 .	5	$8,080 .
6	Subtotal (line 4 + line 5 = line 6) .	6	$8,080 .
7	Total taxable FUTA wages (line 3 – line 6 = line 7). See instructions .	7	$7,000 .
8	FUTA tax before adjustments (line 7 x 0.006 = line 8) .	8	$42 .

Part 3: **Determine your adjustments. If any line does NOT apply, leave it blank.**

9	If ALL of the taxable FUTA wages you paid were excluded from state unemployment tax, multiply line 7 by 0.054 (line 7 × 0.054 = line 9). Go to line 12 .	9	.
10	If SOME of the taxable FUTA wages you paid were excluded from state unemployment tax, OR you paid ANY state unemployment tax late (after the due date for filing Form 940), complete the worksheet in the instructions. Enter the amount from line 7 of the worksheet .	10	.
11	If credit reduction applies, enter the total from Schedule A (Form 940) .	11	.

Part 4: **Determine your FUTA tax and balance due or overpayment. If any line does NOT apply, leave it blank.**

12	Total FUTA tax after adjustments (lines 8 + 9 + 10 + 11 = line 12) .	12	$42 .
13	FUTA tax deposited for the year, including any overpayment applied from a prior year .	13	.
14	Balance due. If line 12 is more than line 13, enter the excess on line 14. • If line 14 is more than $500, you must deposit your tax. • If line 14 is $500 or less, you may pay with this return. See instructions .	14	$42 .
15	Overpayment. If line 13 is more than line 12, enter the excess on line 15 and check a box below	15	.

▶ You **MUST** complete both pages of this form and **SIGN** it.

Check one: ☐ Apply to next return. ☐ Send a refund.

Next ▶

For Privacy Act and Paperwork Reduction Act Notice, see the back of the Payment Voucher.   Cat. No. 11234O   Form **940** (2021)

DRAFT AS June 28, 2021 DO NOT FILE

850212

Name *(not your trade name)*	Employer identification number (EIN)
SONJA OLSON	92-1234567

Part 5: Report your FUTA tax liability by quarter only if line 12 is more than $500. If not, go to Part 6.

16 Report the amount of your FUTA tax liability for each quarter; do NOT enter the amount you deposited. If you had no liability for a quarter, leave the line blank.

16a 1st quarter (January 1 – March 31)   .   .   .   .   **16a** [.]

16b 2nd quarter (April 1 – June 30)   .   .   .   .   **16b** [.]

16c 3rd quarter (July 1 – September 30)   .   .   .   .   **16c** [.]

16d 4th quarter (October 1 – December 31)   .   .   .   .   **16d** [.]

17 Total tax liability for the year (lines 16a + 16b + 16c + 16d = line 17) **17** [.]   Total must equal line 12.

Part 6: May we speak with your third-party designee?

Do you want to allow an employee, a paid tax preparer, or another person to discuss this return with the IRS? See the instructions for details.

☐ **Yes.** Designee's name and phone number

Select a 5-digit personal identification number (PIN) to use when talking to the IRS. [ ][ ][ ][ ][ ]

☐ **No.**

Part 7: Sign here. You MUST complete both pages of this form and SIGN it.

Under penalties of perjury, I declare that I have examined this return, including accompanying schedules and statements, and to the best of my knowledge and belief, it is true, correct, and complete, and that no part of any payment made to a state unemployment fund claimed as a credit was, or is to be, deducted from the payments made to employees. Declaration of preparer (other than taxpayer) is based on all information of which preparer has any knowledge.

X Sign your name here   *Sonja Olson*

Print your name here   SONJA OLSON

Print your title here   OWNER

Date   1 / 11 /2020

Best daytime phone   612-222-2222

(watermark: DRAFT AS OF June 28, 2021 DO NOT FILE)

✂ ▼ **Detach Here and Mail With Your Payment and Form 940.** ▼ ✂

Form **940-V**	**Payment Voucher**	OMB No. 1545-0028
Department of the Treasury Internal Revenue Service	▶ Don't staple or attach this voucher to your payment.	20**21**

1 Enter your employer identification number (EIN).	2 Enter the amount of your payment. ▶ Make your check or money order payable to "**United States Treasury**"	Dollars	Cents
92-1234567		$42	

3 Enter your business name (individual name if sole proprietor).
SONJA OLSON

Enter your address.
421 PORTLAND AVENUE

Enter your city, state, and ZIP code; or your city, foreign country name, foreign province/county, and foreign postal code.
BOISE, ID 83701

22222	VOID ☐	a Employee's social security number	For Official Use Only ▶ OMB No. 1545-0008		

b Employer identification number (EIN) 92-1234567		1 Wages, tips, other compensation $15,080	2 Federal income tax withheld $260.00
c Employer's name, address, and ZIP code SONJA OLSON 421 PORTLAND AVENUE BOISE, ID 83701		3 Social security wages $15,080	4 Social security tax withheld $934.96
		5 Medicare wages and tips $15,080	6 Medicare tax withheld $218.66
		7 Social security tips	8 Allocated tips
d Control number		9	10 Dependent care benefits
e Employee's first name and initial JILL	Last name BROWN Suff.	11 Nonqualified plans	12a See instructions for box 12
		13 Statutory employee ☐ Retirement plan ☐ Third-party sick pay ☐	12b
421 PORTLAND AVENUE BOISE, ID 83701		14 Other	12c
			12d
f Employee's address and ZIP code			

15 State Employer's state ID number	16 State wages, tips, etc.	17 State income tax	18 Local wages, tips, etc.	19 Local income tax	20 Locality name

Form **W-2** Wage and Tax Statement   **2021**   Department of the Treasury—Internal Revenue Service

Copy A—For Social Security Administration. Send this entire page with Form W-3 to the Social Security Administration; photocopies are **not** acceptable.

For Privacy Act and Paperwork Reduction Act Notice, see the separate instructions.

Cat. No. 10134D

Do Not Cut, Fold, or Staple Forms on This Page

DO NOT STAPLE

33333	a Control number	For Official Use Only ▶ OMB No. 1545-0008		

b Kind of Payer (Check one) ▶	941 ☑ Military ☐ 943 ☐ 944 ☐ CT-1 ☐ Hshld. emp. ☐ Medicare govt. emp. ☐	Kind of Employer (Check one) ▶	None apply ☑ 501c non-govt. ☐ State/local non-501c ☐ State/local 501c ☐ Federal govt. ☐	Third-party sick pay (Check if applicable) ☐
c Total number of Forms W-2	d Establishment number	1 Wages, tips, other compensation $15,080.00	2 Federal income tax withheld $292.76	
e Employer identification number (EIN) 92-1234567		3 Social security wages $15,080.00	4 Social security tax withheld $934.96	
f Employer's name SONJA OLSON		5 Medicare wages and tips $15,080.00	6 Medicare tax withheld $218.66	
		7 Social security tips	8 Allocated tips	
421 PORTLAND AVENUE BOISE, ID 83701		9	10 Dependent care benefits	
		11 Nonqualified plans	12a Deferred compensation	
g Employer's address and ZIP code				
h Other EIN used this year		13 For third-party sick pay use only	12b	
15 State Employer's state ID number		14 Income tax withheld by payer of third-party sick pay		
16 State wages, tips, etc.	17 State income tax	18 Local wages, tips, etc.	19 Local income tax	
Employer's contact person		Employer's telephone number	For Official Use Only	
Employer's fax number		Employer's email address		

Under penalties of perjury, I declare that I have examined this return and accompanying documents, and, to the best of my knowledge and belief, they are true, correct, and complete.

Signature ▶ *Sonja Olson*   Title ▶ OWNER   Date ▶ 01/01/2021

For Employee Clarisse

Form **941 for 2021:** **Employer's QUARTERLY Federal Tax Return**
(Rev. June 2021)   Department of the Treasury — Internal Revenue Service

951121

OMB No. 1545-0029

Employer identification number (EIN) 9 2 – 1 2 3 4 5 6 7

Name *(not your trade name)* SONJA OLSON

Trade name *(if any)*

Address 421 PORTLAND AVENUE
Number   Street   Suite or room number

BOISE   ID   83701
City   State   ZIP code

Foreign country name   Foreign province/county   Foreign postal code

Report for this Quarter of 2021
(Check one.)

✓ **1:** January, February, March

☐ **2:** April, May, June

☐ **3:** July, August, September

☐ **4:** October, November, December

Go to *www.irs.gov/Form941* for instructions and the latest information.

Read the separate instructions before you complete Form 941. Type or print within the boxes.

Part 1: **Answer these questions for this quarter.**

1 Number of employees who received wages, tips, or other compensation for the pay period including: *June 12* (Quarter 2), *Sept. 12* (Quarter 3), or *Dec. 12* (Quarter 4) . . . . . . 1 | 1

2 Wages, tips, and other compensation . . . . 2 | $325 . 00

3 Federal income tax withheld from wages, tips, and other compensation . . . . . . 3 | .

4 If no wages, tips, and other compensation are subject to social security or Medicare tax ☒ Check and go to line 6.

		Column 1		Column 2	
5a	Taxable social security wages* . .	.	× 0.124 =	.	
5a	(i) Qualified sick leave wages* .	.	× 0.062 =	.	
5a	(ii) Qualified family leave wages* .	.	× 0.062 =	.	
5b	Taxable social security tips . . .	.	× 0.124 =	.	
5c	Taxable Medicare wages & tips . .	.	× 0.029 =	.	
5d	Taxable wages & tips subject to Additional Medicare Tax withholding	.	× 0.009 =	.	

*Include taxable qualified sick and family leave wages for leave taken after March 31, 2021, on line 5a. Use lines 5a(i) and 5a(ii) **only** for wages paid after March 31, 2020, for leave taken before April 1, 2021.*

5e Total social security and Medicare taxes. Add Column 2 from lines 5a, 5a(i), 5a(ii), 5b, 5c, and 5d 5e | $0 .

5f Section 3121(q) Notice and Demand—Tax due on unreported tips (see instructions) . . 5f | .

6 Total taxes before adjustments. Add lines 3, 5e, and 5f . . . . 6 | $0 .

7 Current quarter's adjustment for fractions of cents . . . . 7 |

8 Current quarter's adjustment for sick pay . . . . 8 | .

9 Current quarter's adjustments for tips and group-term life insurance . . . . . 9 | .

10 Total taxes after adjustments. Combine lines 6 through 9 . . . . 10 | .

11a Qualified small business payroll tax credit for increasing research activities. Attach Form 8974 11a | .

11b Nonrefundable portion of credit for qualified sick and family leave wages for leave taken before April 1, 2021 . . . . 11b | .

11c Nonrefundable portion of employee retention credit . . . . 11c | .

▶ **You MUST complete all three pages of Form 941 and SIGN it.**   Next ▶

For Privacy Act and Paperwork Reduction Act Notice, see the back of the Payment Voucher.   Cat. No. 17001Z   Form **941** (Rev. 6-2021)

951221

Name *(not your trade name)*	Employer identification number (EIN)
SONJA OLSON	92-1234567

Part 1:   Answer these questions for this quarter. *(continued)*

11d Nonrefundable portion of credit for qualified sick and family leave wages for leave taken after March 31, 2021 . . . . **11d** [.]

11e Nonrefundable portion of COBRA premium assistance credit (see instructions for applicable quarters) . . . . **11e** [.]

11f Number of individuals provided COBRA premium assistance [   ]

11g Total nonrefundable credits. Add lines 11a, 11b, 11c, 11d, and 11e . . . . **11g** [.]

12 Total taxes after adjustments and nonrefundable credits. Subtract line 11g from line 10 . **12** [.]

13a Total deposits for this quarter, including overpayment applied from a prior quarter and overpayments applied from Form 941-X, 941-X (PR), 944-X, or 944-X (SP) filed in the current quarter **13a** [.]

13b Reserved for future use . . . . **13b** [.]

13c Refundable portion of credit for qualified sick and family leave wages for leave taken before April 1, 2021 . . . . **13c** [.]

13d Refundable portion of employee retention credit . . . . **13d** [.]

13e Refundable portion of credit for qualified sick and family leave wages for leave taken after March 31, 2021 . . . . **13e** [.]

13f Refundable portion of COBRA premium assistance credit (see instructions for applicable quarters) . . . . **13f** [.]

13g Total deposits and refundable credits. Add lines 13a, 13c, 13d, 13e, and 13f . . . . . **13g** [.]

13h Total advances received from filing Form(s) 7200 for the quarter . . . . **13h** [.]

13i Total deposits and refundable credits less advances. Subtract line 13h from line 13g . . . . **13i** [.]

14 Balance due. If line 12 is more than line 13i, enter the difference and see instructions . . . **14** [$0 .]

15 Overpayment. If line 13i is more than line 12, enter the difference [.] Check one: ☐ Apply to next return. ☐ Send a refund.

Part 2:   Tell us about your deposit schedule and tax liability for this quarter.

If you're unsure about whether you're a monthly schedule depositor or a semiweekly schedule depositor, see section 11 of Pub. 15.

16 Check one: ☒ **Line 12 on this return is less than $2,500 or line 12 on the return for the prior quarter was less than $2,500, and you didn't incur a $100,000 next-day deposit obligation during the current quarter.** If line 12 for the prior quarter was less than $2,500 but line 12 on this return is $100,000 or more, you must provide a record of your federal tax liability. If you're a monthly schedule depositor, complete the deposit schedule below; if you're a semiweekly schedule depositor, attach Schedule B (Form 941). Go to Part 3.

☐ **You were a monthly schedule depositor for the entire quarter.** Enter your tax liability for each month and total liability for the quarter, then go to Part 3.

Tax liability: Month 1 [.]

Month 2 [.]

Month 3 [.]

Total liability for quarter [.]   Total must equal line 12.

☐ **You were a semiweekly schedule depositor for any part of this quarter.** Complete Schedule B (Form 941), Report of Tax Liability for Semiweekly Schedule Depositors, and attach it to Form 941. Go to Part 3.

▶ **You MUST complete all three pages of Form 941 and SIGN it.**   Next ▶

Form **941** (Rev. 6-2021)

951921

Name *(not your trade name)*	Employer identification number (EIN)
SONJA OLSON	92-1234567

Part 3:   Tell us about your business. If a question does NOT apply to your business, leave it blank.

17   If your business has closed or you stopped paying wages . . . . ☐ Check here, and

enter the final date you paid wages [/ /] ; also attach a statement to your return. See instructions.

18a   If you're a seasonal employer and you don't have to file a return for every quarter of the year . . . ☐ Check here.

18b   If you're eligible for the employee retention credit solely because your business is a recovery startup business ☐ Check here.

19	Qualified health plan expenses allocable to qualified sick leave wages for leave taken before April 1, 2021	19	.
20	Qualified health plan expenses allocable to qualified family leave wages for leave taken before April 1, 2021	20	.
21	Qualified wages for the employee retention credit	21	.
22	Qualified health plan expenses for the employee retention credit	22	.
23	Qualified sick leave wages for leave taken after March 31, 2021	23	.
24	Qualified health plan expenses allocable to qualified sick leave wages reported on line 23	24	.
25	Amounts under certain collectively bargained agreements allocable to qualified sick leave wages reported on line 23	25	.
26	Qualified family leave wages for leave taken after March 31, 2021	26	.
27	Qualified health plan expenses allocable to qualified family leave wages reported on line 26	27	.
28	Amounts under certain collectively bargained agreements allocable to qualified family leave wages reported on line 26	28	.

Part 4:   May we speak with your third-party designee?

Do you want to allow an employee, a paid tax preparer, or another person to discuss this return with the IRS? See the instructions for details.

☐ Yes. Designee's name and phone number [   ] [   ]

Select a 5-digit personal identification number (PIN) to use when talking to the IRS. ☐ ☐ ☐ ☐ ☐

☐ No.

Part 5:   Sign here. You MUST complete all three pages of Form 941 and SIGN it.

Under penalties of perjury, I declare that I have examined this return, including accompanying schedules and statements, and to the best of my knowledge and belief, it is true, correct, and complete. Declaration of preparer (other than taxpayer) is based on all information of which preparer has any knowledge.

X

Sign your name here   *Sonja Olson*

Print your name here   SONJA OLSON

Print your title here   OWNER

Date   4 / 11 / 2020

Best daytime phone   612-222-2222

Paid Preparer Use Only   Check if you're self-employed . . . ☐

Preparer's name	[ ]	PTIN	[ ]
Preparer's signature	[ ]	Date	[/ /]
Firm's name (or yours if self-employed)	[ ]	EIN	[ ]
Address	[ ]	Phone	[ ]
City	[ ]	State	[ ]	ZIP code	[ ]

Page **3**   Form **941** (Rev. 6-2021)

22222	VOID ☐	a Employee's social security number	For Official Use Only ▶ OMB No. 1545-0008		

b Employer identification number (EIN) 92-1234567	1 Wages, tips, other compensation $1,300	2 Federal income tax withheld

c Employer's name, address, and ZIP code SONJA OLSON 421 PORTLAND AVENUE BOISE, ID 83701	3 Social security wages	4 Social security tax withheld
	5 Medicare wages and tips	6 Medicare tax withheld
	7 Social security tips	8 Allocated tips

d Control number	9	10 Dependent care benefits

e Employee's first name and initial CLARISSE	Last name OLSON	Suff.	11 Nonqualified plans	12a See instructions for box 12

	13 Statutory employee ☐ Retirement plan ☐ Third-party sick pay ☐	12b
421 PORTLAND AVENUE BOISE, ID 83701	14 Other	12c
		12d

f Employee's address and ZIP code

15 State Employer's state ID number	16 State wages, tips, etc.	17 State income tax	18 Local wages, tips, etc.	19 Local income tax	20 Locality name

Form **W-2** **Wage and Tax Statement**   **2021**

Copy A—**For Social Security Administration.** Send this entire page with Form W-3 to the Social Security Administration; photocopies are **not** acceptable.

Department of the Treasury—Internal Revenue Service **For Privacy Act and Paperwork Reduction Act Notice, see the separate instructions.**

Cat. No. 10134D

Do Not Cut, Fold, or Staple Forms on This Page

DO NOT STAPLE

33333	a Control number	For Official Use Only ▶ OMB No. 1545-0008

b Kind of Payer (Check one)	941 ☑ Military ☐ 943 ☐ 944 ☐ CT-1 ☐ Hshld. emp. ☐ Medicare govt. emp. ☐	Kind of Employer (Check one)	None apply ☑ 501c non-govt. ☐ State/local non-501c ☐ State/local 501c ☐ Federal govt. ☐	Third-party sick pay (Check if applicable) ☐

c Total number of Forms W-2	d Establishment number	1 Wages, tips, other compensation $1,300	2 Federal income tax withheld

e Employer identification number (EIN) 92-1234567	3 Social security wages	4 Social security tax withheld

f Employer's name SONJA OLSON 421 PORTLAND AVENUE BOISE, ID 83701	5 Medicare wages and tips	6 Medicare tax withheld
	7 Social security tips	8 Allocated tips
	9	10 Dependent care benefits
	11 Nonqualified plans	12a Deferred compensation

g Employer's address and ZIP code		
h Other EIN used this year	13 For third-party sick pay use only	12b

15 State Employer's state ID number	14 Income tax withheld by payer of third-party sick pay

16 State wages, tips, etc.	17 State income tax	18 Local wages, tips, etc.	19 Local income tax

Employer's contact person	Employer's telephone number	For Official Use Only
Employer's fax number	Employer's email address	

Under penalties of perjury, I declare that I have examined this return and accompanying documents, and, to the best of my knowledge and belief, they are true, correct, and complete.

Signature ▶ *Sonja Olson*   Title ▶ OWNER   Date ▶ 01/01/2021

For Employee Ophelia

Form **944 for 2021:** **Employer's ANNUAL Federal Tax Return**

Department of the Treasury — Internal Revenue Service

OMB No. 1545-2007

Employer identification number (EIN)   4 1 – 1 2 3 4 5 6 7

Name (not your trade name)   SUSAN PROVIDER

Trade name (if any)

Address   1470 ASHLAND AVENUE

Number   Street   Suite or room number

ST. PAUL   MN   55105

City   State   ZIP code

Foreign country name   Foreign province/county   Foreign postal code

Who Must File Form 944

You must file annual Form 944 instead of filing quarterly Forms 941 **only if the IRS notified you in writing.**

Go to *www.irs.gov/Form944* for instructions and the latest information.

Read the separate instructions before you complete Form 944. Type or print within the boxes.

Part 1: Answer these questions for this year. Employers in American Samoa, Guam, the Commonwealth of the Northern Mariana Islands, the U.S. Virgin Islands, and Puerto Rico can skip lines 1 and 2, unless you have employees who are subject to U.S. income tax withholding.

1	Wages, tips, and other compensation	**1** $1,000 .
2	Federal income tax withheld from wages, tips, and other compensation	**2** .
3	If no wages, tips, and other compensation are subject to social security or Medicare tax	**3** ☐ Check and go to line 5.
4	Taxable social security and Medicare wages and tips:	

		Column 1		Column 2
4a	Taxable social security wages*	$1,000 .	× 0.124 =	$124 .
4a (i)	Qualified sick leave wages*	.	× 0.062 =	.
4a (ii)	Qualified family leave wages*	.	× 0.062 =	.
4b	Taxable social security tips	.	× 0.124 =	.
4c	Taxable Medicare wages & tips	$1,000 .	× 0.029 =	$29 .
4d	Taxable wages & tips subject to Additional Medicare Tax withholding	.	× 0.009 =	.

*Include taxable qualified sick and family leave wages for leave taken after March 31, 2021, on line 4a. Use lines 4a(i) and 4a(ii) **only** to report wages paid for leave taken before April 1, 2021.

4e	**Total social security and Medicare taxes.** Add Column 2 from lines 4a, 4a(i), 4a(ii), 4b, 4c, and 4d	**4e** $153 .
5	**Total taxes before adjustments.** Add lines 2 and 4e	**5** $153 .
6	**Current year's adjustments** (see instructions)	**6** .
7	**Total taxes after adjustments.** Combine lines 5 and 6	**7** $153 .
8a	Qualified small business payroll tax credit for increasing research activities. Attach Form 8974	**8a** .
8b	Nonrefundable portion of credit for qualified sick and family leave wages for leave taken before April 1, 2021	**8b** .
8c	Nonrefundable portion of employee retention credit	**8c** .
8d	Nonrefundable portion of credit for qualified sick and family leave wages for leave taken after March 31, 2021	**8d** .

▶ **You MUST complete all three pages of Form 944 and SIGN it.**

Next ▶

For Privacy Act and Paperwork Reduction Act Notice, see the back of the Payment Voucher.   Cat. No. 39316N   Form **944** (2021)

Name (not your trade name)	Employer identification number (EIN)
SUSAN PROVIDER	41-1234567

Part 1: Answer these questions for this year. *(continued)*

8e	Nonrefundable portion of COBRA premium assistance credit	8e	.
8f	Number of individuals provided COBRA premium assistance		
8g	Total nonrefundable credits. Add lines 8a, 8b, 8c, 8d, and 8e	8g	.
9	Total taxes after adjustments and nonrefundable credits. Subtract line 8g from line 7 . .	9	$153 .
10a	Total deposits for this year, including overpayment applied from a prior year and overpayments applied from Form 944-X, 944-X (SP), 941-X, or 941-X (PR)	10a	.
10b	Reserved for future use	10b	
10c	Reserved for future use	10c	
10d	Refundable portion of credit for qualified sick and family leave wages for leave taken before April 1, 2021	10d	.
10e	Refundable portion of employee retention credit	10e	
10f	Refundable portion of credit for qualified sick and family leave wages for leave taken after March 31, 2021	10f	.
10g	Refundable portion of COBRA premium assistance credit	10g	.
10h	Total deposits and refundable credits. Add lines 10a, 10d, 10e, 10f, and 10g	10h	.
10i	Total advances received from filing Form(s) 7200 for the year	10i	.
10j	Total deposits and refundable credits less advances. Subtract line 10i from line 10h . .	10j	.
11	Balance due. If line 9 is more than line 10j, enter the difference and see instructions . . .	11	$153 .
12	Overpayment. If line 10j is more than line 9, enter the difference		

12 Overpayment. If line 10j is more than line 9, enter the difference [.]   Check one: ☐ Apply to next return. ☐ Send a refund.

Part 2: Tell us about your deposit schedule and tax liability for this year.

13 Check one: [X] Line 9 is less than $2,500. Go to Part 3.

☐ Line 9 is $2,500 or more. Enter your tax liability for each month. If you're a semiweekly schedule depositor or you became one because you accumulated $100,000 or more of liability on any day during a deposit period, you must complete Form 945-A instead of the boxes below.

	Jan.		Apr.		July		Oct.
13a	.	13d	.	13g	.	13j	.
	Feb.		May		Aug.		Nov.
13b	.	13e	.	13h	.	13k	.
	Mar.		June		Sept.		Dec.
13c	.	13f	.	13i	.	13l	.

Total liability for year. Add lines 13a through 13l. Total must equal line 9.   13m [.]

▶ You MUST complete all three pages of Form 944 and SIGN it.   Next ▶

Page **2**   Form **944** (2021)

DRAFT AS OF June 30, 2021 DO NOT FILE

Name *(not your trade name)*	Employer identification number (EIN)
SUSAN PROVIDER	41-1234567

Part 3: Tell us about your business. If any question does NOT apply to your business, leave it blank.

14   If your business has closed or you stopped paying wages . . . . ☐ Check here, and

enter the final date you paid wages [/ /] ; also attach a statement to your return. See instructions.

15   Qualified health plan expenses allocable to qualified sick leave wages for leave taken before April 1, 2021   **15** [.]

16   Qualified health plan expenses allocable to qualified family leave wages for leave taken before April 1, 2021   **16** [.]

17   Qualified wages for the employee retention credit . . . .   **17** [.]

18   Qualified health plan expenses for the employee retention credit . . . .   **18** [.]

19   Qualified sick leave wages for leave taken after March 31, 2021 . . . .   **19** [.]

20   Qualified health plan expenses allocable to qualified sick leave wages reported on line 19   **20** [.]

21   Amounts under certain collectively bargained agreements allocable to qualified sick leave wages reported on line 19   **21** [.]

22   Qualified family leave wages for leave taken after March 31, 2021 . . . .   **22** [.]

23   Qualified health plan expenses allocable to qualified family leave wages reported on line 22   **23** [.]

24   Amounts under certain collectively bargained agreements allocable to qualified family leave wages reported on line 22 . . . .   **24** [   ]

25   If you're eligible for the employee retention credit in the third quarter solely because your business is a recovery startup business, enter the total of any amounts included on lines 8c and 10e for the third quarter . . . .   **25** [.]

26   If you're eligible for the employee retention credit in the fourth quarter solely because your business is a recovery startup business, enter the total of any amounts included on lines 8c and 10e for the fourth quarter . . . .   **26** [.]

Part 4: May we speak with your third-party designee?

Do you want to allow an employee, a paid tax preparer, or another person to discuss this return with the IRS? See the instructions for details.

☐ Yes. Designee's name and phone number [   ] [   ]

Select a 5-digit personal identification number (PIN) to use when talking to the IRS. [ ] [ ] [ ] [ ] [ ]

☐ No.

Part 5: Sign here. You MUST complete all three pages of Form 944 and SIGN it.

Under penalties of perjury, I declare that I have examined this return, including accompanying schedules and statements, and to the best of my knowledge and belief, it is true, correct, and complete. Declaration of preparer (other than taxpayer) is based on all information of which preparer has any knowledge.

X   Sign your name here   *Susan Provider*

Print your name here   SUSAN PROVIDER

Print your title here   OWNER

Date   4/11/2021

Best daytime phone   612-221-1111

Paid Preparer Use Only   Check if you're self-employed ☐

Preparer's name	[ ]	PTIN [ ]
Preparer's signature	[ ]	Date [ ]
Firm's name (or yours if self-employed)	[ ]	EIN [ ]
Address	[ ]	Phone [ ]
City	[ ] State [ ]	ZIP code [ ]

Form **944** (2021)

CHAPTER 9

Amending Your Tax Return:
Form 1040X

If you discover that you made a mistake on your tax returns in an earlier year, either by not claiming all your business income or by not deducting all your business expenses, you may be able to do something about it.

Don't amend your return if you realize later you made a math error. The IRS will correct math errors when processing your original return. If you didn't include a required form or schedule, the IRS will send you a request for the missing item. If you are waiting for a refund from your original return, don't file your amended return until after you receive the refund. You may cash the refund check from your original return. Amended returns take up to 16 weeks to process.

You can amend your tax return by filing **Form 1040X** within three years of the date you filed the original return or two years from the time you paid the taxes on your original return, whichever is later. If you filed your return before April 15, it will be treated as if you had filed it on April 15. If you obtained an extension, you can count from the date you actually filed. This means that most people have until April 15, 2022 to file an amended return for the years 2020, 2019, and 2018. After April 15, it will be too late for most providers to file an amended return for 2018.

Don't be shy about filing an amended return. The IRS doesn't audit them any more often than original returns. If you think you may have missed some business deductions, check the list of more than 1,000 deductions in the *Record-Keeping Guide*. If you find that you were entitled to deductions that you didn't claim and you have adequate records to back this up, don't hesitate to file an amended return.

You must file a separate **Form 1040X** for each annual tax return that you are amending. If you're entitled to a refund and your original return also showed a refund, you'll get another refund check in addition to interest on the amount owed to you.

If you're claiming unclaimed depreciation on your amended tax return, you must use bonus depreciation rules (see chapter 3). The IRS allows you to elect to use the Section 179 rule when amending your tax return. See chapter 3.

When you file **Form 1040X**, you must send with it copies of any tax forms for the year that is affected by the amended **Form 1040X**. (Don't send copies of your original tax forms, just amended versions of the forms that show changes.) A change on

Schedule C will affect Schedule SE and Form 1040. A change in your Time-Space percentage will affect Form 4562, Form 8829, and Schedule A. For more information, see the instructions for Form 1040X, which also tell you where to mail your amended return. You can track the status of your amended return three weeks after you file by going online at www.irs.gov/Filing/Wheres-My-Amended-Return or by phone at 866-464-2050.

Amending your federal tax return will probably mean that you must also amend your state tax return. Check with your state for information on amending your state return.

How Much Will It Be Worth?

Here's how to estimate how much you might save by amending your federal tax return:

- If you're in the 12% federal tax bracket for 2021 (if married filing jointly, making less than $81,050):

  12% + 14% (net self-employment tax) = 26%.

  You'll get a refund of about $0.26 on every additional dollar of deductions you claim on your amended return.

- If you're in the 22% federal tax bracket for 2021 (if married filing jointly, making between $81,051 and $172,750):

  22% + 14% (net self-employment tax) = 36%.

  You'll get a refund of about $0.36 on every additional dollar of deductions you claim on your amended return.

Example of an Amended Return

Here is an example of how to amend your tax return, based on the sample tax return shown in appendix A.

Example

Sandy James filed her tax return (see appendix A) on April 15, 2022. In September 2022 she realizes that although she uses a 400-square-foot room exclusively for business, she didn't claim that on her last tax return. Here's her new Time-Space percentage:

Percentage for exclusive-use room: 400 ÷ 2,200 = 18%
Time-Space percentage for rest of home: 1,800 ÷ 2,200 = 81.8% x 39% Time percentage = 32%
Revised Time-Space percentage: 18% + 32% = 50%

Now Sandy must redo all the forms she filled out last tax season that are affected by this change:

- **Form 8829**
  Line 7 will now be 50%. Adjust the expenses on this form using this 50% Time-Space percentage. Line 36 will now be $7,641.

- **Form 4562**
  Recalculate the furniture and fence using the 50% Time-Space percentage. Line 22 will now be $9,206.

- **Schedule C**
  Line 13 will now be $9,206.
  Line 16b will now be $50.
  Line 21 will now be $65.
  Line 22 will now be $450.
  Line 27a will now be $11,351.
  Line 29 will now be $44,142.
  Line 30 from **Form 8829** will now be $7,641.
  Line 31 will now be $36,501, a reduction of net profit of $2,412.

- **Schedule SE**
  Line 12 will now be $5,158.

- **Schedule A**
  Since Sandy took the standard deduction, she won't file **Schedule A**.

See the sample **Form 1040X** to see how Sandy saved $583 in federal taxes by amending her return.

Because Sandy's business profit is lower, she is able to reduce her self-employment tax as well as her federal income tax. Do not fill out lines 23–31 unless you are changing the number of your exemptions.

For more information about the tax issues discussed in this chapter, refer to the related topics in the other chapters of this book and the Redleaf Press *Family Child Care Record-Keeping Guide.*

Form **1040-X**			

Form 1040-X (Rev. July 2021)

Department of the Treasury—Internal Revenue Service

Amended U.S. Individual Income Tax Return

▶ Use this revision to amend 2019 or later tax returns.
▶ Go to *www.irs.gov/Form1040X* for instructions and the latest information.

OMB No. 1545-0074

This return is for calendar year (enter year) **2018**   **or fiscal year** (enter month and year ended) _____

Your first name and middle initial	Last name	Your social security number
SANDY	JAMES	123 45 6789

If joint return, spouse's first name and middle initial	Last name	Spouse's social security number
BILL	JAMES	987 65 4321

Current home address (number and street). If you have a P.O. box, see instructions.	Apt. no.	Your phone number
687 HOOVER STREET		212-541-7742

City, town or post office, state, and ZIP code. If you have a foreign address, also complete spaces below. See instructions.
HUDSON, OH 43287

Foreign country name	Foreign province/state/county	Foreign postal code

Amended return filing status. You **must** check one box even if you are not changing your filing status. **Caution:** In general, you can't change your filing status from married filing jointly to married filing separately after the return due date.

☐ Single   ☒ Married filing jointly   ☐ Married filing separately (MFS)   ☐ Head of household (HOH)   ☐ Qualifying widow(er) (QW)

If you checked the MFS box, enter the name of your spouse. If you checked the HOH or QW box, enter the child's name if the qualifying person is a child but not your dependent ▶

Enter on lines 1 through 23, columns A through C, the amounts for the return year entered above.
Use Part III on page 2 to explain any changes.

			A. Original amount reported or as previously adjusted (see instructions)	**B. Net change**—amount of increase or (decrease)—explain in Part III	**C. Correct amount**
Income and Deductions					
1	Adjusted gross income. If a net operating loss (NOL) carryback is included, check here ▶ ☐	1	77,164	(2,242)	74,923
2	Itemized deductions or standard deduction	2	25,100	---	25,100
3	Subtract line 2 from line 1	3	52,064	(2,242)	49,822
4a	Reserved for future use	4a			
b	Qualified business income deduction	4b	7,783	(483)	7,300
5	Taxable income. Subtract line 4b from line 3. If the result is zero or less, enter -0-	5	44,281	(1,758)	42,522
Tax Liability					
6	Tax. Enter method(s) used to figure tax (see instructions):	6	4,951	(243)	4,708
7	Nonrefundable credits. If a general business credit carryback is included, check here ▶ ☐	7		---	
8	Subtract line 7 from line 6. If the result is zero or less, enter -0-	8	4,951	(243)	4,708
9	Reserved for future use	9			
10	Other taxes	10	5,498	(340)	5,158
11	Total tax. Add lines 8 and 10	11	10,449	(583)	9,866
Payments					
12	Federal income tax withheld and excess social security and tier 1 RRTA tax withheld. (**If changing,** see instructions.)	12	9,000	---	9,000
13	Estimated tax payments, including amount applied from prior year's return	13			
14	Earned income credit (EIC)	14			
15	Refundable credits from: ☐ Schedule 8812 Form(s) ☐ 2439 ☐ 4136 ☐ 8863 ☐ 8885 ☐ 8962 or ☐ other (specify): _____	15			
16	Total amount paid with request for extension of time to file, tax paid with original return, and additional tax paid after return was filed	16			1,485
17	Total payments. Add lines 12 through 15, column C, and line 16	17			10,449
Refund or Amount You Owe					
18	Overpayment, if any, as shown on original return or as previously adjusted by the IRS	18			---
19	Subtract line 18 from line 17. (If less than zero, see instructions.)	19			
20	**Amount you owe.** If line 11, column C, is more than line 19, enter the difference	20			
21	If line 11, column C, is less than line 19, enter the difference. This is the amount **overpaid** on this return	21			
22	Amount of line 21 you want **refunded to you**	22			583
23	Amount of line 21 you want **applied to your** (enter year): _____ estimated tax	23			

Complete and sign this form on page 2.

For Paperwork Reduction Act Notice, see separate instructions.   Cat. No. 11360L   Form **1040-X** (Rev. 7-2021)

Form 1040-X (Rev. 7-2021)   Page **2**

Part I   Dependents

Complete this part to change any information relating to your dependents.
This would include a change in the number of dependents.
Enter the information for the return year entered at the top of page 1.

		A. Original number of dependents reported or as previously adjusted	**B. Net change —** amount of increase or (decrease)	**C. Correct number**
24	Reserved for future use	24		
25	Your dependent children who lived with you	25		
26	Your dependent children who didn't live with you due to divorce or separation	26		
27	Other dependents	27		
28	Reserved for future use	28		
29	Reserved for future use	29		

30 List **ALL** dependents (children and others) claimed on this amended return.

Dependents (see instructions):				(d) ✓ if qualifies for (see instructions):	
If more than four dependents, see instructions and check here ▶ ☐	**(a)** First name Last name	**(b)** Social security number	**(c)** Relationship to you	Child tax credit	Credit for other dependents
				☐	☐
				☐	☐
				☐	☐
				☐	☐

Part II   Presidential Election Campaign Fund (for the return year entered at the top of page 1)

Checking below won't increase your tax or reduce your refund.

☐ Check here if you didn't previously want $3 to go to the fund, but now do.
☐ Check here if this is a joint return and your spouse did not previously want $3 to go to the fund, but now does.

Part III   Explanation of Changes. In the space provided below, tell us why you are filing Form 1040-X.

▶ Attach any supporting documents and new or changed forms and schedules.

The business use of home was miscalculated and is 50% rather than 39%.

Remember to keep a copy of this form for your records.

Under penalties of perjury, I declare that I have filed an original return, and that I have examined this amended return, including accompanying schedules and statements, and to the best of my knowledge and belief, this amended return is true, correct, and complete. Declaration of preparer (other than taxpayer) is based on all information about which the preparer has any knowledge.

Sign Here

▶ *Sandy James*   9/30/2022
Your signature   Date   Your occupation

▶ *Bill James*   9/30/2022
Spouse's signature. If a joint return, **both** must sign.   Date   Spouse's occupation

Paid Preparer Use Only

Print/Type preparer's name	Preparer's signature	Date	Check ☐ if self-employed	PTIN
Firm's name ▶			Firm's EIN ▶	
Firm's address ▶			Phone no.	

For forms and publications, visit *www.irs.gov/Forms*.   Form **1040-X** (Rev. 7-2021)

CHAPTER 10

Recovering Your Unclaimed Depreciation: Form 3115

This chapter explains how to use **Form 3115 Application for Change in Accounting Method** to take advantage of any depreciation deductions you may have overlooked in previous years. Several IRS rulings (specifically, Revenue Procedure 2011-14) state that you can use **Form 3115** to deduct all the depreciation you haven't claimed for items that you've used in your business (with some restrictions; see below). Before these rulings, the only way you could deduct unclaimed depreciation without incurring a fee was to file an amended tax return—and you can only do that for the last three years.

If you have any unclaimed depreciation from earlier years, you can use **Form 3115** to deduct it on your tax return. (Note that you can't file **Form 3115** electronically.) Since family child care providers are entitled to depreciate a wide range of small and large household items, it's easy to overlook depreciation opportunities, yet by claiming them now, you could reap hundreds of dollars of deductions on this year's tax return.

For example, let's say that you started your business in 2011, and in 2012 you bought a sofa for $800; however, you've never claimed any depreciation for it. If your Time-Space percentage for 2012–2020 was 40%, you would have been entitled to depreciate $320 of the cost of the sofa ($800 x 40%), using seven-year accelerated depreciation (see chapter 3). Since you didn't claim any of this depreciation, you can use **Form 3115** to claim the entire $320 on your tax return. (You'll find a completed sample of **Form 3115** at the end of this chapter.)

Put items you owned before you went into business in one of two categories: items valued at $200 or less and items valued at $201 or more. You are entitled to deduct in one year under the Start-Up Rule up to $5,000 worth of items you owned before you went into business valued at $200 or less. Amounts above this must be amortized over 180 months. For example, let's say you started your business in 2012 and at that time had 100 items each individually valued at less than $200 for a total of $7,000. **Note**: These numbers are after applying your Time-Space percentage. You can use **Form 3115** to deduct $5,000 of the $7,000 and amortize the other $2,000 over 180 months (15 years). Because it has been eight years (96 months), you can also deduct on **Form 3115** an additional $1,067 ($2,000 ÷ 180 months x 96 months = $1,067). On your 2021 tax return, you can also deduct $133 ($2,000 ÷ 180 months x 12 months = $133), representing the ninth year on **Form 4562**. Continue to deduct $133 on **Form 4562** for the remaining six years.

For items valued at more than $200, use the depreciation rules in effect in the year your business began to claim previously unclaimed depreciation using **Form 3115**. For example, if your business began in 2012, you would use the fifteen-year depreciation rule for a fence, patio, or driveway. If you purchased an $8,000 fence in 2012 and your Time-Space percentage was 40%, you were entitled to depreciate $3,200 over 15 years. You can use **Form 3115** to recapture about $1,700 for 2012–2019. You could claim an additional $213 for the tenth year of depreciation on **Form 4562**. Continue deducting $213 for the remaining 5 years. See my article "How to Recapture Previously Unclaimed Depreciation" (http://tomcopelandblog.com/?p=14623&preview=true) for more details.

For information about what kinds of property you can depreciate, see chapter 3 of this book (and refer to the *Record-Keeping Guide* for a comprehensive list). Here's a sampling of the items that family child care providers can typically depreciate:

- the home

- home appliances, such as a washer, dryer, freezer, stove, or refrigerator

- fences, outdoor play equipment, lawn mowers, snowblowers

- furniture, such as beds, chairs, or sofas

- televisions, DVD players, computers, home entertainment systems

- home improvements, such as remodeling or a new furnace

You can deduct unclaimed depreciation for property that you never previously depreciated and for property that would have been only partly depreciated. For example, let's say that you remodeled your basement in January 2015 but didn't start claiming depreciation until 2021 because you weren't aware that you could depreciate this expense. You would continue to claim the depreciation on your tax return (as year seven under the 39-year home improvement rules).

If you used the wrong depreciation method in earlier years, you can also use **Form 3115** to correct it. Let's say that you began depreciating a carpet over 39 years, and you realized several years later that you could have depreciated it over seven years. You can use **Form 3115** to correct this error.

Let's say that you started depreciating the carpet in 2017 over 39 years and discovered your error in 2021. You can file **Form 3115** to correct the error and in 2021 you would continue depreciating the carpet under the seven-year method by using the fifth-year percentage (8.93%) as shown on the depreciation tables in chapter 3.

Requirements for Using Form 3115

To be eligible to deduct your previously unclaimed depreciation by filing **Form 3115**, you must meet the following requirements:

1. You must still be in business.
If you go out of business for a year or two and then start up again, you can't use **Form 3115** to recapture any depreciation for the years before you closed your business. You also can't use **Form 3115** if you closed your child care business and used your home for some other business (such as renting out rooms).

2. You must own the property you are deducting.
You must own the property in question at the start of the year in which you deduct the unclaimed depreciation. For example, let's say that you began your business in 2015 and

have never claimed any depreciation on your home. You decide to file **Form 3115** with your tax return to claim your home depreciation for the years 2015 to 2020. To be eligible to do this, you must still own the home and be in business on January 1, 2021.

If you sell the home before January 1, 2021, you can't claim any deductions on **Form 3115** on your 2021 tax return. If you sell the home during 2021, you can still deduct your home depreciation for the years 2015–2019 by filing **Form 3115** with your 2021 tax return. If you had sold the home in 2020, you can file **Form 3115** with an amended 2020 tax return to claim the unclaimed depreciation. (You can file an amended return only up to three years after filing the original return.) Filing **Form 3115** is only allowed to be done on an amended return for the year the property was disposed.

3. You must be using the property you are deducting in your business.

You must have been using the item in your business on January 1, 2020. For example, if you used a sewing machine in your business from 2015 to 2019 but haven't used it since then, you can't use **Form 3115** to claim the unclaimed depreciation for it now.

You *can* use **Form 3115** for items you continue to use in your business after their depreciation life is over. For example, if you've been using a sofa in your business for more than seven years (its depreciation period), you can still use **Form 3115**, as long as you've used it for your business in the current year.

4. You must file Form 3115 by the tax deadline (including any extensions) for the year in which you are deducting your previously unclaimed depreciation.

To claim your past year's depreciation on your current tax return, you must file **Form 3115** no later than the due date of that tax return. In other words, to deduct previously unclaimed depreciation on your tax return, you must file **Form 3115** by April 15. If you file for an extension on your tax return, you could file **Form 3115** as late as October 15 and still claim the deductions on your tax return.

There is one way you could claim the deductions using **Form 3115** if you haven't filed it with your original tax return. You can amend your tax return up to October 15 using **Form 1040X**, attach **Form 3115** to your amended return, and file **Form 3115** before sending in your amended return. Write on the top of your amended return "Filed Pursuant to IRS Tax Code Section 301.9100-2."

There's no time limit for your right to claim your depreciation from previous years. You can do it anytime you discover that you haven't claimed earlier depreciation. If you file your tax return on April 15 and don't file **Form 3115** by that date, you can always claim the depreciation on your next tax return, as long as you're still in business, still own the property, and continue to use it in your business.

5. You can't claim an expense that you've already deducted.

You can't reclaim depreciation if you have already deducted the property under Section 179 (see chapter 3). For example, if you bought a computer in 2013 and deducted the entire business-use portion of its cost that year, you can't use **Form 3115** because you've already claimed all the expense you're entitled to deduct for that computer. You also can't use **Form 3115** to go back and use Section 179 on property you purchased in earlier years. You can use Section 179 only in the year you purchase the property.

6. You must not have depreciated the item for at least two years before using Form 3115.

To take advantage of filing **Form 3115**, you must not have claimed depreciation on the items you are claiming for at least two years immediately preceding the year you use **Form 3115**. In other words, if you didn't claim depreciation on your furniture and appliances from 2015 to 2019, but you did claim depreciation on them in 2020, you can't use **Form 3115**.

7. You must use the proper depreciation method.

You can't use **Form 3115** to change the depreciation rules on an item that you've already started depreciating. For example, if you began depreciating a swing set in 2010 under straight-line rules, you can't use **Form 3115** to switch to accelerated depreciation and claim higher deductions for the earlier years.

Unless you've already started depreciating the item under straight-line rules, you must generally use accelerated depreciation rules on **Form 3115** to calculate your unclaimed depreciation for previous years. This is because you can't generally use straight-line depreciation for an item unless you chose this method in the first year you used the item in your business. If you didn't have the option of using straight-line depreciation in the first year you used the item, you must abide by the rules that were in effect at that time. Here are the rules you must use when claiming depreciation on **Form 3115**:

- Home (nonresidential real property): 39-year (or 31.5-year) straight-line
- Home improvements (nonresidential real property): 39-year (or 31.5-year) straight-line
- Land improvements (asset class 00.3): 15-year 150% declining balance
- Computers (asset class 00.12 information systems): if used 50% or less in business, 5-year straight-line; if used more than 50% in business, 5-year 200% declining balance
- Other personal property (asset class 00.11 office furniture, entertainment/recreation items, fixtures, and equipment): 7-year 200% declining balance
- Cars (asset class 00.22): if used 50% or less in business, 5-year straight-line; if used more than 50% in business, 5-year 200% declining balance

Check Your State Rules

If you claim **Form 3115** depreciation deductions on your federal tax return, check to see if your state tax rules will permit you to include these deductions when calculating your state tax return. Some states don't allow you to transfer these deductions to your state tax return.

Unclaimed Depreciation and Losses on Schedule C

Although depreciation of personal property can always be used to claim a loss for your business, depreciation of a home or home improvement is not allowed to create a loss on **Schedule C**. You must follow the usual instructions on **Form 8829** about deduction limitations. You may have to carry forward some of your deductions to your **Form 8829** for next tax season (see page 54). For a detailed explanation of how to depreciate property, see chapter 3.

In certain situations, it might be allowable for the depreciation of a home or home improvement to create a loss on **Schedule C**. For example, let's say that you didn't claim any home depreciation for the years 2016–2020, and this year you're using **Form 3115** to claim that depreciation. You discover that the home depreciation deductions that you're claiming for 2016–2018 would have created a loss for your business if you had claimed them in those years; however, you would have been able to carry those deductions forward to 2019–2020 because your business made enough profit to cover the deductions in the later years. In a case like this, it may be allowable to claim all the home depreciation from 2016 to 2020 on this year's tax return because they would have been allowed in previous years. You can enter the allowable amount on **Form 8829**, line 22, column b. (Enter "Section 481[a] Adjustment" on this line.)

If the depreciation of a home or home improvement would not have been allowed in prior years due to the **Form 8829** deduction limitations, enter the carry-forward amount on line 31 of your 2021 **Form 8829** (Enter "Section 481[a] Adjustment" on this line.) You must still follow the usual instructions on **Form 8829** about deduction limitations, so you may have to carry forward some of your deductions to your **Form 8829** for next tax season.

Claiming Depreciation on Vehicles

You can use **Form 3115** to claim depreciation on your vehicle only if you used the actual vehicle expenses method of claiming car expenses in earlier years or if you never claimed any car expenses. You can't claim past depreciation on your car if you used the standard mileage rate method. In calculating how much vehicle depreciation you can take, you must apply the yearly limitations on vehicle depreciation.

> **Will Filing Form 3115 Increase My Chances of Being Audited?**
> Your chances of being audited at all are very slim, and it's unlikely that you will be audited just because you file **Form 3115**—so don't base your decision about whether to claim depreciation on this. (If all your records are in order, you have nothing to worry about anyway.) If you don't claim all the depreciation you're entitled to, you're paying more taxes than you should.

What If You Don't Have the Receipts Anymore?

You need to calculate depreciation based on the lower of the cost of an item or its fair market value at the time you started using it for business (see chapter 3). But what if you don't know the cost of the item? Let's say that you've been using your freezer in your business since 2011, but you've never depreciated it and didn't save the receipt when you bought it because you didn't know it was deductible. What can you do?

Start by looking for other records you may have that show how much you paid for the item, such as a credit card statement, repair service contract, canceled check, or statement from the store where you purchased the item. If you can't find any of those kinds of records, estimate the value of the property when you began using it. Look up newspaper ads for used freezers from that year or visit a thrift store to get an idea of the fair market value of a used freezer.

See if you have any old family photos that show that you owned the item in 2011 or earlier. If your estimated fair market value of the item in 2011 is reasonable, you should be okay. Don't be aggressive by inflating the value of your item. The IRS should accept a reasonable estimate of its value, as long as you have some kind of evidence that you owned the item from 2011 to 2021.

Maximize Your Reclaimed Depreciation

Previously unclaimed depreciation could be one of your biggest deductions this year. Here are some ways to ensure that you'll be able to claim all the depreciation that you're entitled to:

- Capture the biggest unclaimed depreciation first. This will probably be your home or home improvements. Don't worry that this will increase your taxes when you sell your home. The tax consequences of selling your home will be the same regardless of whether you've claimed all the depreciation you're entitled to (see chapter 12). The IRS rules state that all allowable depreciation must be treated as if it had been claimed, so any property that you haven't depreciated will be treated as if it had been depreciated. Therefore, you will have to pay the same amount later, and you should claim your depreciation today.

- Save all your receipts for home purchases, home improvements, furniture, appliances, and outdoor play equipment. To document items you bought in earlier years, dig out the receipts, canceled checks, or credit card statements. (It's easy to track these purchases and improvements if you use the *Inventory-Keeper*, which provides a room-by-room listing of depreciable items.)

- Don't throw away any household property you have used in earlier years for your business and are still using in your business. Remember, you can claim depreciation on an item this year only if you still own it as of January 1 of last year.

How important is it to deduct your unclaimed depreciation? Here's an example. Let's say that you've never depreciated the following property:

- Your home, which has a business basis of $30,000 ($100,000 adjusted basis x 30% Time-Space percentage)

- Your major appliances (washer, dryer, freezer, refrigerator, stove, microwave oven), which have a business basis of $1,000

- Your furniture (sofa, chairs, tables, bed, lawn mower), which has a business basis of $1,000

Applying 39-year straight-line rules to the house and 7-year 200% declining balance rules to the appliances and furniture, you would be entitled to a business deduction of about $1,019 for each year that you've used these items in your business. This would translate into a tax savings of $265 per year if you're in the 12% tax bracket (12% federal income tax and 14% net self-employment tax) and $367 if you're in the 22% tax bracket (22% federal income tax and 14% net self-employment tax). In addition, there may be state income tax savings. As you can see, your tax savings will rise quickly for every year that you haven't claimed the depreciation for this property.

Although **Form 3115** isn't the simplest tax form to fill out, you have a lot to gain by filing it. Even if you have to pay a tax preparer to do it for you, it may be well worth the extra cost. If you've been reluctant to claim all the depreciation you're entitled to, you should seriously consider filing this form; it can mean a substantial one-time business deduction.

How to Fill Out Form 3115

If you're filing jointly, enter the names and Social Security numbers of both spouses in the same order they appear on your **Form 1040**. The principal business activity code number is 62440. Enter "1/1/21" as the date when the change begins. Enter "12/31/21" as the date when the change ends.

Check the box to indicate the applicant:
Check Individual (unless you are incorporated).

Check the appropriate box to indicate the type of accounting method change being requested:
Check Depreciation or Amortization.

Part I

Line 1: Enter "7" for the DCN.

Line 2: Check the No column.

Line 3: Check the Yes column.

Part II

Line 4: Check the No column.

Line 5: Check the No column.

Line 6a: Check the No column, go to 7a.

Line 7a: Check the Yes column.

Line 7b: Check the "Not under exam" box.

Line 8a: Check the No column, go to line 9.

Line 9: Leave blank.

Line 10: Check the No column.

Line 11a: Check the No column, go to line 12.

Line 12: Check the No column.

Line 13: Check the No column.

Lines 14–16a: Attach a statement to the form to answer these questions. See the example shown later in this chapter.

Line 17: Check the Yes column.

Line 18: Check the No column.

Line 19: Leave blank.

Part III

Lines 20 and 23: Leave blank. Do not attach any documents.

Part IV

Line 25: Check the No column.

Line 26: Enter amount of recaptured depreciation you are claiming. See the example shown later in this chapter.

Line 27: Check the Yes column.

Line 28: Check the No column.

Schedule A: Change in Overall Method of Accounting
Leave the rest of page 4, pages 5–7, and the top of page 8 blank.

Transfer Your Unclaimed Depreciation to Schedule C
Enter the amount from **Form 3115**, Part IV, line 26, on one of the blank lines of **Schedule C**, Part V. Title that entry "Section 481(a) Adjustment." Include this amount in the total you enter on **Schedule C**, line 27 (other expenses).

Professional Help Is Recommended

The IRS rulings that allow you to claim previously unclaimed depreciation on **Form 3115** are relatively new, and they may require clarification. If you file **Form 3115**, you should consult a tax preparer to help you with it. If you aren't using a tax preparer, it would be worth it to hire one just to do (or review) your **Form 3115**.

Two Examples of How to Fill Out Form 3115
The following examples show you how to fill out the remaining lines on **Form 3115**. In the first example, the depreciation period is over; in the second, it is still in progress.

EXAMPLE 1

This example is shown on the forms and the attachment at the end of this chapter.

Karin Roth has been in business since 2012, and her Time-Space percentage each year has been 35%. In 2012 she bought a washer for $400 and a dryer for $300. She has never claimed any depreciation for these items. To claim it on her tax return, she'll have to file **Form 3115** by April 15 (unless she takes an extension). To answer questions 12, 13, and 25, Karin will write an attachment to **Form 3115** (see example at end of chapter). To calculate the proper amount of her depreciation, Karin will consult chapter 3. As her attachment shows, she was entitled to deduct $245 in depreciation over eight years. Because the eight-year recovery period has expired, she can claim all $245 as a deduction this year.

Karin will enter "–$245" on **Form 3115**, Part IV, line 26. Then she will enter $245 on one of the blank lines of her **Schedule C**, Part V, and write "Section 481(a) Adjustment" on that line.

EXAMPLE 2

In this case, Karin bought the washer and dryer in 2014, and her Time-Space percentages for the years 2016–2019 are as follows: 35%; 38%; 35%; 40%. Karin will fill out **Form 3115** in the same way, and her depreciation calculation will look like this:

2016: $700 x 35% = $245 x 14.29% = $35.01
2017: $700 x 38% = $266 x 24.49% = $65.14
2018: $700 x 35% = $245 x 17.49% = $42.85
2019: $700 x 40% = $280 x 12.49% = $34.97
Total depreciation allowed 2015–2018: $177.97

In this case, Karin will enter "–$178" on **Form 3115**, Part IV, line 26, and will claim this amount on her **Schedule C**, Part V. Karin is also entitled to claim $25 for the fifth year of depreciation on the washer and dryer for last year:

2020: $700 x 40% = $280 x 8.93% = $25

Karin will enter this $25 on line 1 of her **Form 4562**. Since there is still one more year of depreciation left, she will also be entitled to claim the sixth year of depreciation on the washer and dryer on her **Form 4562** next tax season:

2021: $700 x 40% = $280 x 8.92% = $24.98

Next year she will enter this $25 on line 17 of her **Form 4562**. (Although no attachment is shown for this example, Karin would complete **Form 3115** and the attachment in exactly the same way as example 1, except for her entry for question 26.)

How to File Form 3115

In the past, if you wanted to deduct previously unclaimed depreciation, you had to pay a hefty fee and get the consent of the commissioner of the IRS to change your accounting method. Now there is no fee for filing **Form 3115** and you can get automatic consent, if you proceed as follows:

1. Fill out **Form 3115**. Attach the original of **Form 3115** with your tax return.

2. Mail a copy of **Form 3115** by the filing deadline (April 15 or your extension deadline) to:

   Internal Revenue Service
   Ogden, UT 84201
   M/S 6111

   Since you won't receive any acknowledgment that the IRS has received the form, send it by certified mail with a return receipt request in case you have to prove that it was delivered. If your **Form 3115** isn't postmarked by the deadline, the IRS will deny the deductions on your tax return. (You could file again next year and claim the deductions.) If for any reason the IRS does not consent to your **Form 3115**, it will notify you.

3. Attach a list of your previously unclaimed or underclaimed property to **Form 3115**, as shown at the end of this chapter. Be sure to include your name and Social Security number and indicate that this is an attachment to **Form 3115**.

A Note to Tax Professionals

The two types of unclaimed depreciation are **Schedule C** operating expenses depreciation (furniture, appliances, and other personal property) and **Form 8829** operating expenses depreciation (home and home improvements).

Calculate how much of each type of depreciation the provider was entitled to deduct for each unclaimed year. Check to see whether claiming this depreciation would have created a loss on **Form 8829** for each year in question. Higher **Schedule C** depreciation deductions may affect the provider's ability to claim some of the deductions on **Form 8829**.

After taking this into account, check to see if the provider is allowed to deduct all unclaimed depreciation on **Form 8829** each year. If so, the provider won't need to recalculate **Form 8829** each year. If not, she will need to recalculate the allowed deductions on **Form 8829** and carry forward any unallowed deductions to the next year's **Form 8829**. There may be a number of years of carry-forward deductions. The provider should keep copies of the recalculated **Form 8829**s as backup supporting statements.

Although **Form 8829** was introduced in 1991, the earlier rules were the same about the limitation on claiming home expenses that create a business loss. Consider the potential complexity of these calculations before agreeing to file **Form 3115**.

For more information about the tax issues discussed in this chapter, refer to the related topics in the other chapters of this book and the Redleaf Press *Family Child Care Record-Keeping Guide*.

| Form **3115**
(Rev. December 2018)
Department of the Treasury
Internal Revenue Service | **Application for Change in Accounting Method**
▶ Go to *www.irs.gov/Form3115* for instructions and the latest information. | OMB No. 1545-2070 |

Name of filer (name of parent corporation if a consolidated group) (see instructions) **HANK AND KARIN ROTH**	**Identification number** (see instructions) **468-78-9123**
	Principal business activity code number (see instructions) **62441**
Number, street, and room or suite no. If a P.O. box, see the instructions. **466 WOBBLY LANE**	Tax year of change begins (MM/DD/YYYY) **1/1/2020**
City or town, state, and ZIP code **DULUTH, MN 55671**	Tax year of change ends (MM/DD/YYYY) **12/31/2020** Name of contact person (see instructions)
Name of applicant(s) (if different than filer) and identification number(s) (see instructions)	Contact person's telephone number

If the applicant is a member of a consolidated group, check this box . . . . ▶ ☐

If **Form 2848,** Power of Attorney and Declaration of Representative, is attached (see instructions for when Form 2848 is required), check this box . . . . ▶ ☐

Check the box to indicate the type of applicant.

☑ Individual
☐ Corporation
☐ Controlled foreign corporation (Sec. 957)
☐ 10/50 corporation (Sec. 904(d)(2)(E))
☐ Qualified personal service corporation (Sec. 448(d)(2))
☐ Exempt organization. Enter Code section ▶

☐ Cooperative (Sec. 1381)
☐ Partnership
☐ S corporation
☐ Insurance co. (Sec. 816(a))
☐ Insurance co. (Sec. 831)
☐ Other (specify) ▶ _____

Check the appropriate box to indicate the type of accounting method change being requested.
See instructions.

☑ Depreciation or Amortization
☐ Financial Products and/or Financial Activities of Financial Institutions
☐ Other (specify) ▶ _____

Caution: To be eligible for approval of the requested change in method of accounting, the taxpayer must provide all information that is relevant to the taxpayer or to the taxpayer's requested change in method of accounting. This includes **(1)** all relevant information requested on this Form 3115 (including its instructions), and **(2)** any other relevant information, even if not specifically requested on Form 3115.
  The taxpayer must attach all applicable statements requested throughout this form.

Part I	**Information for Automatic Change Request**	Yes	No
1	Enter the applicable designated automatic accounting method change number ("DCN") for the requested automatic change. Enter only one DCN, except as provided for in guidance published by the IRS. If the requested change has no DCN, check "Other," and provide both a description of the change and a citation of the IRS guidance providing the automatic change. See instructions.		

a (1) DCN: **7**   (2) DCN: ____   (3) DCN: ____   (4) DCN: ____   (5) DCN: ____   (6) DCN: ____
  (7) DCN: ____   (8) DCN: ____   (9) DCN: ____   (10) DCN: ____   (11) DCN: ____   (12) DCN: ____

b	Other ☐ Description ▶ _____		
2	Do any of the eligibility rules restrict the applicant from filing the requested change using the automatic change procedures (see instructions)? If "Yes," attach an explanation.		✓
3	Has the filer provided all the information and statements required **(a)** on this form and **(b)** by the List of Automatic Changes under which the applicant is requesting a change? See instructions.	✓	
	Note: Complete Part II and Part IV of this form, and, Schedules A through E, if applicable.		

Part II	**Information for All Requests**	Yes	No
4	During the tax year of change, did or will the applicant **(a)** cease to engage in the trade or business to which the requested change relates, or **(b)** terminate its existence? See instructions.		✓
5	Is the applicant requesting to change to the principal method in the tax year of change under Regulations section 1.381(c)(4)-1(d)(1) or 1.381(c)(5)-1(d)(1)? . . . . If "No," go to line 6a. If "Yes," the applicant cannot file a Form 3115 for this change. See instructions.		✓

Sign Here

Under penalties of perjury, I declare that I have examined this application, including accompanying schedules and statements, and to the best of my knowledge and belief, the application contains all the relevant facts relating to the application, and it is true, correct, and complete. Declaration of preparer (other than applicant) is based on all information of which preparer has any knowledge.

| Signature of filer (and spouse, if joint return)
Hank Roth Karin Roth | Date
1/10/2021 | Name and title (print or type)
HANK ROTH, KARIN ROTH |

| **Preparer**
(other than
filer/applicant) | Print/Type preparer's name | Preparer's signature | Date |
| | Firm's name ▶ | | |

For Privacy Act and Paperwork Reduction Act Notice, see the instructions.   Cat. No. 19280E   Form **3115** (Rev. 12-2018)

Form 3115 (Rev. 12-2018)   Page **2**

Part II   Information for All Requests *(continued)*

		Yes	No
6a	Does the applicant (or any present or former consolidated group in which the applicant was a member during the applicable tax year(s)) have any federal income tax return(s) under examination (see instructions)? . . . . . If "No," go to line 7a.		✓
b	Is the method of accounting the applicant is requesting to change an issue under consideration (with respect to either the applicant or any present or former consolidated group in which the applicant was a member during the applicable tax year(s))? See instructions.		
c	Enter the name and telephone number of the examining agent and the tax year(s) under examination. Name ▶ _____ Telephone number ▶ _____ Tax year(s) ▶ _____		
d	Has a copy of this Form 3115 been provided to the examining agent identified on line 6c?		
7a	Does audit protection apply to the applicant's requested change in method of accounting? See instructions. . . If "No," attach an explanation.	✓	
b	If "Yes," check the applicable box and attach the required statement.		

☑ Not under exam   ☐ 3-month window   ☐ 120 day: Date examination ended ▶ _____
☐ Method not before director   ☐ Negative adjustment   ☐ CAP: Date member joined group ▶ _____
☐ Audit protection at end of exam   ☐ Other

		Yes	No
8a	Does the applicant (or any present or former consolidated group in which the applicant was a member during the applicable tax year(s)) have any federal income tax return(s) before Appeals and/or a federal court? . . . . . If "No," go to line 9.		✓
b	Is the method of accounting the applicant is requesting to change an issue under consideration by Appeals and/or a federal court (for either the applicant or any present or former consolidated group in which the applicant was a member for the tax year(s) the applicant was a member)? See instructions. . . . . If "Yes," attach an explanation.		
c	If "Yes," enter the name of the (check the box) ☐ Appeals officer and/or ☐ counsel for the government, telephone number, and the tax year(s) before Appeals and/or a federal court. Name ▶ _____ Telephone number ▶ _____ Tax year(s) ▶ _____		
d	Has a copy of this Form 3115 been provided to the Appeals officer and/or counsel for the government identified on line 8c?		
9	If the applicant answered "Yes" to line 6a and/or 8a with respect to any present or former consolidated group, attach a statement that provides each parent corporation's **(a)** name, **(b)** identification number, **(c)** address, and **(d)** tax year(s) during which the applicant was a member that is under examination, before an Appeals office, and/or before a federal court.		
10	If for federal income tax purposes, the applicant is either an entity (including a limited liability company) treated as a partnership or an S corporation, is it requesting a change from a method of accounting that is an issue under consideration in an examination, before Appeals, or before a federal court, with respect to a federal income tax return of a partner, member, or shareholder of that entity?		✓
11a	Has the applicant, its predecessor, or a related party requested or made (under either an automatic or non-automatic change procedure) a change in method of accounting within any of the five tax years ending with the tax year of change? . . . . If "No," go to line 12.		✓
b	If "Yes," for each trade or business, attach a description of each requested change in method of accounting (including the tax year of change) and state whether the applicant received consent.		
c	If any application was withdrawn, not perfected, or denied, or if a Consent Agreement granting a change was not signed and returned to the IRS, or the change was not made or not made in the requested year of change, attach an explanation.		
12	Does the applicant, its predecessor, or a related party currently have pending any request (including any concurrently filed request) for a private letter ruling, change in method of accounting, or technical advice? . . . If "Yes," for each request attach a statement providing **(a)** the name(s) of the taxpayer, **(b)** identification number(s), **(c)** the type of request (private letter ruling, change in method of accounting, or technical advice), and **(d)** the specific issue(s) in the request(s).		✓
13	Is the applicant requesting to change its **overall** method of accounting? . . . . If "Yes," complete Schedule A on page 4 of the form.		✓

Form **3115** (Rev. 12-2018)

Form 3115 (Rev. 12-2018)   Page **3**

Part II	**Information for All Requests** *(continued)*	Yes	No

14 If the applicant is either **(i) not** changing its overall method of accounting, or **(ii)** changing its overall method of accounting **and** changing to a special method of accounting for one or more items, attach a detailed and complete description for each of the following (see instructions):

  a The item(s) being changed.

  b The applicant's present method for the item(s) being changed.

  c The applicant's proposed method for the item(s) being changed.

  d The applicant's present overall method of accounting (cash, accrual, or hybrid).

15a Attach a detailed and complete description of the applicant's trade(s) or business(es). See section 446(d).

  b If the applicant has more than one trade or business, as defined in Regulations section 1.446-1(d), describe **(i)** whether each trade or business is accounted for separately; **(ii)** the goods and services provided by each trade or business and any other types of activities engaged in that generate gross income; **(iii)** the overall method of accounting for each trade or business; and **(iv)** which trade or business is requesting to change its accounting method as part of this application or a separate application.

  Note: If you are requesting an automatic method change, see the instructions to see if you are required to complete lines 16a–16c.

16a Attach a full explanation of the legal basis supporting the proposed method for the item being changed. Include a detailed and complete description of the facts that explains how the law specifically applies to the applicant's situation and that demonstrates that the applicant is authorized to use the proposed method.

  b Include all authority (statutes, regulations, published rulings, court cases, etc.) supporting the proposed method.

  c Include either a discussion of the contrary authorities or a statement that no contrary authority exists.

17 Will the proposed method of accounting be used for the applicant's books and records and financial statements? For insurance companies, see the instructions. . . . . ✓ |

  If "No," attach an explanation.

18 Does the applicant request a conference with the IRS National Office if the IRS National Office proposes an adverse response?   ✓

19a If the applicant is changing to either the overall cash method, an overall accrual method, or is changing its method of accounting for any property subject to section 263A, any long-term contract subject to section 460 (see 19b), or inventories subject to section 474, enter the applicant's gross receipts for the 3 tax years preceding the tax year of change.

1st preceding year ended: mo. yr.	2nd preceding year ended: mo. yr.	3rd preceding year ended: mo. yr.
$	$	$

  b If the applicant is changing its method of accounting for any long-term contract subject to section 460, in addition to completing 19a, enter the applicant's gross receipts for the 4th tax year preceding the tax year of change:

  4th preceding year ended: mo. _____ yr. _____ $ _____

Part III	**Information for Non-Automatic Change Request**	Yes	No

20 Is the applicant's requested change described in any revenue procedure, revenue ruling, notice, regulation, or other published guidance as an automatic change request? . . . .

  If "Yes," attach an explanation describing why the applicant is submitting its request under the non-automatic change procedures.

21 Attach a copy of all documents related to the proposed change (see instructions).

22 Attach a statement of the applicant's reasons for the proposed change.

23 If the applicant is a member of a consolidated group for the year of change, do all other members of the consolidated group use the proposed method of accounting for the item being changed? . . . .

  If "No," attach an explanation.

24a Enter the amount of **user fee** attached to this application (see instructions). ▶ $ _____

  b If the applicant qualifies for a reduced user fee, attach the required information or certification (see instructions).

Form 3115 (Rev. 12-2018)   Page **4**

Part IV	Section 481(a) Adjustment	Yes	No
25	Does published guidance require the applicant (or permit the applicant and the applicant is electing) to implement the requested change in method of accounting on a cut-off basis? . . . . If "Yes," attach an explanation and do not complete lines 26, 27, and 28 below.		✓
26	Enter the section 481(a) adjustment. Indicate whether the adjustment is an increase (+) or a decrease (-) in income. ▶ $ ___245___ Attach a summary of the computation and an explanation of the methodology used to determine the section 481(a) adjustment. If it is based on more than one component, show the computation for each component. If more than one applicant is applying for the method change on the application, attach a list of the **(a)** name, **(b)** identification number, and **(c)** the amount of the section 481(a) adjustment attributable to each applicant.		
27	Is the applicant making an election to take the entire amount of the adjustment into account in the tax year of change? If "Yes," check the box for the applicable elective provision used to make the election (see instructions). ☐ $50,000 de minimis election ☐ Eligible acquisition transaction election	✓	
28	Is any part of the section 481(a) adjustment attributable to transactions between members of an affiliated group, a consolidated group, a controlled group, or other related parties? . . . . If "Yes," attach an explanation.		✓

Attachment to Form 3115 for Tax Year 2021
Hank and Karin Roth
SS #123-45-6789, 987-65-4321

Answers to Questions:

14a) Applicant is deducting unclaimed depreciation for a washer bought for $400 in 2012 and a dryer bought for $300 in the same year.

14b) Present method: Applicant has previously not depreciated this property.

14c) Proposed method: Applicant is depreciating this property under the 7-year MACRS 200% declining balance method under Section 168.

14d) Overall method of accounting: Cash basis.

15a) The applicant is a family child care provider. She takes care of children in her home. The business activity code is 624410.

16) Revenue Procedure 2018-13, section 6.01.

26) Depreciation Calculation

Washer (asset class 00.11):	$400
Dryer (asset class 00.11):	$300
Total:	$700

The Time-Space percentage was 35% for all the years of depreciation.

2012: $700 x 35% = $245 x 14.29%   = $35.01
2013: $700 x 35% = $245 x 24.49%   = $60.00
2014: $700 x 35% = $245 x 17.49%   = $42.85
2015: $700 x 35% = $245 x 12.49%   = $30.60
2016: $700 x 35% = $245 x 8.93%   = $21.88
2017: $700 x 35% = $245 x 8.92%   = $21.85
2018: $700 x 35% = $245 x 8.93%   = $21.88
2019: $700 x 35% = $245 x 4.46%   = $10.93
Total depreciation allowed 2012–2019   = $245.00

Schedule E—Change in Depreciation or Amortization. See instructions.

Applicants requesting approval to change their method of accounting for depreciation or amortization complete this section. Applicants **must** provide this information for each item or class of property for which a change is requested.

Note: See the *Summary of the List of Automatic Accounting Method Changes* in the instructions for information regarding automatic changes under sections 56, 167, 168, 197, 1400I, 1400L, or former section 168. **Do not** file Form 3115 with respect to certain late elections and election revocations. See instructions.

1   Is depreciation for the property determined under Regulations section 1.167(a)-11 (CLADR)? . . . .   ☐ Yes ☑ No
    If "Yes," the only changes permitted are under Regulations section 1.167(a)-11(c)(1)(iii).

2   Is any of the depreciation or amortization required to be capitalized under any Code section, such as
    section 263A? . . . .   ☐ Yes ☑ No
    If "Yes," enter the applicable section ▶ _____

3   Has a depreciation, amortization, expense, or disposition election been made for the property, such as
    the election under sections 168(f)(1), 168(i)(4), 179, 179C, or Regulations section 1.168(i)-8(d)? . . . .   ☐ Yes ☑ No
    If "Yes," state the election made ▶ _____

4a To the extent not already provided, attach a statement describing the property subject to the change. Include in the description the type of property, the year the property was placed in service, and the property's use in the applicant's trade or business or income-producing activity.

  b   If the property is residential rental property, did the applicant live in the property before renting it?   . .   ☐ Yes ☐ No
  c   Is the property public utility property? . . . .   ☐ Yes ☑ No

5   To the extent not already provided in the applicant's description of its present method, attach a statement explaining how the property is treated under the applicant's present method (for example, depreciable property, inventory property, supplies under Regulations section 1.162-3, nondepreciable section 263(a) property, property deductible as a current expense, etc.).

6   If the property is not currently treated as depreciable or amortizable property, attach a statement of the facts supporting the proposed change to depreciate or amortize the property.

7   If the property is currently treated and/or will be treated as depreciable or amortizable property, provide the following information for both the present (if applicable) and proposed methods:

  a   The Code section under which the property is or will be depreciated or amortized (for example, section 168(g)).

  b   The applicable asset class from Rev. Proc. 87-56, 1987-2 C.B. 674, for each asset depreciated under section 168 (MACRS) or under section 1400L; the applicable asset class from Rev. Proc. 83-35, 1983-1 C.B. 745, for each asset depreciated under former section 168 (ACRS); an explanation why no asset class is identified for each asset for which an asset class has not been identified by the applicant.

  c   The facts to support the asset class for the proposed method.

  d   The depreciation or amortization method of the property, including the applicable Code section (for example, 200% declining balance method under section 168(b)(1)).

  e   The useful life, recovery period, or amortization period of the property.

  f   The applicable convention of the property.

  g   Whether the additional first-year special depreciation allowance (for example, as provided by section 168(k), 168(l), 168(m), 168(n), 1400L(b), or 1400N(d)) was or will be claimed for the property. If not, also provide an explanation as to why no special depreciation allowance was or will be claimed.

  h   Whether the property was or will be in a single asset account, a multiple asset account, or a general asset account.

Form **3115** (Rev. 12-2018)

Schedule E

Lines 6–7a: Attach a statement to the form to answer these questions.

PPROPOSED METHOD

Line 6:   Applicant is depreciating this property under the 7-year MACRS 200% declining balance method under Section 168.

Line 7a: Section 168.

Line 7b: Washer (asset class 00.11) and Dryer (asset class 00.11).

Line 7c: Assets used for child care business.

Line 7d: 200% declining balance method under Section 168.

Line 7e: Recovery period of 7 years.

Line 7f: Half year convention.

Line 7g: No special depreciation allowance will be taken because an election was made to elect out for this asset class.

Line 7h: Single asset account.

CHAPTER 11

Selling Your Business Property: Form 4797

If you sold items you used for your business this year, you will need to report the sale by filing **Form 4797** Sales of Business Property with your income tax forms. You should fill out **Form 4797** if you experienced any of the following situations last year:

* An item you're depreciating wears out before the end of its depreciation period.

* You sell your car.

* You sell your home or land.

* You sell property that was used in your business while you were still in business.

* Your business use drops to 50% or less for an item you depreciated under Section 179 or listed property (such as your car) that used the accelerated rules, and you must recapture (pay back) some of the depreciation you've claimed.

To illustrate these situations, we'll look at nine examples. Examples 1 and 2 show how to handle an item that wears out before the end of its depreciation period. Examples 3 through 6 deal with selling items you're using in your business. Examples 7 and 8 show how to handle the sale of a vehicle, and example 9 explains how to recapture depreciation.

Selling Your Home

The IRS rules issued in December 2002 have greatly simplified the tax consequences of selling your home. Most family child care providers will now be able to avoid paying any taxes on the profit made by selling a home but will still have to pay taxes on the home depreciation that has been claimed since May 6, 1997. For more information, see chapter 12.

Where you report the sale depends on several factors.

* If you sold any business property that you had previously deducted (such as under the $2,500 rule) or other business property that you owned for less than one year, report the sale in Part II of **Form 4797**.

* If you sold any business property at a loss, report it in Part I of **Form 4797**.

* If you sold any business property at a gain that was your home, improvement to your home or land, report it in Part III of **Form 4797**, using lines 20–24, 26, and 30–32.

- If the business property that was sold at a gain was not your home, improvement to your home, or land, report it in Part III of **Form 4797**, using lines 20–25 and 30–32.

An Item Wears Out during the Depreciation Period

Example 1

You've been providing child care since 2014. In January 2016 you install a new deck for $2,000. In March 2020 the deck is rotted out, and you demolish it. Later that year you build a new deck and start depreciating it (see chapter 3 for instructions). You were depreciating the first deck over 39 years as a home improvement. Your Time-Space percentages have been as follows: 2016: 30%; 2017: 28%; 2018: 27%; 2019: 31%; 2020: 32%; 2021: 33%. Your depreciation deductions for 2016–2020 were as follows:

```
2016: $2,000 x 30% = $600 x 2.461% = $14.77
2017: $2,000 x 28% = $560 x 2.564% = $14.36
2018: $2,000 x 27% = $540 x 2.564% = $13.85
2019: $2,000 x 31% = $620 x 2.564% = $15.90
2020: $2,000 x 32% = $640 x 2.564% = $16.41
```

Total claimed so far: $75.29

For 2021 you must first calculate the amount of depreciation you're entitled to for the last year you used the old deck in your business (2021):

$2,000 x 33% = $660 x 2.564% = $16.92

Under the Half-Year Convention rules (see chapter 3), you can claim only half the normal depreciation for 2021 (you last used the deck in March 2021). Therefore, enter $8.46 ($16.92 x 50% = $8.46) on **Form 4562**, line 17, as your depreciation for 2021.

So far you've claimed a total of $83.75 for the old deck ($75.29 for 2016–2020 and $8.46 for 2021). Since the deck has now worn out, you're also entitled to claim the rest of the depreciation for the deck this year. The remaining depreciation you haven't yet claimed amounts to $576.25 ($2,000 x 33% Time-Space percentage for 2021 = $660 – $83.75).

You'll claim this $576.25 as a loss on Part I of **Form 4797** because the deck was used in business for more than one year. (See example form at the end of chapter 11.) It is a loss because you weren't able to claim all the depreciation before the deck wore out. You'll carry over the total of this amount and any other amounts you enter here to **Form 1040, Schedule 1**, line 4, where it will reduce your taxable income and thus your taxes.

If you are no longer in business when the deck wears out, you won't be able to claim this remaining depreciation; you can only claim a business loss if you're still in business.

Example 2

In 2018 you bought a microwave oven for $300 and started using it in your business. In 2021 the oven breaks down; you discard it and buy a new one. Your Time-Space percentages have been as follows: 2018: 35%; 2019: 38%; 2020: 37%; 2021: 36%. You've been depreciating the oven under seven-year 200% declining balance rules. Your depreciation deductions for 2018–2020 were as follows:

```
2018: $300 x 35% = $105 x 14.29% =    $15.00
2019: $300 x 38% = $114 x 24.49% =    $27.92
2020: $300 x 37% = $111 x 17.49% =    $19.41
```

Total claimed so far: $62.33

In 2021 the business basis of the microwave oven is $108 ($300 x 36% Time-Space percentage), so you can claim $6.74 in depreciation ($108 x 12.49% x 50%) on **Form 4562**, line 17. You can claim the remaining depreciation, $38.93 ($108 – $62.33 – $6.74), as a loss on Part I of **Form 4797**. You'll carry over this loss (and any other amounts in this section) to **Form 1040, Schedule 1**, line 4. (This example is not shown on the forms at the end of this chapter.)

You Sell an Item You've Used for Business

You must follow special rules when you sell items you've used in your business, and the reporting procedures differ depending on whether you have a gain or a loss on the sale. To determine that, follow these steps:

1. If you bought the item while you were in business, start with its original cost. If you bought it before you went into business, use the lesser of its original cost or its fair market value when you began using it for business. (This will usually be the item's fair market value.) This is the basis of the item.

2. Determine the total depreciation you were entitled to claim on the item while using it for your business, using straight-line depreciation rules. Determine the total depreciation you actually claimed for the item. Use the larger of these two amounts for the next step.

3. Subtract the item's total depreciation (step 2) from the item's basis (step 1). You must subtract all the depreciation you could have claimed, even if you didn't claim it all. The result is the item's adjusted basis.

4. Subtract the adjusted basis (step 3) from the price you got for the item when you sold it.

4a. If you did the steps above using the original cost, the result is your gain or loss on the sale.

4b. If you did the steps above using the fair market value when you began using it for business and the result is a loss, that is your loss on the sale.

4c. If you did the steps above using the fair market value when you began using it for business and the result is a gain, repeat the steps above using the original cost. If the second result is still a gain, use this second calculation for your gain. If this second calculation shows a loss, you have neither a gain nor a loss.

IF YOU'RE NO LONGER IN BUSINESS

If you sell an item after you're no longer in business (or no longer using the item in your business), use the above calculations to determine if you have a gain or a loss, adjusting the basis of the item by any depreciation you were entitled to claim. If you have a gain, enter it on **Schedule D** and **Form 1040** but not on **Form 4797**. If you have a loss, you have no further forms to fill out. Since you're no longer using the item in your business, you can't claim a deduction for a business loss.

IF THE ITEM WAS ORIGINALLY A GIFT

If someone gave you the item as a gift, use the donor's basis to determine your gain or loss for the item. Using the steps above, use the donor's adjusted basis (usually the original cost) of the item as your "original cost" or its fair market value when it was given to you.

- If someone bought a $1,000 swing set in 2017 and gave it to you in that same year, you would use $1,000 as its basis and follow the calculations above.

- If someone bought a $1,000 swing set in 2013 and gave it to you in 2017, its 2017 fair market value would be less than $1,000. If you estimate it to be worth $600 in 2017, you would use $600 as your fair market value basis instead of the $1,000 purchase price.

Example 3: Item Used 100% for Business and Sold at a Gain

You started your business in 2016. In 2019 you buy a swing set to use 100% for your business. You're still in business on May 1, 2021, when you sell the swing set for $900.

$1,000	purchase price of swing set (2019)
− $475	depreciation claimed 2019–2021 (7-year 200% declining balance)

	2019: $1,000 x 14.29%	= $142.90
	2020: $1,000 x 24.49%	=$244.90
	2021: $1,000 x 17.49% x 50%	=$87.45
	Total:	$475.25

$525	adjusted basis of swing set
$900	sale price of swing set in 2021
− $525	adjusted basis
$375	gain

Report this gain on **Form 4797**, Part III, and carry it over to line 13 (see end-of-chapter example), along with any other amounts you've reported in this section. The amounts on line 13 will be totaled on line 18 and carried over to **Schedule 1**, line 4, where they will increase your taxable income. Since this is not a business gain, you won't owe any additional self-employment tax on it.

Charitable Contributions

If you give an item to a charitable organization, either while you're in business or after you've closed your business, your deduction for it would be the lower of the fair market value of the item at the time you donated it or the adjusted basis of the item. Since a self-employed person can't claim a business deduction for a charitable contribution, report the donation on **Schedule A**, line 16.

For example, if you had given the swing set in example 3 to a charity on May 1, 2020, you could claim a charitable deduction of $525 ($1,000 – $475 depreciation = $525 adjusted basis) if its fair market value at that time was more than $525. If it was worth $500 at that time, you would deduct $500.

If you give an item away but *not* to a charitable organization before it's fully depreciated, you can't take any more depreciation deductions for that item.

Example 4: Item Used 40% for Business and Sold at a Gain

How would example 3 change if your own children also used the swing set and your Time-Space percentage was 40% each year?

$400   business basis of swing set ($1,000 purchase price x 40% Time-Space percentage)
– $190   depreciation claimed 2019–2021 (7-year 200% declining balance)

2019: $400 x 14.29%   = $57.16
2020: $400 x 24.49%   = $97.96
2021: $400 x 17.49% x 50%   = $34.98   (only a half year of depreciation because it
                                                             was sold during the year)

Total: $190.10

$210   adjusted business basis of swing set

$360   business basis of swing set sale ($900 x 40%)
– $210   adjusted business basis
$150   gain

You'll report this gain on **Form 4797**, Part III (see example at end of chapter) and **Schedule 1**. Since you've also used the swing set for personal use, there may also be personal tax consequences:

$600   personal basis of swing set ($1,000 purchase price x 60% personal use)
$540   personal basis of swing set sale ($900 x 60%)

$540   personal basis of sale
– $600   personal basis of purchase
($60)   personal loss

Since you can't deduct a personal loss, in this case you won't fill out any other forms; however, if you had a personal gain on the sale, you'd report it as income on **Form 8949** and **Schedule D**.

Example 5: Item Used 100% for Business and Sold at a Loss

How would Example 3 change if you sold the swing set in 2021 for $500?

$500   sale price of swing set in 2021
– $525   adjusted basis
($25)   loss

In this case, you would deduct the $25 loss as a business loss on **Form 4797**, Part I. (This example is not shown on the forms at the end of this chapter.)

Example 6: Item Used 40% for Business and Sold at a Loss

How would Example 3 change if you sold the swing set for $400, your own children used the swing set, and your Time-Space percentage was 40% each year?

$160   business percentage of sale price ($400 x 40%)
– $210   adjusted business basis
($150)   business loss

Enter this $30 as a loss on **Form 4797**, Part I (see example at end of chapter).

What If You Sell an Item at a Garage Sale?

The tax impact of selling an item at a garage sale is the same as in examples 3 through 6. You must take depreciation into account and calculate an adjusted basis for the item:

- If you never used the item in your business, report any gain you made on the sale on **Form 8949** and **Form 1040**. If you have a loss on the sale, don't report it on any tax form.

- If you're in business and you sell an item used in your business, report the business gain or loss on **Form 4797** and any personal gain on **Form 8949**.

- If you're no longer in business and you sell an item used in your business for a profit, report it as a gain on **Form 8949**. If you have a loss on the sale, don't report it on any tax form.

You Sell a Vehicle You've Used for Business

Calculating a gain or loss on the sale of a vehicle is a little more complicated than it is for other items; however, you need to follow the special rules about selling a vehicle and often they'll allow you to claim a business loss and save taxes. The procedure you'll follow will depend on which method you've used to deduct your vehicle expenses.

ACTUAL VEHICLE EXPENSES METHOD

If you used the actual vehicle expenses method to claim your vehicle expenses, you have claimed a depreciation deduction. When the vehicle is sold, you will take your depreciation deductions into account as shown in the previous examples.

STANDARD MILEAGE RATE METHOD

If you used the standard mileage rate method to claim your vehicle expenses, you must do a special calculation to determine how much depreciation to apply to the sale. Each year you use the standard mileage rate method, part of the deduction is considered to be depreciation. Here are the depreciation amounts for the last several years:

2021	$0.26 per mile
2020	$0.27 per mile
2019	$0.26 per mile
2018	$0.25 per mile
2017	$0.25 per mile
2015–16	$0.24 per mile
2014	$0.22 per mile
2012–13	$0.23 per mile
2011	$0.22 per mile
2010	$0.23 per mile
2008–2009	$0.21 per mile
2007	$0.19 per mile
2004–2006	$0.17 per mile

Multiply your business miles for each year you used your vehicle in business by the appropriate depreciation amount. Add these results together to get the total depreciation you will use to determine the adjusted basis of your vehicle.

Example 7: Sale of a Vehicle (Standard Mileage Rate)

In 2016 you buy a $15,000 vehicle and use it for business. You drive it 1,500 business miles in 2016, 1,400 miles in 2017, 1,700 miles in 2018, 1,452 miles in 2019, 1,130 miles in 2020, and 800 miles in 2021. You sell the vehicle in September 2021 for $4,000.

You use the standard mileage rate method every year, and your average business-use percentage since you owned it is 20%. Here's how you would calculate your gain or loss on the sale:

Depreciation per year

1,500 miles in 2016 x $0.24 =	$360
1,400 miles in 2017 x $0.25 =	$350
1,700 miles in 2018 x $0.25 =	$425
1,452 miles in 2019 x $0.26 =	$377.52
1,130 miles in 2020 x $0.27 =	$305.10
800 miles in 2021 x $0.26 =	$208
Total:	$2,025.62

$3,000	business basis of vehicle ($15,000 purchase price x 20% business use)
− $2,026	depreciation claimed as part of standard mileage rate method
$974	adjusted business basis

$800	business sale price of vehicle sold ($4,000 x 20% business use)
− $974	adjusted business basis
($174)	business loss

You can deduct this loss as a business loss on **Form 4797**, Part I.

Example 8: Sale of a Vehicle (Actual Vehicle Expenses)

If you had used the actual vehicle expenses method instead, you'd use the depreciation that you could have claimed over the years (even if you didn't actually claim it). This example is otherwise like example 7 except that you're depreciating the vehicle based on 20% business use. After six years of use, you would have claimed the full amount of depreciation ($15,000 purchase price x 20% = $3,000).

$3,000	business basis of vehicle
− $3,000	depreciation claimed under actual vehicle expenses method
0	adjusted basis

$800	business basis of vehicle sold
− 0	adjusted basis
$800	business gain

You would report this gain as shown in example 3.

You Have to Recapture Some Depreciation

For a description of the many circumstances under which you might have to recapture depreciation, see chapter 3. This example is one of the most common scenarios: you used Section 179 to deduct the entire business portion of an item in the year you bought it, and then your business-use percentage dropped to 50% or below before the end of the item's depreciation period. In this case, you'll have to recapture some of the depreciation you've claimed by filling out Part IV of **Form 4797**.

Example 9: Business Use Drops below 50% after Using Section 179

In 2019 you used Section 179 to deduct a $1,000 set of children's furniture. Since you expected to use it 100% for business purposes, you deducted the entire $1,000 in 2019. In 2021 your own children began using the furniture 60% of the time. Since your business-use percentage dropped below 50% in 2021, you must recapture some of the Section 179 deduction you claimed by filling out lines 33–35 of **Form 4797** as follows:

Line 33: Enter "$1,000."

Line 34: Enter the amount of depreciation you would have been entitled to claim each year through 2020, under straight-line rules, if you had not used Section 179.

2019: $1,000 x 100% business use = $1,000 x 7.14% = $ 71.40
2020: $1,000 x 100% business use = $1,000 x 14.29% = <u>$142.90</u>
Total: $214.30

Line 35: Subtract line 34 from line 33:

$1,000 – $214.30 = $785.70

Part IV	Recapture Amounts Under Sections 179 and 280F(b)(2) When Business Use Drops to 50% or Less (see instructions)		(a) Section 179	(b) Section 280F(b)(2)
33	Section 179 expense deduction or depreciation allowable in prior years.	33	$1,000	
34	Recomputed depreciation. See instructions	34	$214	
35	Recapture amount. Subtract line 34 from line 33. See the instructions for where to report . .	35	$786	

Form **4797** (2021)

Also enter $786 on **Schedule C**, line 6 (other income). You'll have to pay self-employment tax and income tax on this amount. You should still claim $57.16 as a depreciation deduction for 2021 on **Form 4562**.

If you went out of business by the end of 2021, you'd report the $786 as income on **Schedule C** and wouldn't be able to take any further depreciation deductions on the furniture.

If you remain in business, you'd report the $786 as income but would now be able to claim depreciation on the furniture in 2022 and beyond. (2022 would be the fourth year of depreciation; you'd be able to deduct $57.12 [$1,000 x 40% Time-Space percentage = $400 x 14.28% = $57.12]. You'd enter this amount on **Form 4562**, line 17.)

For more information about the tax issues discussed in this chapter, refer to the related topics in the other chapters of this book and the Redleaf Press *Family Child Care Record-Keeping Guide*.

Form **4797**	**Sales of Business Property**	OMB No. 1545-0184
Department of the Treasury Internal Revenue Service	(Also Involuntary Conversions and Recapture Amounts Under Sections 179 and 280F(b)(2)) ▶ Attach to your tax return. ▶ Go to *www.irs.gov/Form4797* for instructions and the latest information.	**2021** Attachment Sequence No. **27**

Name(s) shown on return	Identifying number
LUPE and BETH SERANNO	621-33-7454

1a	Enter the gross proceeds from sales or exchanges reported to you for 2021 on Form(s) 1099-B or 1099-S (or substitute statement) that you are including on line 2, 10, or 20. See instructions	**1a**
b	Enter the total amount of gain that you are including on lines 2, 10, and 24 due to the partial dispositions of MACRS assets .	**1b**
c	Enter the total amount of loss that you are including on lines 2 and 10 due to the partial dispositions of MACRS assets .	**1c**

Part I **Sales or Exchanges of Property Used in a Trade or Business and Involuntary Conversions From Other Than Casualty or Theft—Most Property Held More Than 1 Year** (see instructions)

2	**(a)** Description of property	**(b)** Date acquired (mo., day, yr.)	**(c)** Date sold (mo., day, yr.)	**(d)** Gross sales price	**(e)** Depreciation allowed or allowable since acquisition	**(f)** Cost or other basis, plus improvements and expense of sale	**(g) Gain or (loss)** Subtract (f) from the sum of (d) and (e)
	#1 DECK	01/01/2015	03/01/2021	$0	$84	$660	($576)
	#6 SWING SET	01/01/2019	05/01/2021	$160	$190	$400	($50)
	#7 VEHICLE	01/08/2018	09/01/2021	$800	$2,026	$3,000	($174)

3	Gain, if any, from Form 4684, line 39	**3**	
4	Section 1231 gain from installment sales from Form 6252, line 26 or 37	**4**	
5	Section 1231 gain or (loss) from like-kind exchanges from Form 8824 .	**5**	
6	Gain, if any, from line 32, from other than casualty or theft .	**6**	0
7	Combine lines 2 through 6. Enter the gain or (loss) here and on the appropriate line as follows .	**7**	($800)

Partnerships and S corporations. Report the gain or (loss) following the instructions for Form 1065, Schedule K, line 10, or Form 1120-S, Schedule K, line 9. Skip lines 8, 9, 11, and 12 below.

Individuals, partners, S corporation shareholders, and all others. If line 7 is zero or a loss, enter the amount from line 7 on line 11 below and skip lines 8 and 9. If line 7 is a gain and you didn't have any prior year section 1231 losses, or they were recaptured in an earlier year, enter the gain from line 7 as a long-term capital gain on the Schedule D filed with your return and skip lines 8, 9, 11, and 12 below.

8	Nonrecaptured net section 1231 losses from prior years. See instructions .	**8**	
9	Subtract line 8 from line 7. If zero or less, enter -0-. If line 9 is zero, enter the gain from line 7 on line 12 below. If line 9 is more than zero, enter the amount from line 8 on line 12 below and enter the gain from line 9 as a long-term capital gain on the Schedule D filed with your return. See instructions.	**9**	

Part II **Ordinary Gains and Losses** (see instructions)

10	Ordinary gains and losses not included on lines 11 through 16 (include property held 1 year or less):		
11	Loss, if any, from line 7 .	**11** (	$800)
12	Gain, if any, from line 7 or amount from line 8, if applicable .	**12**	
13	Gain, if any, from line 31 .	**13**	$525
14	Net gain or (loss) from Form 4684, lines 31 and 38a .	**14**	
15	Ordinary gain from installment sales from Form 6252, line 25 or 36 .	**15**	
16	Ordinary gain or (loss) from like-kind exchanges from Form 8824 .	**16**	
17	Combine lines 10 through 16.	**17**	($275)
18	For all except individual returns, enter the amount from line 17 on the appropriate line of your return and skip lines a and b below. For individual returns, complete lines a and b below.		
a	If the loss on line 11 includes a loss from Form 4684, line 35, column (b)(ii), enter that part of the loss here. Enter the loss from income-producing property on Schedule A (Form 1040), line 16. (Do not include any loss on property used as an employee.) Identify as from "Form 4797, line 18a." See instructions .	**18a**	
b	Redetermine the gain or (loss) on line 17 excluding the loss, if any, on line 18a. Enter here and on Schedule 1 (Form 1040), Part I, line 4 .	**18b**	($275)

For Paperwork Reduction Act Notice, see separate instructions.   Cat. No. 13086I   Form **4797** (2021)

Form 4797 (2021)   Page **2**

Part III — Gain From Disposition of Property Under Sections 1245, 1250, 1252, 1254, and 1255
(see instructions)

19	(a) Description of section 1245, 1250, 1252, 1254, or 1255 property:		(b) Date acquired (mo., day, yr.)	(c) Date sold (mo., day, yr.)
A	#3 SWING SET		01/01/2019	05/01/2021
B	#4 SWING SET		01/01/2019	05/01/2021
C				
D				

	These columns relate to the properties on lines 19A through 19D. ▶		Property A	Property B	Property C	Property D
20	Gross sales price (**Note:** *See line 1a before completing.*)	20	$900	$360		
21	Cost or other basis plus expense of sale	21	$1,000	$400		
22	Depreciation (or depletion) allowed or allowable	22	$475	$190		
23	Adjusted basis. Subtract line 22 from line 21	23	$525	$210		
24	Total gain. Subtract line 23 from line 20	24	$375	$150		
25	**If section 1245 property:**					
a	Depreciation allowed or allowable from line 22	25a	$475	$190		
b	Enter the **smaller** of line 24 or 25a	25b	$375	$150		
26	**If section 1250 property:** If straight line depreciation was used, enter -0- on line 26g, except for a corporation subject to section 291.					
a	Additional depreciation after 1975. See instructions	26a				
b	Applicable percentage multiplied by the **smaller** of line 24 or line 26a. See instructions	26b				
c	Subtract line 26a from line 24. If residential rental property **or** line 24 isn't more than line 26a, skip lines 26d and 26e	26c				
d	Additional depreciation after 1969 and before 1976	26d				
e	Enter the **smaller** of line 26c or 26d	26e				
f	Section 291 amount (corporations only)	26f				
g	Add lines 26b, 26e, and 26f	26g				
27	**If section 1252 property:** Skip this section if you didn't dispose of farmland or if this form is being completed for a partnership.					
a	Soil, water, and land clearing expenses	27a				
b	Line 27a multiplied by applicable percentage. See instructions	27b				
c	Enter the **smaller** of line 24 or 27b	27c				
28	**If section 1254 property:**					
a	Intangible drilling and development costs, expenditures for development of mines and other natural deposits, mining exploration costs, and depletion. See instructions	28a				
b	Enter the **smaller** of line 24 or 28a	28b				
29	**If section 1255 property:**					
a	Applicable percentage of payments excluded from income under section 126. See instructions	29a				
b	Enter the **smaller** of line 24 or 29a. See instructions	29b				

Summary of Part III Gains. Complete property columns A through D through line 29b before going to line 30.

30	Total gains for all properties. Add property columns A through D, line 24	30	$525
31	Add property columns A through D, lines 25b, 26g, 27c, 28b, and 29b. Enter here and on line 13	31	$525
32	Subtract line 31 from line 30. Enter the portion from casualty or theft on Form 4684, line 33. Enter the portion from other than casualty or theft on Form 4797, line 6	32	$0

Part IV — Recapture Amounts Under Sections 179 and 280F(b)(2) When Business Use Drops to 50% or Less
(see instructions)

			(a) Section 179	(b) Section 280F(b)(2)
33	Section 179 expense deduction or depreciation allowable in prior years	33		
34	Recomputed depreciation. See instructions	34		
35	Recapture amount. Subtract line 34 from line 33. See the instructions for where to report	35		

Form **4797** (2021)

SCHEDULE 1
(Form 1040)

Department of the Treasury
Internal Revenue Service

Additional Income and Adjustments to Income

▶ Attach to Form 1040, 1040-SR, or 1040-NR.
▶ Go to *www.irs.gov/Form1040* for instructions and the latest information.

OMB No. 1545-0074

2021

Attachment
Sequence No. **01**

Name(s) shown on Form 1040, 1040-SR, or 1040-NR
LUPE and BETH SERRANO

Your social security number
621-33-7454

Part I   Additional Income

1	Taxable refunds, credits, or offsets of state and local income taxes	**1**	
2a	Alimony received	**2a**	
b	Date of original divorce or separation agreement (see instructions) ▶ _____		
3	Business income or (loss). Attach Schedule C	**3**	98,839
4	Other gains or (losses). Attach Form 4797	**4**	($275)
5	Rental real estate, royalties, partnerships, S corporations, trusts, etc. Attach Schedule E	**5**	
6	Farm income or (loss). Attach Schedule F	**6**	
7	Unemployment compensation	**7**	
8	Other income:		
a	Net operating loss	**8a** ( )	
b	Gambling income	**8b**	
c	Cancellation of debt	**8c**	
d	Foreign earned income exclusion from Form 2555	**8d** ( )	
e	Taxable Health Savings Account distribution	**8e**	
f	Alaska Permanent Fund dividends	**8f**	
g	Jury duty pay	**8g**	
h	Prizes and awards	**8h**	
i	Activity not engaged in for profit income	**8i**	
j	Stock options	**8j**	
k	Income from the rental of personal property if you engaged in the rental for profit but were not in the business of renting such property	**8k**	
l	Olympic and Paralympic medals and USOC prize money (see instructions)	**8l**	
m	Section 951(a) inclusion (see instructions)	**8m**	
n	Section 951A(a) inclusion (see instructions)	**8n**	
o	Section 461(l) excess business loss adjustment	**8o**	
p	Taxable distributions from an ABLE account (see instructions) .	**8p**	
z	Other income. List type and amount ▶ _____ _____	**8z**	
9	Total other income. Add lines 8a through 8z	**9**	
10	Combine lines 1 through 7 and 9. Enter here and on Form 1040, 1040-SR, or 1040-NR, line 8	**10**	98,564

For Paperwork Reduction Act Notice, see your tax return instructions.   Cat. No. 71479F   **Schedule 1 (Form 1040) 2021**

DRAFT AS OF July 21, 2021 DO NOT FILE

Part II   Adjustments to Income

11	Educator expenses	**11**	
12	Certain business expenses of reservists, performing artists, and fee-basis government officials. Attach Form 2106	**12**	
13	Health savings account deduction. Attach Form 8889	**13**	
14	Moving expenses for members of the Armed Forces. Attach Form 3903	**14**	
15	Deductible part of self-employment tax. Attach Schedule SE	**15**	6,983
16	Self-employed SEP, SIMPLE, and qualified plans	**16**	
17	Self-employed health insurance deduction	**17**	
18	Penalty on early withdrawal of savings	**18**	
19a	Alimony paid	**19a**	
b	Recipient's SSN . . . . ▶		
c	Date of original divorce or separation agreement (see instructions) ▶		
20	IRA deduction	**20**	
21	Student loan interest deduction	**21**	
22	Reserved for future use	**22**	
23	Archer MSA deduction	**23**	
24	Other adjustments:		
a	Jury duty pay (see instructions)	**24a**	
b	Deductible expenses related to income reported on line 8k from the rental of personal property engaged in for profit	**24b**	
c	Nontaxable amount of the value of Olympic and Paralympic medals and USOC prize money reported on line 8l	**24c**	
d	Reforestation amortization and expenses	**24d**	
e	Repayment of supplemental unemployment benefits under the Trade Act of 1974	**24e**	
f	Contributions to section 501(c)(18)(D) pension plans	**24f**	
g	Contributions by certain chaplains to section 403(b) plans . .	**24g**	
h	Attorney fees and court costs for actions involving certain unlawful discrimination claims (see instructions)	**24h**	
i	Attorney fees and court costs you paid in connection with an award from the IRS for information you provided that helped the IRS detect tax law violations	**24i**	
j	Housing deduction from Form 2555	**24j**	
k	Excess deductions of section 67(e) expenses from Schedule K-1 (Form 1041)	**24k**	
z	Other adjustments. List type and amount ▶ _____	**24z**	
25	Total other adjustments. Add lines 24a through 24z	**25**	
26	Add lines 11 through 23 and 25. These are your **adjustments to income.** Enter here and on Form 1040 or 1040-SR, line 10, or Form 1040-NR, line 10a	**26**	6,983

Schedule 1 (Form 1040) 2021

CHAPTER 12

Selling Your Home:
Form 4797 and Schedule D

When you sell your home, you potentially face two taxes. The first tax is on the depreciation you claimed (or were entitled to claim) for all the years you used your home for your business. The second tax is on the profit of the sale of your home. Almost every provider must pay the first tax, and some may have to pay the second tax.

The Tax on the Depreciation of Your Home

When you use your home for business, you are entitled to depreciate its value. You always want to depreciate your home because doing so will usually generate a substantial deduction each year.

Here's a very simple example. You purchase your home for $200,000. Each year, your Time-Space percentage is 35%. You run your family child care business for seven years and then stop offering child care. Years later you sell your home:

$200,000 x 35% = $70,000
Homes are depreciated over 39 years: $70,000 ÷ 39 = $1,795
You used your home for your business for 7 years: $1,795 x 7 years = $12,565

Over the seven years, you were entitled to claim $12,565 of business deductions. (See chapter 3 for a discussion of how to depreciate your home.) As a result, when you sell your home, you will owe taxes on $12,565.

The tax rate you will pay on this amount depends on your tax bracket in the year you sell your home. The current tax rates are as follows:

*   10% if you are in the 10% tax bracket

*   12% if you are in the 12% tax bracket

*   22% if you are in the 22% tax bracket

*   24% if you are in the 24% tax bracket

*   25% if you are in the 32% or higher tax bracket (see page 132 for a description of the 2021 tax brackets)

If you sold your home in 2021 and you were in the 12% tax bracket, you would owe $1,508 in taxes ($12,565 x 12% = $1,508).

Important Note: Always Depreciate Your Home!

In the above example, you would owe $1,508 in taxes even if you didn't claim house depreciation for the seven years you were in business; this tax is due if you were entitled to claim house depreciation—even if you didn't! The IRS rules clearly state that if you were entitled to claim house depreciation in any tax year, you will be treated as if you did when you sell your home. You will owe this tax even if you do not offer child care services for many years before you sell your home. The only situation in which you would not be entitled to claim house depreciation (and therefore not have to pay taxes on it when you sell your home) is if you showed a loss in your business in any year. For example, if you showed a business loss for the last two tax years, you wouldn't owe any tax on depreciation for those years.

When you consider the above information, you should realize that you always want to depreciate your home, no matter what! You will owe the same amount in taxes on your home later, even if you didn't depreciate it. Depreciating your home can mean a significant tax deduction each year, so don't let anyone tell you it's not a good idea. If you did not depreciate your home in earlier years, you can amend your tax return (going back one year) or use **Form 3115** (see chapter 10) to claim the depreciation (going back many years). The amount of depreciation subject to tax is the lower of the amount of depreciation claimed or the gain from the sale of the home.

Note: The tax on house depreciation is only due for depreciation claimed—or entitled to be claimed—after May 6, 1997.

The Tax on the Profit on the Sale of Your Home

Normally, when you sell something for a profit, you will owe a tax on this profit. So, if you bought your home for $200,000 and sold it for $275,000, you earned a profit of $75,000 that would be subject to taxes.

However, there is a rule that may allow you to avoid paying taxes on the first $250,000 ($500,000 if you are married) of the profit on the sale of your home. To take advantage of this rule, you must meet two tests. First, you must be able to show that you owned your home for two of the last five years before you sold it. Second, you must show that you lived in your home (as your main home) for two of the last five years before you sold it.

Because most providers will not make a profit of $250,000 (or $500,000) on the sale of their homes, it may appear that they will not have to pay tax on the profit. Unfortunately, it's not that simple. The tax rules regarding the sale of your home are extremely complicated when you have used your home for your child care business.

Get Professional Help

I strongly recommend that providers get help from a tax professional if they sell their home. I would not rely on any tax software (TurboTax, H&R Block, and so on) to correctly calculate your taxes. IRS **Publication 523 Selling Your Home** (www.irs.gov/pub523) does cover this topic, but you will find it extremely difficult to fill out the proper forms correctly even if you try to follow these directions. I wish the sale of home rules were simpler! I apologize for not alerting readers to the possibility of owing taxes on the profit on the sale of the home in earlier editions of this book.

Other Points to Consider

The longer you use your home for business after May 6, 1997, the more tax you'll have to pay on depreciation when you sell your home. For example, let's say that the basis of your home is $100,000, you use 39-year depreciation rules, and your Time-Space percentage is 35%. If you sell your home five years after May 6, 1997, you'll owe tax on $4,485. If you sell it ten years after May 6, 1997, you'll owe tax on $8,970. If you sell it fifteen years after May 6, 1997, you'll owe tax on $13,455. (This assumes that your gain on the sale is at least equal to these amounts.)

HOME IMPROVEMENTS

If you've made home improvements while living in your home, you can reduce the profit on the sale of your home. You can increase the basis of the home by the cost of the improvement and then decrease the basis by the amount of depreciation you claimed (or were entitled to claim) on the improvement. The more home improvements you make on your home, the lower your gain will be when you sell your home.

Like-Kind Exchanges

One way to avoid paying the tax on the sale of a home is to conduct a like-kind exchange. If you expect to make a profit on the sale of your home over the limits of $250,000 or $500,000, you may want to consider a like-kind exchange. The Tax Code states that "no gain or loss shall be recognized if property held for productive use in trade or business . . . is exchanged solely for property of a like-kind to be held for productive use in trade or business." This means that you can exchange your old home for a new one and avoid some of the taxes you would otherwise owe, even if you don't meet the two-year test. (Doing a like-kind exchange does allow you to defer paying taxes on depreciation claimed after May 6, 1997, but eventually you will have to pay tax on this depreciation.) To take advantage of the like-kind exchange rules, you have to intend to continue providing child care in your new home.

The best way to do a like-kind exchange is to hire an intermediary to handle the transactions and ensure that all the proper rules are followed. You are allowed 180 days after closing on your old home, but before you've received the money from the sale, to conduct a like-kind exchange. Once you've accepted the money from the sale of your home, you can no longer do a like-kind exchange.

Conducting a like-kind exchange is far more complicated than described here. You should hire a qualified intermediary to handle this complicated transaction. I strongly urge you to talk to a tax professional before you sell your home and use a tax preparer, lawyer, or real estate professional to help you follow the requirements of the law.

The cost of hiring a qualified intermediary may be expensive, so if your taxable gain from selling the home is not large, it may not be worth doing a like-kind exchange.

Changes in Marital Status

Changes in your marital status can complicate the tax impact of selling your home. If you're planning to marry or divorce, you should consult a tax professional to find out how the home sale rules will apply in your situation.

In June 2013 the U.S. Supreme Court struck down the Defense of Marriage Act (DOMA) and ended federal discrimination against same-sex couples who are legally married under state law. This means a family child care provider who is legally married to a same-sex partner can take advantage of the ability to depreciate her home, even if the home is in her spouse's name. It also means that the same provider will be taxed on this depreciation when the home is sold.

For more information about the tax issues discussed in this chapter, refer to the related topics in the other chapters of this book and the Redleaf Press *Family Child Care Record-Keeping Guide*.

CHAPTER 13

Closing Your Child Care Business

From a tax point of view, it's almost as easy to close your child care business as it is to start it. You don't need to notify the IRS of your decision to quit. (Check your state revenue department to see if your state has any special requirements.) If you ended your business in 2021, however, there are some tax issues that you should review carefully, especially in regard to depreciation.

Depreciation Issues

General Depreciation Rule

In general, if you go out of business before you have fully depreciated your property, you stop claiming depreciation and forfeit the ability to claim the remainder of the depreciation. In addition, you don't have to report any of the depreciation you have already claimed as income. This includes any depreciation you claimed using the 50% or 100% bonus depreciation rules. There are two exceptions to this general depreciation rule: Section 179 depreciation and accelerated depreciation on a vehicle (see next page).

The Half-Year Convention

For items you've been depreciating under the Half-Year Convention rules (see chapter 3), you can claim only a half-year's worth of the normal depreciation in the year you end your business. The items covered by this convention include personal property (non-real estate used in your business), land improvements, and vehicles.

For example, you bought a washer in 2019 for $500 and used it in your business until you closed your business in 2021. Your Time-Space percentage in 2021 is 35%, and you've been using straight-line depreciation. Your depreciation deduction for the washer in 2021 would normally be $25 ($500 x 35% x 14.29% [Year 3 depreciation rate] = $25); however, if you went out of business last year, you can only claim half of this amount, or $12.50.

The Mid-Month Convention

For items you've been depreciating under the Mid-Month Convention rules (see chapter 3), you can claim only a prorated part of the normal depreciation in the year you end your business, based on the month you quit. The items covered by this convention include your home and home improvements.

For example, you bought a new roof in 2020 for $6,000 and went out of business in July 2021. Your Time-Space percentage in 2021 is 30%. Your normal depreciation for all of 2021 would be $46.15 ($6,000 x 30% x 2.564%). You are considered to be in business for 6.5 months in 2021, because the month you go out of business counts for half of a month. Thus, multiply $46.15 by 6.5 months and divide by 12 months. The result, $25.00, is your depreciation deduction for 2021.

Section 179

If you used Section 179 rules (see chapter 3) on any items while you were in business, check to see whether the recovery period has run out for each item. This period is five years for computers and vehicles, and seven years for furniture, appliances, TVs, VCRs, DVD players, and large play equipment. If the recovery period is still in effect, you'll have to pay additional taxes to recapture the unused depreciation (see chapter 11).

Recapturing Accelerated Depreciation on a Vehicle

If you use accelerated depreciation (the 200% declining balance method) to depreciate a vehicle you use more than 50% for business, and your business use of the vehicle falls below 50% during the five-year recovery period, you will have to recapture some of the depreciation you claimed and report it as income. Use the rules for recapturing depreciation described in chapter 11. You would also need to recapture some depreciation if you had used the 50% or 100% bonus depreciation rules on the vehicle. You do not have to recapture depreciation if you used the 50% or 100% bonus depreciation rules on any other property.

Going Out of Business Checklist

If you closed your business in 2021, here's a checklist of some other business reminders and tax issues that could affect your tax return:

❑ Make sure you've taken all the depreciation you're entitled to on your home and other property used in your business. If you haven't, use **Form 3115** to take these deductions in 2021 (see chapter 10). They can add up to a large amount, and if you went out of business in 2021, this will be your last chance to claim them.

❑ If you paid employees in 2021 (including your spouse and children), be sure to file **Form 941** or **Form 944** to report wages for Social Security and Medicare taxes for the quarter you quit. Check the box at the top of the form to indicate that you won't be filing any more of these forms. File **Form 940** at the end of the year, as usual. You must file **Form W-2** by the date the next **Form 941** is due and file **Form W-3** one month later (see chapter 8).

❑ If you weren't in business until December 31, adjust the number of hours on **Form 8829**, line 5. For example, if you ended your business on August 31, write in 5,856 hours (the number of hours from January 1 to August 31). Enter on **Form 8829** only expenses that you incurred during this time period. In this case, you would enter only 66% (5,832 hours ÷ 8,760 total hours in the year) of your mortgage interest, real estate taxes, and homeowners insurance, and you would enter your actual expenses for utilities, home repairs, and maintenance for these months.

❑ It's a good idea to send a letter to the parents of the children in your care officially informing them of your decision to end your business. Keep a copy of the letter for your files. Take photographs that show you have converted your play areas back to personal use.

❑ If you're planning to sell your home in the next few years, consult a tax professional about how to reduce your tax liability when selling your home.

❑ Since you'll file your final business forms this tax season, you won't need to file **Schedule C**, **Form 4562**, **Form 8829**, or **Schedule SE** for 2022.

❑ If you have any carryover expenses from **Form 8829** in your last year of business, you won't be able to claim them after your business ends.

❑ Notify your state regulatory department, local child care resource and referral agency, Food Program sponsor, and local family child care association that you are going out of business so they can update their records.

❑ If you sell any items you've used in your business *before* you go out of business, you may be entitled to a business deduction or (more rarely) need to report some additional business income. See chapter 11 for details.

❑ Contact your insurance agent to review your policies (homeowners, business liability, and car) to see if you are entitled to a refund.

The IRS does not consider you to have gone out of business if you simply move from one home to another and continue your child care business in your new home. Your business has continued, even if you're operating at a new location. You'll still file one **Schedule C**, **Form 4562**, and **Schedule SE**. You will need to file two **Form 8829**s, showing your Time-Space percentage and expenses for each home separately.

If you go out of business and later decide to start up again, just start claiming your income and expenses as if you were beginning your business for the first time. To claim depreciation for items that you used before, use the lower of the item's fair market value or its adjusted basis at the time you start using it again for your business (see chapter 3).

For more information about the tax issues discussed in this chapter, refer to the related topics in the other chapters of this book and the Redleaf Press *Family Child Care Record-Keeping Guide*.

CHAPTER 14

Dealing with an Audit

Although your chances of being audited are less than 1%, if you are audited, your best defense is to have good records for your business. You should keep documents such as receipts, bills, record books, and menus for at least three years after the date you file your tax return. Keep the records for items you are depreciating (such as your home, personal property, and business equipment) for the depreciation period plus three years. In other words, if you began depreciating your stove in 2016, you should keep the receipt for eight years (the depreciation period) plus three years, or until the year 2027.

You may wish to bring another person with you to the audit, such as your spouse, a friend, your tax preparer, a certified public accountant, an enrolled agent, an enrolled federal tax accountant, or an attorney. Sometimes it can help to have another person in the room, especially someone who is more objective or familiar with the audit process.

When auditing a family child care business, IRS auditors often target the following five areas of the tax return:

- unreported income
- Time-Space percentage
- food expenses
- shared business and personal expenses
- business mileage

Unreported Income

The first thing the auditor is likely to do is ask you to identify the source of all the deposits to your personal and business bank accounts. You should mark the source of every deposit on the deposit slip, your check register, or your computer software program, even if they are simply transfers from one account to another. Label each business deposit by the parent's name. If you can't account for a deposit, the IRS is likely to assume that it is business income and will tax it.

Time-Space Percentage

The auditor may challenge your Time-Space percentage. You need to have records showing the hours you worked and that the space you are claiming was used on a regular basis for your business. The higher your Time-Space percentage is, the more closely the IRS will examine your records. Don't let the auditor challenge your right to count the hours you spent cooking, cleaning, and planning activities for your business (see chapter 1).

Food Expenses

With the passage of the standard meal allowance rule (see chapter 4), the IRS may be less likely to challenge your food expenses in an audit. The only question is likely to be whether you can prove that you served the number of meals and snacks you are claiming. The meals reimbursed by the Food Program will appear on your monthly claim forms, but you must keep very careful daily records of all the meals and snacks you serve that aren't reimbursed by the Food Program. If you are claiming food expenses based on the actual cost of food, be sure to keep all your business and personal food receipts.

Shared Business and Personal Expenses

The auditor may try to claim that some of your business expenses are personal, especially items such as household supplies and repairs. To support your case, you can take pictures that show children using the item or get letters from parents.

Business Mileage

Auditors have sometimes held that a provider can't deduct any miles for a trip in which some personal items were purchased; however, this is not what the law says. It says that you may deduct all the miles for a trip if it is *primarily* for business purposes.

Avoiding an Audit

No one wants to be audited by the IRS. It's a scary prospect that most of us would do just about anything to avoid. Instead of worrying about whether you'll be audited, focus on keeping the proper records for your business. If your records are complete and organized, you have nothing to fear from an audit.

For example, I often hear people say, "I don't claim all my allowable expenses because I'm afraid I'll be audited" or "I used a lower Time-Space percentage than I really had because I didn't want to trigger an audit." It isn't a good idea to think like this. You have little control over *if* you'll be audited; your real concern should be "If I'm audited, do I have the records to back up my deductions?" If the answer is yes, you have little to worry about.

People also ask, "If I claim many deductions that I haven't claimed before, my expenses will be a lot higher than usual. Will the IRS notice and audit my return?" Again, don't worry about this. Just claim the deductions you're entitled to and keep the records to back them up.

In an audit you can submit records and receipts for expenses that you didn't originally claim on your tax return to offset any deductions the auditor disallows (or even to give you a refund). For example, you could claim a higher Time-Space percentage or a larger business food expense. (If you discover additional deductions after the audit is completed, ask the IRS to reopen your case. If the IRS won't do this, you can file an amended return up to three years after you filed the original return, even after being audited.)

Errors by Your Tax Preparer

You're always responsible for paying the proper taxes, even if your tax preparer has made a mistake on your return. That's why it's important to make sure you understand what your tax preparer has done. If the mistake was the tax preparer's error, a good tax preparer will pay some, if not all, of the interest that is because of the mistake. (Tax preparers aren't required to pay this, however.) If you knew that what your tax preparer did was wrong, you should pay the penalty. If you didn't know that it was wrong, ask your tax preparer to pay the penalty. (It's best to find out your tax preparer's policy on this issue when you hire the preparer.)

You Have the Right to Appeal

Remember that some auditors aren't familiar with the unique way the tax rules apply to family child care businesses, so an auditor may not be aware of all the deductions you're entitled to. When this happens, some providers have told the auditor, "Tom Copeland said I could do it in his *Tax Workbook*!" Although I've tried to interpret the tax laws and show you how to apply them in a reasonable manner, in any specific situation they may be subject to various interpretations. If there's a dispute, ask your auditor to justify his or her interpretation with a written reference. (If you need more help, refer to the resources listed below.)

If you don't agree with your auditor's findings, you have a right to ask that the auditor's supervisor review the problem. If you aren't satisfied with the supervisor's decision, you have the right to appeal. Do your best to settle the matter with the auditor and the supervisor first.

Appealing the decision is a relatively simple matter. Tell your auditor that you want to appeal. Better yet, put your request for an appeal in writing. When you appeal, your auditor will write up the facts of your case and pass them on to an appeals officer; however, your auditor (or your auditor's supervisor) may offer to settle your case before sending it to appeal.

Appearing before the appeals officer is an informal affair. Bring your tax preparer (or even better, have your tax preparer appear without you). If you can't resolve the case here, you can appeal to the U.S. Tax Court. There is a $60 filing fee to appeal to the Tax Court (there's no fee for the appeals up to this point). You can choose to go before the "S-Court," which handles disputes that involve only a few thousand dollars. Although you don't need a lawyer to appear before the Tax Court, it's common to hire professional assistance at this level. (For more information on this process, refer to **Publication 556**.)

Get the Help You Need

If you're audited, you don't have to do it alone; get the help you need. We recommend that you hire a tax professional to assist you. To be qualified to represent you before the IRS, this person must be an enrolled agent, a certified public accountant, or an attorney.

- Check my website, www.tomcopelandblog.com, for a wealth of resource materials and a special section on audits. This site has copies of all the IRS rulings and Tax Court cases that involve family child care businesses.

- Get the text of the IRS **Child Care Provider Audit Technique Guide** at my website (www.tomcopelandblog.com) or the IRS website (www.irs.gov/pub/irs-utl /child_care_provider.pdf). Although this guide doesn't have the force of law, it can help you understand what your auditor may be looking for. You can challenge its interpretations, but if you do you should be prepared to cite some other authority for your position. (The statements in the **Child Care Provider Audit Technique Guide** may need to be modified based on new laws, Tax Court cases, IRS Revenue Rulings, and IRS Revenue Procedures that have been released since its publication.)

IRS Taxpayer Advocate Service

If you have one of the following problems or an ongoing issue with the IRS that hasn't been resolved through normal processes, you can call the IRS Taxpayer Advocate Service (877-777-4778, 24 hours a day) for help:

- You're suffering, or are about to suffer, a significant hardship.
- You're facing an immediate threat of adverse action.
- You're about to incur significant costs (including fees for professional representation).
- You haven't received a response or resolution by the date promised.
- You've experienced a delay of more than 30 days to resolve an issue.

For more information about the tax issues discussed in this chapter, refer to the related topics in the other chapters of this book and the Redleaf Press *Family Child Care Record-Keeping Guide.*

PART IV

Appendixes

Sample Tax Return

Sandy James began her child care business on January 1, 2017. She has one child of her own, Vanessa, age three, and she cares for six children, ages two through eight. Sandy's husband, Bill, earned $41,000 in 2021 as a construction worker. His **Form W-2** shows that he had $9,000 withheld in federal taxes and $1,200 withheld in state taxes. He paid $4,104 in medical bills in 2021. Sandy's Time-Space percentage is 39%. In 2021 Sandy and Bill received a federal stimulus check for $4,200. Of this, $1,400 was for Bill, $1,400 was for Sandy, and $1,400 was for their child. None of this is taxable income and will not appear on their tax return. Let's see how Sandy should fill out her tax forms.

Sandy's first task will be to organize her records by income and expense categories, using the worksheets in the Tax Organizer. Next, she'll place the worksheets next to the proper tax form. A step-by-step process of how she'll fill out her tax forms follows. You can also refer to the copies of her completed forms at the end of this appendix.

In this example, the numbers on the tax forms will be rounded to the nearest dollar, as you should also do on your tax forms. (The deductions in this sample tax return aren't intended to be used as a guideline. Your deductions may be significantly more or less than shown here.)

Form 8829 Expenses for Business Use of Your Home

Lines 1–7: Sandy has a Time-Space percentage of 39%.

Line 8: Sandy carries forward her tentative profit from **Schedule C**, line 29, to this line on **Form 8829**.

Lines 16–17: Because Sandy is claiming the standard deduction, she will enter her mortgage interest and real estate taxes on lines 16 and 17. If she chose to itemize her personal expenses on **Schedule A**, she would enter these expenses on lines 10 and 11. Sandy enters her deductible mortgage interest ($5,000) and real estate taxes ($3,000) in column (b) because they also have a personal component.

Lines 18–25: Homeowners insurance ($1,500) and utilities (gas, electricity, water, sewer, cable TV, and trash hauling = $2,000) go in column (b) because they have a personal component. A $15 replacement of a window broken by a child in her care is a 100% business expense and goes on line 20, column (a). A screen door that cost $85 to repair was damaged by normal wear and tear and goes on line 20, column (b). Sandy multiplies the total of the items in column (b) ($11,585) by her Time-Space percentage (39%) from line 7. She adds to the result ($4,518) the $15 from column (a) and enters the total ($4,533) on line 26.

Lines 30, and 37–42:   Sandy purchased her home in 2009 for $150,000 ($15,000 of this was the value of the land). In 2011 she remodeled her kitchen for $8,000. In 2012 she hired a contractor to paint her living room and bedrooms for $750. Here's how she'll calculate her depreciation for her home:

$150,000	Purchase price of home
+ $8,000	Kitchen improvement done before business began
$158,000	
– $15,000	Land
$143,000	Basis of home
x 39%	Time-Space percentage
$55,770	Business basis of home
x 2.564%	(Because Sandy began depreciating her home after May 13, 1993, she uses 39-year depreciation rules. This is the percentage she uses after the first year.)
$1,430	Home depreciation

Since the painting was a repair, it isn't added to this calculation. Sandy can't claim a business expense for it because it was done before she began her business.

Enter the $1,430 on **Form 8829**, line 42.

Sandy skips to Part III to enter her home depreciation. Sandy enters "2.564%" on line 41 because that's the percentage for a full year of depreciation for a home that was first used for business in 2018. She enters "$1,430" on line 42 and line 30.

Line 36:   When she finishes this form, Sandy will transfer the amount on line 36 ($5,963) to **Schedule C**, line 30. Then she'll be able to calculate her net profit on **Schedule C**.

Sandy could choose to use the IRS Simplified Method or claim her expenses from **Form 8829** on her **Schedule C**. If she used the Simplified Method, her maximum deduction for house expenses would be $585 (300 square feet x $5 x 39%). Since her actual house expenses ($5,963 – **Form 8829**, line 36) are more than this, she will use her **Form 8829** expenses.

Form 4562 Depreciation and Amortization

Sandy added a new deck in March 2021 that cost $9,000. This is a home improvement that would normally be depreciated over 39 years. However, because Sandy cares for six children and one of her own, she determines she uses her deck more than half the time in her business. She tracked the actual use of her deck for two months and calculated that she used it 80% of the time for her business. She is therefore eligible for the Section 179 exception that allows her to deduct the business portion on the deck in one year (See pages 72–73).

$9,000 deck x 80% business use = $7,200.

Enter this on **Form 4562**, line 6. The amount to enter on line 11 is Sandy's profit from **Schedule C** ($38,913 minus this Section 179 deduction = $31,713).

OTHER PERSONAL PROPERTY

In 2018 Sandy began depreciating some appliances and furniture worth $3,300. She owned these items before she went into business and began using them in her business in 2018. Here's how she'll calculate her depreciation for these expenses:

Furniture/appliances: $3,300 purchased before 2018

$3,300 x 39% (T/S%) = $1,254

$1,254 x 12.49% (7-year 200% DB method, year 4) = $157

Sandy will enter "$157" on line 17.

LAND IMPROVEMENTS

In June 2021 Sandy bought a $3,600 fence for her backyard. She will use the 100% bonus depreciation rule.

$3,600 x 39% (T/S%) = $1,404
Enter on **Form 4562**, line 14.

Part V: Sandy will record her vehicle mileage in Part V, Section B.

Schedule C Profit or Loss from Business

PART I INCOME

Sandy earned $68,080 in parent fees last year. Of this amount, she received $80 in January 2021 for care she provided in December. Another $140 is a bounced check that a parent never honored. Sandy also received $2,300 in reimbursements from the Food Program. Here's how she'll report this income:

Line 1b: $68,080

— $80   Received

$68,000

— $140   Bounced check

$67,860

Line 6: $2,300

PART II EXPENSES

Line 8: **Advertising**: Sandy paid $150 for business cards, newspaper ads, and so on.

Line 9: **Automobile expenses**: The value of Sandy's vehicle on January 1, 2018 (when she first used it for business), was $4,000. She drove the vehicle 14,472 miles in 2021, and 3,604 of those miles were for business trips. Sandy's actual vehicle expenses were

Gas, oil, repairs	$600
Vehicle insurance	$800
Extra vehicle insurance for her business	$200
Vehicle loan interest	$237
Parking for business trips	$15
Vehicle property tax	$150

Here's how Sandy will calculate her deduction for vehicle expenses—first, to decide whether to use the standard mileage rate method or the actual vehicle expenses method, she calculates her vehicle expenses using both methods:

STANDARD MILEAGE RATE METHOD

3,604 business miles (Jan–Dec) x $0.56	=	$2,018.24
Vehicle loan interest:		
$237 x 24.9% (3,604 ÷ 14,472)	=	$59
Parking		$15
Vehicle property tax:		
$150 x 24.9%	=	$37
Total		$2,129.00

ACTUAL VEHICLE EXPENSES METHOD

3,546 miles ÷ 14,241 miles = 24.9% business use

Gas, oil, repairs	$600	
Vehicle insurance	$800	
Vehicle loan interest	$237	
Vehicle property tax	$150	
Total	$1,787	x 24.9% = $447
Extra vehicle insurance		$200
Parking		$15
Total		$662

Vehicle depreciation (5-year straight-line, year 3):

$4,000
x 24.9%
$996   x 20.0% = $198

Total $860

Sandy will use the standard mileage rate method because it gives her a larger deduction ($2,129 vs. $860). She enters "$2,129" on **Schedule C**, line 9. Sandy will not fill out Part IV because she must fill out **Form 4562**.

Line 13: **Depreciation**: Sandy enters "$8,761" from **Form 4562**, line 22.

Line 15: **Insurance**: Sandy paid $427 for business liability insurance premiums. This is 100% deductible.

Line 16b: **Interest**: Sandy paid $100 in interest on her credit card for her dining room furniture.

$100 x 39% Time-Space percentage = $39

Line 17: **Legal and professional services**: Last year Sandy paid a tax preparer to file her tax return. The tax preparer charged her $500 to file her business tax forms and $250 to file her personal tax forms. Sandy will enter "$500" here.

Line 18: **Office expenses**: Sandy purchased the following items last year:

Notebooks, calculator, copies, postage	$84.00
Subscriptions to child care magazines	$40.00
Child care books/calendar (*Tax Workbook,* *Record-Keeping Guide,* and *KidKare Software*)	$133.90
Membership fee in local child care association	$15.00
Training workshops	$37.00
Long-distance calls to parents of children in her care	$25.39
Total:	$335.29

Since these expenses were used 100% for her business, she will enter "$335" on line 18. Sandy also spent $300 on her monthly phone bill, but none of this is deductible.

Line 20b: **Rent of business property**: Sandy purchased Netflix and showed movies for the children in her care. $95.88 x 39% Time-Space percentage = $37.39. Enter "$38" on line 20b.

Line 21: **Repairs and maintenance**: Sandy spent $130 on a service contract for her refrigerator and microwave oven.

$130 x 39% Time-Space percentage = $51.00

Line 22: **Supplies**: Sandy purchased the following supplies last year:

Kitchen supplies (soap, scrubbers, napkins)	$50
Can opener	$20
Children's games and toys	$440
Total:	$510

Since these items were also used for personal purposes, she can claim only her Time-Space percentage:

$510 x 39% = $211

This year Sandy also purchased the following:

Arts and crafts supplies	$240
Household supplies (paper towels, toilet paper, etc.)	$150
Total:	$390

Sandy calculated that these items were used 50% in her business ($390 x .50 = $195). This gives her a new total of $406 ($211 + $195), which she enters on line 22.

Line 24: **Travel**: Sandy traveled to a three-day family child care conference in Orlando in July and incurred these expenses:

Plane ticket	$675	
Hotel	$520	
Taxis	$40	
Total:	$1,235	Enter on line 24a.

IRS Publication 1542 Per Diem Rates lists the amount of meal expenses you can claim for a business trip without having to keep food receipts. The general meal rate is $55 per day, but some cities have a higher rate. Orlando, Florida, has a higher rate of $66 per day, so Sandy can claim $198 ($66 x 3 days) with this method. But she can deduct only 50% of meal expenses, so she enters "$99" on line 24b (see page 109).

Line 27: **Other Expenses**: In April 2021 Sandy purchased a $2,000 swing set used by her business and her own children. Under the $2,500 rule she can deduct the business portion of $780 ($2,000 x 39% = $780) here. No need to depreciate it. To elect this rule she must attach a statement to her tax return (see page 237).

In February 2021 Sandy purchased two computers for $1,500 each used 100% in her business. Because of the $2,500 rule, Sandy can deduct her two computers in full and doesn't have to depreciate it.

On the blank lines of Part V, Sandy has entered the following line items:

Food for children in her care	$5,802
Swing set	$780
Two computers	$3,000
Fire extinguisher (required by licensing)	$45
Security locks	$102
Cleaning supplies	$422
Activity expenses	$380
Toys	$600
Total:	$11,131

Sandy will enter "$11,131" on line 27a.

Schedule SE Self-Employment Tax

This form is easy to complete. Sandy transfers her net profit from **Schedule C**, line 31, onto line 2 of this form and follows the directions to calculate her self-employment tax of $5,498. Then she transfers this total to **Form 1040 Schedule 2**, line 4.

Schedule A Itemized Deductions

Because the 2021 standard deduction for married couples filing jointly is $25,100, Sandy and Bill will not itemize their taxes on **Schedule A** and will use the standard deduction.

Schedule EIC Earned Income Credit

Sandy and Bill earned more than the limit of $47,646 in adjusted gross income (**Form 1040**, line 11), so they aren't eligible for this credit.

Form 1040 U.S. Individual Income Tax Return

Sandy and Bill can now transfer the amounts from their other tax forms to **Form 1040**. She will also fill out **Schedule 1** and **Schedule 2**.

Form 8995 Qualified Income Deduction Simplified Computation

All providers who show a profit on **Schedule C** should fill out this form.

Line 1:   Enter profit from **Schedule C**, line 31 = $38,913

Line 5:   Multiply line 4 by 20%: $38,913 x 20% = $7,783

Line 11: The formula for this line is: Total income ($77,164 from **Form 1040**, line 11) minus the standard deduction ($25,100 from **Form 1040**, line 12) = $52,064

Line 13: Enter the same amount on line 13.

Line 14: Multiply line 13 by 20% = $10,413

Line 15: Enter the lesser of line 10 or line 14: $7,783

Form **8829**	**Expenses for Business Use of Your Home**	OMB No. 1545-0074
Department of the Treasury Internal Revenue Service (99)	▶ File only with Schedule C (Form 1040). Use a separate Form 8829 for each home you used for business during the year. ▶ Go to *www.irs.gov/Form8829* for instructions and the latest information.	**20****21** Attachment Sequence No. **176**

Name(s) of proprietor(s)	Your social security number
SANDY JAMES	123-45-6789

Part I — Part of Your Home Used for Business

1	Area used regularly and exclusively for business, regularly for daycare, or for storage of inventory or product samples (see instructions)	**1**	2,200
2	Total area of home	**2**	2,200
3	Divide line 1 by line 2. Enter the result as a percentage	**3**	100 %
	For daycare facilities not used exclusively for business, go to line 4. All others, go to line 7.		
4	Multiply days used for daycare during year by hours used per day **4** 3,399 **hr.**		
5	If you started or stopped using your home for daycare during the year, see instructions; otherwise, enter 8,760 **5** 8,760 **hr.**		
6	Divide line 4 by line 5. Enter the result as a decimal amount **6** .39		
7	Business percentage. For daycare facilities not used exclusively for business, multiply line 6 by line 3 (enter the result as a percentage). All others, enter the amount from line 3 ▶	**7**	39 %

Part II — Figure Your Allowable Deduction

8	Enter the amount from Schedule C, line 29, **plus** any gain derived from the business use of your home, **minus** any loss from the trade or business not derived from the business use of your home. See instructions.	**8**	$38,913

See instructions for columns (a) and (b) before completing lines 9–22.

			(a) Direct expenses	(b) Indirect expenses		
9	Casualty losses (see instructions)	**9**				
10	Deductible mortgage interest (see instructions)	**10**				
11	Real estate taxes (see instructions)	**11**				
12	Add lines 9, 10, and 11	**12**				
13	Multiply line 12, column (b), by line 7			**13**		
14	Add line 12, column (a), and line 13				**14**	
15	Subtract line 14 from line 8. If zero or less, enter -0-				**15**	$38,913
16	Excess mortgage interest (see instructions)	**16**		$5,000		
17	Excess real estate taxes (see instructions)	**17**		$3,000		
18	Insurance	**18**		$1,500		
19	Rent	**19**				
20	Repairs and maintenance	**20**	$15	$85		
21	Utilities	**21**		$2,000		
22	Other expenses (see instructions)	**22**				
23	Add lines 16 through 22	**23**	$15			
24	Multiply line 23, column (b), by line 7			**24**	$4,518	
25	Carryover of prior year operating expenses (see instructions)			**25**	$0	
26	Add line 23, column (a), line 24, and line 25				**26**	$4,533
27	Allowable operating expenses. Enter the **smaller** of line 15 or line 26				**27**	$4,533
28	Limit on excess casualty losses and depreciation. Subtract line 27 from line 15				**28**	$34,380
29	Excess casualty losses (see instructions)			**29**		
30	Depreciation of your home from line 42 below			**30**	$1,430	
31	Carryover of prior year excess casualty losses and depreciation (see instructions)			**31**		
32	Add lines 29 through 31				**32**	$1,430
33	Allowable excess casualty losses and depreciation. Enter the **smaller** of line 28 or line 32				**33**	$1,430
34	Add lines 14, 27, and 33				**34**	$5,963
35	Casualty loss portion, if any, from lines 14 and 33. Carry amount to **Form 4684.** See instructions				**35**	
36	**Allowable expenses for business use of your home.** Subtract line 35 from line 34. Enter here and on Schedule C, line 30. If your home was used for more than one business, see instructions. ▶				**36**	$5,963

Part III — Depreciation of Your Home

37	Enter the **smaller** of your home's adjusted basis or its fair market value. See instructions	**37**	$158,000
38	Value of land included on line 37	**38**	$15,000
39	Basis of building. Subtract line 38 from line 37	**39**	$143,000
40	Business basis of building. Multiply line 39 by line 7	**40**	$55,770
41	Depreciation percentage (see instructions)	**41**	2.564 %
42	Depreciation allowable (see instructions). Multiply line 40 by line 41. Enter here and on line 30 above	**42**	$1,430

Part IV — Carryover of Unallowed Expenses to 2022

43	Operating expenses. Subtract line 27 from line 26. If less than zero, enter -0-	**43**	
44	Excess casualty losses and depreciation. Subtract line 33 from line 32. If less than zero, enter -0-	**44**	

For Paperwork Reduction Act Notice, see your tax return instructions.   Cat. No. 13232M   Form **8829** (2021)

Form **4562**	Depreciation and Amortization		OMB No. 1545-0172

Form 4562
Department of the Treasury
Internal Revenue Service   (99)

Depreciation and Amortization
(Including Information on Listed Property)
▶ Attach to your tax return.
▶ Go to *www.irs.gov/Form4562* for instructions and the latest information.

OMB No. 1545-0172
2021
Attachment
Sequence No. **179**

Name(s) shown on return	Business or activity to which this form relates	Identifying number
SANDY JAMES	FAMILY CHILD CARE	123-45-6789

Part I   Election To Expense Certain Property Under Section 179
Note: If you have any listed property, complete Part V before you complete Part I.

1	Maximum amount (see instructions)	**1**	$1,000,000
2	Total cost of section 179 property placed in service (see instructions)	**2**	
3	Threshold cost of section 179 property before reduction in limitation (see instructions)	**3**	$500,000
4	Reduction in limitation. Subtract line 3 from line 2. If zero or less, enter -0-	**4**	0
5	Dollar limitation for tax year. Subtract line 4 from line 1. If zero or less, enter -0-. If married filing separately, see instructions	**5**	$500,000

6	(a) Description of property	(b) Cost (business use only)	(c) Elected cost	
	Deck	$7,200	$7,200	

7	Listed property. Enter the amount from line 29 . . . . **7**		
8	Total elected cost of section 179 property. Add amounts in column (c), lines 6 and 7	**8**	$7,200
9	Tentative deduction. Enter the **smaller** of line 5 or line 8	**9**	$7,200
10	Carryover of disallowed deduction from line 13 of your 2020 Form 4562	**10**	
11	Business income limitation. Enter the smaller of business income (not less than zero) or line 5. See instructions	**11**	$31,713
12	Section 179 expense deduction. Add lines 9 and 10, but don't enter more than line 11	**12**	$7,200
13	Carryover of disallowed deduction to 2022. Add lines 9 and 10, less line 12 ▶	**13**	

Note: Don't use Part II or Part III below for listed property. Instead, use Part V.

Part II   Special Depreciation Allowance and Other Depreciation (Don't include listed property. See instructions.)

14	Special depreciation allowance for qualified property (other than listed property) placed in service during the tax year. See instructions	**14**	$1,404
15	Property subject to section 168(f)(1) election	**15**	
16	Other depreciation (including ACRS)	**16**	

Part III   MACRS Depreciation (Don't include listed property. See instructions.)

Section A

17	MACRS deductions for assets placed in service in tax years beginning before 2021	**17**	$157
18	If you are electing to group any assets placed in service during the tax year into one or more general asset accounts, check here . . . . ▶ ☐		

Section B—Assets Placed in Service During 2021 Tax Year Using the General Depreciation System

(a) Classification of property	(b) Month and year placed in service	(c) Basis for depreciation (business/investment use only—see instructions)	(d) Recovery period	(e) Convention	(f) Method	(g) Depreciation deduction
19a 3-year property						
b 5-year property						
c 7-year property						
d 10-year property						
e 15-year property						
f 20-year property						
g 25-year property			25 yrs.		S/L	
h Residential rental property			27.5 yrs.	MM	S/L	
			27.5 yrs.	MM	S/L	
i Nonresidential real property			39 yrs.	MM	S/L	
				MM	S/L	

Section C—Assets Placed in Service During 2021 Tax Year Using the Alternative Depreciation System

20a Class life					S/L	
b 12-year			12 yrs.		S/L	
c 30-year			30 yrs.	MM	S/L	
d 40-year			40 yrs.	MM	S/L	

Part IV   Summary (See instructions.)

21	Listed property. Enter amount from line 28	**21**	
22	**Total.** Add amounts from line 12, lines 14 through 17, lines 19 and 20 in column (g), and line 21. Enter here and on the appropriate lines of your return. Partnerships and S corporations—see instructions .	**22**	$8,761
23	For assets shown above and placed in service during the current year, enter the portion of the basis attributable to section 263A costs	**23**	

For Paperwork Reduction Act Notice, see separate instructions.	Cat. No. 12906N	Form **4562** (2021)

DRAFT AS OF June 30, 2021 DO NOT FILE

Form 4562 (2021)   Page **2**

Part V — Listed Property (Include automobiles, certain other vehicles, certain aircraft, and property used for entertainment, recreation, or amusement.)

Note: For any vehicle for which you are using the standard mileage rate or deducting lease expense, complete **only** 24a, 24b, columns (a) through (c) of Section A, all of Section B, and Section C if applicable.

Section A—Depreciation and Other Information (Caution: See the instructions for limits for passenger automobiles.)

24a Do you have evidence to support the business/investment use claimed? ☐ **Yes** ☐ **No**   **24b** If "Yes," is the evidence written? ☐ **Yes** ☐ **No**

(a) Type of property (list vehicles first)	(b) Date placed in service	(c) Business/investment use percentage	(d) Cost or other basis	(e) Basis for depreciation (business/investment use only)	(f) Recovery period	(g) Method/Convention	(h) Depreciation deduction	(i) Elected section 179 cost
25 Special depreciation allowance for qualified listed property placed in service during the tax year and used more than 50% in a qualified business use. See instructions			**25**					
26 Property used more than 50% in a qualified business use:								
		%						
		%						
		%						
27 Property used 50% or less in a qualified business use:								
Automobile	1-1-18	24.9 %				S/L –		
		%				S/L –		
		%				S/L –		

28 Add amounts in column (h), lines 25 through 27. Enter here and on line 21, page 1 . **28**

29 Add amounts in column (i), line 26. Enter here and on line 7, page 1 . . . . **29**

Section B—Information on Use of Vehicles

Complete this section for vehicles used by a sole proprietor, partner, or other "more than 5% owner," or related person. If you provided vehicles to your employees, first answer the questions in Section C to see if you meet an exception to completing this section for those vehicles.

	(a) Vehicle 1		(b) Vehicle 2		(c) Vehicle 3		(d) Vehicle 4		(e) Vehicle 5		(f) Vehicle 6	
30 Total business/investment miles driven during the year (**don't** include commuting miles)	3,604											
31 Total commuting miles driven during the year												
32 Total other personal (noncommuting) miles driven	10,868											
33 Total miles driven during the year. Add lines 30 through 32	14,472											
	Yes	No	Yes	No	Yes	No	Yes	No	Yes	No	Yes	No
34 Was the vehicle available for personal use during off-duty hours?	✓											
35 Was the vehicle used primarily by a more than 5% owner or related person?	✓											
36 Is another vehicle available for personal use?	✓											

Section C—Questions for Employers Who Provide Vehicles for Use by Their Employees

Answer these questions to determine if you meet an exception to completing Section B for vehicles used by employees who **aren't** more than 5% owners or related persons. See instructions.

		Yes	No
37	Do you maintain a written policy statement that prohibits all personal use of vehicles, including commuting, by your employees?		
38	Do you maintain a written policy statement that prohibits personal use of vehicles, except commuting, by your employees? See the instructions for vehicles used by corporate officers, directors, or 1% or more owners		
39	Do you treat all use of vehicles by employees as personal use?		
40	Do you provide more than five vehicles to your employees, obtain information from your employees about the use of the vehicles, and retain the information received?		
41	Do you meet the requirements concerning qualified automobile demonstration use? See instructions.		

Note: If your answer to 37, 38, 39, 40, or 41 is "Yes," don't complete Section B for the covered vehicles.

Part VI — Amortization

(a) Description of costs	(b) Date amortization begins	(c) Amortizable amount	(d) Code section	(e) Amortization period or percentage	(f) Amortization for this year
42 Amortization of costs that begins during your 2021 tax year (see instructions):					

43 Amortization of costs that began before your 2021 tax year **43**

44 Total. Add amounts in column (f). See the instructions for where to report **44**

Form **4562** (2021)

SCHEDULE C (Form 1040) Department of the Treasury Internal Revenue Service (99)	**Profit or Loss From Business** (Sole Proprietorship) ▶ Go to *www.irs.gov/ScheduleC* for instructions and the latest information. ▶ **Attach to Form 1040, 1040-SR, 1040-NR, or 1041; partnerships must generally file Form 1065.**	OMB No. 1545-0074 20**21** Attachment Sequence No. **09**

Name of proprietor **SANDY JAMES**	Social security number (SSN) **123-45-6789**

A	Principal business or profession, including product or service (see instructions) **FAMILY CHILD CARE**	**B** Enter code from instructions ▶	6	2	4	4	1	0

C	Business name. If no separate business name, leave blank.	**D** Employer ID number (EIN) (see instr.)

E	Business address (including suite or room no.) ▶ 687 HOOVER ROAD
	City, town or post office, state, and ZIP code HUDSON, OH 42383

F Accounting method: **(1)** ☑ Cash **(2)** ☐ Accrual **(3)** ☐ Other (specify) ▶ _____

G Did you "materially participate" in the operation of this business during 2021? If "No," see instructions for limit on losses . ☑ Yes ☐ No

H If you started or acquired this business during 2021, check here . . . . ▶ ☐

I Did you make any payments in 2021 that would require you to file Form(s) 1099? See instructions . . . . ☐ Yes ☑ No

J If "Yes," did you or will you file required Form(s) 1099? . . . . ☐ Yes ☐ No

Part I   Income

1	Gross receipts or sales. See instructions for line 1 and check the box if this income was reported to you on Form W-2 and the "Statutory employee" box on that form was checked . . . . ▶ ☐	**1**	$67,860
2	Returns and allowances	**2**	$67,860
3	Subtract line 2 from line 1	**3**	
4	Cost of goods sold (from line 42)	**4**	$67,860
5	**Gross profit.** Subtract line 4 from line 3	**5**	
6	Other income, including federal and state gasoline or fuel tax credit or refund (see instructions)	**6**	$2,300
7	**Gross income.** Add lines 5 and 6 . . . . ▶	**7**	$70,160

Part II   Expenses. Enter expenses for business use of your home **only** on line 30.

8	Advertising	**8**	$150	**18**	Office expense (see instructions) .	**18**	$335
9	Car and truck expenses (see instructions) . . .	**9**	$2,129	**19**	Pension and profit-sharing plans .	**19**	
				20	Rent or lease (see instructions):		
10	Commissions and fees .	**10**		**a**	Vehicles, machinery, and equipment	**20a**	
11	Contract labor (see instructions)	**11**		**b**	Other business property . . .	**20b**	$38
12	Depletion	**12**		**21**	Repairs and maintenance . . .	**21**	$51
13	Depreciation and section 179 expense deduction (not included in Part III) (see instructions)	**13**	$8,761	**22**	Supplies (not included in Part III) .	**22**	$406
				23	Taxes and licenses	**23**	
				24	Travel and meals:		
14	Employee benefit programs (other than on line 19) .	**14**		**a**	Travel	**24a**	$1,235
15	Insurance (other than health)	**15**	$410	**b**	Deductible meals (see instructions)	**24b**	$99
16	Interest (see instructions):			**25**	Utilities	**25**	
a	Mortgage (paid to banks, etc.)	**16a**		**26**	Wages (less employment credits)	**26**	
b	Other	**16b**	$39	**27a**	Other expenses (from line 48) . .	**27a**	$11,131
17	Legal and professional services	**17**	$500	**b**	**Reserved for future use** . . .	**27b**	

28	**Total expenses** before expenses for business use of home. Add lines 8 through 27a . . . . . ▶	**28**	$25,284
29	Tentative profit or (loss). Subtract line 28 from line 7	**29**	$44,876
30	Expenses for business use of your home. Do not report these expenses elsewhere. Attach Form 8829 unless using the simplified method. See instructions. **Simplified method filers only:** Enter the total square footage of (a) your home: _____ and (b) the part of your home used for business: _____ . Use the Simplified Method Worksheet in the instructions to figure the amount to enter on line 30	**30**	$5,963
31	**Net profit or (loss).** Subtract line 30 from line 29. • If a profit, enter on both **Schedule 1 (Form 1040), line 3,** and on **Schedule SE, line 2.** (If you checked the box on line 1, see instructions). Estates and trusts, enter on **Form 1041, line 3.** • If a loss, you **must** go to line 32.	**31**	$38,913
32	If you have a loss, check the box that describes your investment in this activity. See instructions. • If you checked 32a, enter the loss on both **Schedule 1 (Form 1040), line 3,** and on **Schedule SE, line 2.** (If you checked the box on line 1, see the line 31 instructions.) Estates and trusts, enter on **Form 1041, line 3.** • If you checked 32b, you **must** attach Form 6198. Your loss may be limited.	**32a** ☐ All investment is at risk. **32b** ☐ Some investment is not at risk.

For Paperwork Reduction Act Notice, see the separate instructions.   Cat. No. 11334P   Schedule C (Form 1040) 2021

Schedule C (Form 1040) 2021   Page **2**

Part III   Cost of Goods Sold (see instructions)

33   Method(s) used to value closing inventory: **a** ☐ Cost   **b** ☐ Lower of cost or market   **c** ☐ Other (attach explanation)

34   Was there any change in determining quantities, costs, or valuations between opening and closing inventory? If "Yes," attach explanation . . . . ☐ Yes   ☐ No

35	Inventory at beginning of year. If different from last year's closing inventory, attach explanation . . .	35	
36	Purchases less cost of items withdrawn for personal use	36	
37	Cost of labor. Do not include any amounts paid to yourself	37	
38	Materials and supplies	38	
39	Other costs	39	
40	Add lines 35 through 39	40	
41	Inventory at end of year	41	
42	**Cost of goods sold.** Subtract line 41 from line 40. Enter the result here and on line 4	42	

Part IV   Information on Your Vehicle. Complete this part **only** if you are claiming car or truck expenses on line 9 and are not required to file Form 4562 for this business. See the instructions for line 13 to find out if you must file Form 4562.

43   When did you place your vehicle in service for business purposes? (month/day/year)   ▶ _____ / _____ / _____

44   Of the total number of miles you drove your vehicle during 2021, enter the number of miles you used your vehicle for:

a Business _____ **b** Commuting (see instructions) _____ **c** Other _____

45   Was your vehicle available for personal use during off-duty hours? . . . . ☐ Yes   ☐ No

46   Do you (or your spouse) have another vehicle available for personal use?. . . . . ☐ Yes   ☐ No

47a   Do you have evidence to support your deduction? . . . . ☐ Yes   ☐ No

  b   If "Yes," is the evidence written? . . . . ☐ Yes   ☐ No

Part V   Other Expenses. List below business expenses not included on lines 8–26 or line 30.

SWING SET	$708
COMPUTER	$1,596
FENCE	$1,404
TIER II PROVIDER FOOD	$5,802
HOUSEHOLD ITEMS	$147
CLEANING SUPPLIES	$422
ACTIVITY SUPPLIES	$380
TOYS	$600
48 **Total other expenses.** Enter here and on line 27a **48**	$11,131

Schedule C (Form 1040) 2021

SCHEDULE SE
(Form 1040)

Department of the Treasury
Internal Revenue Service (99)

Self-Employment Tax

▶ Go to *www.irs.gov/ScheduleSE* for instructions and the latest information.
▶ Attach to Form 1040, 1040-SR, or 1040-NR.

OMB No. 1545-0074

2021

Attachment
Sequence No. **17**

Name of person with self-employment income (as shown on Form 1040, 1040-SR, or 1040-NR)	Social security number of person with **self-employment** income ▶
SANDY JAMES	123-45-6789

Part I   Self-Employment Tax

Note: If your only income subject to self-employment tax is **church employee income,** see instructions for how to report your income and the definition of church employee income.

A   If you are a minister, member of a religious order, or Christian Science practitioner **and** you filed Form 4361, but you had $400 or more of **other** net earnings from self-employment, check here and continue with Part I . . . . ▶ ☐

Skip lines 1a and 1b if you use the farm optional method in Part II. See instructions.

1a	Net farm profit or (loss) from Schedule F, line 34, and farm partnerships, Schedule K-1 (Form 1065), box 14, code A	**1a**	
b	If you received social security retirement or disability benefits, enter the amount of Conservation Reserve Program payments included on Schedule F, line 4b, or listed on Schedule K-1 (Form 1065), box 20, code AH	**1b**	( )

Skip line 2 if you use the nonfarm optional method in Part II. See instructions.

2	Net profit or (loss) from Schedule C, line 31; and Schedule K-1 (Form 1065), box 14, code A (other than farming). See instructions for other income to report or if you are a minister or member of a religious order	**2**	$38,913
3	Combine lines 1a, 1b, and 2	**3**	$38,913
4a	If line 3 is more than zero, multiply line 3 by 92.35% (0.9235). Otherwise, enter amount from line 3 .	**4a**	$35,936
	Note: If line 4a is less than $400 due to Conservation Reserve Program payments on line 1b, see instructions.		
b	If you elect one or both of the optional methods, enter the total of lines 15 and 17 here	**4b**	
c	Combine lines 4a and 4b. If less than $400, **stop;** you don't owe self-employment tax. **Exception:** If less than $400 and you had **church employee income,** enter -0- and continue . . . . ▶	**4c**	
5a	Enter your **church employee income** from Form W-2. See instructions for definition of church employee income **5a**		
b	Multiply line 5a by 92.35% (0.9235). If less than $100, enter -0-	**5b**	
6	Add lines 4c and 5b	**6**	
7	Maximum amount of combined wages and self-employment earnings subject to social security tax or the 6.2% portion of the 7.65% railroad retirement (tier 1) tax for 2021	**7**	142,800
8a	Total social security wages and tips (total of boxes 3 and 7 on Form(s) W-2) and railroad retirement (tier 1) compensation. If $142,800 or more, skip lines 8b through 10, and go to line 11 . . . . **8a**		
b	Unreported tips subject to social security tax from Form 4137, line 10 . . . **8b**		
c	Wages subject to social security tax from Form 8919, line 10 . . . . . . **8c**		
d	Add lines 8a, 8b, and 8c	**8d**	
9	Subtract line 8d from line 7. If zero or less, enter -0- here and on line 10 and go to line 11 . . . ▶	**9**	
10	Multiply the **smaller** of line 6 or line 9 by 12.4% (0.124)	**10**	
11	Multiply line 6 by 2.9% (0.029)	**11**	
12	**Self-employment tax.** Add lines 10 and 11. Enter here and on **Schedule 2 (Form 1040), line 4** . .	**12**	$5,498
13	**Deduction for one-half of self-employment tax.** Multiply line 12 by 50% (0.50). Enter here and on **Schedule 1 (Form 1040), line 15** **13** 2,749		

Part II   Optional Methods To Figure Net Earnings (see instructions)

Farm Optional Method. You may use this method **only** if **(a)** your gross farm income[1] wasn't more than $8,820, **or (b)** your net farm profits[2] were less than $6,367.

14	Maximum income for optional methods	**14**	5,880
15	Enter the **smaller** of: two-thirds (²⁄₃) of gross farm income[1] (not less than zero) **or** $5,880. Also, include this amount on line 4b above	**15**	

Nonfarm Optional Method. You may use this method **only** if **(a)** your net nonfarm profits[3] were less than $6,367 and also less than 72.189% of your gross nonfarm income,[4] **and (b)** you had net earnings from self-employment of at least $400 in 2 of the prior 3 years. **Caution:** You may use this method no more than five times.

16	Subtract line 15 from line 14	**16**	
17	Enter the **smaller** of: two-thirds (²⁄₃) of gross nonfarm income[4] (not less than zero) **or** the amount on line 16. Also, include this amount on line 4b above	**17**	

[1] From Sch. F, line 9; and Sch. K-1 (Form 1065), box 14, code B.
[2] From Sch. F, line 34; and Sch. K-1 (Form 1065), box 14, code A—minus the amount you would have entered on line 1b had you not used the optional method.
[3] From Sch. C, line 31; and Sch. K-1 (Form 1065), box 14, code A.
[4] From Sch. C, line 7; and Sch. K-1 (Form 1065), box 14, code C.

For Paperwork Reduction Act Notice, see your tax return instructions.   Cat. No. 11358Z   Schedule SE (Form 1040) 2021

Form **1040**	Department of the Treasury—Internal Revenue Service (99) **U.S. Individual Income Tax Return**	**2021**	OMB No. 1545-0074	IRS Use Only—Do not write or staple in this space.

Filing Status
Check only one box.

☐ Single ☐ Married filing jointly ☐ Married filing separately (MFS) ☐ Head of household (HOH) ☐ Qualifying widow(er) (QW)

If you checked the MFS box, enter the name of your spouse. If you checked the HOH or QW box, enter the child's name if the qualifying person is a child but not your dependent ▶

Your first name and middle initial	Last name	Your social security number
SANDY	JAMES	123 45 6789

If joint return, spouse's first name and middle initial	Last name	Spouse's social security number
BILL	JAMES	987 65 4321

Home address (number and street). If you have a P.O. box, see instructions.
687 Hoover Street   Apt. no.

City, town, or post office. If you have a foreign address, also complete spaces below.   State   ZIP code
Hudson, Ohio 42387

Foreign country name   Foreign province/state/county   Foreign postal code

Presidential Election Campaign
Check here if you, or your spouse if filing jointly, want $3 to go to this fund. Checking a box below will not change your tax or refund.
☐ You ☐ Spouse

At any time during 2021, did you receive, sell, exchange, or otherwise dispose of any financial interest in any virtual currency?   ☐ Yes ☐ No

Standard Deduction

Someone can claim: ☐ You as a dependent ☐ Your spouse as a dependent
☐ Spouse itemizes on a separate return or you were a dual-status alien

Age/Blindness You: ☐ Were born before January 2, 1957 ☐ Are blind   Spouse: ☐ Was born before January 2, 1957 ☐ Is blind

Dependents (see instructions):
If more than four dependents, see instructions and check here ▶ ☐

(1) First name Last name	(2) Social security number	(3) Relationship to you	(4) ✔ if qualifies for (see instructions): Child tax credit	Credit for other dependents
Vanessa James	124 56 4411	Daughter	☑	☐
			☐	☐
			☐	☐
			☐	☐

Attach Sch. B if required.

Standard Deduction for—
• Single or Married filing separately, $12,550
• Married filing jointly or Qualifying widow(er), $25,100
• Head of household, $18,800
• If you checked any box under *Standard Deduction,* see instructions.

1	Wages, salaries, tips, etc. Attach Form(s) W-2	1	$41,000
2a	Tax-exempt interest ... 2a	b Taxable interest ... 2b	
3a	Qualified dividends ... 3a	b Ordinary dividends ... 3b	
4a	IRA distributions ... 4a	b Taxable amount ... 4b	
5a	Pensions and annuities ... 5a	b Taxable amount ... 5b	
6a	Social security benefits ... 6a	b Taxable amount ... 6b	
7	Capital gain or (loss). Attach Schedule D if required. If not required, check here ▶ ☐	7	
8	Other income from Schedule 1, line 10	8	$38,913
9	Add lines 1, 2b, 3b, 4b, 5b, 6b, 7, and 8. This is your **total income** ▶	9	$79,913
10	Adjustments to income from Schedule 1, line 26	10	$2,749
11	Subtract line 10 from line 9. This is your **adjusted gross income** ▶	11	$77,164
12a	Standard deduction or itemized deductions (from Schedule A) ... 12a $25,100		
b	Charitable contributions if you take the standard deduction (see instructions) 12b		
c	Add lines 12a and 12b	12c	$25,100
13	Qualified business income deduction from Form 8995 or Form 8995-A	13	$7,783
14	Add lines 12c and 13	14	$32,883
15	**Taxable income.** Subtract line 14 from line 11. If zero or less, enter -0-	15	$44,281

For Disclosure, Privacy Act, and Paperwork Reduction Act Notice, see separate instructions.   Cat. No. 11320B   Form **1040** (2021)

Form 1040 (2021)   Page **2**

16	**Tax** (see instructions). Check if any from Form(s): 1 ☐ 8814 2 ☐ 4972 3 ☐ _____		16	$4,916
17	Amount from Schedule 2, line 3		17	
18	Add lines 16 and 17		18	$4,916
19	Nonrefundable child tax credit or credit for other dependents from Schedule 8812		19	
20	Amount from Schedule 3, line 8		20	
21	Add lines 19 and 20		21	
22	Subtract line 21 from line 18. If zero or less, enter -0-		22	$4,916
23	Other taxes, including self-employment tax, from Schedule 2, line 21		23	$5,498
24	Add lines 22 and 23. This is your **total tax** ▶		24	$10,414
25	Federal income tax withheld from:			
a	Form(s) W-2	25a		
b	Form(s) 1099	25b		
c	Other forms (see instructions)	25c		
d	Add lines 25a through 25c		25d	$9,000
26	2021 estimated tax payments and amount applied from 2020 return		26	
27a	Earned income credit (EIC)	27a		
	Check here if you had not reached the age of 19 by December 31, 2021, and satisfy all other requirements for claiming the EIC. See instructions ▶ ☐			
b	Nontaxable combat pay election	27b		
c	Prior year (2019) earned income	27c		
28	Refundable child tax credit or additional child tax credit from Schedule 8812	28		
29	American opportunity credit from Form 8863, line 8	29		
30	Recovery rebate credit. See instructions	30		
31	Amount from Schedule 3, line 15	31		
32	Add lines 27a and 28 through 31. These are your **total other payments and refundable credits** ▶		32	---
33	Add lines 25d, 26, and 32. These are your **total payments** ▶		33	$9,000

If you have a qualifying child, attach Sch. EIC.

Refund

Direct deposit? See instructions.

34	If line 33 is more than line 24, subtract line 24 from line 33. This is the amount you **overpaid**		34	
35a	Amount of line 34 you want **refunded to you.** If Form 8888 is attached, check here ▶ ☐		35a	
▶ b	Routing number _____ ▶ c Type: ☐ Checking ☐ Savings			
▶ d	Account number _____			
36	Amount of line 34 you want **applied to your 2022 estimated tax** ▶	36		

Amount You Owe

37	**Amount you owe.** Subtract line 33 from line 24. For details on how to pay, see instructions ▶		37	$1,414
38	Estimated tax penalty (see instructions) ▶	38		

Third Party Designee

Do you want to allow another person to discuss this return with the IRS? See instructions . . . . ▶ ☐ **Yes.** Complete below. ☐ **No**

Designee's name ▶ _____   Phone no. ▶ _____   Personal identification number (PIN) ▶ _____

Sign Here

Under penalties of perjury, I declare that I have examined this return and accompanying schedules and statements, and to the best of my knowledge and belief, they are true, correct, and complete. Declaration of preparer (other than taxpayer) is based on all information of which preparer has any knowledge.

Joint return? See instructions. Keep a copy for your records.

Your signature	Date	Your occupation	If the IRS sent you an Identity Protection PIN, enter it here (see inst.) ▶
Sandy James	4/3/2022	child care provider	
Spouse's signature. If a joint return, **both** must sign.	Date	Spouse's occupation	If the IRS sent your spouse an Identity Protection PIN, enter it here (see inst.) ▶
Bill James	4/3/2022	Construction	

Phone no. _____   Email address _____

Paid Preparer Use Only

Preparer's name	Preparer's signature	Date	PTIN	Check if: ☐ Self-employed
Firm's name ▶			Phone no.	
Firm's address ▶			Firm's EIN ▶	

Go to *www.irs.gov/Form1040* for instructions and the latest information.   Form **1040** (2021)

| SCHEDULE 1
(Form 1040)

Department of the Treasury
Internal Revenue Service | **Additional Income and Adjustments to Income**

▶ Attach to Form 1040, 1040-SR, or 1040-NR.
▶ Go to *www.irs.gov/Form1040* for instructions and the latest information. | OMB No. 1545-0074

20**21**

Attachment
Sequence No. **01** |

Name(s) shown on Form 1040, 1040-SR, or 1040-NR	Your social security number
SANDY and BILL JAMES	123-45-6789

Part I   Additional Income

DRAFT AS OF July 21, 2021 DO NOT FILE

1	Taxable refunds, credits, or offsets of state and local income taxes	**1**	
2a	Alimony received	**2a**	
b	Date of original divorce or separation agreement (see instructions) ▶ _____		
3	Business income or (loss). Attach Schedule C	**3**	$38,913
4	Other gains or (losses). Attach Form 4797	**4**	
5	Rental real estate, royalties, partnerships, S corporations, trusts, etc. Attach Schedule E	**5**	
6	Farm income or (loss). Attach Schedule F	**6**	
7	Unemployment compensation	**7**	
8	Other income:		
a	Net operating loss	**8a** ( )	
b	Gambling income	**8b**	
c	Cancellation of debt	**8c**	
d	Foreign earned income exclusion from Form 2555	**8d** ( )	
e	Taxable Health Savings Account distribution	**8e**	
f	Alaska Permanent Fund dividends	**8f**	
g	Jury duty pay	**8g**	
h	Prizes and awards	**8h**	
i	Activity not engaged in for profit income	**8i**	
j	Stock options	**8j**	
k	Income from the rental of personal property if you engaged in the rental for profit but were not in the business of renting such property	**8k**	
l	Olympic and Paralympic medals and USOC prize money (see instructions)	**8l**	
m	Section 951(a) inclusion (see instructions)	**8m**	
n	Section 951A(a) inclusion (see instructions)	**8n**	
o	Section 461(l) excess business loss adjustment	**8o**	
p	Taxable distributions from an ABLE account (see instructions) .	**8p**	
z	Other income. List type and amount ▶ _____	**8z**	
9	Total other income. Add lines 8a through 8z	**9**	
10	Combine lines 1 through 7 and 9. Enter here and on Form 1040, 1040-SR, or 1040-NR, line 8	**10**	$38,913

| For Paperwork Reduction Act Notice, see your tax return instructions. | Cat. No. 71479F | Schedule 1 (Form 1040) 2021 |

Schedule 1 (Form 1040) 2021   Page **2**

Part II   Adjustments to Income

11	Educator expenses	11	
12	Certain business expenses of reservists, performing artists, and fee-basis government officials. Attach Form 2106	12	
13	Health savings account deduction. Attach Form 8889	13	
14	Moving expenses for members of the Armed Forces. Attach Form 3903 . . .	14	
15	Deductible part of self-employment tax. Attach Schedule SE	15	$2,749
16	Self-employed SEP, SIMPLE, and qualified plans	16	
17	Self-employed health insurance deduction	17	
18	Penalty on early withdrawal of savings	18	
19a	Alimony paid	19a	
b	Recipient's SSN . . . . ▶		
c	Date of original divorce or separation agreement (see instructions) ▶		
20	IRA deduction	20	
21	Student loan interest deduction	21	
22	Reserved for future use	22	
23	Archer MSA deduction	23	
24	Other adjustments:		
a	Jury duty pay (see instructions)	24a	
b	Deductible expenses related to income reported on line 8k from the rental of personal property engaged in for profit	24b	
c	Nontaxable amount of the value of Olympic and Paralympic medals and USOC prize money reported on line 8l	24c	
d	Reforestation amortization and expenses	24d	
e	Repayment of supplemental unemployment benefits under the Trade Act of 1974	24e	
f	Contributions to section 501(c)(18)(D) pension plans	24f	
g	Contributions by certain chaplains to section 403(b) plans . .	24g	
h	Attorney fees and court costs for actions involving certain unlawful discrimination claims (see instructions)	24h	
i	Attorney fees and court costs you paid in connection with an award from the IRS for information you provided that helped the IRS detect tax law violations	24i	
j	Housing deduction from Form 2555	24j	
k	Excess deductions of section 67(e) expenses from Schedule K-1 (Form 1041)	24k	
z	Other adjustments. List type and amount ▶ _____	24z	
25	Total other adjustments. Add lines 24a through 24z	25	
26	Add lines 11 through 23 and 25. These are your **adjustments to income.** Enter here and on Form 1040 or 1040-SR, line 10, or Form 1040-NR, line 10a	26	$2,749

Schedule 1 (Form 1040) 2021

SCHEDULE 2
(Form 1040)

Department of the Treasury
Internal Revenue Service

Additional Taxes

▶ Attach to Form 1040, 1040-SR, or 1040-NR.
▶ Go to *www.irs.gov/Form1040* for instructions and the latest information.

OMB No. 1545-0074

2021

Attachment
Sequence No. **02**

Name(s) shown on Form 1040, 1040-SR, or 1040-NR
Sandy and Bill James

Your social security number
123-45-6789

Part I   Tax

1	Alternative minimum tax. Attach Form 6251	**1**	
2	Excess advance premium tax credit repayment. Attach Form 8962	**2**	
3	Add lines 1 and 2. Enter here and on Form 1040, 1040-SR, or 1040-NR, line 17 . .	**3**	

Part II   Other Taxes

4	Self-employment tax. Attach Schedule SE	**4**	$5,498
5	Social security and Medicare tax on unreported tip income. Attach Form 4137	**5**	
6	Uncollected social security and Medicare tax on wages. Attach Form 8919	**6**	
7	Total additional social security and Medicare tax. Add lines 5 and 6	**7**	
8	Additional tax on IRAs or other tax-favored accounts. Attach Form 5329 if required	**8**	
9	Household employment taxes. Attach Schedule H	**9**	
10	Repayment of first-time homebuyer credit. Attach Form 5405 if required	**10**	
11	Additional Medicare Tax. Attach Form 8959	**11**	
12	Net investment income tax. Attach Form 8960	**12**	
13	Uncollected social security and Medicare or RRTA tax on tips or group-term life insurance from Form W-2, box 12	**13**	
14	Interest on tax due on installment income from the sale of certain residential lots and timeshares	**14**	
15	Interest on the deferred tax on gain from certain installment sales with a sales price over $150,000	**15**	
16	Recapture of low-income housing credit. Attach Form 8611	**16**	

(continued on page 2)

For Paperwork Reduction Act Notice, see your tax return instructions.   Cat. No. 71478U   Schedule 2 (Form 1040) 2021

Schedule 2 (Form 1040) 2021 | Page **2**

Part II Other Taxes *(continued)*

17 Other additional taxes:

a Recapture of other credits. List type, form number, and amount ▶ _____ | **17a**

b Recapture of federal mortgage subsidy. If you sold your home in 2021, see instructions | **17b**

c Additional tax on HSA distributions. Attach Form 8889 | **17c**

d Additional tax on an HSA because you didn't remain an eligible individual. Attach Form 8889 | **17d**

e Additional tax on Archer MSA distributions. Attach Form 8853 | **17e**

f Additional tax on Medicare Advantage MSA distributions. Attach Form 8853 | **17f**

g Recapture of a charitable contribution deduction related to a fractional interest in tangible personal property | **17g**

h Income you received from a nonqualified deferred compensation plan that fails to meet the requirements of section 409A | **17h**

i Compensation you received from a nonqualified deferred compensation plan described in section 457A | **17i**

j Section 72(m)(5) excess benefits tax | **17j**

k Golden parachute payments | **17k**

l Tax on accumulation distribution of trusts | **17l**

m Excise tax on insider stock compensation from an expatriated corporation | **17m**

n Look-back interest under section 167(g) or 460(b) from Form 8697 or 8866 | **17n**

o Tax on non-effectively connected income for any part of the year you were a nonresident alien from Form 1040-NR | **17o**

p Any interest from Form 8621, line 16f, relating to distributions from, and dispositions of, stock of a section 1291 fund | **17p**

q Any interest from Form 8621, line 24 | **17q**

z Any other taxes. List type and amount ▶ _____ | **17z**

18 Total additional taxes. Add lines 17a through 17z | **18**

19 Additional tax from Schedule 8812 | **19**

20 Section 965 net tax liability installment from Form 965-A | **20**

21 Add lines 4, 7 through 16, 18, and 19. These are your **total other taxes.** Enter here and on Form 1040 or 1040-SR, line 23, or Form 1040-NR, line 23b | **21** | $5,498

Schedule 2 (Form 1040) 2021

Form **8995** Department of the Treasury Internal Revenue Service	**Qualified Business Income Deduction** **Simplified Computation** ▶ Attach to your tax return. ▶ Go to *www.irs.gov/Form8995* for instructions and the latest information.	OMB No. 1545-2294 **2021** Attachment Sequence No. **55**

Name(s) shown on return	Your taxpayer identification number

Note. You can claim the qualified business income deduction **only** if you have qualified business income from a qualified trade or business, real estate investment trust dividends, publicly traded partnership income, or a domestic production activities deduction passed through from an agricultural or horticultural cooperative. See instructions.

Use this form if your taxable income, before your qualified business income deduction, is at or below $164,900 ($164,925 if married filing separately; $329,800 if married filing jointly), and you aren't a patron of an agricultural or horticultural cooperative.

1	(a) Trade, business, or aggregation name	(b) Taxpayer identification number	(c) Qualified business income or (loss)
i	Family Child Care		$38,913
ii			
iii			
iv			
v			

2	Total qualified business income or (loss). Combine lines 1i through 1v, column (c)	**2**	$38,913	
3	Qualified business net (loss) carryforward from the prior year	**3**	( )	
4	Total qualified business income. Combine lines 2 and 3. If zero or less, enter -0-	**4**	$38,913	
5	Qualified business income component. Multiply line 4 by 20% (0.20)			**5** $7,783
6	Qualified REIT dividends and publicly traded partnership (PTP) income or (loss) (see instructions)	**6**	---	
7	Qualified REIT dividends and qualified PTP (loss) carryforward from the prior year	**7**	(---)	
8	Total qualified REIT dividends and PTP income. Combine lines 6 and 7. If zero or less, enter -0-	**8**	---	
9	REIT and PTP component. Multiply line 8 by 20% (0.20)			**9** $0
10	Qualified business income deduction before the income limitation. Add lines 5 and 9			**10** $7,783
11	Taxable income before qualified business income deduction (see instructions)	**11**	$52,064	
12	Net capital gain (see instructions)	**12**	---	
13	Subtract line 12 from line 11. If zero or less, enter -0-	**13**	$52,064	
14	Income limitation. Multiply line 13 by 20% (0.20)			**14** $10,413
15	Qualified business income deduction. Enter the smaller of line 10 or line 14. Also enter this amount on the applicable line of your return (see instructions) ▶			**15** $7,783
16	Total qualified business (loss) carryforward. Combine lines 2 and 3. If greater than zero, enter -0-			**16** ( )
17	Total qualified REIT dividends and PTP (loss) carryforward. Combine lines 6 and 7. If greater than zero, enter -0-			**17** ( )

For Privacy Act and Paperwork Reduction Act Notice, see instructions.   Cat. No. 37806C   Form **8995** (2021)

$2,500 Election

For the year ending December 31, 2022 I am electing the de minimus safe harbor rule under Treas. Reg. Section 1.263(a)-1(f) for my business expenses of less than $2,500.

Sandy James   4/3/2022
_____   _____
Sandy James   Date

Taxpayer identification number: 26-389187
Address: 687 Hoover Street, Hudson, Ohio 42387

How and When to Depreciate an Item

Step 1: Does It Cost More Than $2,500?

If the answer is yes, go to step 2. If no, attach statement (see page 237) and deduct it in one year. If it's part of a home improvement, see step 4.

Step 2: Is It a Repair?

The definition of a repair was greatly expanded in 2014. If the answer is yes, deduct it in one year, regardless of the cost. If not, go to step 3.

Step 3: Choose a Depreciation Category

Office equipment (computer, printer, copy machine)

Personal property (furniture, appliances, play equipment)

Land improvement (fence, patio, driveway)

Home improvement (house, deck, new addition, major remodeling)

Home

Step 4: Follow the Directions for Each Depreciation Category

Office equipment:

- Costing less than $2,500: deduct in one year and attach statement to your tax return.

- Costing more than $2,500:

    ○ If you use less than 50% for your business, depreciate over five years.

    ○ If you use 50% or more for your business:

       • use the Section 179 rule, or

       • use the 100% bonus depreciation rule and deduct in one year, or

       • depreciate over five years.

Personal property (other property used in your business):

- Costing less than $2,500: deduct in one year and attach statement to your tax return.

- Costing more than $2,500:

    ○ use 100% bonus depreciation rule and deduct in one year, or

    ○ depreciate over seven years.

- If you use 50% or more for your business:
  - can use the Section 179 rule.

Land improvement:

- Costing less than $2,500: deduct in one year and attach statement to your tax return.
- Costing more than $2,500:
  - Does the Safe Harbor for Small Taxpayers rule apply (see page 247)?
    - If yes, deduct in one year.
    - If no, use the 100% bonus depreciation rule and deduct in one year, or depreciate over 15 years.

Home improvement:

- Costing less than $2,500: deduct in one year and attach statement to your tax return.
- Costing more than $2,500:
  - Does the Safe Harbor for Small Taxpayers rule apply (see page 247)?
    - If yes, deduct in one year.
    - If no, depreciate over 39 years, or if used more than 50% for business, use the Section 179 rule.

Home:

- Depreciate over 39 years.

IRS Resources

You can call the IRS Business and Specialty Tax Line at 800-829-4933 with any tax question. This toll-free number for business questions should make it easier for you to get through to an IRS employee who can answer your questions. If you aren't sure if the answer you are given is correct, ask the IRS employee to tell you which IRS publication or part of the Tax Code the answer is based on. If you have a hearing impairment and TDD equipment, you can call 800-829-4059. If you live outside the United States and have a tax question, call your U.S. Embassy. In Puerto Rico call 787-622-8929.

You can find IRS forms and publications at local IRS offices, banks, libraries, and post offices. You can also call 800-829-3676 to have any IRS form mailed to you. The IRS has its own website (www.irs.gov) from which you can download any IRS form, publication, or instruction book. The site also has other information that may help you with your taxes.

You can also get IRS tax forms by fax. Dial 703-368-9694 from the voice unit of your fax machine and follow the voice prompts. Tax forms must be on plain paper, not thermal paper, to be acceptable for filing. (You can copy the form if necessary.) For help with transmission problems, call the Fed World Help Desk at 703-487-4608.

If you want to report that another taxpayer (an illegal child care provider, for example) is cheating, call the IRS criminal investigation informant hotline at 800-829-0433. Your name will be kept confidential, and you are eligible for a reward if the IRS collects taxes due.

Below is a list of the IRS publications and Tax Court cases that address family child care tax issues. You can find copies at www.tomcopelandblog.com.

Child Care Provider Audit Technique Guide

This guide from the IRS is a must if you are audited. It contains guidance on the many unique tax issues facing child care providers. You can find the guide at www .tomcopelandblog.com.

Publication 587 Business Use of Your Home

Under the section Day-Care Facility, this publication clarifies that providers who have applied for, have been granted, or are exempt from a license, certification, or registration under applicable state law can claim home expenses as shown on **Form 8829**. This publication also discusses how to calculate the Time-Space percentage in filling out **Form 8829**. It includes a discussion of how to claim food expenses and report Food Program income.

Instructions for Form 8829 Expenses for Business Use of Your Home
Under the section Special Computation for Certain Day-Care Facilities, the instructions spell out how to calculate the Time-Space percentage of the home when at least one of the rooms in the home is used exclusively for the business.

IRS Revenue Ruling 92-3
This Revenue Ruling, based on an audit of a family child care provider, clarifies how to calculate the Time-Space percentage. It also defines what "regular use" means.

Tax Court Cases
Robert Neilson and Dorothy Neilson v. Commissioner, 94-1, 1990
In this case, the court ruled that a provider could claim 75 hours a week (including preparation and cleanup time) in determining her Time-Space percentage. The court also allowed the provider to deduct a portion of her lawn care expenses.

Uphus and Walker v. Commissioner
Tax Court Memo 1994-71, February 23, 1994
In these two cases, the court ruled that providers could claim rooms (laundry room, basement storage area, garage, and furnace area) as regularly used for the business even if the children in care never entered the rooms. The use of these rooms by the provider for business purposes was enough to meet the regular-use test.

Hewett v. Commissioner
Tax Court Memo 1996-110
In this case, the court allowed a taxpayer to claim an exclusive-use area for a grand piano that occupied a small recessed section of the living room and had no partition separating it from the rest of the home. The court ruled that it wasn't necessary to have a physical barrier to prove that an area was used exclusively for business.

Scott C. and Patricia A. Simpson v. Commissioner
Tax Court Memo 1997-223, May 12, 1997
In this case, a new provider was not allowed to claim most of her first two years of expenses because they were not related to her business. These expenses included a cross-country ski machine, personal food expenses, payments to wineries, and much more. Despite the loss of many deductions, the court did allow her to show a loss of $2,000–$3,000 for these two years. The court also acknowledged that cable TV and water were proper business deductions.

Peter and Maureen Speltz v. Commissioner
Tax Court Summary Opinion 2006-25
A provider hired her husband and set up a medical reimbursement plan without paying him a salary. The court ruled that the plan was valid, the husband was a bona fide employee, and the provider was allowed to deduct thousands of dollars in medical expenses.

Jonelle Broady v. Commissioner
Tax Court Summary Opinion 2008-63
An illegal provider was entitled to claim business expenses such as advertising, car expenses, office supplies, repairs and maintenance, and supplies and food. Illegal providers are not entitled to claim expenses associated with the home.

Tax Help on the Internet
Commercial internet services have special sites on which you can get tax assistance; however, be careful about accepting advice from these sources, because none of the information is guaranteed.

State Tax Information and Forms
If you need state tax information and forms, contact your state tax office.

List of IRS Forms and Publications

Here's a list of the IRS forms and publications that are mentioned in this book:

Form W-5 Earned Income Credit Advance Payment Certificate
Form W-10 Dependent Care Provider's Identification and Certification
Form 1040 U.S. Individual Income Tax Return
Form 1040-ES Estimated Tax for Individuals
Form 1040-SE Self-Employment Tax
Form 1040X Amended U.S. Individual Income Tax Return
Form 3115 Application for Change in Accounting Method
Form 4562 Depreciation and Amortization
Form 4684 Casualties and Thefts
Form 4797 Sales of Business Property
Form 4868 Application for Automatic Extension of Time to File U.S. Individual Income Tax Return
Form 5305-SEP Simplified Employee Pension
Form 5695 Residential Energy Credits
Form 8109 Federal Tax Deposit Coupon
Form 8812 Additional Child Tax Credit
Form 8824 Like-Kind Exchange
Form 8829 Expenses for Business Use of Your Home
Form 8863 Education Credits
Form 8880 Credit for Qualified Retirement Savings Contributions
Form 8949 Sales and Other Dispositions of Capital Assets
Publication 463 Travel, Entertainment, Gift, and Car Expenses
Publication 505 Tax Withholding and Estimated Tax
Publication 523 Selling Your Home
Publication 534 Depreciating Property Placed in Service Before 1987
Publication 544 Sales and Other Dispositions of Assets
Publication 556 Examination of Returns, Appeal Rights, and Claims for Refund
Publication 583 Starting a Business and Keeping Records
Publication 587 Business Use of Your Home

Publication 590 Individual Retirement Arrangements

Publication 596 Earned Income Credit

Publication 946 How to Depreciate Property

Publication 1542 Per Diem Rates

Schedule A Itemized Deductions

Schedule B Interest and Dividend Income

Schedule C Profit or Loss from Business

Schedule D Capital Gains and Losses

Schedule EIC Earned Income Credit

Schedule SE Self-Employment Tax

Schedule 1

Schedule 2

Schedule 3

Employee and Payroll Tax Forms

Circular E Employer's Tax Guide

Form I-9 Employment Eligibility Verification

Form SS-4 Application for Employer Identification Number

Form SS-5 Application for a Social Security Card

Form W-2 Wages and Tax Statement

Form W-3 Transmittal of Income and Tax Statements

Form W-4 Employee's Withholding Allowance Certificate

Form 940 Employer's Annual Federal Unemployment Tax Return (FUTA)

Form 941 Employer's Quarterly Federal Tax Return

Form 944 Employer's Annual Federal Tax Return

Form 1099-NEC Non-employee Compensation

Finding and Working
with a Tax Professional

Tax Professional Directory

The National Association for Family Child Care (NAFCC) maintains a list of tax professionals around the country who have experience filing tax returns for family child care providers. This list is posted at www.nafcc.org. It is available for members only.

Working with a Tax Professional

When hiring or working with a tax professional, follow these guidelines:

- Get referrals from other providers who have a good tax professional.

- Ask the professionals you are considering about their training, experience, and knowledge of the unique tax laws that affect family child care providers (see pages xvi–xvii).

- Always review your tax return before signing it, and ask questions if you don't understand something on your return.

- Never sign a blank tax form or one that has been filled out in pencil.

- Keep a copy of your return for your records.

- Remember that you are ultimately responsible for your tax return even if your tax professional makes an error.

- Watch out for the following warning signs of an unscrupulous tax professional:
    Someone who says that he or she can obtain larger refunds than other preparers.
    Someone who bases his or her fee on a percentage of the amount of the refund.
    Someone who refuses to sign your return or give you a copy for your records.

PART V

Tax Forms

Form **W-10**
(Rev. October 2020)
Department of the Treasury
Internal Revenue Service

Dependent Care Provider's Identification and Certification

▶ Do **NOT** file Form W-10 with your tax return. Instead, keep it for your records.
▶ Go to *www.irs.gov/FormW10* for the latest information.

Part I	**Dependent Care Provider's Identification** (see instructions)	
Please Print or Type	Name of dependent care provider	Provider's taxpayer identification number
	Address (number, street, and apt. no.)	If the above number is a social security number, check here ▶ . . . . . . ☐
	City, state, and ZIP code	

Certification and Signature of Dependent Care Provider. Under penalties of perjury, I, as the dependent care provider, certify that my name, address, and taxpayer identification number shown above are correct.

Please Sign Here	Dependent care provider's signature	Date

Part II	**Name and Address of Person Requesting Part I Information** (see instructions)

Name, street address, apt. no., city, state, and ZIP code of person requesting information

_____

For calendar year 2021, I paid $ _____ (amount paid) to

_____ (name of provider) for the care of

_____ (name of child(ren)).

_____   _____
Signature of Parent   Date

_____   _____
Signature of Provider   Date

_____

Electing the $2,500 Safe Harbor Rule

If you bought items costing $2,500 or less that you want to deduct in 2021, rather than depreciating, attach this statement to your 2021 tax return.

For the year ending December 31, 2021, I am electing the de minimis safe harbor under Treas. Reg. Section 1.263(a)-1(f) for my business expenses of less than $2,500.

_____   _____
Signature   Date

Taxpayer identification number:

Address:

Form 1040

Department of the Treasury—Internal Revenue Service   (99)

U.S. Individual Income Tax Return   **2021**   OMB No. 1545-0074   IRS Use Only—Do not write or staple in this space.

Filing Status
Check only one box.

☐ Single   ☐ Married filing jointly   ☐ Married filing separately (MFS)   ☐ Head of household (HOH)   ☐ Qualifying widow(er) (QW)

If you checked the MFS box, enter the name of your spouse. If you checked the HOH or QW box, enter the child's name if the qualifying person is a child but not your dependent ▶

Your first name and middle initial	Last name	Your social security number
If joint return, spouse's first name and middle initial	Last name	Spouse's social security number

Home address (number and street). If you have a P.O. box, see instructions.		Apt. no.	**Presidential Election Campaign**
City, town, or post office. If you have a foreign address, also complete spaces below.	State	ZIP code	Check here if you, or your spouse if filing jointly, want $3 to go to this fund. Checking a box below will not change your tax or refund.
Foreign country name	Foreign province/state/county	Foreign postal code	☐ You ☐ Spouse

At any time during 2021, did you receive, sell, exchange, or otherwise dispose of any financial interest in any virtual currency?   ☐ Yes   ☐ No

Standard Deduction

Someone can claim: ☐ You as a dependent   ☐ Your spouse as a dependent
☐ Spouse itemizes on a separate return or you were a dual-status alien

Age/Blindness   You: ☐ Were born before January 2, 1957   ☐ Are blind   Spouse: ☐ Was born before January 2, 1957   ☐ Is blind

Dependents (see instructions):
If more than four dependents, see instructions and check here ▶ ☐

(1) First name Last name	(2) Social security number	(3) Relationship to you	(4) ✔ if qualifies for (see instructions):	
			Child tax credit	Credit for other dependents
			☐	☐
			☐	☐
			☐	☐
			☐	☐

Attach Sch. B if required.

1	Wages, salaries, tips, etc. Attach Form(s) W-2			1	
2a	Tax exempt interest	2a	**b** Taxable interest	2b	
3a	Qualified dividends	3a	**b** Ordinary dividends	3b	
4a	IRA distributions	4a	**b** Taxable amount	4b	
5a	Pensions and annuities	5a	**b** Taxable amount	5b	
6a	Social security benefits	6a	**b** Taxable amount	6b	
7	Capital gain or (loss). Attach Schedule D if required. If not required, check here ▶ ☐			7	
8	Other income from Schedule 1, line 10			8	
9	Add lines 1, 2b, 3b, 4b, 5b, 6b, 7, and 8. This is your **total income** ▶			9	
10	Adjustments to income from Schedule 1, line 26			10	
11	Subtract line 10 from line 9. This is your **adjusted gross income** ▶			11	

Standard Deduction for—
- Single or Married filing separately, $12,550
- Married filing jointly or Qualifying widow(er), $25,100
- Head of household, $18,800
- If you checked any box under *Standard Deduction,* see instructions.

12a	**Standard deduction or itemized deductions** (from Schedule A)	12a			
b	Charitable contributions if you take the standard deduction (see instructions)	12b			
c	Add lines 12a and 12b			12c	
13	Qualified business income deduction from Form 8995 or Form 8995-A			13	
14	Add lines 12c and 13			14	
15	**Taxable income.** Subtract line 14 from line 11. If zero or less, enter -0-			15	

For Disclosure, Privacy Act, and Paperwork Reduction Act Notice, see separate instructions.   Cat. No. 11320B   Form **1040** (2021)

Form 1040 (2021)   Page **2**

16	**Tax** (see instructions). Check if any from Form(s): **1** ☐ 8814 **2** ☐ 4972 **3** ☐ _____			16	
17	Amount from Schedule 2, line 3			17	
18	Add lines 16 and 17			18	
19	Nonrefundable child tax credit or credit for other dependents from Schedule 8812			19	
20	Amount from Schedule 3, line 8			20	
21	Add lines 19 and 20			21	
22	Subtract line 21 from line 18. If zero or less, enter -0-			22	
23	Other taxes, including self-employment tax, from Schedule 2, line 21			23	
24	Add lines 22 and 23. This is your **total tax** ▶			24	
25	Federal income tax withheld from:				
a	Form(s) W-2		25a		
b	Form(s) 1099		25b		
c	Other forms (see instructions)		25c		
d	Add lines 25a through 25c			25d	

If you have a qualifying child, attach Sch. EIC.

26	2021 estimated tax payments and amount applied from 2020 return			26	
27a	Earned income credit (EIC)		27a		
	Check here if you had not reached the age of 19 by December 31, 2021, and satisfy all other requirements for claiming the EIC. See instructions ▶ ☐				
b	Nontaxable combat pay election	27b			
c	Prior year (2019) earned income	27c			
28	Refundable child tax credit or additional child tax credit from Schedule 8812		28		
29	American opportunity credit from Form 8863, line 8		29		
30	Recovery rebate credit. See instructions		30		
31	Amount from Schedule 3, line 15		31		
32	Add lines 27a and 28 through 31. These are your **total other payments and refundable credits** ▶			32	
33	Add lines 25d, 26, and 32. These are your **total payments** ▶			33	

Refund

34	If line 33 is more than line 24, subtract line 24 from line 33. This is the amount you **overpaid**			34	
35a	Amount of line 34 you want **refunded to you.** If Form 8888 is attached, check here ▶ ☐			35a	

Direct deposit? See instructions.

▶ b Routing number _____ ▶ c Type: ☐ Checking ☐ Savings
▶ d Account number _____

36	Amount of line 34 you want **applied to your 2022 estimated tax** ▶	36	

Amount You Owe

37	**Amount you owe.** Subtract line 33 from line 24. For details on how to pay, see instructions ▶		37	
38	Estimated tax penalty (see instructions) ▶	38		

Third Party Designee

Do you want to allow another person to discuss this return with the IRS? See instructions ▶ ☐ **Yes.** Complete below. ☐ **No**

Designee's name ▶ _____ Phone no. ▶ _____ Personal identification number (PIN) ▶ _____

Sign Here

Under penalties of perjury, I declare that I have examined this return and accompanying schedules and statements, and to the best of my knowledge and belief, they are true, correct, and complete. Declaration of preparer (other than taxpayer) is based on all information of which preparer has any knowledge.

Joint return? See instructions. Keep a copy for your records.

Your signature	Date	Your occupation	If the IRS sent you an Identity Protection PIN, enter it here (see inst.) ▶ _____
Spouse's signature. If a joint return, **both** must sign.	Date	Spouse's occupation	If the IRS sent your spouse an Identity Protection PIN, enter it here (see inst.) ▶ _____
Phone no.		Email address	

Paid Preparer Use Only

Preparer's name	Preparer's signature	Date	PTIN	Check if: ☐ Self-employed
Firm's name ▶			Phone no.	
Firm's address ▶			Firm's EIN ▶	

Go to *www.irs.gov/Form1040* for instructions and the latest information.   Form **1040** (2021)

SCHEDULE C
(Form 1040)

Department of the Treasury
Internal Revenue Service (99)

Profit or Loss From Business
(Sole Proprietorship)

▶ Go to *www.irs.gov/ScheduleC* for instructions and the latest information.
▶ **Attach to Form 1040, 1040-SR, 1040-NR, or 1041; partnerships must generally file Form 1065.**

OMB No. 1545-0074

2021

Attachment
Sequence No. **09**

Name of proprietor

Social security number (SSN)

A Principal business or profession, including product or service (see instructions)	**B** Enter code from instructions ▶
C Business name. If no separate business name, leave blank.	**D** Employer ID number (EIN) (see instr.)

E Business address (including suite or room no.) ▶
City, town or post office, state, and ZIP code

F Accounting method: **(1)** ☐ Cash   **(2)** ☐ Accrual   **(3)** ☐ Other (specify) ▶

G Did you "materially participate" in the operation of this business during 2021? If "No," see instructions for limit on losses   .   ☐ Yes   ☐ No

H If you started or acquired this business during 2021, check here   .   .   .   .   ▶ ☐

I Did you make any payments in 2021 that would require you to file Form(s) 1099? See instructions   .   .   .   .   .   .   ☐ Yes   ☐ No

J If "Yes," did you or will you file required Form(s) 1099?   .   .   .   .   ☐ Yes   ☐ No

Part I   Income

1	Gross receipts or sales. See instructions for line 1 and check the box if this income was reported to you on Form W-2 and the "Statutory employee" box on that form was checked . . . . ▶ ☐	**1**	
2	Returns and allowances	**2**	
3	Subtract line 2 from line 1	**3**	
4	Cost of goods sold (from line 42)	**4**	
5	**Gross profit.** Subtract line 4 from line 3	**5**	
6	Other income, including federal and state gasoline or fuel tax credit or refund (see instructions) . . .	**6**	
7	**Gross income.** Add lines 5 and 6 . . . . ▶	**7**	

Part II   Expenses. Enter expenses for business use of your home **only** on line 30.

8	Advertising	**8**		**18**	Office expense (see instructions) .	**18**	
9	Car and truck expenses (see instructions) . . .	**9**		**19**	Pension and profit-sharing plans .	**19**	
				20	Rent or lease (see instructions):		
10	Commissions and fees .	**10**		**a**	Vehicles, machinery, and equipment	**20a**	
11	Contract labor (see instructions)	**11**		**b**	Other business property . . .	**20b**	
12	Depletion	**12**		**21**	Repairs and maintenance . . .	**21**	
13	Depreciation and section 179 expense deduction (not included in Part III) (see instructions)	**13**		**22**	Supplies (not included in Part III) .	**22**	
				23	Taxes and licenses	**23**	
				24	Travel and meals:		
14	Employee benefit programs (other than on line 19) .	**14**		**a**	Travel	**24a**	
15	Insurance (other than health)	**15**		**b**	Deductible meals (see instructions)	**24b**	
16	Interest (see instructions):			**25**	Utilities	**25**	
a	Mortgage (paid to banks, etc.)	**16a**		**26**	Wages (less employment credits)	**26**	
b	Other	**16b**		**27a**	Other expenses (from line 48) . .	**27a**	
17	Legal and professional services	**17**		**b**	**Reserved for future use** . . .	**27b**	

28	**Total expenses** before expenses for business use of home. Add lines 8 through 27a . . . . ▶	**28**	
29	Tentative profit or (loss). Subtract line 28 from line 7	**29**	
30	Expenses for business use of your home. Do not report these expenses elsewhere. Attach Form 8829 unless using the simplified method. See instructions. **Simplified method filers only:** Enter the total square footage of (a) your home: _____ and (b) the part of your home used for business: _____ . Use the Simplified Method Worksheet in the instructions to figure the amount to enter on line 30	**30**	
31	**Net profit or (loss).** Subtract line 30 from line 29. • If a profit, enter on both **Schedule 1 (Form 1040), line 3,** and on **Schedule SE, line 2.** (If you checked the box on line 1, see instructions). Estates and trusts, enter on **Form 1041, line 3.** • If a loss, you **must** go to line 32.	**31**	
32	If you have a loss, check the box that describes your investment in this activity. See instructions. • If you checked 32a, enter the loss on both **Schedule 1 (Form 1040), line 3,** and on **Schedule SE, line 2.** (If you checked the box on line 1, see the line 31 instructions.) Estates and trusts, enter on **Form 1041, line 3.** • If you checked 32b, you **must** attach **Form 6198.** Your loss may be limited.	**32a** ☐ All investment is at risk. **32b** ☐ Some investment is not at risk.	

For Paperwork Reduction Act Notice, see the separate instructions.   Cat. No. 11334P   Schedule C (Form 1040) 2021

Schedule C (Form 1040) 2021   Page **2**

Part III	**Cost of Goods Sold** (see instructions)

33 Method(s) used to
value closing inventory: **a** ☐ Cost   **b** ☐ Lower of cost or market   **c** ☐ Other (attach explanation)

34 Was there any change in determining quantities, costs, or valuations between opening and closing inventory?
If "Yes," attach explanation . . . .   ☐ **Yes**   ☐ **No**

35	Inventory at beginning of year. If different from last year's closing inventory, attach explanation . . .	**35**	
36	Purchases less cost of items withdrawn for personal use	**36**	
37	Cost of labor. Do not include any amounts paid to yourself	**37**	
38	Materials and supplies	**38**	
39	Other costs	**39**	
40	Add lines 35 through 39	**40**	
41	Inventory at end of year	**41**	
42	**Cost of goods sold.** Subtract line 41 from line 40. Enter the result here and on line 4	**42**	

Part IV	**Information on Your Vehicle.** Complete this part **only** if you are claiming car or truck expenses on line 9 and are not required to file Form 4562 for this business. See the instructions for line 13 to find out if you must file Form 4562.

43 When did you place your vehicle in service for business purposes? (month/day/year)   ▶ _____ / _____ / _____

44 Of the total number of miles you drove your vehicle during 2021, enter the number of miles you used your vehicle for:

a Business _____   **b** Commuting (see instructions) _____   **c** Other _____

45 Was your vehicle available for personal use during off-duty hours? . . . .   ☐ **Yes**   ☐ **No**

46 Do you (or your spouse) have another vehicle available for personal use?. . . . .   ☐ **Yes**   ☐ **No**

47a Do you have evidence to support your deduction? . . . .   ☐ **Yes**   ☐ **No**

b If "Yes," is the evidence written? . . . .   ☐ **Yes**   ☐ **No**

Part V	**Other Expenses.** List below business expenses not included on lines 8–26 or line 30.

--	
--	
--	
--	
--	
--	
--	
48 **Total other expenses.** Enter here and on line 27a **48**	

Schedule C (Form 1040) 2021

SCHEDULE SE
(Form 1040)

Department of the Treasury
Internal Revenue Service (99)

Self-Employment Tax

▶ Go to *www.irs.gov/ScheduleSE* for instructions and the latest information.
▶ Attach to Form 1040, 1040-SR, or 1040-NR.

OMB No. 1545-0074

2021

Attachment
Sequence No. **17**

Name of person with self-employment income (as shown on Form 1040, 1040-SR, or 1040-NR)

Social security number of person
with **self-employment** income ▶

Part I	Self-Employment Tax

Note: If your only income subject to self-employment tax is **church employee income,** see instructions for how to report your income and the definition of church employee income.

A If you are a minister, member of a religious order, or Christian Science practitioner **and** you filed Form 4361, but you had $400 or more of **other** net earnings from self-employment, check here and continue with Part I . . . . ▶ ☐

Skip lines 1a and 1b if you use the farm optional method in Part II. See instructions.

1a Net farm profit or (loss) from Schedule F, line 34, and farm partnerships, Schedule K-1 (Form 1065), box 14, code A . . . . | **1a** |

b If you received social security retirement or disability benefits, enter the amount of Conservation Reserve Program payments included on Schedule F, line 4b, or listed on Schedule K-1 (Form 1065), box 20, code AH | **1b** ( )

Skip line 2 if you use the nonfarm optional method in Part II. See instructions.

2 Net profit or (loss) from Schedule C, line 31; and Schedule K-1 (Form 1065), box 14, code A (other than farming). See instructions for other income to report or if you are a minister or member of a religious order | **2** |

3 Combine lines 1a, 1b, and 2 . . . . | **3** |

4a If line 3 is more than zero, multiply line 3 by 92.35% (0.9235). Otherwise, enter amount from line 3 . | **4a** |

Note: If line 4a is less than $400 due to Conservation Reserve Program payments on line 1b, see instructions.

b If you elect one or both of the optional methods, enter the total of lines 15 and 17 here . . . . . | **4b** |

c Combine lines 4a and 4b. If less than $400, **stop;** you don't owe self-employment tax. **Exception:** If less than $400 and you had **church employee income,** enter -0- and continue . . . . ▶ | **4c** |

5a Enter your **church employee income** from Form W-2. See instructions for definition of church employee income . . . . | **5a** | | **5b** |

b Multiply line 5a by 92.35% (0.9235). If less than $100, enter -0- . . . . | **5b** |

6 Add lines 4c and 5b . . . . | **6** |

7 Maximum amount of combined wages and self-employment earnings subject to social security tax or the 6.2% portion of the 7.65% railroad retirement (tier 1) tax for 2021 . . . . | **7** | 142,800

8a Total social security wages and tips (total of boxes 3 and 7 on Form(s) W-2) and railroad retirement (tier 1) compensation. If $142,800 or more, skip lines 8b through 10, and go to line 11 . . . . | **8a** |

b Unreported tips subject to social security tax from Form 4137, line 10 . . . | **8b** |

c Wages subject to social security tax from Form 8919, line 10 . . . . . | **8c** |

d Add lines 8a, 8b, and 8c . . . . | **8d** |

9 Subtract line 8d from line 7. If zero or less, enter -0- here and on line 10 and go to line 11 . . . ▶ | **9** |

10 Multiply the **smaller** of line 6 or line 9 by 12.4% (0.124) . . . . | **10** |

11 Multiply line 6 by 2.9% (0.029) . . . . | **11** |

12 **Self-employment tax.** Add lines 10 and 11. Enter here and on **Schedule 2 (Form 1040), line 4** . . | **12** |

13 **Deduction for one-half of self-employment tax.**
Multiply line 12 by 50% (0.50). Enter here and on **Schedule 1 (Form 1040), line 15** . . . . | **13** |

Part II	Optional Methods To Figure Net Earnings (see instructions)

Farm Optional Method. You may use this method **only** if **(a)** your gross farm income[1] wasn't more than $8,820, **or (b)** your net farm profits[2] were less than $6,367.

14 Maximum income for optional methods . . . . | **14** | 5,880

15 Enter the **smaller** of: two-thirds (⅔) of gross farm income[1] (not less than zero) or $5,880. Also, include this amount on line 4b above . . . . | **15** |

Nonfarm Optional Method. You may use this method **only** if **(a)** your net nonfarm profits[3] were less than $6,367 and also less than 72.189% of your gross nonfarm income,[4] **and (b)** you had net earnings from self-employment of at least $400 in 2 of the prior 3 years. **Caution:** You may use this method no more than five times.

16 Subtract line 15 from line 14 . . . . | **16** |

17 Enter the **smaller** of: two-thirds (⅔) of gross nonfarm income[4] (not less than zero) **or** the amount on line 16. Also, include this amount on line 4b above . . . . | **17** |

[1] From Sch. F, line 9; and Sch. K-1 (Form 1065), box 14, code B.
[2] From Sch. F, line 34; and Sch. K-1 (Form 1065), box 14, code A—minus the amount you would have entered on line 1b had you not used the optional method.
[3] From Sch. C, line 31; and Sch. K-1 (Form 1065), box 14, code A.
[4] From Sch. C, line 7; and Sch. K-1 (Form 1065), box 14, code C.

For Paperwork Reduction Act Notice, see your tax return instructions.

Cat. No. 11358Z

Schedule SE (Form 1040) 2021

Form **4562**	**Depreciation and Amortization**	OMB No. 1545-0172
Department of the Treasury Internal Revenue Service (99)	**(Including Information on Listed Property)** ▶ Attach to your tax return. ▶ Go to *www.irs.gov/Form4562* for instructions and the latest information.	**2021** Attachment Sequence No. **179**

Name(s) shown on return	Business or activity to which this form relates	Identifying number

Part I Election To Expense Certain Property Under Section 179
Note: If you have any listed property, complete Part V before you complete Part I.

1	Maximum amount (see instructions)	**1**
2	Total cost of section 179 property placed in service (see instructions)	**2**
3	Threshold cost of section 179 property before reduction in limitation (see instructions) .	**3**
4	Reduction in limitation. Subtract line 3 from line 2. If zero or less, enter -0-	**4**
5	Dollar limitation for tax year. Subtract line 4 from line 1. If zero or less, enter -0-. If married filing separately, see instructions	**5**

6	(a) Description of property	(b) Cost (business use only)	(c) Elected cost

7	Listed property. Enter the amount from line 29 . . . . **7**	
8	Total elected cost of section 179 property. Add amounts in column (c), lines 6 and 7	**8**
9	Tentative deduction. Enter the **smaller** of line 5 or line 8	**9**
10	Carryover of disallowed deduction from line 13 of your 2020 Form 4562	**10**
11	Business income limitation. Enter the smaller of business income (not less than zero) or line 5. See instructions	**11**
12	Section 179 expense deduction. Add lines 9 and 10, but don't enter more than line 11	**12**
13	Carryover of disallowed deduction to 2022. Add lines 9 and 10, less line 12 ▶ **13**	

Note: Don't use Part II or Part III below for listed property. Instead, use Part V.

Part II Special Depreciation Allowance and Other Depreciation (Don't include listed property. See instructions.)

14	Special depreciation allowance for qualified property (other than listed property) placed in service during the tax year. See instructions	**14**
15	Property subject to section 168(f)(1) election	**15**
16	Other depreciation (including ACRS)	**16**

Part III MACRS Depreciation (Don't include listed property. See instructions.)

Section A

17	MACRS deductions for assets placed in service in tax years beginning before 2021	**17**
18	If you are electing to group any assets placed in service during the tax year into one or more general asset accounts, check here . . . . ▶ ☐	

Section B—Assets Placed in Service During 2021 Tax Year Using the General Depreciation System

(a) Classification of property	(b) Month and year placed in service	(c) Basis for depreciation (business/investment use only—see instructions)	(d) Recovery period	(e) Convention	(f) Method	(g) Depreciation deduction
19a 3-year property						
b 5-year property						
c 7-year property						
d 10-year property						
e 15-year property						
f 20-year property						
g 25-year property			25 yrs.		S/L	
h Residential rental property			27.5 yrs.	MM	S/L	
			27.5 yrs.	MM	S/L	
i Nonresidential real property			39 yrs.	MM	S/L	
				MM	S/L	

Section C—Assets Placed in Service During 2021 Tax Year Using the Alternative Depreciation System

20a Class life					S/L	
b 12-year			12 yrs.		S/L	
c 30-year			30 yrs.	MM	S/L	
d 40-year			40 yrs.	MM	S/L	

Part IV Summary (See instructions.)

21	Listed property. Enter amount from line 28	**21**
22	**Total.** Add amounts from line 12, lines 14 through 17, lines 19 and 20 in column (g), and line 21. Enter here and on the appropriate lines of your return. Partnerships and S corporations—see instructions	**22**
23	For assets shown above and placed in service during the current year, enter the portion of the basis attributable to section 263A costs **23**	

For Paperwork Reduction Act Notice, see separate instructions.   Cat. No. 12906N   Form **4562** (2021)

Form 4562 (2021)   Page **2**

Part V	Listed Property	(Include automobiles, certain other vehicles, certain aircraft, and property used for entertainment, recreation, or amusement.)

Note: For any vehicle for which you are using the standard mileage rate or deducting lease expense, complete **only** 24a, 24b, columns (a) through (c) of Section A, all of Section B, and Section C if applicable.

Section A—Depreciation and Other Information (Caution: See the instructions for limits for passenger automobiles.)

24a Do you have evidence to support the business/investment use claimed? ☐ **Yes** ☐ **No** **24b** If "Yes," is the evidence written? ☐ **Yes** ☐ **No**

(a) Type of property (list vehicles first)	(b) Date placed in service	(c) Business/ investment use percentage	(d) Cost or other basis	(e) Basis for depreciation (business/investment use only)	(f) Recovery period	(g) Method/ Convention	(h) Depreciation deduction	(i) Elected section 179 cost
25 Special depreciation allowance for qualified listed property placed in service during the tax year and used more than 50% in a qualified business use. See instructions . **25**								
26 Property used more than 50% in a qualified business use:								
		%						
		%						
		%						
27 Property used 50% or less in a qualified business use:								
		%				S/L –		
		%				S/L –		
		%				S/L –		
28 Add amounts in column (h), lines 25 through 27. Enter here and on line 21, page 1 . **28**								
29 Add amounts in column (i), line 26. Enter here and on line 7, page 1							**29**	

Section B—Information on Use of Vehicles

Complete this section for vehicles used by a sole proprietor, partner, or other "more than 5% owner," or related person. If you provided vehicles to your employees, first answer the questions in Section C to see if you meet an exception to completing this section for those vehicles.

		(a) Vehicle 1		(b) Vehicle 2		(c) Vehicle 3		(d) Vehicle 4		(e) Vehicle 5		(f) Vehicle 6	
30	Total business/investment miles driven during the year (**don't** include commuting miles) .												
31	Total commuting miles driven during the year												
32	Total other personal (noncommuting) miles driven												
33	Total miles driven during the year. Add lines 30 through 32												
34	Was the vehicle available for personal use during off-duty hours?	Yes	No	Yes	No	Yes	No	Yes	No	Yes	No	Yes	No
35	Was the vehicle used primarily by a more than 5% owner or related person? . .												
36	Is another vehicle available for personal use?												

Section C—Questions for Employers Who Provide Vehicles for Use by Their Employees

Answer these questions to determine if you meet an exception to completing Section B for vehicles used by employees who **aren't** more than 5% owners or related persons. See instructions.

		Yes	No
37	Do you maintain a written policy statement that prohibits all personal use of vehicles, including commuting, by your employees?		
38	Do you maintain a written policy statement that prohibits personal use of vehicles, except commuting, by your employees? See the instructions for vehicles used by corporate officers, directors, or 1% or more owners . .		
39	Do you treat all use of vehicles by employees as personal use?		
40	Do you provide more than five vehicles to your employees, obtain information from your employees about the use of the vehicles, and retain the information received?		
41	Do you meet the requirements concerning qualified automobile demonstration use? See instructions.		

Note: If your answer to 37, 38, 39, 40, or 41 is "Yes," don't complete Section B for the covered vehicles.

Part VI	Amortization

(a) Description of costs	(b) Date amortization begins	(c) Amortizable amount	(d) Code section	(e) Amortization period or percentage	(f) Amortization for this year
42 Amortization of costs that begins during your 2021 tax year (see instructions):					
43 Amortization of costs that began before your 2021 tax year **43**					
44 **Total.** Add amounts in column (f). See the instructions for where to report **44**					

Form **4562** (2021)

Form **8829**

Department of the Treasury
Internal Revenue Service (99)

Expenses for Business Use of Your Home

▶ File only with Schedule C (Form 1040). Use a separate Form 8829 for each
home you used for business during the year.
▶ Go to *www.irs.gov/Form8829* for instructions and the latest information.

OMB No. 1545-0074

2021

Attachment
Sequence No. **176**

Name(s) of proprietor(s)

Your social security number

Part I	Part of Your Home Used for Business		
1	Area used regularly and exclusively for business, regularly for daycare, or for storage of inventory or product samples (see instructions)	1	
2	Total area of home	2	
3	Divide line 1 by line 2. Enter the result as a percentage	3	%

For daycare facilities not used exclusively for business, go to line 4. All others, go to line 7.

4	Multiply days used for daycare during year by hours used per day	4		hr.	
5	If you started or stopped using your home for daycare during the year, see instructions; otherwise, enter 8,760	5		hr.	
6	Divide line 4 by line 5. Enter the result as a decimal amount	6	.		
7	Business percentage. For daycare facilities not used exclusively for business, multiply line 6 by line 3 (enter the result as a percentage). All others, enter the amount from line 3 ▶	7			%

Part II	Figure Your Allowable Deduction				
8	Enter the amount from Schedule C, line 29, **plus** any gain derived from the business use of your home, **minus** any loss from the trade or business not derived from the business use of your home. See instructions.			8	

See instructions for columns (a) and (b) before completing lines 9–22.

			(a) Direct expenses	**(b)** Indirect expenses	
9	Casualty losses (see instructions)	9			
10	Deductible mortgage interest (see instructions)	10			
11	Real estate taxes (see instructions)	11			
12	Add lines 9, 10, and 11	12			
13	Multiply line 12, column (b), by line 7		13		
14	Add line 12, column (a), and line 13			14	
15	Subtract line 14 from line 8. If zero or less, enter -0-			15	
16	Excess mortgage interest (see instructions)	16			
17	Excess real estate taxes (see instructions)	17			
18	Insurance	18			
19	Rent	19			
20	Repairs and maintenance	20			
21	Utilities	21			
22	Other expenses (see instructions)	22			
23	Add lines 16 through 22	23			
24	Multiply line 23, column (b), by line 7		24		
25	Carryover of prior year operating expenses (see instructions)		25		
26	Add line 23, column (a), line 24, and line 25			26	
27	Allowable operating expenses. Enter the **smaller** of line 15 or line 26			27	
28	Limit on excess casualty losses and depreciation. Subtract line 27 from line 15			28	
29	Excess casualty losses (see instructions)	29			
30	Depreciation of your home from line 42 below	30			
31	Carryover of prior year excess casualty losses and depreciation (see instructions)	31			
32	Add lines 29 through 31			32	
33	Allowable excess casualty losses and depreciation. Enter the **smaller** of line 28 or line 32			33	
34	Add lines 14, 27, and 33			34	
35	Casualty loss portion, if any, from lines 14 and 33. Carry amount to **Form 4684.** See instructions			35	
36	**Allowable expenses for business use of your home.** Subtract line 35 from line 34. Enter here and on Schedule C, line 30. If your home was used for more than one business, see instructions. ▶			36	

Part III	Depreciation of Your Home		
37	Enter the **smaller** of your home's adjusted basis or its fair market value. See instructions	37	
38	Value of land included on line 37	38	
39	Basis of building. Subtract line 38 from line 37	39	
40	Business basis of building. Multiply line 39 by line 7	40	
41	Depreciation percentage (see instructions)	41	%
42	Depreciation allowable (see instructions). Multiply line 40 by line 41. Enter here and on line 30 above	42	

Part IV	Carryover of Unallowed Expenses to 2022		
43	Operating expenses. Subtract line 27 from line 26. If less than zero, enter -0-	43	
44	Excess casualty losses and depreciation. Subtract line 33 from line 32. If less than zero, enter -0-.	44	

For Paperwork Reduction Act Notice, see your tax return instructions.   Cat. No. 13232M   Form **8829** (2021)

Form **8995**	Qualified Business Income Deduction Simplified Computation	OMB No. 1545-2294
Department of the Treasury Internal Revenue Service	▶ Attach to your tax return. ▶ Go to *www.irs.gov/Form8995* for instructions and the latest information.	**2021** Attachment Sequence No. **55**

Name(s) shown on return	Your taxpayer identification number

Note. You can claim the qualified business income deduction **only** if you have qualified business income from a qualified trade or business, real estate investment trust dividends, publicly traded partnership income, or a domestic production activities deduction passed through from an agricultural or horticultural cooperative. See instructions.

Use this form if your taxable income, before your qualified business income deduction, is at or below $164,900 ($164,925 if married filing separately; $329,800 if married filing jointly), and you aren't a patron of an agricultural or horticultural cooperative.

DRAFT AS OF October 19, 2021 DO NOT FILE

1	(a) Trade, business, or aggregation name	(b) Taxpayer identification number	(c) Qualified business income or (loss)
i			
ii			
iii			
iv			
v			

2	Total qualified business income or (loss). Combine lines 1i through 1v, column (c)	2		
3	Qualified business net (loss) carryforward from the prior year	3	( )	
4	Total qualified business income. Combine lines 2 and 3. If zero or less, enter -0-	4		
5	Qualified business income component. Multiply line 4 by 20% (0.20)		5	
6	Qualified REIT dividends and publicly traded partnership (PTP) income or (loss) (see instructions)	6		
7	Qualified REIT dividends and qualified PTP (loss) carryforward from the prior year	7	( )	
8	Total qualified REIT dividends and PTP income. Combine lines 6 and 7. If zero or less, enter -0-	8		
9	REIT and PTP component. Multiply line 8 by 20% (0.20)		9	
10	Qualified business income deduction before the income limitation. Add lines 5 and 9		10	
11	Taxable income before qualified business income deduction (see instructions)	11		
12	Net capital gain (see instructions)	12		
13	Subtract line 12 from line 11. If zero or less, enter -0-	13		
14	Income limitation. Multiply line 13 by 20% (0.20)		14	
15	Qualified business income deduction. Enter the smaller of line 10 or line 14. Also enter this amount on the applicable line of your return (see instructions) . . . . ▶		15	
16	Total qualified business (loss) carryforward. Combine lines 2 and 3. If greater than zero, enter -0- . .		16	( )
17	Total qualified REIT dividends and PTP (loss) carryforward. Combine lines 6 and 7. If greater than zero, enter -0-		17	( )

For Privacy Act and Paperwork Reduction Act Notice, see instructions.	Cat. No. 37806C	Form **8995** (2021)

Using Redleaf Record-Keeping Tools

This chart shows how the books in the Redleaf business series work together to help you prepare and pay your taxes and communicate with the IRS. If you use these resources throughout the tax year, it will be much easier to complete your tax forms at the end of the year.

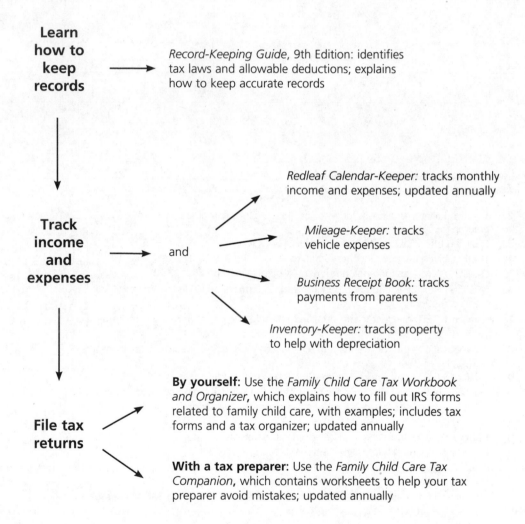

Learn how to keep records → *Record-Keeping Guide*, 9th Edition: identifies tax laws and allowable deductions; explains how to keep accurate records

Track income and expenses → and →

Redleaf Calendar-Keeper: tracks monthly income and expenses; updated annually

Mileage-Keeper: tracks vehicle expenses

Business Receipt Book: tracks payments from parents

Inventory-Keeper: tracks property to help with depreciation

File tax returns →

By yourself: Use the *Family Child Care Tax Workbook and Organizer*, which explains how to fill out IRS forms related to family child care, with examples; includes tax forms and a tax organizer; updated annually

With a tax preparer: Use the *Family Child Care Tax Companion*, which contains worksheets to help your tax preparer avoid mistakes; updated annually